A Personal Look at the Civil War in Rhea and Meigs Counties, Tennessee

Compiled by
Bettye J. Broyles

Rhea County Historical and
Genealogical Society

Heritage Books
2024

HERITAGE BOOKS
AN IMPRINT OF HERITAGE BOOKS, INC.

Books, CDs, and more—Worldwide

For our listing of thousands of titles see our website
at
www.HeritageBooks.com

A Facsimile Reprint
Published 2024 by
HERITAGE BOOKS, INC.
Publishing Division
5810 Ruatan Street
Berwyn Heights, MD 20740

International Standard Book Number
Paperbound: 978-0-7884-8715-6

FOREWORD

This publication is not intended as a "history" of the Civil War, but is merely a collection of letters (representing both North and South), reminiscences, diaries, and newspaper articles pertaining to Rhea and Meigs counties during the war.

Much has been written about the famous battles or skirmishes, but little attention has been directed toward the people at home and what the wives and children of the soldiers were going through. Although there are many letters from the "field" to loved ones at home, most of the letters are from those at home to the soldiers.

The following article from ***The Daily Times*** (Chattanooga) of 4 July 1890 describes the contributions made by women of Virginia, but could just as easily have been written about the women of Rhea and Meigs counties.

"The history of the war would not be complete without a tribute to the Confederate women. It would be injustice to them to say that they were simply patriotic, for while they were all patriots the greatest; they gave the Southern cause the benefit of much more than their good wishes. No women at any time in the history of the world ever surrendered as much for a cause as did the women of the South. There have been instances where hundreds have indeed made every sacrifice, but this is the only instance where a nation of women worked and fought for a nation. There was undoubtedly no one woman in the entire South during the last year of the war of whom it could have been said she lived in luxury. The wife of the President of the Confederacy sold her family silver for the cause. The invalid wife of the General of the Confederate Army spent her small strength in knitting socks for the Confederate soldiers. Little girls occupied their hours in picking lint for Confederate soldiers wounds. Saints—good, beautiful, patient, cheering, they proved angels on battlefields and in the hospitals. They starved at home in order to send their scanty food to the army. Worn and broken by privation, they wrote letters beaming with hope and gladness to the camp and resounding with defiance to the foe. No country ever had such loving daughters, no cause such tireless champions. They were the last to be reconstructed. Some of them have never been reconstructed. Some of them never will be reconstructed."

The letters also are an important source of information about sick, wounded, or deceased relatives or other members of a particular company. It is also interesting to note that most, if not all, of these soldiers would never have seen or visited the distant places had they not been in the service.

Copies of most of the letters in Part II were contributed by several individuals, while others were transcribed from microfilm. A few items were found in the files of the Rhea County Historical and Genealogical Society (Neal and Brown Letters, Allen Letters, King and Frazier Reminiscences, Brown Reminiscences, and Roddy Reminiscences) or the Clyde Roddy Library in Dayton (Clack Diary).

The newspaper articles in Part I were transcribed from various issues of ***The Athens Post*** (microfilm obtained from State Archives in Nashville). The newspaper ceased to be published in the fall of 1863 due to the arrest of the Editor, Sam P. Ivins, and was not reissued again until 1867. Unfortunately, several issues are missing from the microfilm; therefore, descriptions of all the companies raised in Rhea and Meigs counties could not be included.

Several references were found to articles in the ***Cleveland Banner***, but issues of this newspaper were not available from the State Archives.

The letters were copied exactly as written, with all the misspelled words, poor english, and lack of punctuation. In most cases, the hand-writing was easy to read, although a few left a little to be desired. The fact that they were written with a pencil made a few letters more difficult to read, especially when they were on blue paper.

Short biographical sketches have been included for each of the letter-writers, and an attempt has been made to identify the individuals mentioned in the letters. Sometimes, where only a first name was used, this was not possible.

For a detained account of the various companies from Rhea and Meigs counties, please refer to ***Rhea and Meigs Counties (Tennessee) in the Confederate War*** by V.C. Allen published in 1908 (reprinted in 1995 by the Rhea County Historical and Genealogical Society).

The Historical Society would like to thank all of those contributors who made this publication possible: Eugene Colville [Colville and Paine letters], Mary Jane Erwin [Guinn letterr and ledger], Sarah B. Jones [Taylor, Blevins, and Cross letters], Stewart Lillard [Lillard and Stewart letters], Donald Locke [Locke letter], Jane Moore [Everett letters], Tom Morgan [Morgan letters], Cecil B. Smith [Gannaway Poem], Seth Tallent [Clack Diary and Roddy Reminiscences], and Cathy Winkleman [Howell Diary].

Bettye J. Broyles

CONTENTS

A PERSONAL LOOK AT THE CIVIL WAR

— *PART I* —

NEWSPAPER ARTICLES

The following newspaper articles were all found in various issues of ***The Athens Post*** (transcribed from microfilm; date of issue appears under title). Several articles, particularly obituaries or death notices, have been interspersed with the letters. Many of the individuals mentioned in the articles were the authors of the letters.

The articles offer some insight into the personal feelings and the activities of the citizens of Rhea and Meigs counties in the few months prior to secession and the first three years of the war. They also show what the women of the two counties were doing to contribute to the comfort of the soldiers.

Many of the articles are of a general nature (i.e., instructions for making soap, beef jerkey, etc.) and show the ingenuity of the people during a difficult time. There are also several articles and unsigned letters discussing the war or a particular battle in which the soldiers from Rhea or Meigs County participated. The articles have been arranged chronologically rather than by subject.

COUNTY MEETING

[21 December 1860]

A large number of the citizens of Rhea County, of all political parties, assembled at the Courthouse in Washington, on Saturday the 15th instant. On motion of James A. Wallace, Esq., Dr. John W. Thompson was called to the Chair and W.E. Colville requested to act as Secretary. The Chairman then explained the object of the meeting in a few brief and appropriate remarks.

On motion, the following named gentlemen were appointed by the Chairman as a Committee to draft resolutions for the consideration of the meeting, to wit: A.W. Frazier, Jas A. Wallace, S.J. Frazier, Franklin Locke, Jas A. Darwin, W.T. Gass, R.N. Gillespie, and W.E. Colville– who, after retiring for a short time, returned and reported the following preamble and resolutions, to wit:

WHEREAS. In consideration of the great excitement that pervades the whole country, and threatens the Union of these States with certain destruction, we consider it our duty to declare our attachment to the present form of government as the best ever devised by man, and our hostility to all measures tending to overthrow or destroy it– therefore,

RESOLVED, That the election of Lincoln is not a sufficient cause for a dissolution of the Union, and that however much we may deplore it, yet, as it was in accordance with the Constitution, we will abide by and submit to his administration so long as it is just and equal to all.

RESOLVED, That we favor and will contend for the Constitution as it is– the Union as transmitted to us by our sires, as they intended it should be, and the execution of the laws as expounded and interpreted by the Supreme Court; and being impossed with the belief that in this we are right, declare that nothing less will satisfy us.

RESOLVED, That when our rights are trampled upon, or disregarded by the Executive power of the Government, that our safest and most effectual remedy lies in the Constitutional powers of impeachment, and not in the withdrawal from the Union.

RESOLVED, That those States which have nullified the Fugitive Slave Law have violated a plain provision of the Constitution; have attempted to defeat one of the great objects of Government, namely, the protection and security of property, and have been guilty of treason to the General Government, and have greatly impared the rights of the South; but that we believe our remedy to be within the Union and not by secession from it. But when we have asserted our rights, and exhausted all our Constitutional remedies without redress, and there is no other hope within the Union, then, as a last resort, may revolution be justified.

RESOLVED, That the course of South Carolina has been hasty and precipitable, and unjust to her sister States in desiring to forsake them in their hour of danger, and thus leave them with diminished forces to resist the aggressive spirit of Northern fanatics.

RESOLVED, That we freely endorse that portion of President Buchanan's message relating to disunion and secession, and the remedies proposed by him for existing evils.

RESOLVED, That we believe it to be the duty of the Legislature of the State of Tennessee to use their utmost exertions to call a Convention of the Southern States, for the purpose of devising some means of remedying the wrongs of the South, and of allaying the excitement that at present distracts and divides our country.

RESOLVED, That the proceedings of this meeting be published in The Athens Post, Cleveland Banner, Chattanooga Advertiser and the Gazette.

On motion, the vote was taken upon the resolutions separately, when the 2d, 4th, 6th, and 8th were unanimously adopted; the 1st, 3d, and 7th had each one vote against them, and the 5th had three nays. The resolutions were then voted for as a whole with but one dissenting vote.

During the absence of the Committee, the meeting was addressed by the Rev. G.A. Caldwell, of Athens, in an able, interesting and patriotic speech. After reading the report of Committee, addresses were delivered by Rev. J.W. Thompson, Rev. T.H. McCallie, of Chattanooga, Col. W.T. Gass, Rev. O. Bean, S.J.A. Frazier, and Jas A. Wallace, Esqs. Meeting then adjourned.

John W. Thompson, Chairman
W. E. Colville, Secretary

- - - - - - - - - - - - - - -

MEETING IN MEIGS
[1 February 1861]

At a meeting of a portion of the citizens of Meigs County, irrespective of party, held in the town of Decatur, January 28th 1861, Maj. William M. Rogers was requested to act as Chairman, and Dr. D.A. Gallaher, as Secretary.

On motion of R. McKenzie, it was unanimously resolved that this meeting is in favor of the Convention as called by the Legislature of Tennessee, and is also in favor of that Convention passing an Ordinance of Secession.

On motion of Col. G.W. McKenzie, Dr. Jno M. Lillard was unanimously nominated as a candidate to represent this Senatorial District in said Convention, and Dr. A.W. Hodges was also unanimously nominated to represent the Floating District composed of the counties of Meigs, McMinn and Polk.

After an able speech from Dr. Lillard, on motion of I.G. Cross, Esq., a copy of the proceedings was ordered to be sent to The Athens Post, Cleveland Banner and Nashville Union and American, for publication.

On motion of Samuel Blevins, the meeting adjourned.

Wm M. Rogers, Chairman
D. A. Gallaher, Secretary

A CARD

To the Voters of the Senatorial District composed of the Counties of Monroe, Meigs, McMinn, and Polk.

On yesterday at a meeting of members of all parties at the Courthouse in Decatur, I was selected to run for the Delegate in this District, as an Anti-Coercion States Rights Separate State Action Candidate. I agreed to do so in the event there was no candidate already in the field favoring the doctrine. This morning's mail beings letters that Wm M. Stakely, of Monroe, is a candidate, and holds the above doctrine. I therefore decline, as the time is too short and precious to have any wrangling. I make this public because the proceedings of the meeting referred to, I learn, will be published. In haste,

Yours truly, Jno M. Lillard

[NOTE: A similar letter was written by A.W. Hodge]

- - - - - - - - - - - - -

MEETING IN MEIGS
[5 April 1861]

At a meeting of the States Rights party in Meigs County, at the Courthouse in Decatur, on Monday the 1st of April 1861, the following proceedings were had, towit:

Major Jacob Peake was called to act as Chairman and Isaac S. Binyon called to act as Secretary, who were conducted to their respective chairs.

On motion, the Chair appointed the following Committee to draft resolutions to be submitted to the meeting, towit: John M. Lillard, Jno R. Fooshee, Frank McCorkle, Sam M. Cox, Pryor Neal, Jesse Martin, and James E. Fike, who retired and prepared and reported the following preamble and resolutions, towit:

WHEREAS, The time is fast approaching when Tennessee will be called upon to vote for Governor, Congressman, and others; and we deem it our privilege, as well as our duty, to give some expression of our sentiments on the crisis that is now on our country. — Therefore,

RESOLVED, That we are opposed to coercion of the seceded States by the United States, and that the holding of the forts and arsenals in the seceded states, or an attempt to collect revenue therein, is tantamount to coercion and hereby enter our protest against it.

RESOLVED, That non-action at present is fraught with danger, civil war and bloodshed, and we believe the only true course is to give such guarantees as will satisfy the whole South, or a recognition of an independent government in the Seceded States; and hereby declare our preference for the former, but if not obtained then we are for the latter, and will use all honorable means to place Tennessee with the Southern galaxy.

RESOLVED, That we will support any honorable man for Governor or Congress, no matter what has been his former political creed, who endorses our doctrines.

RESOLVED, That the Chairman of this meeting appoint one delegate from each civil district to attend the Nashville Convention, and three delegates from each civil district to attend the Congressional Convention.

Which resolves, as reported, were unanimously adopted. The Chair appointed the following delegates, to-wit:

Congressional:
1st District– J.B. Collins, H. Leonard, ----- Moody
2nd District– Jerry McKenzie, E.S. Chattin, E. Grubb
3rd District– W.S. Russell, Jesse Martin, J.M. Lillard
4th District– I.G. Cross, N.J. Lillard, F. McCorkle
5th District– Rufus Kincade, J.R. Fooshee, Wm Peake
6th District– Pryor Neal, R.R. Davis, J.E. Fike
7th District– A.F. Boggess, B.W. Smith, John McCallon
8th District– Jeff Hornsby, Ed Ford, Jo Moss

Delegates to Nashville:
1st District– J. B. Collins
2nd District– R. S. Holt
3rd District– Wm O. Allen
4th District– G. W. McKenzie
5th District– William Peake
6th District– R. R. Davis
7th District– Lea Neal
8th District– Jeff Hornsby

On motion, the Chairman and Secretary were added to both lists of delegates.

On motion, the proceedings of this meeting were ordered to be printed in The Athens Post, Cleveland Banner, and Nashville Union and American.

On motion, the meeting adjourned *sine die*.

Jacob Peake, Chairman
Isaac S. Binyon, Secretary

- - - - - - - - - - - - -

MEETING IN RHEA COUNTY
[12 April 1861]

On Monday, the 1st inst., the Union men of Rhea County met at the Courthouse in Washington, for the purpose of selecting delegates to attend the approaching State and District Conventions. James A. Darwin, Esq. was called to the Chair and W.E. Colville appointed Secretary.

On motion, the Chair appointed a Committee of three to select delegates to attend the Convention to be held at Athens or Cleveland, on the 11th day of May, 1861. After a short absence, the Committee reported the following names towit:

1st District– Jesse P. Thompson, Benjamin Robinson
2nd District– A.D. Paul, Edward Pyott, Smith Brady
3rd District– R.J. Gaines, Thomas McPherson
4th District– P.W. Miller, J.G. Frazier, D. Walker, John Wheeler
5th District– J.P. Collins, M. Howerton
6th District– Franklin Locke, J.A. Wallace
7th District– Henry Fisher, Samuel Howell
8th District– William Morgan, Stephen Gray
9th District– Dan Knox, William Palmer
10th District– Dr. John Ragsdale, Nicholas Keith

On motion, the Chair appointed delegates to the State Convention, to be held at Nashville, on the 2nd day of May 1861, to wit:
1st District– A. J. Cawood
2th District– Dr. J. W. Gillespie
3rd District– R. Clack
4th District– R. B. Shirley
5th District– J. A. Darwin
6th District– W. E. Colville, W. P. Darwin
7th District– Samuel Howell
8th District– Wash Morgan Jr.
9th District– Dan Knox
10th District– R. F. McDonald

The following resolutions were then read by the Chair and unanimously adopted.

RESOLVED, That we, a portion of the Union men of Rhea County, do cordially approve the patriotic cause of Hon. R.B. Brabson, Representative in Congress for this Congressional District, on the vital question of Union or Disunion which has been precipated upon the country by reckless demagogues, North and South.

RESOLVED, That J.L. Hopkins is the first choice of the Union party of Rhea County, and that the delegates be requested to present his name to the Convention as candidate, and use all honorable means to secure him the nomination.

RESOLVED, That we request the Athens Post and the Chattanooga Gazette to publish the proceedings of this meeting.

J. A. Darwin, Chairman
W. E. Colville, Secretary

- - - - - - - - - - - - -

A WORD TO UNION MEN
[12 April 1861]

The parties of Tennessee are "Union" and "Disunion" – nothing more, nothing less. Union men, thank God, have a majority of more than 60,000, and they are composed of Whigs and Democrats. It is necessary that their action in the approaching canvass should be entirely harmonious– there should be no dissentions in the ranks. In order that such should be the case, there should be as nearly as practicable, an equal division of candidates. Such a cause will leave no ground for Whigs to say "it is a Democratic move," or for Democrats to say "it is a Whig move." Let the people select upon the above stated basis, good and undoubted men, and all will move on smoothly. Tennessee, in her official armor, will be more terrible to treason and to traitors than an "army with Banners."

[signed] KINGSTON, TENN.

- - - - - - - - - - - - -

MEETING IN MEIGS
[19 April 1861]

At a meeting of a portion of the Union party of Meigs County, at Decatur, on the first Monday of April, 1861, the following proceedings were had, to wit:

On motion, J.F. Zeigler was called to the Chair and R.E. Cate appointed secretary. The chairman then explained the object of the meeting in a few plain but pertinent remarks– when, upon motion, the Chair appointed the following delegates to attend the Union Convention to be held in Nashville for the purpose of nominating a candidate for Governor–

1st District– J.N. Witt, Z. Martin
2nd District– H. Whitmore, Wm C. Grubb
3rd District– Josiah Howser, Col. A. Cox
4th District– Wm J. Abel, Thomas Locke
5th District– Dr. G.M. Clementson, W.P. Moore
6th District– F. Grigsby, Thos Cecil
7th District– Gen. J.M. Culler, Sam Bryant
8th District– E. Ford, J. Holloman

On motion, the Chair appointed the following delegates to the Congress and Union Convention to meet at such time and place as may hereafter be designated, for the purpose of nominating a candidate for Congress for the Third Congressional District:

1st District– Nat Witt, W.L. Hutchison, T. Miller
2nd District– T.J. Matthews, D. Wamac, E. Martin, J.W. Williams, A. Grubb
3rd District– Dr. E.D. Gilbert, A. Denton, Wm Evans, A. Perry, A. Goforth
4th District– L. Locke, A. Cate, J. Cooley, P. Allen, J. Bishop
5th District– Dr. G.M. Clementson, Dr. E. Collins, P. Holloman, J. Rowden, J.H. Walker
6th District– J.M. Cecil, M.R. Isley, A. Guinn, J. Lovelace, George Guinn
7th District– M. Bryant, ---- Black, A. F. Boggess, J. J. McCallon, Dr. E.S. Shipley
8th District– E. Ford, E. Rowden, Amos Moss, J. Holloman, Wm Wann

On motion, the Chairman, Secretary, and Dr. John C. Everett were added to both lists of delegates.

On motion, Dr. W.R. Horley, of the Nashville Democrat, was appointed our proxy to cast the vote of this County for any sound Union man for Governor, in case none of our delegates attend the Convention at Nashville.

On motion, a copy of these proceedings were ordered to be furnished to the Athens Post and Nashville Democrat for publication.

On motion, the meeting adjourned *sine die*.

J. F. Zeigler, Chairman
R. E. Cate, Secretary

- - - - - - - - - - -

MEETING IN MEIGS COUNTY
[26 April 1861]

We were at Decatur on Monday and Tuesday. There was a large number of persons present on Monday. "The War," of course, was the all-absorbing topic of conversation, although the excitement was less than we expected– attributable, no doubt, to the fact that there is but little diversity of sentiment. So far as we could learn, and we took some pains, the people of Meigs are unanimous in the determination to resist the policy of the Lincoln administration to overrun, "seize, hold and possess," the South. We noticed a military company, armed with percussion muskets, drilling under Capt. N.J. Lillard. We understood this Company has tendered its services to the State.

Maj. L. R. Hurst and Gen. James T. Lane addressed the people at the Courthouse on Monday, on public affairs. Both are for the State taking immediate action. But we have neither time or space to notice their remarks at length– Major Hurst is a candidate for Joint Representative, unless Meigs presents one of her own citizens. Gen. Lane is a candidate for the State Senate.

We have said above that there was no undue excitement among the people– We are glad to record it, for if there ever was a time when the people should be one in heart, one in sentiment, and one in purpose, it is now.

- - - - - - - - - - - - -

MEETING AT TEN MILE [MEIGS COUNTY]
[3 May 1861]

A large portion of the citizens of Ten Mile Stand and vicinity met pursuant to appointment, on Saturday, the 27th inst. to give expression to their sentiments on the perilous condition of affairs.

On motion of J.B. McCallon, A.F. Boggess was called to the Chair and S.J. Bryan was requested to act as Secretary. The Chairman then explained the object of the meeting in a few plain but pertinent remarks.

On motion of N.C. Redman, the Chair appointed the following Committee, viz: J.C. Sharp, G.R. Griffith, Dr. M.C. Clark, G.P. Sharp, Lea Neal, W.P. Proffitt and S.J. Bryan, who reported the following preamble and resolutions, which were adopted.

WHEREAS, A crisis is upon the County of paramount importance, affecting the interest, rights and liberties of every citizen; and, whereas, the revolution is upon us, of a character and magnitude hitherto unknown, demanding not only an expression, but prompt action from every patriot: Therefore,

RESOLVED, That with sorrow we have seen the rapid succession of evils that have befallen our Country, until our once proud Republic is shaken to its centre, and its Constitution, the piller and paladium of our liberties, is

trampled under foot with impunity, until our Union under it is disolved, though with pain we say it; there is no Union to love but that that was.
RESOLVED, That with indignation we have seen the vasillating course and iniquitous coercive policy of Abe Lincoln, President innaugurate of these once United States, but corrupt Executive of sectionalism, whose Courts has inaugurated a Civil War of which no eye of faith nor spirit of prophecy can see an end.
RESOLVED, That in this emergency we hail with pride the patriotic and gallant answer of His Excellency Isham G. Harris, the Executive of Tennessee, in reply to the base and tyrannical call of Abe Lincoln for Tennessee sons to engage in fraternal butchery, and that we will, to the extent of our abilities, sustain our Executive in this answer.
RESOLVED, That we are in favor of immediate withdrawal from the Northern faction of the old Confederacy and standing in arms with our Southern brethern, under the banner of Tennessee, and follow its fortunes and share its fate, whether in victory or in defeat, resisting coercion to the latter and until peace is restored.
RESOLVED, That we are opposed to joining the Southern Confederacy further than a union of arms for defence or the accomplishment of our cherished object, peace. The chrisis is upon us, and we will fight out of it, and then consult as to our future civil relations.
RESOLVED, That as danger threatens us, of any character, it becomes every community to be in readiness to defend themselves and families, their property, and each other, from any insurrection or danger that may arise at home, and for this purpose we organize a Home Guard.

On motion of Morgan Bryan, a copy of these proceedings were ordered to be sent to The Athens Post and Cleveland Banner for publication.

A. F. Boggess, Chairman
S. J. Bryan, Secretary

- - - - - - - - - - - - -

ADVICE TO VOLUNTEERS
HOW TO PREPARE FOR THE CAMPAIGN

[10 May 1861]

A writer, who signs himself "An Old Soldier," gives the folling advice to young soldiers:
1. Remember that in a campaign more men die from sickness than by the bullet.
2. Line your blankets with one thickness of brown drilling. This adds but four ounces in weight and doubles the warmth.
3. Buy a small Inda rubber blanket (only $1.50) to lay on the ground or to throw over your shoulders when on guard duty during a rain storm. Most of the eastern troops are provided with these–– straw to lie on is not always to be had.
4. The best military hat in use is the light colored soft felt; the crown being sufficiently high to allow space for air above the brain. You can fasten it up as a continental in fair weather, or turn it down when it is wet or very sunny.
5. Let your beard grow, so as to protect the throat and lungs.
6. Keep your entire person clean; this prevents fevers and bowel complaints in warm climates. Wash your body each day, if possible. Avoid strong coffee and oily meat. Gen. Scott said that the too free use of these (together with neglect in keeping the skin clean) cost many a soldier his life in Mexico.
7. A sudden check of perspiration by chilly or night air often causes fever and death. When thus exposed, do not forget your blanket.

- - - - - - - - - - - - -

IMPORTANT TO FOOT SOLDIERS

[17 May 1861]

1. Blistering, burning, soreness and tenderness of the soles of the feet may almost invariably be prevented, even when marching for days together and above a heated road by soaping the sole of the stocking—that is, covering it with a thin coating of the cheapest brown soap. This, at the same time, keeps the skin of the sole cool, hardens it and prevents inflamation. Coarse cotton socks are the best for walking.
2. Don't wear woolen socks when you are marching, not even thin ones, no matter in what climate.
3. The boot or shoes should have a thick sole; it is not sufficient that they should be simply "double soled." The soles should be at least an inch thick; if three-fourths of an inch or an inch, all the better; they are more expensive, but if well made will last a long time, and even in the warmest weather will be found easy to walk in, the feet easily becoming accustomed to their weight.

- - - - - - - - - - - - -

MURDER

[17 May 1861]

There was a murder committed in Washington, Tenn., on Saturday, 11th inst., by B.M.C. Collins upon James Sexton. Said Collins has made his escape, and the citizens of Rhea County will give a suitable reward for his apprehension.

B.M.C. Collins is about six feet high, slim, spare made, weighs about 130 to 140 pounds, singular mouth, shows his teeth in talking, high prominent cheek bones, dark complexion, black hair, awkward in his movements, bad countenance and loves his liquor.

[signed] W. E. Colville & others

- - - - - - - - - - - - -

DR. W. M. WILSON
SURGEON AND PATHOLOGICAL DENTIST
Rhea County, Tennessee
[17 May 1861]

Will practice all the various branches of his profession in all the Counties of East Tennessee. Address, Washinhgton, Tennessee.
N.B.— All work warranted to be done in the best and most approved style.

- - - - - - - - - - - - -

PAY OF VOLUNTEERS IN CONFEDERATE ARMY
[14 June 1861]

Colonel	$ 165 per month
Lieutenant Colonel	170 per month
Captain	108 per month
First Lieutenant	90 per month
Second Lieutenant	80 per month
First Sergeant	21 per month
Other Sergeants	17 per month
Corps and artificers	13 per month
Privates	11 per month
	[with yearly allowance of clothing and one ration per day]
Quartermasters	108 per month
Commissary	108 per month

- - - - - - - - - - - - -

OFFICIAL VOTE
[14 June 1861]

MEIGS COUNTY

Districts	Separation	Representation	No Sep	No Rep
1 st	13	13	139	139
2nd	72	74	44	44
3rd	68	68	47	47
4th	128	126	3	4
5th	54	54	0	0
6th	72	72	17	17
7th	51	51	1	1
8th	23	23	16	16
	481	478	267	268
	267	268		
Majority	214	210		

In Meigs, the majority for Separation is 214— Capt. Lillard's Company, 100 men, now in Virginia.

RHEA COUNTY

Separation		360
Representation		336
No Separation		202
No Representation		217
Majority for Separation	158	
Majority for Representation	119	

One company of Volunteers, numbering 100 men, was raised in Rhea, and their vote, of course, is not in the above.

- - - - - - - - - - - - -

INSTRUCTIONS TO POST MASTERS
[21 June 1861]

By the vote of the citizens cast on the 8th inst., Tennessee has become a member of the Southern Confederacy. The following are the instructions to Post Masters of that Confederacy, which you will please observe and be governed by:

NEW POSTAGE ACTS: NOTICE TO THE PUBLIC AND INSTRUCTIONS TO POSTMASTERS

The following laws have been enacted by the Congress of the Confederate States of America:

Letter Postage

An Act to prescribe the Rates of Postage in the Confederate States of America, and for other purposes: "The Congress of the Confederate States of America do enact, that from and after such period as the Post Master General may by proclamation announce, there shall be charged the following rates of postage, towit: for every single sealed letter, and for every letter in manuscript or paper of any kind, upon which information shall be asked for or communicated in writing or by marks or signs, conveyed in the mail for any distance between places within the Confederate States of America, not exceeding five hundred miles, five cents; and for any distance exceeding five hundred miles, double that rate; and every letter or parcel not exceeding half an ounce in weight shall be deemed a single letter, and every additional weight of half an ounce, shall be charged with additional single postage; *and all packages containing other than printed or written matter — and money packages are included in this class— shall be rated by weight as letters are rated,* and shall be charged the rates of postage on letters; and all drop-letters, placed in any post office not for transmission but for delivery only, shall be charged with postage at the rate of two cents each; and in all the foregoing cases the postage must be prepaid by stamps; and all letters which shall hereafter be advertised as remaining over or uncalled for in any post office, shall be charged with two cents each addition to the regular postage, both to be accounted for as other postage of this Confederacy."

[signed] W.D. McNISH
Post Master, Nashville, Tenn.

- - - - - - - - - - - - -

HORRIBLE AFFAIR
[21 June 1861]

Yesterday evening, two gentlemen named Beard and Arehart, were standing on Gay Steet [in Knoxville] near the store of T.C. Champe Esq. A musket was fired from the Daguerrian Gallery of Thos H. Smiley. The shot, it is supposed, was aimed at Mr. Beard, but struck young Arehart in the shoulder, inflicting a serious, if not fatal wound.

[James] Arehart is a member of Capt. Colville's Company, from Rhea County.

A man named Marcum has been arrested and charged with the commission of the deed. It was a cold blooded attempt at assination and created intense excitement. It required great effort to keep the populace from inflicting on the accused summary punishment. He was however handed over to the civil authorities and is now in prison awaiting his trial.

- - - - - - - - - - - - -

ANOTHER COMPANY FROM MEIGS
[21 June 1861]

Captain A.F. Boggess' Company of volunteers left Decatur for Knoxville on the 13th instant. There was a very large number of people, both ladies and gentlemen, in attendance. The Company, being formed, was marched to the Baptist Church where the Rev. Mr. Rose talked to them a few minutes, closing with one of the most fervent prayers for their safety and their success; after which, MISS CATTIE LOCKE, of Ten Mile Stand, appeared with a beautiful Flag, and after making the following Address, she presented it to the Company. Turning to Captain and his Company, Miss Cattie said:

Capt. Boggess— You, with your gallant corps of volunteers, composed of our fathers, brothers and companions, have been called from your peaceful pursuits and are now ready to take up the line of march to the tented field, to meet the enemies and would be oppressors of Southern freemen, and threatened invaders of our peaceful homes in the sunny South. And although we are prevented from sharing with you the dangers of camplife, we desire to cheer you in your departure, by giving you every assurance of our approval of your determination to meet our common enemy, and for that purpose, as a token of our unwavering confidence in your patriotism and valor, and of our firm faith in the righteousness of your cause, I am assigned the pleasant duty of presenting to you this beautiful Flag, wrought by the fair hands of the daughters of Meigs County, to accompany you in the dangers and horrors of your campaign and when surrounded by dangers, may it be your monitor to prompt you to maintain the ancient character and renown of our beloved Tennessee, and may your achievements reflect upon you honors as bright as those stars confer upon the field of blue which they stud, and be assured that the hearts that prompt its presentation beat high with anticipation for your success and safe return, and I trust our prayers on your behalf will not fall unheeded or unheard in His sight who rules even in the hour of battle. Your country calls for your service– its voice is of paramount importance, and though it costs our hearts bitter pangs and our eyes a profusion of tears, we say to you, kindred, countrymen, go– not that we love you less, but that we love our country and liberty more. Go, and may you early return with peace perched upon your victorious banner, and may the glory of the ancient Tenth Legion be yours.

While the speaker was addressing the Company, a gentle breeze stirred the silken banner, which waved above her head, displaying the names of those young ladies who assisted in making it, inscribed on the eleven stars– among which was the name of the Speaker that stood beneath it– and we believe there was no one among that vast assembly who looked upon her calm, placid, but firm countenance, comparing with the beautiful flag that floated above her, that did not feel the genial influence which women may wield. Every one present seemed interested. Perfect silence reigned during the while, and a tear might have been seen starting from the most resolute and firm. There was no ear that did not listen, no heart that was not moved.

JOHN M. LILLARD, First Lieutenant in the Company, briefly and patriotically responded, returning thanks for the presentation of the colors wrought by the fair hands of the daughters of Meigs County, for whom he would every danger; and while that banner continued to wave at the head of their column, or while those names written upon the stars could be seen or remembered, they would be prompted to act, and that flag they would defend with their lives. He hoped to return it to the hand that gave it, with peace and liberty perched upon it.

- - - - - - - - - - - - -

ANOTHER FLAG FOR CAPT. BOGGESS' COMPANY
[21 June 1861]

Editor Post: Among the various things transpiring in our valley, nothing of more interest has presented itself than the arrival of Capt. Boggess' Company of Volunteers, from Meigs County. This gallant little band, composed in part of middle aged men, but mostly of younger men, who may indeed be said to be the flower of Meigs

County, reached Mouse Creek on Thursday evening last, in time to partake of the sumptous dinner prepared for them by the ladies of our vicinity, who were generally present to share the honors of waiting upon them in person. During the night they remained at Mouse Creek the ladies made them a beautiful flag.— The next morning, after the citizens of the neighborhood had met to see them take the cars, Capt. Boggess drew up his Company in front of the Depot platform for the purpose of receiving the Flag.—

Upon being loudly called for, Major L. R. Hurst made them a speech of five or ten minutes' length, in his peculiar happy style. After which, Miss SALLIE HURST, who had been appointed to present the colors, appeared upon the platform with her military cap on, holding the banner in her hand— Miss Martha E. Cate by her side, supporting the flag presented the Company by the ladies of Meigs County. Beneath the folds of these two beautiful banners, Miss Sallie said:

Gentlemen Soldiers: I am here in behalf of the ladies of Mouse Creek, to present this flag to Captain Boggess' Company, from Meigs County, who have volunteered to defend the rights and the honor of our glorious South. Patriotism has prompted you to leave your domestic cares and the loved ones at home, to fight the battles of your Country. You should remember that the race is not always to the swift, nor the battle to the strong, but to him that looks to the God of battles.

Through you, Dr. Lillard, I present this Flag. I am sure it will never be dishonored. When in the heat and storm of battle, look upon the Flag and think of the warm hearts left behind you and press forward to victory and glory.

Dr. JOHN M. LILLARD, holding the Flag in his hand, his eyes, in tears, fixed upon the fifteen stars, replied in behalf of the Company:

Miss Sallie: To you and the fair ones of Mouse Creek who have made and presented this beautiful flag to Capt. Boggess' Company, I on behalf of the Company, thank you. You behold, also, the beautiful Flag we have, presented to our Company on the eve of our departure from Meigs County, on yesterday. These two flags, wrought by the hands of the fair daughters of Meigs and McMinn, we will take, with the belief that your prayers during our absence will ascend to the God of battles for our success and the preservation of our lives and safe return home to our loved ones. Should we be engaged in deadly conflict with the enemies of our beloved South, these two banners, entwining their folds together over our heads, will give strength to our arms and fire to our hearts to drive back those who would ravage and subjugate our beloved South. Rest assured this Company will not dishonor this flag, and we trust we may never be lowered in your estimation, but that our conduct in this contest may meet your highest expectation. Again, on behalf of the Company, I thank you.

- - - - - - - - - - - - -

LETTER FROM AN EAST TENNESSEE VOLUNTEER

[21 June 1861]

Camp Davis, Near Lynchburg, Va.
June 11, 1861

Editor Post: I take this opportunity of complying with a request made by divers of my friends before I left, to write to them—and as your paper has a circulation amongst them all, I hope you will allow me to give, through your columns, a short account of ourselves to our friends. We received orders from the commander in charge of the troops at Harper's Ferry to march there as soon as we could get conveyance. The officers and men of our Regiment are well pleased with our place of destination. We expected, a few days ago, to be ordered to Manassas Junction. We expect to be placed where fighting will be done, and we have the men that will do it up right. A short time now will tell what it will be with the North, feathers or fuss. We are, as a body of men, the most healthy I have ever seen, and thus far have met with the best luck. Only one man has lost his life as yet of all our troops. He belonged to Col. Vaughn's Company, from Monroe County, by the name of Harrell, occasioned by the train running off the track as we came here from Knoxville.

Day before yesterday Capt. Pearce B. Anderson marched a fine Company of men into our camps, and remained in only for a few hours. He has since left for some important point. He is much like the same man that he was when he lived in our midst, except the gray hair—but all is right and young within him. From some cause he left the troops that he came here with and was ordered by the Governor to raise a Company of Artillery, which he done in a few days.

The soldiers are much gratified that Tennessee has gone out of the Union of Abolitionism and joined her true friends and brethern of the South. I hope, now that the majority have spoked in our favor, that our enemies, if any we have, at home will be as true to the government under which they live as they used to say we ought to be— they are now legally and constitutionally subjects of the Confederate States, and it is a bad rule that wont work both ways. They said we were rebels for opposing the Lincoln government before our connection was dissolved; now it is dissolved; would it not be treason in them to oppose this government, now thus constitutionally made by the will of the people? I would write many other things, but know that you have seen them in print.

Yours &c, S.M. BOGGESS

- - - - - - - - - - - - -

DISCONTINUED

[28 June 1861]

We learn that the mail route between Athens and Sulphur Springs has been discontinued. Sulphur Springs and Prestonville will be supplied through Washington, Rhea County. Our friends at Sewee and Moore's X Roads will please advise us as to their papers.

- - - - - - - - - - - - -

THE SKIRMISH AT NEW CREEK DEPOT

[28 June 1861]

Brigade Headquarters, Camp Davis
Romney, June 19, 1861

Colonel: I have the honor to report that on yesterday I directed Col. J. C. Vaughn, of the 3rd Tennessee Regiment, to take two Companies from his own and two from the 13th Virginia Regiment and at 8 o'clock, p.m., to proceed to New Creek Depot, 18 miles West of Cumberland, on the Baltimore and Ohio Railroad, disperse the forces there collected, bring away the two pieces of artillery, and burn the Railroad bridge.

The directions, I am happy to assure you, were carried out to the letter, and the march of 38 miles accomplished between 8 p.m. and 12 the next day.— Some 250 of the Federal troops, after a slight stand, retired in disorder, with a loss of a few men. The bridge was then burned, and Col. Vaughn retired, bringing with him two pieces of artillery and a stand of colors.

To Col. Vaughn, his officers and men, I am much indebted for the handsome manner in which my orders were carried out.

Enclosed you will find the report of Col. Vaughn.
I am, Sir, very respectfully,
Your obedient servant
[signed] A. P. Hill
Col. 3d Reg't, Commanding Brigade,
Col. E. K. Smith, A.A. General

- - - - - - - - - - - - -

HEADQUARTERS, 3d TENN. REGT. COL. HILL'S BRIGADE, JUNE 19, 1861

[28 June 1861]

A.P. Hill, Col. Commanding Brigade, C.S.A., Romney, Va.:

Sir: I have the honor to report that on yesterday, at 8 o'clock, p.m., in pursuance of your order, I took two companies of the 13th Virginia Volunteers, C.S.A., commanded by Capts. Crittendon and White, and also two Companies of 3d Tennessee Regiment Volunteers, C.S. A., commanded by Capts. Lillard and Mathas, and advanced 18 miles West, to the line of the enemy, upon the Baltimore and Ohio Railroad, and found them posted in some strength, with two pieces of artillery, on the North bank of the Potomac, at the 21st Railroad bridge, on said road.— The enemy had no pickets posted. At 5 o'clock, a.m., after reconnoitering, I gave the order to charge the enemy, which command, I beg leave to say, was gallantly executed and in good order, but with great enthusiasm.

As we appeared in sight, at a distance of 400 yards, the enemy broke and fled in all directions, firing as they run only a few random shots, one of which, however, I regret to say, entered the arm of private Smith, of Capt. Lillard's Company, which was in advance, wounding him slightly. The enemy did not wait to fire their artillery, which we captured, consisting of two loaded guns, both of which, however, were spiked by the enemy before they fled. From the best information their number was between two and three hundred.

I do not know the loss of the enemy, but several of them were seen to fall.— We did not take any prisoners, owing to the start the enemy got, and of our having left in the rear all the horses belonging to the command. I then ordered the 21st railroad bridge to be burnt, which was done, and in a few minutes only the piers remained. In further pursuance of your order, I then retired, bringing with me the two guns. The enemy's flag, which I forgot to mention, was captured, and other articles of little value. I cannot close without bringing to your notice the gallant conduct of both officers and men, who were each at their posts, and burning to engage the enemy, and, when the order to charge was given, rushed forward with enthusiasm, wading the river to their waists. I arrived here this evening, the spirits of my men in no wise flagged.

Respectfully, your obd't serv't
[signed] John C. Vaughn
Colonel Commanding,
Third Tennessee Volunteers. C.S.A.

- - - - - - - - - - - - -

FROM MEIGS COUNTY

[5 July 1861]

Editor, Athens Post: Dear Sir– Being County Court, a number of citizens were here today, who repaired to the Courthouse immediately after dinner and held the following meeting extempore:

On motion, Rev. Z. Rose was called to the Chair and W.L. McKinley requested to act as Secretary. Thereupon, the Chairman explained, briefly but pertinently, the object of the meeting.

On motion, the Chair appointed the following Committee to report resolutions expressive of the sense of the meeting, to wit: J.R. Fooshee, G.W. McKenzie, Caleb Moore, William W. Lillard, and A.W. Hodges, who reported the following preamble and resolutions:

WHEREAS, The people of Tennessee will again, on the 1st Thursday in August next, be called upon to elect a Governor of the State, and believing it to be our duty to express our choice to fill that high and responsible position– Therefore,

RESOLVED, That we, the people of Meigs County, regardless of old political parties, endorse the action of our present Governor, and admire his bold and manly stand against the aggressive and unconstitutional acts of a

Black Republican President, and heartily endorse his actions to place Tennessee in a State of defense against inroads of a Northern army.
RESOLVED, That, as we endorse the course of our patriotic Governor, Isham G. Harris, it is our desire that he again permit us to place him in the Gubernatorial chair.
RESOLVED, That we do not wish any opposition to be made to his reelection, as it is our desire to bury all old party differences and to be a united people henceforth.
RESOLVED, That we do not think it necessary for Governor Harris to canvass the State, as we think he would better subserve the interests of the State in these times of trouble at his post in giving advise and directions to our defensive operations against a fanatical enemy.
RESOLVED, That in the event he should not be a candidate again for reelection, we will cordially and heartily support any good Southern man.

When, on motion, it was ordered that the Secretary furnish copies of the proceedings of this meeting, to be published in the Athens Post and Cleveland Banner. Then, on motion, the meeting adjourned, *sine die*.

Z. Rose, Chairman
W.L. McKinley, Secretary
July 1, 1861

- - - - - - - - - - - - -

MEETING IN RHEA
[9 July 1861]

A portion of the Southern Rights Men of Rhea County having assembled at the Courthouse in Washington, on Monday the 5th day of July, 1861, John B. Murphy, Esq. was called to the Chair, Onslow Bean appointed Secretary. On motion, P. Killough, T.J. Haney, John Howell, Joseph Parks, R.N. Gillespie and Martin White were appointed a Committee to draft suitable resolutions. After having retired a few minutes, the Committee returned and reported, through Mr. P. Killough, their Chairman, the following preamble and resolutions, viz:

WHEREAS, the election for State officers is drawing near, and it behooves all true Southern men to give an expression of opinion as to their preferences for the candidates to the various offices in the State, therefore,
RESOLVED, That although there are hundreds of other good and true men in both the former old parties for whom we would have cheerfully voted, yet, reviewing all the circumstances by which we are surrounded, and taking everything into consideration, we consider Isham G. Harris, the present incumbent, "the right man in the right place," and will support him for Governor of Tennessee in preference to all others. He has been tried and found true in these trying times; and while the citizens of some of our sister States have wept and mourned over the imbecility and degeneracy of their Governors, it has been the pride of Tennesseans to point with a triumphant air to Isham G. Harris, and exclaim "behold Tennessee's jewel."

Isham G. Harris

RESOLVED, That we will support good and true men to the Confederate Congress, to the State Senate, and the House of Representatives, who are right now and who are in favor of sustaining the South in this her hour of peril, and resisting Abe Lincoln and his minions to the last extremity, it matters not what have been their former antecedents; the only questions that we will ask of a candidate now will be "Are you for the South now? are you in favor of resisting Abe Lincoln until death?" and we respectfully request our friends to bury all party differences.
RESOLVED, That a copy of these resolutions be sent to the Athens Post for publication, and that the Cleveland Banner and Union and American be requested to copy.

J. B. Murphy, Chairman
O. Bean, Secretary

- - - - - - - - - - - - -

THE FIGHT NEAR WINCHESTER
[12 July 1861]

Mr. Frazier, of Meigs County, a member of Capt. Lillard's Company, and Chaplain to the 3rd Tennessee Regiment, arrived here on Thursday evening, direct from Winchester. The account of Jackson's collision with Patterson's advance, and the capture of one entire company of the enemy, is correct. . . . Mr. Frazier was at Winchester when the prisoners arrived. . . .

- - - - - - - - - - - - -

DEAD IN THE SERVICE
[12 July 1861]

We learn from the mountains that a Mr. Hall, of Capt. Ragsdale's Company, was killed a few days since, by being thrown from a wagon.

Mr. Bradley, of Capt. Colville's Company, died of pneumonia, from exposure while recovering from measels.

- - - - - - - - - - - - -

FROM CAPT. LOWRY'S COMPANY
[19 July 1861]

Below is an extract from a letter from Mr. J. A. PECK, a member of Capt. Lowry's Company, and formerly employed on this paper [*Athens Post*]:

CAMP KEY, Fentress Co., July 11

S.P. Ivins: I avail myself of the first opportunity to drop you a line. Captain Willie Lowry's Infantry Company and Captain Rowen's Cavalry are now stationed at this point— "Three Forks of Wolf River." We were on the road the greater portion of eight days. Had quite a time, too, but all got here safe. We have a plesant place for camps. The water is splendid and right at hand. Provisions of all kinds are very plenty and extraordinarily cheap. We are all well, doing well, and as fat as cub bears.

Captains Boggess and Allen's Infantry Company's arrived here today about 12 o'clock, the two numbering two hundred and twenty-seven men. We have now in "Camp Key" 500 men and four other Companies expected every hour.

I wish you would send me the *Post* for twelve months and I will pay you when I return.

Respects to all. J.A.P.

- - - - - - - - - - - - -

FROM THE VOLUNTEERS
[19 July 1861]

CAMP EDWARDS
near Jacksboro, July 9

Sam P. Ivins: . . . We have three companies of Infantry at this point, to wit, Capt. Snapp's, Capt. Hannah's, and Capt. Colville's, besides Capt. Ragsdale's Cavalry Company. There has been a great reaction in public sentiment since our advent into the neighborhood of the mountain. With a few exceptions, if the people were let alone they would be for acquiescence. In fact, some of the leaders so express themselves. I think all will be right here in a week or two. Kentucky on the border is still threatening to drive us back— indeed, they are arming the citizens. In Knox and Whitfield Counties they have already received some fifteen hundred stand of arms. It is thought there will be an effort to send arms through some of the mountain passes into East Tennessee. If so, you may look out for a considerable fuss.

We have a good many men sick, mostly with measels. Yours truly, — [not signed]

- - - - - - - - - - - - -

REPORT FROM JIMTOWN
[16 August 1861]

Reports reached here last Monday morning that Paul McDermott, a member of Capt. Lowry's Company, now stationed in the neighborhood of Jimtown, had been attacked by three men, while separated from his comrads, and killed. Also, that George W. Bridges, of whose departure for Washington we made mention last week, has been captured on the Kentucky line by a detachment of Capt. Rowan's Company; that Rowan's men had been subsequently cut off, and that the encampment of the troops was being surrounded and menanced by large bodies of Union men, &c. . . .

- - - - - - - - - - - - -

TO THE CLERKS OF THE COUNTY COURTS OF THE STATE OF TENNESSEE
[16 August 1861]

You are hereby requested to issue to each Constable in your respective counties, an order requiring him to make dilligent enquiry at each house in his civil district for all muskets, bayonets, rifles, swords and pistols belonging to the State of Tennessee, to take them into possession and deliver them to you.

A reward of one dollar will be paid to the Constable for each musket and bayonet or rifle, and fifty cents for each sword or pistol thus reclaimed.

You will forward the arms thus obtained at public expense, to the military authorities of Nashville, Knoxville and Memphis as may be most convenient, and will inform the Military and Finance Board, by letter, of the result of your action, and of the expense incurred. A check for the amount will be promptly forwarded.

[signed] ISHAM G. HARRIS, Governor &c.

- - - - - - - - - - - - -

FROM THIRD TENNESSEE REGIMENT
[16 August 1861]

Camp Fairfax, Va.,
Aug. 9, 1861

Editor Post: Dear Sir:

I have just arrived in camp from one of our regular turns as an advance picket guard, to a point known as Falls Church, four miles from Alexandria. This trip we perform by turn, one Company at a time, until the Regiment has been gone through. Our cavalry say the enemys pickets only comes out two miles this side of Alexandria. One of the Lieutenants rode up to our pickets yesterdy, about three miles this side of Alexandria, and gave himself up as a prisoner.

Our Third Tennessee Regiment is very much improving in health since we come to this place. We are also receiving daily recruits to it, and of the right sort of material. I would just say to our friends at home, no danger of subjugation or of being whipped here. We have got much of the Yankees' valuable property and many of their soldiers. The property is of vast use to us, but the prisoners none.

I will give you a list of Capt. Lillard's Company, with reference to the health of each, which you will please publish for the satisfaction of their friends:

[NOTE: after the vast majority of names was written "here and well." In order to shorten the following list, this notation has been omitted; any different notation is shown in parenthesis following the name. B.J.B.]

I.G. Cross, 1st Lt.; D.M Blevins, 2nd Lt.; B.F. Taylor, 3rd Lt.; S.R. Baldwin, Orderly Sgt; H.T. Blevins, 2d Sgt.; Roswell Chambers, 3d Sgt.; B.F. Lillard, 4th Sgt.; J.H. Guinn, 1st Corp.; J.C.C. Blevins, 2d Corp. (at Winchester, sick); W.N. King, 3d Corp.; L.R. Blevins, 4th Corp.

Privates: M. Aheart (at Winchester, not well), G.W. Atchley (left at Winchester with the sick), T.B. Allen, A. Armstrong, J.B. Boggess, S.M. Boggess, J.M. Buckner, A. Buckner, B.F. Bean, J.P. Blevins, J.K. Blevins Jr., J.W. Crain, G.W. Cate, S.M. Cox, Wm Carroll, M.V. Copeland, J.C. Cowan, J.V. Guinn, L.B. Guinn, E. Guthman, S.H. Howell, Smith Hutton, E.L. Hodge, J. Horrid, R. Hackler, Abijah Howard (here, not well), John Howard, B.F. Hudson, J.S. Hairwood, J.A. Key, J.S.V. Lillard, John Lillard, Thomas S. Latham, James Lamar, Amos Lamar, Frank McCorkle, Lafayette McCorkle, S.M. McGinnis, J.C. Moore, G.W. Marshall, H.L.W. Martin, E. Massengill, J.G. Monsey (at Winchester, sick), Wm Martin, William Melton, J.N. Melton, L.C. Nance, Jacob Nance, Henry Nailer (at Lynchburg, sick), A. Owens, James Parks, J.A. Pearce, N. Perry, J.T. Russell, T.J. Russell, C. Rhinehart, W.B. Runyan, W.A. Smith, R. Stewart, M.V. Stewart, Frank Sharp, R.G. Snyder, Tyre Spradlin, J.K.P. Slaughter, R.S.A. Swan, John Taylor, John Thomas, A.J. Vincent, H. Vincent, Wm Vincent, John Vincent, Jack Vickery, C.A. Wright, John Weeks, James King, Wm Clark, Wm Godsey, John V. Baugh. None others recalled.

There has been, since I commenced writing this letter, great excitement created in camp, in consequene of Prince Napoleon of France being here. I am so informed by Col. Vaughn. It indicates something.

I know you would be delighted to see some things we have seen, and in others you would not. Our boys, in the most part, are well satisfied and faring well and would be content with any thing they could stand up to, being made of purely Southern material. [unsigned]

- - - - - - - - - - - - -

RECEIPT FOR CHEAP COFFEE
[16 August 1861]

Take sweet potatoes, cut them up and dry them so they may be beaten as fine as ground coffee, from which take one third coffee and two thirds pulverized potatoes. It cannot be detected. N. SHARP

- - - - - - - - - - - - -

PRIVATE LETTER FROM MANASSAS
[23 August 1861]

BULL RUN, VA., July 27, 1861

Dear Sister: I write you a line, which will inform you that I am well. You have, doubtless, heard and read of the great battle at Manassas, on last Sunday, in which I participated from beginning to ending. It commenced about two miles to our right, and our Brigade was ordered to the left wing, which caused us to run double-quick about seven miles. We finally reached the battery, and after hard fighting for several hours we charged upon it, and then had a hard fight to hold the piece, but finally the Cavalry come to our aid and the Hessians dispersed in great disorder. (Grand sight to behold.) They pursued the enemy for several miles, cutting them down on the right and on the left, taking, in all, about 2000 prisoners that day and many more the next. Firing ceased about 5 o'clock, and the horrors of war were fully presented to our view, for the dead and the dying were as thick as hail stones. Many were the brave men that fell on the ill-fated old fields round and about Manassas Junction. Our General, Bee, Lieut. Col. Booth, of our Regiment, Aril McCarty, of our Company, killed, and about one dozen of them wounded. Our Company suffered as much as any, for we was in the heat of battle, all occasionally retiring and again rallying. They had greatly the advantage of us in the position, as they picked it themselves. We buried all our dead that we could find, in boxes—some we never found. Our army dug holes and buried the most of the enemy's dead— some are yet unburied, just lying on the field as they fell. We captured in all about 60 cannons, 3000 prisoners, many horses, wagons, guns, ammunition, and many other things too tedious to mention. I refer you to the newspapers for I am at a loss to know how to describe the battle. Jeff Davis came in late in the evening and pursued the enemy with the horsemen and says it was the greatest victory on record. One shot cut my pants, another cut the corner of a little book in my breast pocket, neither of which did me any harm. The cannon balls, grape shot and bomb shells fell thick all around me. The way they whistled in the air are indescribable. When the battle was over I was so exhausted that if I had been pushed over I don't know that I could have risen again. But my life was miraculously preserved, and I felt grateful, which might be attributable to the intercession at the throan of Grace by kind sisters. But I must close. When I see you again I will tell you what I can't write. We are not allowed to mail letters here. I will send this by hand to where it can be mailed. Cousin Eli Hoyle and Sam Hoyle were both in the battle and fought like men. The former was slightly wounded in the shoulder. Dr. Hoyle is well. We are on the battle ground now, in camps. Your brother, D.H. HOYLE

- - - - - - - - - - - - -

CLOTHING FOR THE SOLDIERS

[30 August 1861]

All who can do so, should, at the earliest possible day, make up something like the following, for their friends and relatives, omitting such, of course, as have heretofore been furnished.

Two pairs of pants of heavy brown or grey mixed jeans, lined, if thought advisable, with domestic.

One roundabout, or army jacket, of the same material, lined throughout, with side and vest pockets. It should be long enough to come some four inches below the waist band of the pants, and large enough to be worn over the vest or outside shirt.

One heavy vest, of jeans, linsey or kersey.

One overshirt, of some woolen or mixed goods.

One or two pair of drawers, as the case may require.

Two pair of heavy woolen socks.

One good blanket— lined is advisable.

An overcoat, or a loose sack coat, or hunting shirt with belt.

- - - - - - - - - - - - -

THE SOLDIERS

[30 August 1861]

In another place will be found a Proclamation from Governor Harris, in reference to winter clothing for the Volunteer Soldiers. Woolen socks, Drawers, and Under-shirt will be most needed. While we hope to see it do more, McMinn County must at the least furnish a supply ample for the number of Volunteers she has sent to the field. We know Monroe, Polk, Meigs, and Rhea will promptly provide.

Many of the brave volunteers will probably have to encounter the rigors of the approaching winter mid bleak and inhospitable mountains, and unless warmly clad, must endure sufferings such as we who are permitted to enjoy the comforts of home can hardly appreciate.— but whether engaged in the Valley of the Potomac, among our own Alpine ranges, or on the more distant plains and praries of Missouri or whether of our own county, town, or state; the gallant men who compose our armies are all brothers, engaged in the same noble cause, and should be alike the objects of our sympathy and encouragement and the recipients of every substantial comfort we can possibly give them.

Some friends have suggested a county organization for the purpose indicated. But we think more can be accomplished by every household resolving itself into a special committee, with full power to go ahead as far as it may be able. And in this way, the women folks, upon whom much depends, of both town and country, can labor efficiently, each contributing such articles as to them may seem best.

We know they will all alike promptly respond to the call, for woman's heart is always the same, whether it beat beneath a silken boddice or a cotton gown— ever ready to engage in good and patriotic works.

If, however, the families of each civil district think they can do more by an organized effort, let that plan at once be adopted.

Jack Frost will soon be on his accustomed tour through the mountains, stripping the purple foliage from the trees and heralding the approach of dread winter, and the Boys will sadly feel the need of the articles named unless speedily provided.

- - - - - - - - - - - - -

FROM RHEA

[30 August 1861]

Sulphur Springs, Aug. 22m 1861

Editor Post: Nothing of a striking nature has turned up here since I last wrote you, save the other day we wrre thrown somewhat into a ferment on hearing that the Union men (I should say Lincolmites) in this, Roane, and some of the upper and Mountain counties, were on the :Forward March," to what point or for what purpose the Lord only knows. The Home Guard of Meigs, under the command of Elisha Sharp and Abijah Boggess, hearing also of their movements, put off in hot pursuit, "armed and equipped as the law directs," en route for *Jimtown*.

After the first day's march, finding the track too cold, or else no track at all, the order was given to retire, which they did. It would have done your soul good to have seen those venerable old fellows at the head of their little army. They seemed to be in the true spirit of the enterprise, and looked as though they felt that our cause was a just and righteous one, and that the dragon's teeth and winds that Lincoln has been sowing broadcast, has now fully ripened into a harbest of whirlwids and should be reaped or paid back to his Goths and Bandals—his slab-sided hirelings—the full measure of whose patrotism is $11 per month and stealage, with compound interest.

Messers. Caldwell, Preston, Cawood and Wasson are getting up another Company here, and report already more than fifty good men and true who are ready at a moment's notice to go where duty calls. This will make the fourth Company for the Volunteer County — the gallant old Rhea — long may she wave!

The spirit of rebellion is cooling down in this section, and I hope the day is not far distant when East Tennessee will be as free and show us united a front as any section of the Confederate States of America.

Yours &c OLD '76

- - - - - - - - - - - - -

FOR COFFEE DRINKERS
[6 September 1861]

We are assured by a gentleman, who has often drank the beverage, that no substitute for coffee is equal to the infusion of the pea. Let the peas be well roasted without burning, then pound them. Cook the broken peas like coffee, and without admixture; boil well, drink with milk and sugar. Those who are fond of chocolate generally like the pea coffee.

- - - - - - - - - - - - -

THE CHEROKEES
[6 September 1861]

The latest advices from this Nation brings intelligence that at the council held on the 20th of August, it was decided, in a full vote, to unite with the Southern Confederacy. There were only two votes in the negative.

- - - - - - - - - - - - -

RHEA SOLDIERS' AID SOCIETY
[6 September 1861]

Pursuant to previous notice, a portion of the ladies of Washington and vicinity met for the purpose of forming themselves into a "Soldiers' Aid Society," for furnishing the gallant men who have gone forth to battle for our liberties, our rights, and our homes, with suitable winter clothes– when the names of the following ladies were handed in: – Mrs. Parks, Peterson, Evans, Early, Chambers, Nanny, Darwin, Smith, Ball, Roe, Rudd, Howard, Gillespie, Locke, Rawlings, Hoyl; Misses Munsa Gist, Mollie Kelley, Sarah Evans, Mag Sykes, Minerva Frazier, Scrap Hoyal, Susanna Chambers, Charity Chambers, Margaret Ball, A.A. Gillespie, O.J. Locke, Jennie Hoyal, Nep James, Lucy Evans, Cussa Evans, Eliza Evans.

On motion, Mrs. Joseph Parks was chosen President, and Mrs. Minerva Early and Miss Jennie Hoyal, Vice Presidents; Miss A.A. Gillespie, Secretary, and Mrs. H. Gillespie, Treasurer.

They request the ladies of Rhea County, in each Civil district, to form themselves into Societies for knitting and making winter clothing of all kinds for the soldiers, and that as many of the ladies from all parts of the County as can conveniently be present at their next meeting in Washington, on the 11th of this month, bringing whatever contributions of clothing they may have to spare.

Rhea County has already three gallant companies in the field. Winter will soon be here, and the gallant men who compose these companies must not freeze.– No. Let every woman in Rhea ply the needle and the shuttle, until every one of these noble men has a good warm suit of clothes. Never let it be said that the ladies of Rhea have allowed one single one of our boys to suffer for want of clothing. We cannot wield the battle blade upon the field, but we have an important work to perform in this great war for our independence. Ours is to clothe and contribute to the wants and comforts of the soldiers. By this we can do much. Let us, then, set about and push on the good work. We know that all the ladies of Rhea need is a hint – Forward the good work, then.

- - - - - - - - - - - - -

POULTICE FOR WOUNDS
[13 September 1861]

A poultice made of the common red, or garden beet, and immediately applied to a wound, will prevent tetanus or lockjaw. The poultice should be renewed as often as it becomes dry, and continued until all inflamation is drawn out or destroyed.

- - - - - - - - - - - - -

ORGANIZATION OF THE THIRD REGIMENT
[13 September 1861]

The Third Regiment of East Tennessee Volunteers was organized yesterday, at Camp Lillard, near Knoxville, by the election of the following officers: Colonel, John M. Lillard; Lieutenant Colonel, James J. Odell; and Major, Thomas McConnell.

- - - - - - - - - - - - -

SIMPLE SALVE FOR SOLDIERS' FEET
[27 September 1861]

The Scientific American has received the following receipt for making an excellent composition for annointing the feet of soldiers during long marching:— Take equal parts of gum camphor, olive oil and beeswax, and mix them together, warm until they are united and become a salve. At night wash the feet well, dry them, and apply the salve, and put on clean stockings and sleep with them on. Next day the feet will be in excellent trim for marching.

- - - - - - - - - - - - -

HINTS FOR THE MONTH
[27 September 1861]

Prepared for the War! should be written over the door of every farm building.— Save all the provender you can, that will nurish man or beast.

Take care of your straw, chaff, bran, everything, and don't feed extravagantly because you have full cribs.

Fix up your shelters for the protection of stock during the winter.

Repair all farm houses.

Take care of your stock.

Don't indulge any longer in mutton, but look to the wool and guard against hard times. Set all the old folks to knitting stockings for the soldiers. Half a pound of wool will make four pair heavy winter socks, and they will be sorely needed. We have no Yankee knitting looms, and must rely upon our fingers.

Prepare early to sow a large area in wheat, rye, and barley.

Sow large turnip patches. Red top will do well sown any time in September.— Save all your peas and pea vines.

Cotton:— Pick it out as rapidly as it opens, and don't let a bale of it leave your gin house until the blockade is raised, and it can be made available by your Government.

Work day and night— not to make money, but to be able to protect the soldier and his family, and secure our own independene.

- - - - - - - - - - - - -

CHEROKEES

[27 September 1861]

At New Orleans, John Ross, Chief of the Cherokee Indians, published a statement that at a mass meeting on the 21st ult. his people authorized their authorities to form an alliance with the Confederate government, and that a mounted regiment, under Colonel Drew, will be raised for that service.

- - - - - - - - - - - - -

KNOXVILLE DISTRICT

[4 October 1861]

Wm G. Swan, Esq., of Knoxville, is announed by his friends, through the *Register*, as a candidate for the Confederate Congress. Judge Swan was among the earliest and most earnest advocates of the Southern cause, and we believe is now with the Army of the Potomac. [NOTE: Swan's election is mentioned in the KING REMINISCENCES in Part II]

- - - - - - - - - - - - -

WATER-PROOF CLOTHING

[4 October 1861]

Below is a receipt for makimg cloth water-proof . . . to every gallon of spirits of terpentine put 2½ pounds of beeswax, boil well in a pot, remove the fire, and while it is hot put in your goods; move it about until it is well saturated, then hand it up to dry. It will require one gallon of turpentine to every eight yards of goods.

- - - - - - - - - - - - -

SULPHUR SPRINGS SOLDIERS' AID SOCIETY [RHEA COUNTY]

[4 October 1861]

On Saturday, the 4th ultimate, the Ladies of Sulphur Springs and vicinity met for the purpose of organizing a Soldiers' Aid Society, to promote the comfort of our brave sons who are now in actual service. The Rev. S. Phillips being called upon, responded in a neat and appropriate address.

The Society was then organized by the appointment of Mrs. Mary Leuty, President; Mrs. T.K. Munsey and Mrs. John H. Leuty, Vice Presidents; Mrs. C. Day, Treasurer; Mrs. Burton Leuty, Secretary; R.B. Shirley, Shipping Agent.

It is earnestly requested that the Ladies of the 4th [Civil District] cooperate with us. Remember that sands make mountains and every little[bit?] helps. I am happy to state that in the patriotic 4th, none has yet been found who refuses to ---?---, that they pay taxes for this purpose, and it is hoped that none will be found. Although coming in at the eleventh hour, the Sulphur Springs Society are determined not to be left in the background.

PRESTONVILLE SOCIETY

The following are the names of the "Prestonville Society:" Mrs. J.P. Thompson, President; Mrs. Wm Cash and Mrs. Arch McCaleb, Vice Presidents; Miss Mary Roddy, Secretary; Mrs. D.M. Roddy, Treasurer.

Committee – Mrs. A. McCaleb, Mrs. S. Phillips, Mrs. W. Short, Mrs. J. Whittenburg, and Misses S.A. Cash, Brunnette Robinson, M.J. Robinson, Amy Clack, Elizabeth Roddy, and Amy Roddy.

- - - - - - - - - - - - -

OMITTED THIS WEEK

[11 October 1861]

In consequence of the press of legal advertisements on our columns this week, we have been compelled to omit the publication of proceedings of meetings of Ladies, organizing Soldiers Aid Societies, at the following places: — Pikeville, Yellow Creek, Loudon, Sewee, Cantrell's X Roads, and Decatur. They shall appear just as soon as we can find room for them. In the meantime, we hope the good work will go on.

- - - - - - - - - - - - -

THE NEW POSTAGE STAMP

[11 October 1861]

We saw, last evening, says the Richmond *Dispatch*, 5th inst., the first impressions from the lithographic stone, of the new five cent postage stamp for the

Confederate States of America. The likeness of President Davis is admirable, and the lines of the engraving are so perfect as to closely resemble steel plate. We were agreeably surprised at the excellence of the work, as well as the neatness of the design. This new stamp will be colored green. We are informed that a quantity will be ready for delivery about the middle of next week.

- - - - - - - - - - - - -

ATTENTION VOLUNTEERS

[18 October 1861]

The following commends itself to the attention of Volunteers absent from their Regiment. We understand that the furlough system has been so much abused that the government will be more careful and rigid hereafter in its use.

REGIMENTAL HEADQUARTERS
Camp near Bowling Greene, Ky.
Oct. 9, 1861

All absent officers and soldiers, belonging to this Regiment, are directed to join their respective commands in the Regiment immediately. JOHN M. LILLARD, Col.
Commanding 26th Reg't Tenn. Vols
Formerly known as 3d East Tenn

- - - - - - - - - - - - -

LADIES MEETING

[18 October 1861]

A large and respectable number of the ladies of Decatur and vicinity, Meigs County, assembled at Mrs. Leuty's Hotel for the purpose of forming themselves into a Society to aid and assist the Citizen Soldiery of the Confederate Army, by administering to their wants and comfort in the struggle for Southern Independence and Southern Honor. The meeting was organized by calling Mrs. L.E. Frazier and Miss Jennie Lillard to preside, and Miss Mary Russell and Miss Sallie McCorkle to act as Secretaries.

Misses Tenn. McCorkle, Kate Leuty and Malissa Blevins were appointed a Commission on resolutions, whereupon they reported the following:

WHEREAS, Meigs County has nobly responded to the call of the Southern Confederacy, in sending her fathers, sons and brothers to the tented field, some of whom have already sygnalized themselves in the battle of Manasses Plains, and are now watching the enemy close to the Potomac, in view of Washington City, ready for the bloody drama of war which will probably soon take place; while others of her "gallant sons" are in the adjoining sister State of Kentucky, ready to assist in redeeming that proud State from Lincoln misrule. All this, we are aware, is for the protection of loved ones at home, our firesides, &c.–

RESOLVED, That we will pledge ourselves to do all we can to render the lives of our "soldier boys" comfortable, and to soften the rigors of camplife, by furnishing them suitable clothing for active duty, and administering necessaries and comforts if they should be so uncomfortable as to be confined in hospitals from sickness.

RESOLVED, That we tender our thanks to the ladies of Virginia for their motherly and sisterly conduct in administering to the wants of our soldiers; and more recently, to the ladies of Southern Kentucky, who have received the coming of Southern troops in their midst with every expression of affectionate feeling, as it was to them a relief from Northern tyranny and subjugation.

RESOLVED, That we will, if necessary, become, all of us, Florence Nightingales to nurse our citizen soldiers in camp, and subject ourselves to the inconveniences incident thereto.

RESOLVED, That we would earnestly request all the ladies of Meigs County to furnish, at their earliest convenience, all the clothing they can, to send to our soldiers to protect them from the rigours of the coming winter.

RESOLVED, That the presiding officers appoint a Committee of three as a Committee of Correspondence; also a Committee of three as a Committee of Contributions.

The following ladies were appointed a Committee of Correspondence: Misses Tennessee McCorkle, Kate Leuty, and Malissa Blevins.

Mrs. Texas Stewart, Misses Sallie Russell and Eva Lillard, as a Committee on Contributions.

On motion, it was ordered that a copy of these proceedings be furnished by the secretaries to the Athens Post and Cleveland Banner, to be published. The meeting then adjourned to meet on the 12th inst.

L.E. Frazier and M.J. Lillard, Presidents
Mary Russell and Sallie McCorkle, Secretaries

- - - - - - - - - - - - -

SEWEE SOLDIERS AID SOCIETY
[MEIGS COUNTY]

[18 October 1861]

Actuated by the pure motives of promoting the interest of their country, and assuring the brave and gallant soldiers there are those who will ever hold them to memory as sacred and dear, and who possess hearts that will beat fervently, in their sphere, to their valor, by rendering comfortable and agreeable, as much as possible, the cold comforts of camp and the stern realities of war, the ladies of Sewee and vicinity met at Sewee Academy for the purpose of organizing a Soldiers' Aid Society, whereupon the following officers were elected: Mrs. B.W. Smith, President; Miss Amanda C. Latham and Miss Jennie Hutsell, Vice Presidents; Miss Mary Hutsell, Miss Mattie Latham, and Miss Jennie Peake, Secretaries; Mrs. Luke Peake, Principal Treasurer, and Misses Mary Smith and Lottie Peake, Assistants.

The following members were present: Mrs. E. Sharp, Jacob Peake, Sam S. Hutsell, Mary Locke, Henry Latham, A.P. Boggess, I.H. Boggess, John Bryson; Misses Lydia Hutsell, Lou Terrell, S.P. Moore, Catie Locke, Mary Redman, Mary Latham, Sallie Peak, Malinda Smith, Katie Latham, Sallie Moore, Delri Sharp, and Annie Hutsell.

- - - - - - - - - - - - -

YELLOW CREEK SOLDIERS' AID SOCIETY
[RHEA COUNTY]
[18 October 1861]

The Ladies of Yellow Creek, 3rd district of the Volunteer County – the gallant old Rhea – met a few days since to organize a Soldiers' Aid Society, to promote the comfort of our soldiers now in actual service.

After the usual preliminaries, they appointed Mrs. James Rhea, President; Mrs. J. D. Chattin, Miss Kate Clack, and Mrs. D. J. Wilson, Vice-Presidents; Mrs. E. J. Neil and Miss Sallie J. Fouste, Secretaries; Mr. Spencer G. Clack, Treasurer; and Mr. James Rhea, Shipping Agent.

Every lady in the County not belonging to a similar Society is earnestly requested to cooperate with us. Contributions can be sent either to the residence of James Rhea or R.N. Clack, at which places the Society will meet from time to time as may be required.

This district has now forty-five good and true men in actual service, and the ladies (God bless them) with a determination not to be out done in patriotism, have gone about the good work with a zeal and fervency of soul that does honor to true Southern blood.

By the efforts of their Committees, they have enough material reported to make a respectable shipment, which will go to headquarters so soon as it can be manufactured – and strange to relate, this has been done in opposition and under difficulties which even they in their laudable work have to encounter.

Some of the would-be nobobs not only refuse to subscribe, but are actually wielding an influence against them, and plead as an exercise that they have taxes to pay for this purpose. I wonder if the idea ever entered their cranium that money will not clothe a freezing soldier. If our Government could get a sufficient supply of clothing for money it never would have asked assistance.

The only question before us is this: Shall we respond to the call? Will we protect our fathers, brothers and sons from the fierce wintry blasts by dividing with them our blankets and woolen goods? Or shall we let them suffer, in addition to the privations of camp life the still greater privation, an absolute want of clothing in the chilling winds of winter? No, never!

Oat(?) upon such men as refuse to assist in the work upon the niggardly plea "that they pay taxes." Sirs, if you don't wish to subscribe any thing to clothe the brave soldiers who have left their homes and firesides you clutch with such tenacity, stop your croakings. The ladies will get along without your aid! Our Soldiers will be warmly clothed for the winter, for the true Southern spirit in the fair ladies of the third have willed it so, and when you will they will.

Yours, S.G.C.
Lake, P.O. – Sept. 16, 1861

- - - - - - - - - - - - -

MORE CLOTHING FOR THE VOLUNTEERS
[RHEA COUNTY]
[1 November 1861]

A portion of the Southern Rights ladies of the First District [Prestonville] met about five weeks since and organized a Soldiers' Aid Society for the purpose of furnishing our Rhea County Volunteers with suitable clothing for the coming winter. On the 13th, they met at the residence of D.M. Roddy and boxed the clothing ready for shipping.

The following is a list of the different articles: 80 pairs Socks, 36 pairs Pants, 16 pairs Drawers, 20 Shirts, 18 Blankets, 5 Vests, 2 Coats. The box is to be sent to Capt. Crawford's Company– from this County– now in Kentucky assisting that gallant State to rid itself of the Lincoln despotism. This will be by no means our last contributions to the brave Volunteers who have gone forth to keep the foe from our homes and firesides.

Although we cannot share with them the perils of the battlefield, yet we wish to prove to them women who possess true Southern patriotism enough to labor incessantly to promote their comfort and happiness.

- - - - - - - - - - - - -

GRATUITOUS MEDICAL SERVICES
[1 November 1861]

We tender our medical services gratuitously to all families or persons, in the bounds of our practice, who are now or may hereafter be left destitute by the absence of relatives or friends who have entered, or may hereafter enter, the army in defence of the State.

[signed] G.M. CLEMENTSON and M.C. CLARK

- - - - - - - - - - - - -

ANOTHER COMPANY FROM RHEA COUNTY
[8 November 1861]

SULPHUR SPRINGS, Tenn.
Oct. 31, 1861

Editor Post: Yesterday was a day here long to remember. The "Piney Boys," 4th Company from the gallant old Rhea, commanded by Capt. A.J. Cawood, met at this place for the purpose of making a start to Headquarters at Knoxville, and bidding adieu to the loved ones left behind. Before their departure, however, the Ladies, who are ever ready to stimulate us in any good work, presented the Company with a beautiful Banner, through Miss MARY ROBINSON, who delivered the following beautiful and patriotic Address:

Gallant Captain and Brave Piney Boys: The cause that calls you to arms is a just and righteous one. Already has our sunny South been invaded by an unprincipled foe. Already has Southern soil been stained by the blood of the brave and noble sons of the South, who feared not to die in their Country's defense. You, imitating their example, have nobly enlisted at your Country's call. True, you are not the first upon the tented field, yet we expect you not to shrink or falter in the hour of battle. I take pleasure, therefore, Capt. Cawood, to present to the 4th Company of Rhea County Volunteers, through you, this banner.— Although it is not as fine and grand as *some*, I trust 'tis enough that it is the *true* flag of the South; the Striking Colors— red, white, and blue— the proud emblems of love, purity and fidelity— Keep it unstained by any act of cowardice— may you ever be able, when necessary, to bear it to battle with a strong heart and steady mein amid the roar of cannon and rattle of musketry. Cling to it, and if need be, die by it.

Although we are not permitted to share with you the toils and hardships of camp life, our interest in your success is none the less. You are almost ready to bid farewell to your nearest and dearest friends on earth— some their wives, mothers, and sisters; it may be for a short time, but alas! it may be forever— the home of earth you may never see again— the music of home voices may never again greet your eyes, but if heaven orders it so, may angels hands supply your dying wants and waft your immortal spirits to a clime where the noise of battle will be heard no more. Accept now this last favor. May you all live to follow this standard back home and place it in the hands of those who gave it, and be kept in memory of the brave "Piney Boys."

The banner was received by Dr. J.L. ABERNATHY, who responded to the speech as follows:

Called upon to receive this handsome banner, without much time for reflection, I must confess my inability to respond in a style commensurate with the occasion, or the manner your felicitous remarks properly indicate and demand. But any deficiency on my part, in the reception of the beautiful emblem of Southern Independence, I hope and trust will be regarded with that leniency charity is ever ready to bestow upon the unfortunate. For this flag, gotten up, as I learn, in much haste, yet in elegant style, and for the very complementary terms in which you have been pleased to allude to the gallant "Piney Boys," I tender you and the ladies of the vicinity our sincere regard and patriotic devotion. Let me assure you we will ever cherish with proud recollection this occasion, this ensign, and those who gave it— that no stain of dishonor shall tarnish its bright folds— no act of ours will cause you to regret the donation.

When Constantine marched forth to give battle to the pagans of the world he was at a loss for a sign that would animate, inspire his men to heroic action when the hour of conflict was at hand— something that would ever keep prominently before their minds their cause and their duty. In the middle of the night, before a great battle, he is said to have had a vision. He looked up to the blue canopy and beheld, painted with the splendor of the sun, a cross, surrounded by these words: "By this sign I Conquor." Constantine transferred his vision to his banner, and his legion marched on to victory and renown. "By *this* sign" aloft, moving over our heads, we intend to conquor. Wherever these tribands kiss the breeze the land shall be free. It is a beacon of light to the soldier, and we will sustain it with such heroism and devotion as will further illustrate the proud history of Tennessee— A history, though brief, frought with daring deeds of heroes— a history that challenges the admiration of the world. Let us pause a moment to contemplate her annals.

We do not have to go away back in the twilight of history to trace her noble career. Less than a century ago Tennessee was one vast unbroken wilderness, with savages and beasts. Now she has a population of millions living in the highest state of advanced civilization. Unaided by any government, the hardy pioneers pushed across the mountains, that bind our Eastern border, and here planted that germ which by the nourishment and fostering care of wisdom, has developed the present magnificient proportions of a great and mighty commonwealth. Although not one of the original colonies, yet, when they were invaded, her chivalrous sons seized their unerring rifles, marched far down the Atlantic slope to Kings Mountain and there defeated England's bravest warriors, turning the tide of a revolution that liberated America. They were at the Horseshoe, Talladeger, and Emuckfaw. They went down to New Orleans, met the flower of the English army and again drove the haughty Brittons beyond the seas. They passed through the blaze that lit up the national road from Vera Cruz to the ancient halls of Montezuma baptizing themselves in blood, and wining imperishable renown.

Who is not proud of being a Tennessean? On every occasion from her infancy to her present glory and pride of strength, Tennessee has done more than any other State for the national defender of a government that is now seeking her degredation, her ruin, her annihilation! For the first time in her history, she is threatened with invasion. For the first time she is called upon to defend her own virgin soil, and she now sounds the toesin of war, loud and distinct, from the mountains to the Mississippi, calling upon her valiant and ever ready sons to come to the rescue.

The --?-- hordes of the North are exerting every means to bring the miseries of war to our homes. They would crimson our murmuring brooks and flowing rivers with the blood of our fathers, brothers and sons. They would purple fields with the rich blood of those you love.— They would place our mothers, wives and daughters in the merciless power and vengeance of their ruffian soldiers. Will these contingencies ever arise?— Never! while a freeman walks the soil of Tennessee. Never! while the memory of a glorious ancestry lives so fresh and green with a grateful posterity. Never! until freedom and chivalry become contemptible, and tyranny and cowardice decent!

If they attempt our northern border, our black throated "dogs of war" will resound from peak to peak and down the deep gorges of the mountains, and away across the hills and vales to the father of floods. All along the line will be heard the music of the rifles and the melody of muskets.

If they meet our forces at the Gap, they will find another Thermopylae— if not another Waterloo. But if, by superior numbers, they gain an advantage "we will dispute every inch of ground," rase every house, burn every blade of grass, and the last encroachments of liberty shall be our graves. With freedom, the choice between death and dishonor is neither difficult nor doubtful.

Fellow soldiers! This is *our* flag! We will rally around it in the story of battle; we will rally around it in the hour of victory, or the hour of defeat. It shall be a pillow of cloud by day and a pillow of fire by night, and before we ingloriously surrender it let us pour out our blood as a libation upon the altar of our Country. If it should ungloriously trail in the dust, I pray a just God will not permit *one* to return to tell its sad fate.

I now pass this beautiful ensign to the proper officer, accompanied by the words of Lord Nelson, before the fall of Trafalgar: "It is expected every man to do his duty."

After which, the Company went to Brady's Ferry to await the coming of the steamer Tennessee which soon hove in sight, made a landing, and took them on their way amidst loud huzzahs for the Piney Boys.

Yours, OLD '76

- - - - - - - - - - - - -

THE McKINLEY [sic] RANGERS

[15 November 1861]

On Thursday, the 7th inst., this magnificient Company of Cavalry met at Decatur, Tenn., for the purpose of taking their leave for more active duties in the Confederate service. They number nearly 100 strong, most of whom are stout, athletic men, mounted on the best horses in the country. Without being invidious, it may be fairly styled one of the best Cavalry Companies in the State. The following are the commissioned officers:

G. W. McKenzie, Captain
Wiley O. Martin, First Lieutenant
William W. Lillard, Second Lieutenant
David C. Blevins, Third Lieutenant
Non-commissioned officers not yet elected.

After the routine of valuing their horses was gone through with, the Company was paraded and marched through the principal streets of the town by Adjutant Cross, of the 3rd Tennessee Regiment, now in Virginia. The Company then dismounted and repaired to a suitable place, accompanied by a large concourse of people, to receive a flag from the ladies, when Miss ALMYRA LILLARD appeared upon the stand with a plain but neat banner, with the motto of "God Defend the Right" inscribed thereon, and delivered in good style the following address:

Captain McKenzie: I am here on behalf of the ladies of McMinn and Meigs to present to you and your gallant band this flag, to accompany you through the dangers of a bloody conflict.— Through it is not made of fine material, yet we hope you will receive it as though it were of superfine gold— and when surrounded by dangers may it be your monitor to prompt you to maintain the ancient character and renown of our beloved Tennessee. May your achievements reflect upon you honor as bright as those stars confer upon the field of blue which they stud. We present it to you, knowing that it will never be dishonored by trailing in the dust, but that you will honor, protect, yes, and even dare to die by it. And be assured that the hearts that prompt its presentation beat high in anticipation of your success and safe return. I trust that the prayers in your behalf will not fall unheeded by Him who rules even in the hour of battle.

Your Country calls for your services! 'Tis for the loved ones of your fireside circle that you fight. Today you take leave of your homes and all that's near and dear to you, not that you love them less, but that you love your Country more.— Though it grieves you to leave them, trust in God for their protection. As you go, remember you are not alone, but have many brave and noble hearted companions by your side. Yes, we see by your side aged fathers, whose locks are silvered o'er with the frosts of many winters, still the hearts of tenderness and love dwell within. May you, by your kindness, teach them to love you— sympathise with them in their sufferings through the approaching winter, that they may honor you. When far away, and perchance upon the battlefield, look upon this banner and think of the warm hearts left behind you. May it give strength to your arms, fire to your hearts, and enable you to go forth wielding the implements of war, with the sentiments transcribed: "Victory or death:"—

Mothers, will you pray for your sons? Wives, will you pray for your husbands? Sisters, will you not petition God in behalf of that brother that is now about to take up the line of march to the tented field? Patriotism has prompted him to leave you, and it is patriotism that has prompted the thousands of the fair sons of the South that are already upon the field, contending for ours as well as their rights and liberties— and for this I fear we will ever feel our indebtedness to the patriotic sons of Tennessee. Ladies, in God's name, will we not appreciate our liberties if bought again by the blood of our fathers and brothers?

Thirteen cousins upon the plains of Virginia; six in Kentucky, ready I presume, to face the enemy's cannon; one dear brother upon the field of action, I know not where, but I thank heaven, for the assurance that I have, should he fall, it will be with his face to the free and in defence of his Country. Little did I think when I parted with so many of my friends last May that in so short a time I would be called upon to part with almost my last and more dear ties. But, Captain, today we bid you farewell. We place our dearest interests in your hands. They are our fathers, our brothers, our cousins, our schoolmates and associates! O, strive to lead them to victory and honor! And with a heart and feelings inexoressible, I say to you, kindred, countrymen, go, and may the God of battles protect you.

When she had concluded, Lieut. DAVID C. BLEVINS accepted the banner, stepped upon the stand, and responded in behalf of the Company, as follows:

Ladies and Gentlemen: — In behalf of Captain McKenzie, of the Company of which I am a member, in the name of God, my Country, and the ladies, I accept this banner. The cause of our meeting together on this occasion has not been common since the early history of our Country. Heretofore when we assembled together it was to congratulate and commemorate the Anniversaries of our Independence, to meet in the festive Halls on days of thanksgiving, and to thank God for the preservation and perpetuity of our once happy Union; to talk of the liberty we enjoyed and of the great brotherhood that existed in the then United States. It was then that the man of Maine and gentleman of Louisiana met, shook hands, and called each other brother. But how changed are things now! That fraternity is extinguished forever!

And we, the members of this Company, have met together today to start in defence of Southern rights, Southern institutions— our homes and our firesides.

You have met here to bid your friends and relatives farewell, and to urge them on in defence of the holy course which they have espoused. We regret to leave you, but our beloved State— the Volunteer State of Tennessee— calls us to her assistance. Then who could stay at home?

The countenances of you all respond in a voice louder than seven-fold thunder, nous! our rights and constitutional guarantees have alike been disregarded. Our homes, our firesides, nay, our beloved "sunny South," with all her sacred institutions, have been invaded by the ruthless hordes of old Abe Lincoln, with their vulgar motto, "beauty and booty," and that vassalage and destitution should be the scenes that all her peaceful citizens would have to witness. This cruel, unjust and wanton war has been forced upon us through the duplicity and latent schemes of an unprincipled fanatical party at the North.

We are proud of this beautiful banner which the fair ladies of Meigs and adjoining counties have presented us. I know the fair hands that wrought these beautiful stars and bars are my schoolmates, associates, and friends. And I also know that your hearts desire, your prayers, and your wishes are that our armies may be successful, and that peace, liberty and justice may again be restored to your beloved Country. I know, furthermore, that your every heart throbs with patriotic innocence. Then, as I am fourth in command of this Company, it will fall to my lot when we meet the enemy on the contested field to bear this banner to the front. I pledge you that as long as this arm is able to support the same, or hand to grasp the staff, that it shall never be disgraced or trailed in the dust. However, should it please Him who rules men, armies and nations, and disposes of them in accordance with the unalterable fiat of His own will, that I should fall a victim— a martyr— to the Cause of my Country, I pledge you further that this gallant Company will snatch up this banner as a jewell dropped from heaven and bear it on to victory.

Although the dark cloud of political misfortune is lowering over us, and the dogs of war are howling all around, and have already begun eagerly to lap up their prey. Nevertheless, I indulge the proud hope that our early independence will be recognized by other nations, and that peace will be restored to the Country.

And as the basis upon which I predicate my hope, permit me to refer you to the battles of Manassas Plains and Great Bethel, Virginia, as well as Oak Hills and Lexington, Missouri, and ask the mouldering remains of our patriotic heroes who fell in defense of our cause on those battle fields, what of our success? And the response will be, victory has crowned our arms on every field.

But when peace shall again reign throughout our happy land, when Northern patrotism and fanaticism shall have folded their black wings of tyranny and oppression, and fallen trembling and conquered at the feet of Liberty and Independence, it will be that *this star-circled banner, triumphantly shall wave o'er a land that can boast of a Washington's grave.*

After which the large crowd, who were remarkably orderly, mostly departed for their respective homes. In conclusion, it is hardly necessary to say that the "McKinley Rangers," in company with their Confederate brethern in arms in Tennessee and elsewhere, will, whenever and wherever necessary, "cry havoc, and let slip the dogs of war."

- - - - - - - - - - - -

FROM RHEA COUNTY
[29 November 1861]

SULPHUR SPRINGS, TENN.
Nov. 24, 1861

Editor Post: As the late stampede is upon a stand, the general excitement somewhat subsided, and "Richard is himself again," it would not, perhaps be out of place to post you as to the recent fight at Camp Clift.

Last week, or directly after the burning of the bridge, a hint of the movement of Clift and his followers was borne us on the evening winds, and in two days we had as many as a thousand men on the *qui vive*, ready and anxious, this time, to effectually rid the country of ever mother's son of them.

It was the intention of our Minute Men, under the command of Captain's Abernathy, Roddy, Callahan, and Mitchell, of Rhea, and others from Meigs and Bledsoe whose headquarters were at Washington, to sweep the mountain and valley from that point down, untill every one of them was either captured or completely routed.

On Wednesday evening, after the plan was understood, the whole body moved from Washington to Smith's X Roads and sent out pickets towards Clift's Camp, who on next day, were fired on by Col. Wood's Alabama regiment of infantry, mistaking them for Clift's men. Our pickets, it seems, were under the same mistake, as they sent runners back to report that Clift was marching upon us with about 1000 well armed men. I said runners— they *were runners*— and no sooner had they reported than several others at the Cross Roads proved to be the same stripe, and judging from the start he made, in all probability there is one from there who is yet running.

It was on account of not having our colors in a position to be seen by the Colonel, that we were fired upon, and we may be truly thankful it was no worse with us— only one man wounded, H. Clay Darwin, in the foot— a slight wound— only a musket ball nearly spent, which was easily extracted by Dr. Hoyl. From some of the prisoners taken we learn we were only a few hours too late— in fact, everything went to show that we were close on the heels of old Clift himself.

Capt. McKenzie's Company, which is yet on the alert, may yet lift the old gentleman. We learned there were at Camp Clift only about three Companies— Jeff Mathes', Bob Sullivan's and John Morgan's.

We captured most of Sullivan's men, and some say that Sullivan "bit the dust" near the head of the valley, as he was making his way to Kentucky. Many prisoners belonging to the other companies were captured, and what few made their escape, I suppose, are now in search of the long lost descendant of Balaam's quadruped.

Yours, OLD '76

- - - - - - - - - - - - -

VOTE OF MEIGS COUNTY
[29 November 1861]

For Presidental Electors		303
For Congress:	Welcker	28
	Tibbs	87
	Pope	132
	Caldwell	56

- - - - - - - - - - - - -

SOAP
[29 November 1861]

A large supply of soap may be extracted from every cornfield at this season of the year. While a thousand pounds of oak wood yields only two and a half pounds of potash, and soap is made out of potash. A thousand pounds of corn stalks will yield seventeen pounds of potash, and soap is made of potash. A thousand pounds of oak leaves burnt to ashes will yield twenty-four pounds of potash, and soap may be made out of the potash.

- - - - - - - - - - - - -

GUNS — PRISONERS
[6 December 1861]

Our old friend, Capt. Boggess, of the Meigs County Minute Men, arrived here last Saturday, with a large lot of guns, and five prisoners said to be members of Old Clift's Company. Clift himself is said to be still at large, although there are those who think the old fellow was summarily disposed of by some of the parties who were in pursuit of him.

- - - - - - - - - - - - -

LETTER TO SOLDIERS' AID SOCIETY
[6 December 1861]

Camp Bowling Green, Ky.
November 25, 1861

To the Ladies of Rhea County comprising the
Soldiers' Aid Society

The Volunteer Company from Rhea County, the "Rhea Invincibles," have received at your hands valuable contributions of clothing, which conduces greatly to our comfort, health and happiness. – We are also in receipt of clothing and other articles which add greatly to the comfort of the soldier, from the kind and patriotic ladies of Meigs County. We cannot refrain from expressing to you our deep gratitude and sincere thanks for your unbounded generosity, and while your favors thus conferred have so enhanced the comfort and welfare of our brave soldiers, the sentiments thereby conveyed have animated our spirits and incited us to a determination to use greater and nobler exertions to achieve the independence of our country and to defend the homes and happinesss of our fathers and mothers, our kindred and friends, who have not neglected or forgotten us, but are thus nobly assisting us to fight the battles of our country, and as long as the patriotic ladies of the South thus demonstrate their patriotism and willingness to assist us in our great struggle for independence, our course will continue to prosper and be triumphant. – and under such encouragements and with such assistance, we certainly must not, cannot, will not be conquered.

Fully appreciating your Patriotism and the valuable services you have rendered us, we again, in behalf of our Company, tender you our grateful and sincere thanks and acknowledgments, and hope that henceforth we may be better men and brave soldiers. Yours Respectfully,

John Crawford, Captain
Jas Johnson, Quarter Master,
26th Regt. Tenn. Vol.

- - - - - - - - - - - - -

MEIGS COUNTY

[20 December 1861]

Meigs County, with a voting population of less than 800, has 500 volunteers in the service. All honor to gallant Meigs.

- - - - - - - - - - - - -

THE FRANK RAMSEY HOSPITAL

[20 December 1861]

A military hospital has recently been opened at Loudon under charge of our clever and talented friend, Dr. J.L. Abernathy, of the Confederate army. Donations of bed blankets, comforts, and other necessaries for the sick, are needed.

- - - - - - - - - - - - -

THE NEW REGIMENT

[20 December 1861]

A new Regiment was organized Saturday at Camp Key, near this place [Athens]. The following are its field officers: James W. Gillespie, Colonel
D. M. Key, Lieut. Colonel
Lawson Guthrie, Major

The Regiment is composed of the following companies:

Capt. Guthries', Hamilton County
Capt. Goodman's, Polk County
Capt. Cawood's, Rhea County
Capt. Turner's, Roane County
Capt. Neff's, Jefferson & Monroe County
Capt. Hill's, Bledsoe County
Capt. Lafferty's, McMinn County
Capt. Hodge's, Meigs & McMinn County
Capt. McKamey's, Bradley & Polk County
Capt. Phillips', Hawkins County

- - - - - - - - - - - - -

JAMES P. FLEMING

[11 April 1862]

Was killed at Fort Donelson, in battle, February 15th, 1862. James enlisted in the service of his country in Rhea County, Tenn., under Capt. John Crawford— left Rhea County 4th of July, 1861, and professed a change of heart the same day his patrotism and love of liberty urged him to volunteer in defense of his home and country— willing to expose himself to the enemy's roaring cannon and rattling musketry, to save his country from subjugation and ruin. But, unfortunately for him, he fell in the first scene of action in which he was engaged— sealing his faith with his blood. As a child, he was respectful and obedient; as a man, amiable and kind; while a soldier he performed his duties without a murmur. He was elected Orderly Sergeant after the Company got to Bowling Green— as an officer, affectionate— beloved by all who knew him. He died at his post. Weep not for him, our loss is his gain.

Why should we mourn departed friends,
Or shake at Death's alarms?
'Tis but the voice that Jesus sends,
to call us to his arms.

- - - - - - - - - - - - -

MEIGS COUNTY

[2 May 1862]

We spent Monday at Decatur. Court met at 9 o'clock, and at 12 meridian, adjourned till the next regular term. There were but a few persons present. Indeed, more than half the men of Meigs are in the Southern army. The wheat fields between this place and Decatur appear to be seriously injured, especially in the "No-Pone Valley."

The whiskey blockade being rather more strict and efficient at Decatur than some other places we could name, the Court Clerk, Bar, candidates for future honors, and editors present, all were as "sober as Judges"— a fact we take an immense degree of pleasure in recording.

- - - - - - - - - - - - -

FERRY BOATS

[2 May 1862]

In consequence of there being no ferry boats at present on the Tennessee River between Chattanooga and Kingston, the mail routes from Athens to Pikeville and to Sulphur Springs [Rhea County], and the cross route direct to Kingston, was suspended. We trust the obstructions will soon be removed.

Our papers for Bledsoe and Rhea we shall send via Chattanooga until otherwise advised; and our patrons in Meigs thus cut off, will have to send to the railroad for theirs until such time as the routes may be opened again. The effects of the Lincolnite leaders in East Tennessee have resulted in an immense amount of evil, inconvenience and loss to the people.

- - - - - - - - - - - - -

THE MAIL ROUTES
[9 May 1862]

From the following letter it will be seen that the mail routes to Rhea, Meigs, Bledsoe and Roane counties can be resumed:

Hd Qrs. 1st Brig., East Tennessee
Chattanooga, May 1, 1862

Sam P. Ivins, Esq., Athens

I am directed by Brig. Gen'l Leadbetter, commanding here, to say that the Ferry boats belonging at Brady's and Locke's Ferries, and Cotton Port on the Tennessee, will be restored. The Steamer will tow them up on her next trip.

Very respectfully, your ob't servt.
H. Goldthwaite, A.A. Gen'l

- - - - - - - - - - - - -

FERRY BOATS
[23 May 1862]

We are sorry to learn that the boats have not yet been restored to the Ferries on the Tennessee, and consequently the people beyond the river are still deprived of their usual mail facilities. We submit to the military authorities that whatever necessity there may have been for the removal of the boats a few weeks ago, there is no reason now why they should not be returned, and they owe it to good faith and the public interest to have the business promptly attended to.

- - - - - - - - - - - - -

THIRD TENNESSEE REGIMENT
[23 May 1862]

The Third Tennessee Regiment— than which there has been no more gallant or effective in the service— was re-organized on Wednesday, the 14th, for the war.— The following field officers were elected:

J.C. Vaughn, of Monroe, Colonel
N.J. Lillard, of Meigs, Lieutenant Colonel
D.C. Haskins, of Polk, Major

- - - - - - - - - - - - -

A PROFITABLE INVESTMENT
[23 May 1862]

A lady of Greensboro, Alabama, not long since, gave a very fine quilt to Rev. J.J. Hutchison to be sold for the gunboat fund. He offered it for sale in Marion, and got over a hundred dollars for it. The crowd gave it back to him to be sold over again. He carried it to Tuscaloosa and got about five hundred dollars for it and received it back again. He then carried it to Summerfield and got another five hundred and the quilt back again. He then carried it to Selma and sold it for one thousand and five hundred dollars for the benefit of soldiers' families, and we suppose will continue to sell and resell it until he foots up thousands more.

- - - - - - - - - - - - -

DRIED FRUIT
[30 May 1862]

If fruit should be as abundant this year as it promises to be, we suggest that a large quantity of peaches should be dried. The dried fruit will make pleasant food and an agreeable drink for the soldiers. When apples come in, they should also be dried in large quantities.

- - - - - - - - - - - - -

MOUNTED RANGERS WANTED
[13 June 1862]

I have a Company now in camps at Post Oak Springs, Roane County, partly organized, and desire a few more men before a full organization.— My company is attached to Judge Gardenhire's Regiment of Independent Mounted Rangers— said Regiment has been authorized for the defence of our border, from Nashville to Cumberland Gap. We get the bounty, regular Cavalry pay, and are paid for what we capture.

This service offers inducements to young men of daring offered by no other service. Come to the defence of your homes and alters, by meeting the invader upon the border! Address or report to me at Post Oak Springs, Tennessee. J. R. NEAL, Captain

- - - - - - - - - - - - -

LIQUOR LAW
[4 July 1862]

HEADQUARTERS
6th DIST. DEPT. OF E. TENN

Office Deputy Provost Marshal
Athens, June 14, 1862

1. Hereafter no one but Dr. Marshall, Druggist, Athens, McMinn County; W. G. Whitehead, Benton, Polk County; Dr. Edwards, Cleveland, Bradley County; Frank McCorkle, Decatur, Meigs County; and Hugh L. M. Roberts, Washington, Rhea County, will be allowed

to sell liquors in the above named counties; and then only for medical purposes, strictly, and on proper prescriptions.

2. None but regular commissioned army Surgeons will be allowed to prescribe liquors for officers or soldiers, and no one but a well known regular practicing Physician will be permitted to issue prescriptions for citizens.

3. Any one violating these orders will be promptly arrested and punished.

W. L. Lafferty
Capt. and Deputy Provost Marshall
5th Dist., Dept E. Tenn. June 20, 1862

- - - - - - - - - - - - -

TWENTY-SIXTH TENNESSEE REGIMENT
[18 July 1862]

Dr. E. T. Taliaferro, Surgeon of the 26th Tennessee Regiment (Col. Lillard's) arrived here [Athens] last week. Dr. Taliaferro was with the Regiment at the surrender of Fort Donelson and was taken with the balance to Johnson's Island, Lake Erie, four miles from Sandusky City, where most of the men are now confined. He left there on the 25th of June, and reports all in good health. We publish below the names of some of the members of the Regiment, names of friends and post-office of the latter:

A.F. Boggess	Mrs. L.C. Boggess,Ten Mile, Tenn.
T.B. Bowling	Col. S. Peak, Moore's X Roads, Tenn.
J.L. Bottles	Mrs. J.L. Bottles, Broylesville, Tenn.
J.F. Butler	J. Eldridge, Lenoir, Tenn.
H.C. Evans	Hamilton Kraus, Thorn Hill, Tenn.
A.M. Foster	Mrs. A.M. Foster, Ringgold, Ga.
J.R. Gaba	Mrs. J.R. Gaba, Jonesboro, Tenn.
Jas C. Gordon	J.M. Lee or L.M. Gordon, Ringgold
Talbot Greene	Mrs. E. Greene, Jonesboro, Tenn.
H.W. Graham	Mrs. Nancy Graham, Little River, Va.
J.A. Howell	Mrs. Elvina Howell, Decatur, Tenn.
B. Hendrix	Mrs. B. Hendrix, High Point, Ga.
A.C. Hickey	Joseph D. Hickey, Newport, Tenn.
W.L. Gordon	Mrs. M.L. Caldwell, Chattanooga, Tenn.
R.N. McDuffie	Mrs. M.A. McDuffie, Loudon, Tenn.
J. McDuffie	same
Levi Mobley	Mrs. E. Mobley, Thorn Hill, Tenn.
C.D. McFarland	T.C. McFarland, Chattanooga, Tenn
J.N. McNabb	G. McNabb or G.I. Thomas, Newport
W.E. McElwee	Wm McElwee, Post Oak Springs, Tenn.
J.R. Morrell	Stephen Maston, Bristol, Tenn.
Lea Neil	S.J. Bryan, Ten Mile, Tenn.
" "	Pryor Neil, Decatur, Tenn.
G.W. Owings	J.R. Owings, Pond Spring, Ga.
C.L. Reed	Jas J. Reed (Bro), Ringgold, Ga.
George Stuart	D.W. & A. Stuart, Newport, Tenn.
R.U. Saffell	J.E. Bogle, Maryville, Tenn.
B.F. Welker	Mrs. H.A. Welker, Loudon, Tenn.
" "	A.G. Welker, Chattanooga, Tenn.
G.T. Willis	George Willis, Rossville, Ga.
T.B. Brown	Mrs. E.H. Tipton, Selma, Ala.
W.F. Brown	A. Brown, Post Oak Springs, Tenn.
J.W. Rush	Mrs. J.W. Rush, Selma, Ala.

The following named members of other regiments were also confined on Johnson's Island:

E. Winston	Mrs. R.C. Winston, Rogersville, Tenn.
R. Blair	John Blair, Jonesboro, Tenn.
T.M. Hoyl	T.L. Hoyl, Cleveland, Tenn.
L.C. Hoyl	same
S.B. Sullins	Rev. T. Sullins, Athens, Tenn.
J.F. Whitfield	Mrs. J.F. Whitfield, Montgomery, Ala.
W.M. Simpson	Mrs. L. Simpson, Athens, Tenn.

- - - - - - - - - - - - -

WAGONS AND TEAMS
[18 July 1862]

We are authorized by Messers. Bridges and Zimmerman, who are agents of the Confederate Government, to buy or *impress*, to say that the recent order for wagons and teams continues, and if the people do not bring them in and take a fair price, they will be compelled, in the discharge of their duty, to resort to impressment. They desire to buy, and not press. All the farmers who can possibly spare a wagon and team, or parts of each, will please come forward immediately.

- - - - - - - - - - - - -

MAIL TO DECATUR
[1 August 1862]

Being remote from the main channel of mail facilities, it is very important that whatever mail matter may reach your place for Decatur should be promptly forwarded. This, for some time, has not been done. Today the mail brought nothing to this place for Meigs County, as I am advised by the Post Master. Where the wrong is cannot be known here, nor is it believed that the wrong, whatever it may be, is intentional. . . .

- - - - - - - - - - - - -

TO THE PEOPLE OF McMINN, MONROE, RHEA, AND MEIGS
[22 August 1862]

J. H. Hale, of Athens, has been appointed Government Agent to purchase Jeans, Linseys and Socks, for the use of the army, and the people of the above named counties are hereby notified not to sell to other parties than an authorized agent. The soldier must be furnished with comfortable clothing, and the people are urged to manufacture as fast as possible.

By order of Maj. James Glover, Q.M.
D. J. DISMUKES, Agent

- - - - - - - - - - - - -

EXHUMATION OF CORPSES

[22 August 1862]

Our attention has been called to the fact that, in a number of instances, the remains of deceased soldiers killed in the recent battles, or the victim of disease, have been disinterred for transportation to their late homes, at remote distances from Richmond. When a Metalic burial case can be obtained, this transportation may be effected; but otherwise, the expenditure for a wooden coffin, with saw dust or other packing, is just so much money thrown away, if we are correctly informed. We learn that it is rarely the case a corpse forwarded in this way reaches its destination. The rapidity of decomposition impels the railroad authorities to remove the corpse from the train, for reinterment, and thus the anxiety of relatives and friends to secure the remains for burial is defeated, and the heavy expense incurred in providing the coffin, &c., rendered unavailing. The removal of corpses should be deferred until the return of cold weather.

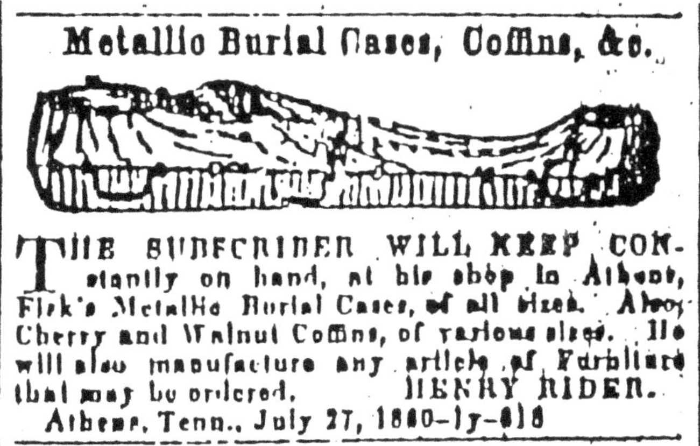

The above advertisement from *The Athens Post* contains a drawing of the metalic burial case mentioned in the last article.

\- - - - - - - - - - - - -

JERKED BEEF FOR THE ARMY

[5 September 1862]

There is a process of curing beef known to Mexicans and old Texans as "jerking." The process is simple. Cut the meat into strips of eight to fourteen inches in length, salt it moderately, then string it upon ropes in the sun, taking it in at night. In three or four days it is ready for use. The transportation would be much easier than that of cattle, as it could be put in barrels, or bales made of "raw hide," or "hickory bark." Beef cured in this manner is always juicy and palatable. It is healthy; a haversack of jerked beef will last a man for days without bread. Cooking is unnecessary, as it is good raw.

\- - - - - - - - - - - - -

$1500 REWARD

[5 September 1862]

HEADQUARTERS, 3d TENN. VOL.
Camp Cross, near Tazewell
Aug. 12, 1862

The following members of the 3d Tennessee Regiment have left their companies without leave. *Thirty Dollars* will be paid for each man delivered at my headquarters wherever they may be, or *Fifteen Dollars* for each one delivered in any jail so their Captain's may get them:

Company A— John Blain, Union Co.; Jno M. Bond, Knox; F.M. Bim, Richmond, Va.; J.M. Murphy, Jefferson; Wm Sharp, Knox; Wm Sullivan, Union

Company B— Chas Denton, Jno Denton, Thos Eakin, Wm Isbel, C.D. McDannel, G.W. Bird, Monroe Co.; Jas Chambliss, Knox; S. McCall, Monroe

Company C— John Duke, Polk Co.

Company D— John Strandridge, N.C.

Company E— Wray Wright, Signor Everett, A.A. Riddle, S.M. Wright, N.M. Young, Wm Burnfield, Blount; Wm Carr, Monroe; L. Runions, Polk; B.F. Grisby, Bradley

Company F— A. Graves, E. Carpenger, L. Evans, W. Carden, H. Cunningham, Monroe

Company G— J. L. Collett, Thomas Hamilton, Henry Shook, McMinn

Company H— J.C. Lewis, Jas H. Gardner, F.M. Wilson, Wm Kirkland, John Horne, Jas H. Cagle, M. Duncan, A.C. Dean, Jas Kirkland, Monroe; A. Balls, Wm Ragland, Roane

Company I— J.W. Vincent, White

Company K— Jas Kirkland, Polk

By Order of J. W. BLEVINS
Adj. of 3d Tenn. Reg't.

\- - - - - - - - - - - - -

3d BATTALION TENNESSEE CAVALRY

[12 September 1862]

Athens
Sept. 8, 1862

All absent members of Capt. Van Dyke's Company, of 3d Battalion Tennessee Cavalry, who are unable to return to Company, must report to the Captain weekly by a certificate from a reliable and practicing Physician, otherwise they will be reported absent without leave, and are liable to be published as deserters.

J.A. TURLEY, 1st Lieut.

\- - - - - - - - - - - - -

GENERAL ORDER
[12 September 1862]

Delinquent subscribers who fail to report themselves at these headquarters by the 1st of October next, will be regarded as deserters and published as such.

SAM P. IVINS
Commander of the *Post*

- - - - - - - - - - - - -

NOTICE
[12 September 1862]

All persons belonging to my Company must report to the command immediately, otherwise I will be compelled to enforce the regulations. By order of James A. Howard, Lt. Col., Commanding Cavalry

G.C. SANDUSKY, Capt.
Lt. Col. Howard's Battery Confederate Cavalry

- - - - - - - - - - - - -

CONSCRIPT
[26 September 1862]

In accordance with Order No. 9, issued by the Governor of Tennessee, I have proceeded to appoint the following named persons as Enrolling Officers for the County of Meigs, towit:

1st District— W.C. Hutcheson
2nd District— Howell Whitmore
3rd District— William S. Russell
4th District— William M. Kilgore
5th District— William S. Peake
6th District— Jacob Peake
7th District— Morgan Bryan
8th District— William Wan

J.B. FOOSHEE, Chairman
County Court, Meigs County

- - - - - - - - - - - - -

HORRIBLE MURDER
[3 October 1862]

Mr. Jacob Womack, an old citizen of Meigs County, near the McMinn line, was murdered by two of his slaves on Tuesday of last week. There was no other white person on the farm at the time, but it appears from the statements of some of the slaves, that on Tuesday afternoon Mr. Womack attempted to correct one of the negroes for some misdemeanor— the negro resisted, knocked his master down, and jumped upon him. He called to another boy, who was within hearing, to come and take his assailant off. The boy ran up, but, instead of assisting his master, handed a knife to the other negro, with which he immediately cut the struggling man's throat from ear to ear, and mangled him in a horrible manner.

The body was taken by the negroes to the creek, sunk and covered with drift and logs— where it was found on the day following, through the disclosures of a third negro who was privy to the concealment. One of the negroes engaged in the killing, we learn, made his escape and is still at large; the other was arrested by the neighbors, and, as soon as the facts were made sufficiently clear, was hung by them on a tree near where the crime was committed. Mr. Womack was some sixty years of age and owned considerable property.

- - - - - - - - - - - - -

MEIGS CONTY
[24 April 1863]

The Circuit Court met at Decatur on Monday. Attendance thin and the session short. The truth is, nearly all the able bodied men are in the army, fighting the battles of freedom. Some counties in East Tennessee have failed to come up to the full measure of their duty, but Meigs is not among that number. Her armor is bright with service, and her escutcheon untarnished. May the terrible struggle soon be terminated, and her gallant sons restored to their homes and firesides.

- - - - - - - - - - - - -

LETTER FROM VICKSBURG
[24 April 1863]

Camp near Vicksburg,
April 12, 1863

Dear Father: — We arrived here safe and sound and found the regiment in very good health. I am very well pleased with the country— a great deal better than I expected to be from what I had heard. We heard before leaving home that it was an awful country, and that the soldiers were all starving. Well, that is all stuff. We get plenty to eat, and that of good substantial diet. We draw bacon, beef, meal, sugar, molasses, peas, and what extras we get we have to pay high for. We pay $5 for coffee, $1.50 for eggs, $2 for butter, $2 per gallon for milk, but as long as we do as well as we are now we ought not to grumble. There is some talk of us moving into Alabama or to Chattanooa, but I would rather stay here until the first of June, as it will be healthy here for that length of time. We have no fears of the Yankees attacking us here, and if they do we are so well fortified that they cant hurt us much. We have preaching every night. I attend regularly. Give all my acquaintances my respects. Tell them I am fat, saucy and well pleased with the country, and camp life generally. John was here the other day. He is all right.

H.W.G.

- - - - - - - - - - - - -

PIN - HOOK FERRY
[24 April 1863]

The Subscriber Respectfully notices the public that this Ferry, the main crossing on the Tennessee River, and on the route leading to Grassy Cove, is now in excellent order and attended by a careful and skillful Ferryman. It has an excellent large Horse Power Boat, and no delay can occur in setting either Travelers or Stock across. He respectfully solicits public attention.

William C. Peake,
Pin Hook, Tennessee River

- - - - - - - - - - - - -

$180 REWARD
[24 April 1863]

The following persons enrolled as Conscripts in the 2d Civil District, Rhea County, have failed to report as the law requires:

LENEAR WASSON— 26 years old, 5 feet 10 inches high, dark complexion, dark eyes, dark hair
ROBERT CLARK— 24 years old, 5 feet 8 inches high, fair complexion, blue eyes, fair hair
JOEL JO PRATT— 20 years old, 6 feet 1 inch high, dark complexion, black eyes, dark hair
WARD HALEY— 36 years old, 6 feet high, fair complexion, blue eyes, fair hair
LEONARD LONG— 36 years old, 5 feet 8 inches high, fair complexion, blue eyes, auburn hair
THOMAS CLARK— 36 years old, 5 feet 8 inches high, fair complexion, blue eyes, fair hair

A reward of $30 each will be paid for the apprehension and delivery of the above named deserters at the Camp of Instructions at Knoxville.

Transportation furnished by the Government.
By order of Leut. Col. E. D. Blake.
JAMES J. CASH
Enrolling Officer, 2d Civil District

- - - - - - - - - - - - -

$150 REWARD
[24 April 1863]

The following persons enrolled as Conscripts in the 3d Civil District, Rhea County, have failed to report as the law requires:

REUBEN W. PORTER— 37 years old, 5 feet 10 inches high, dark complexion, black eyes, light hair
JOSEPH EATON— 37 years old, 5 feet 7 inches high, fair complexion, dark eyes, light hair
W. M. DORTERY— 37 years old, 6 feet 2 inches high, dark complexion, blue eyes, black hair
THOMAS HODGEONS— 23 years old, 5 feet 1 inch high, fair complexion, grey eyes, light hair
GEORGE W. MONROE— 23 years old, 5 feet 7 inches high, fair complexion, blue eyes, dark hair

A reward of $30 each will be paid for the apprehension and delivery of the above named deserters at the Camp of Instruction at Knoxville.

Transportation furnished by the Government.
H. WASSOM
Enrolling Officer, 3d Civil District

- - - - - - - - - - - - -

$210 REWARD
[24 April 1863]

The following persons enrolled as Conscripts in the 10th Civil District, Rhea County, have failed to report as the law requires:

WILLIAM BIRLEY— 24 years old, 6 feet high, light complexion, blue eyes, light hair
HYRAM MORGAN— 19 years old, 6 feet high, dark complexion, black eyes, black hair
W. B. MORGAN— 18 years old, 5 feet 6½ inches high, fair complexion, blue eyes, light hair
G. W. HORSLER— 22 years old, 5 feet 7 inches high, fair complexion, grey eyes, light hair
HENRY MORGAN— 34 years old, 6 feet high, fair complexion, black eyes, dark hair
R. D. MORGAN— 31 years old, 6 feet high, dark complexion, black eyes, black hair

A reward of $30 each will be paid for the apprehension and delivery of the above named deserters at the Camp of Instruction at Knoxville.

Transportation furnished by the Government.
By order of Lt. Col. E. D. Blake
DANIEL HODGES
Enrolling Officer for 10th Civil District

- - - - - - - - - - - - -

$120 REWARD
[24 April 1863]

The following persons enrolled as Conscripts in the 2th Civil District, Meigs County, have failed to report as required by law:

P. N. MATHIS— 33 years old, 5 feet 10 inches high, dark complexion, dark eyes, fair hair
ROBERT COX— 23 years old, 5 feet high, dark complexion, grey eyes, dark hair
JESSE WEIR— 19 years old, 5 feet 7 inches high, dark complexion, dark eyes, dark hair

FREELING WEIR— 18 years old, 5 feet 7 inches high, dark complexion, dark eyes, dark hair

A reward of $30 each will be paid for the apprehension and delivery of the above named deserters at the Camp of Instructions at Knoxville.

Transportation furnished by the Government.

H. WHITMORE
Enrolling Officer, 2d Civil District

- - - - - - - - - - - - -

$330 REWARD
[24 April 1863]

The following persons enrolled as Conscripts in the 5th Civil District, Meigs County, have failed to report as required by law:

SAMPSON ATCHLEY— 31 years old, 5 feet 7½ inches high, dark complexion, grey eyes, black hair
JAMES AIKMON— 29 years old, 5 feet 8½ inches high, fair complexion, black eyes, light hair
JOHN H. HOOD— 21 years old, 5 feet 10 inches high, fair complexion, blue eyes, light hair
RICHARD HOLLAND— 26 years old, 6 feet high, fair complexion, blue eyes, light hair
WILLIAM B. MARSHALL— 27 years old, 6 feet high, dark complexion, black eyes, dark hair
A. B. ROWDEN— 28 years old, 6 feet 1 inch high, fair complexion, blue eyes, light hair
J. W. MOORE— 36 years old, 5 feet 8 inches high, fair complexion, blue eyes, light hair
STEWART JONES— 36 years old, 5 feet 8½ inches high, dark complexion, black eyes, dark hair
FRANKLIN HOYL— 36 years old, 5 feet 10½ inches high, fair complexion, grey eyes, light hair
P. W. VAUGHN— 36 years old, 5 feet 7 inches high, fair complexion, blue eyes, dark hair
W. A. GEORGE— 32 years old, 5 feet 6 inches high, dark complexion, black eyes, dark hair

A reward of $30 each will be paid for the apprehension and delivery of the above named deserters at the Camp of Instruction at Knoxville.

Transportation furnished by the Government.

WILLIAM C. PEAK
Enrolling Officer, 5th Civil District

- - - - - - - - - - - - -

Battles and Leaders of the Civil War

— *PART II* —

LETTERS, REMINISCENCES, AND DIARIES

ALLEN LETTERS

William G. Allen (21 October 1836 - 27 November 1924), son of Valentine and Ann (Frazier) Allen, was married to Mary E. Thomison, daughter of William P. and Nancy (Smith) Thomison, on 15 December 1859, in Rhea County. Allen wrote many articles for the ***Dayton Herald*** and other newspapers describing the activities of the 5th Tennessee Cavalry.

The following summary of his own war experiences was also among his papers now in the collection of the Rhea County Historical and Genealogical Society: "As soon as I could arrange for my wife and settle my Trustee office, I answered Governor Harris' call. I spent 1,169 days doing all I could for the Confederacy, 969 days of that time with Col. George W. McKenzie's 5th Tennessee Cavalry.

"At Richmond, Kentucky, I got my first gunshot wound and had my only hand to hand fight. Here I got my first horse shot from under me in battle. I fought four times in and around Richmond, in fact, at Williamsburg, London, Danville, Linchburg, Georgetown, Lexington, and Parris, where I had my second horse shot from under me by a cannon ball. I posted pickets and lined up for a fight, from Perryville to Big Creek Gap, from Big Creek Gap to Orchard Knob, now a part of Chattanooga.

"On September 7, 1863, just north of Ringgold, on side of White Oak Mountain, my third horse was killed from under me and I still have the scar left in my thigh from an ounce ball. On September 19th, in the bloody battle of Chickamauga, I was pierced through my left arm, left lung, and two minie balls went through my right leg. On May 13 [1864], near Tilton, Georgia, I got another minie ball through my right leg. I carry seven lead scars, one made in Kentucky and six in Georgia.

"On May 27, 1864, I had my fourth horse shot from under me. At Florence, Alabama, I had my fifth horse killed from under me. I rode home on my 18th horse, given me by General Roberson. Six horses were wounded in battle I had to leave them there. One was killed by a falling tree, one was stolen, and one's hoofs came off for want of shoes (feet was worn out). . . ."

William's brothers who also served during the war were Thomas A. Allen, George W. Allen, and Valentine C. Allen IV. All three were in Company I (Lillard's) of the 3rd Tennessee. Their father, Valentine Allen III, was a member of Capt. Darius Waterhouse's Company.

Thomas A. (1838-1897) was one Vaughn's men who escorted President Davis to Washington, Georgia. He was parolled May 8, 1865, by order of President Davis.

George W. (1840-1881) was in the battles of Manassas and Seven Pines, and was wounded at Morristown, Tennessee. Valentine C. was at Vicksburg, was paroled and exchanged in Georgia. He was also with Vaughn's escort for President Davis.

Valentine Allen III (father of William, Thomas, George, and V.C.) was captured and put into a Kingston jail. He was released, but was arrested again and taken to Chattanooga, where he was put in the prison barracks. "The Yankees would not let him take his coat. He was taken from Chattanooga to the Nashville Penitentiary where he languished for three months. Then he was kept in Louisville Penitentiary for three months. General Palmer parolled Valentine Allen, Robert Kile, and Perry Ault out of prison on March 9, 1863, and set these three old, weak and almost naked men on the north side of the Ohio River, forbiding them to go south. Perry Ault died and his family never knew where he was buried. Kyle and Father made shingles at 40 pr 1000 to get a little meat and bread. After I got home on May 10, 1865, I rode to Chattanooga and borrowed $20.00 from Bill Crutchfield. Father came home almost dead" (from William G. Allen papers).

LETTER NO. 1
WILLIAM G. ALLEN TO HIS WIFE, MARY "LIZZIE" ALLEN

Camp Clinch, May 13th 1862

Dear Lizzie

I again embrace the present moments to wright you. I still am blessed with good health, which I am verry thankful for, and I hope by the mercies of an alwise God that the Same blessing may be with you and my Dear Babe. it is with Some degree of reluctance that I am forced to wright you again without hearing from you, when your last letter was So full of Sorrow and Sadness. But I try to wright you once a week at least, and I do want you to do the Same you cannot tell how Sadly I was disappointed on last evening when I arrived back at camps and found no letter from you nor any of my friends. do try and do better in the future. it does not matter whether you hear from me or not, for you cannot expect me to wright to you when I am on a Scout.

We left here on last Tuesday night– crossed the River and marched to Clinton, next day to Jacks Boro, and up to Woodson Gap which is about 15 miles above Jacksboro, Some 25 miles from the Gap. on Saturday we –?-- for Kingston. most all the Boys are sick, we had but one officer a long and his horse got foundered, and I had to take command of the Company. we got back all Safe, our Capt was gon to Knoxville, when we left on the Scout. I Saw George at Woodsons Gap he is well and cannot get his Transfer till the first of next Month, then he will come to our Company.

I learned from Wm Benett that father was going into the Service. I was Sorry to hear it and think that he is Treating himself his family and me wrong he has a large Family, two Boys and myself in the Service already, and I am Sadisfied that he can Serve his Country better at home than any where else, and more I have left you in his care, and if he leaves I Shall try and make Some arraingments to move you on the South Side of the River, But I hope he will reconsider, and think well how and in what Sort of a condition he is leaving Mother and all his Family. will he, can he, leave you all, and be sadisfied. I would answer no with the candor of all my heart, and I do believe when he thinks it all over he will not leave. I no that he wants to Serve his Country, and will not he Show more Patrotism by staying at home and taking care of his Family and making Something for the Army than any other way.

Yes Lizzie I want you to wright to me as Soon as you get this and let me know what your Pah is goin to do and if he is going into the Service any how. wright me where you will be Sadisfied to Stay on the South side [of the] River, if you have any choice. I will try & make Some arrangements about you Staying and if not wright me what you want to do and I will try to Situate you as Comfortable as I can. any thing that is in my Power I will do for you and Willie is all that I live for now, and when I know that you are not Satisfied I am in distress, and moment after moment passes away only by the force of imagination, leaving a space more Sad and doleful for the next and if my time all passed as heavly as when I know that you are in Sorrow many would be the furow that would cross my Brow, and Soon would my head be Silvered with hary hairs, but let me know that all is well at home and well Sadisfied and the Sweet moments pass away in Sun shine and bliss.

Now my Dear wife do you want to know what I think of this war, and many who are taking no part in it. I believe that it will not last long, not longer than 12 mo. for war its self will ware out, and I know from the way that things are progressing that we will not be found acting on the defensive much longer, not longer than we get organized again. Then will the North begin to feel the Ravages of war. And as to myself I feel that I am duty bound to be a Soldier as long as my Country calls me. I feel that I have a wife who would rather See her Self left a widow and her Darling Babe left an orphan than have a husband who would not Serve his Coutry when all that is Holy & Sacred calls him. Yes my Dear wife let me be a Soldier ever ready to do his Duty and if the God of Battles sees fit in his mercys to let the hand of Death come upon him by disease by Swored Ball or Cannon, and my Bones left to bleach on Some lonely Mountain or in Some dark and dismal Swamp who nothing Save the hoot of the owl is herd, then you can Say that he died the death of the noble & Brave Battling for his wife his Babe Home and that is Sacred to him and asks not a place to be buried.

Oh Lizzie, while I am wrighting I see a man of Noble form and look come and bow himself beside a fresh made mound as you and I did when we parted with Little Jinie, and my heart is full mine eyes are all in tears, and my Body nealed beside a Grave with Pen Ink and Paper on the tombstone trying to wright to you. Bless God oh prais him for my Soul is happy, and tears moistens my paper. I cannot tell why nor how I feel, I can only say that I am happy in Jesus. Raise Willie to Love his God. My Dear wife you must excuse me for asking you to pray for me so often for I do feel that you have prayed and God has answered your prayers by blessing my Soul this Beautiful morning a mid So mutch wickedness. I have ever found religion to be precious but more So in Camps, if their is a place on this green Earth where a mans faith is Tried it is in Camps but I feel that I am able by the grace of God to go though mutch wickedness. tell Mother houdy for me when you see her, and that I think often of the prayers that she has sent up to high heaven for me, and I bless God to day that I ever had a praying Mother one who taught me to pray, and if I should fall ere we meet on Earth that we will meet in heaven. Yes that is my every wish, tell her to wright to me how Val is getting. I must close by telling all my friends houdy now my Dear wife I want you to wright to me often. Kiss Willie for me. I am your Husband

W. G. Allen tell all my friends to wright

- - - - - - - - - - - - -

LETTER NO. 2
WILLIAM G. ALLEN TO FATHER [VALENTINE ALLEN III] AND FAMILY

State of Kentucky, Gerrard County
September 30th 1862

Dear Father and Family

I have a chance to send you a few lines by some of our corp who start for Tenn to day. Father I received your kind letter the night of the evacuation of Cumberland Gap, but have not had time to wright you only a few lines. I wrought Bro Thomas on Goos Creek and you a few lines. Since that time we have been very busy, that was one week ago to day as this is monday and the 29th instead of the 30th. We marched on that evening to Manchester. Found all the Feds gon, they left 50 fat beeves burned 45 waggons left 12 not burnt. They also burnt what flour came out of 300 bushel of wheat they had pressed here. We followed on and captured 42 prisoners between here and Boonville. Onsley County.

We stoped at Manchester to get up some rations as our waggons was not with us. we have suffered for something to eat. I rosted corn & apples and drank watter out of mud holes where my horse would not drink because their was a dead horse and mule in it. I have passed through Knox Clay Onsley Laurel Rockcastle Lincoln and Gerrard and saw but two streams of runing water– Cumberland and Rockcastle Rivers– and you could scearsley see that either of them was runing. There has been a drouth in this State and it is not a well watered country no how. I watered my horse out of my hat yesterday out of a hole he could not get too.

We are now in a beautiful country, it is so level and so mutch meadows and fine cattle, in fact it is the prettiest Land I ever saw and if it was only watered I should be tempted when the war was done but East Tenn for me as long as she is not watered, they -----?----- with many friends the Kentuckians are raling to our cause. Regt after Regt are preparing for our cause. Illinois, Ohio & Indiana are sending us some troops, Ky has already --?-rated 45 Regts to General Smith. We leave here to morrow the 30th.

The Cause of the South and Freedom of white men is on the gain. Tenn is almost clear of negro sheiek-ers(?) and Ky soon will be, and thank God for it. Yes Father my blood runs war through my veins when I see and hear how our Cause is prospering, and to know that the Great Tam(?) is with us.

Yesterday was Sunday, we met up with a squad of bushwhackers near Craborchard, of 26 we captured their Capt & 8 men & 15 horses. Their Capt is one of the most notorious men in Ky, we have him here and will hang him. We took him out last night and told him so, told him to get pardon for his sins if he could. We tied the rope to a limb, told him to confess what he had done. he had denied all till now. he said he was a bush whacker & was Capt. had killed 2 men, wounded 2, had robed citizens and wanted time to pray, which was granted him. Father & mother I pray God never to see another such a sight– here is this man who looks to be about 40 years old, rather a good looking man– with two sons one about 16 the other 18, fine looking boys– one on each side taken as bushwhackers, with a Father for Capt– the Boys left a mother yesterday by the roadside upon her knees with prayer & supplication for them & their wicked Father. She wanted to come on but we could not let her come. she has a large family. Father although the proof is so strong against– and the citizens most all say hang him, I never want to see an other such a sight.

We have passed through 2 very nice Towns, Craborchard and Lancaster, met some kind friends at both. one Lady was so mutch excited and rejoiced when she saw the bushwhacker Capt she could not hold her place. she called to me to stop made a negro hold my horse while I followed her into house to hear what sort of man we had. she was excited beond reason, wanted me to stay till her husband came & then stay till morning. We are moving towards Louisville and I think we will join Bragg. General Stevenson is 5 mi west of us at a small place called Brogg(?). I hav not herd from George since I left the Gap. I am your son in haste

W. G. Allen

Please show this to Lizzie I am well

- - - - - - - - - - - - -

LETTER NO. 3
WILLIAM G. ALLEN TO BROTHER

Knoxville, Tenn Feby 27

Dear Bro–

I send to you by Col G.W. McKenzie $950.00. Col will leave the Amount with Frank McKorkle you will please go to Decatur and get it and pay it out as follows: yourself $250, Joseph Parks $200, W.P. Thomison $350, John S Whaley $100, Father $50

Our Boys captured Capt Earley and 20 of his men, they are all in Jail at this place. Capt Earley is a brother to A.P. Earley. is talked here that he will be convicted for counterfitting besides a bush whacker. you take all the trouble on yourself I ask and oblige. wright to me at this place. I want to hear from G.W.

W. G. Allen

- - - - - - - - - - - - -

LETTER NO. 4
GEORGE W. ALLEN TO FATHER

Quarter Masters Dept 3 Tenn
March 11th 1863

Dear Father:

Val and I are well and doing finely, but I am very tired. Just returned to camp after clean clothes. I have been assigned to duty 14 miles from this place at a post. I will move Perminantly tomorrow and leave Val to tend to everything at camp. Genl Stevinson offered to send my name up for Promotion if I will take a field in Texas and a long on Red River to buy and get up Supplies for the Army.

Genl Vaughn gave me a great recomendation to him in writing Genl Stevenson sent it to me this Evening. I have not decided as yet what I will do Col Neute doesnt want me to go, thats his advice and I dont no what to do Val will not help me deside he wont say wether he wants to go or not.

My health is fast improving. I am getting as fat as a bear, no more news of interest, all quiet along our lines. I will return in the morning early, Val will keep you posted on the times. please write me Soon. You Shall hear from me Soon,

Your Son Geo. W. Allen

BROWN AND NEAL LETTERS

Although the Brown family resided in Roane County before and during the War, two of the daughters of William Franklin and Amanda (Renfro) Brown moved to Rhea County after the war.

The letter writer, Mary E. Brown, married Col. John Randolph Neal on 13 November 1862. He was born in Anderson County, Tennessee, on 26 November 1836, the son of John O. and Permelia (Young) Neal.

Upon graduating from Emory and Henry College in Virginia, John began the study of law and was admitted to the bar at the outbreak of the Civil War. In 1861, he enlisted in the Confederate Army as a private in Company D, 6th Tennessee Cavalry, but afterwards became a Lieutenant-Colonel [see article on page 23 concerning a company being organized by Capt. J.R. Neal in 1862].

After the war, John taught school in Virginia, Arkansas, and Tennessee, including one year at Rhea Springs. His law practice became successful, and in 1874, he was elected to represent Rhea, James, Meigs, and Cumberland counties in the State Legislature. John was elected to Congress from the Third District of Tennessee in 1884, and again in 1886.

LETTER NO. 1
JOHN R. NEAL TO MARY E. BROWN

Athens, Tennessee
Aug. 1st, 1861

Dear Mary–

Your letter was not recd for several days after it was written. The delay was occasioned by me being absent at the Springs and hence not getting my mail regularly. I enjoyed myself at the Springs as well as, if not better than I expected, Though I was not able to participate in some of the amusements &c excursions in which others engaged. I found food for thought & reflection amid the beautiful scenery by which I was surrounded. I thought of the past; gazed upon the starring present, and looked forward to the uncertain future. I must confess that I can not see through tho I must, that are before us those bright visions that once cheered my heart and mouved my soul, But I am getting gloomy.

I expect to return to the Springs today. I dont know how long I shall remain, probably a week or ten days. No doubt Post Oak & vicinity wears a sad and dreary appearance especially in a social point of view. Sacrifices must be made, ties must be broken, tears and blood must be shed like water to sustain the cause in which we are engaged. It is now not only a contest between the South and the North, but a contest of Constitutional freedom on the one hand, against a military despotism on the other.

I believe that we will soon have fighting in East Tenn. The Union element, not withstanding all that Lincoln has done, and is doing, not withstanding the Northern defeat at Manassas, is becoming bolder, and I fear that the State authorities will pursue an ---?--- course in regard to it, and thereby bring about a collisian. Companies are being formed & drilled under the U. States flag in this country and the course that has been pursued by some of the Southern Speakers through the country, has aided in bringing about this state of affairs. We however must wait further development.

I shall not insist on a further discussion of the nature of some women, recollect, some not all, but will produce authority to further sustain the position that I assumed. Law, you know, is reason founded on human nature, enacted by wisdom, and sustained by experience. There was a law enacted by the British parliment in regard to obtaining husbands under false pretences. The law enacts That all women, of whatever age, rank, profession, or degree, whether virgins, maids, or widows who shall after this act impose upon, seduce and betray into matrimony any of his Magisty's male subjects, by virtue of scents, paints, cosmetic washes, artificial bust(?), ran(?) stays, or high heeled shoes, shall incur the penalty of the law against witchcraft, & like misdomeanors, and the marriage shall be null & void.

Well then, if women of the character described above do as the law presumes they do do, other women (an the nature[?] of women is the same the world over) who have not the defects enumerated above, will resort to other means to seduce men into matrimony after having . . . [remainder of letter missing]

- - - - - - - - - - - - -

LETTER NO. 2(?)
JOHN R. NEAL TO MARY E. BROWN

[beginning of letter missing;
possibly a continuation of above letter;
definitely John's hndwriting]

. . . adopted to each other than myself and R--- to speak truly. I give way to my feelings with a spirit somewhat akin to that of Raskassins when he painted the picture of Promithius. I regarded life in a different light. Love and contintment had then appeared to me the chief end of woman's existence. When I met you, long absence & seldom communications had partialy affected(?) his memory; & daily intercourse with another whom I had learned to esteem upon first acquaintance for the possession of those qualities of both head & heart Which I admire almost idolitemarly led me to ignore him who had been before the paragon of all I had loved. Sometimes I consol myself with this sentiment from Moore. "The heart like a tendril acoustomed to cling --?-- --?-- withdraw its support from the Confederation till the frail and tattering edifice is almost ready to fall upon our heads and crush us beneath its ruins."

When one considers the disfracted state of our Country, the inevitable cannot turn(?) and agitations that periodically occur. The Civil Wars and revolutions which have become a matter of habit with the French. The internal quarrels and bickerings that have changed Italy that Eden of the world into isolation and ruin, together with the constant changes which affect all the other Nations of the earth, it is with emotions of pleasure and relief that in turn like Noahs(?) --?-- that only permanent --?-- Government. The British and to the British Constitution stands among the nations of the earth like an ancient oak in the world(?) which after having overcome many a blast --?-- overtips the other trees of the forest and commands the respect and admiration of the world. Let it grow where it will, can not flourish alone, But bends toward the nearest --?-- thing which it twins around.

The people here are like Rip Van Winkle– just beginning to arouse from their lethurgy, & to take an active part in the stirring events of their land. On the 5th there will be public speaking here by Col. Trigg & the candidates for the convention. You speak of becoming a candidate, that is, if being solicited by the people. What are your politics? When you were over, you --?-- for the Union. When we reflect upon the history of the American Union, and the arguments brought to bear in favor of the formation of the Federal Government (by the United colonies) by the great men in the famous Con-gress of 74, & its further consolidation in the convention of 86, after the dangers had been passed and it proved to be the Egean shield of our defense(?) & the reverence with which it has(?) been cherished as the guardian of our peace and the protector of our liberties.

A thought of this dissolution of the bond which has bound us together with adamantive(?) chains causes a feeling of pain akin to honor. If we turn again to the causes of the great War of the Revolution we find that the principles of resistence to oppression and defense of the common liberty was the sole origin of its existence. How careful then ought we to be in defense of those rights & liberties, since we have tasted the abundance and propriety of the point of their success & hence can better than they value & appreciate the motives which led to that withdrawal from tyrany. Yet we must guard ----sft with state yielding to the Voice of immediate interest or can . . .

[remainder of letter missing]

\- - - - - - - - - - - - -

LETTER NO. 3
MARY BROWN TO JOHN R. NEAL

Post Oak Springs, Tenn.
Nov. 15th 1861

Dear John:

If you were uncomonly interested in the decision of the very important question, I was quite as much concerned whether or not you would approve of my course. You did not express your mind positively though I suppose you are satisfied, from the fact of your silence. Hearts may agree, though heads may differ.. Here, permit an explanation which to you may be necessary, in order to understand why I have ever spoken as I have on this subject. I would not have referred everything in this matter to you alone, had it not been that peculiarly situated as we now are, I did not wish particularly to do anything in which you did not willingly acquiesce because you regarded it both proper and right.

This led me to waive all privalege or prerogative that custom or tradition may have --?-- woman in due deference. So your superior knowledge of affairs &c &c

The Future can better than other authority perhaps disclose or answer doubtful questions, whether we will remain constant in our attachment to each other. Vows, protestations and oft repeated assurance of eternal constancy will avail nothing.

But if we love with a high and disinterested passion there can be no shadow of doubt as to the ultimate result. Should we in time however find ourselves mistaken in believing this to be true, that we have been deluded into entertaining an imaginary, ephemiral fancy for the reality, absence and such long interval between our meetings, will test and reveal the mock, counterfit passion.

Instead of being love-sick, we should be sick of love. Then we should rather rejoice at having been timely rescued from a lifetime of intense pain and suffering which a marriage devoid of Love would surely entail. I can not say I will remain unchanged; it would be strange though if, Loving as I do, my heart should with no apparent reason withdraw its reciprocal homage.

The whole current of my life must first be unchanneled for it has become a habit, almost a part of my nature, to love. I believe in Platonic Love any way that is affection based on esteem and admiration of the moral and intellectual qualities.

If you like, you may consider my mission as a transcript or picture of my thoughts and feelings but how can you, remembering what I told you, expect to find in them a faithful miror of my heart. You would be more nearly correct when taking just the reverse of what you said. You spoke of going West this winter. I wish it was so I could accompany you for I believe it to be my duty if, by so doing, I could contribute to your happiness or assist you by my feeble efforts through lifes stormy pilgrimage. I would not willingly increase your cares and responsibilities but I might wether the rude falast of adversity quite as bravely as yourself.

Though hitherto unaccustomed to anything that could demand the cultivation of the vurtues of self denial patience, perceverance &c. I flatter myself I possess a spirit that would not be crushed, if so much as depressed or even affected at all by misfortune or poverty. I have hope, energy and industry enough to remove or change whatever may be disagreeable in such a condition. By the way can you not do as well staying at home studying and improving your mind as to go West even if there should be an opening, this coming winter.

You are in error when you suppose there exists a heriditary feud between the people of Kingston and Post Oak. When I have an enemy I would have one worthy of my dislike and not too weak, contemptible and insignificant for hatred. Neither are we altogether governed by the Arabian or chieftain laws of hospitality but rather by the Japanese policy of non-intercourse.

I have another letter from Mr. Frank Foust; he offers an apology for the request he made and still wishes a further correspondence. Also one from a Rev. Mr. Bennett, minister of the Holston Conference, from No. C. His letter I may probably answer, to the others my self respect will allow me now to write.

The people were a good deal alarmed at the startling rumors of Yankee invasion. I hardly know what to think of the destruction of railroad bridges unless they do mean to come through the mountain. It would doubtless be better for our side if they would ---?--- --?-- to use before the fight at Columbus. They are not expecting an attack soon. It is said the authorities speak of returning Lillards regiment to E.T.

I am at a loss to know how to employ the time so as to conduce to the most pleasure and profet this winter. Can you tell me what I must do. I sew some, then read, knit, &c but I get tird of all and have many leisure hours to spare that I would like to spend usefully. Ma wants me to teach the children, but I cant (excuse the term). Talk to me of exercising patience when I never yet found any to cultivate.

Our circuit preacher held a meeting here and in a sermon he preached stated his position of nutrality. The congregation here will not receive him on such a platform. They act on the principal that they who are not for us in this critical and fearful conjusture are against us. By the way speaking of preachers, have you taken orders yet? I dreamed of hearing you preach. I guess you patriotic citizens of McMinn are according to the recomendation of President Davis, keeping this as fast day.

A dispatch was received from Washington yesterday requesting immediate aid of the militia of this place. Several hundred Union men have assembled somewhere in the county and threaten to burn the town. It is said when they commence they intend destroying the grand Metropolis, Post Oak. Shouldn't be surprised if they meet with rather a warm reception should any of the traitors come which I do not now think they will. I felt proud my heart throbbed in joyous exaultation at the news of the victory at Columbus. Is not our success evidence of our being right in our Revolution and ---rriss. The late ---vass will bind & renew in our gallent men redoubled dilligence, thus ensuring victory. Excuse me but the state of the country, the war &c is the most that occupys my mind.

Affectionately

M. Brown

- - - - - - - - - - - - -

LETTER NO. 4
MARY E. BROWN TO JOHN R. NEAL

. . . [first page muissing] . . .

While I do not desire wealth, I confess I acknowledge the full merit of Agurs[?] petition requesting neither poverty nor riches. So one reason for the former, I may mention that I esteem it an assumption of great responsibility ammounting in some cases to absolute commission of crime, for individuals destitute of the means to procure the essentials of life and devoid of all prospects of anniliating this condition to unite their unhappy lots involving others perhaps in their misery–

In your present situation you have no need for me. Instead of proving a helpmate as God ordained woman to be, instead of assisting to improve your fortune I might serve now as an incumberance a burden, clogging the rising of Fordlina's[?] wheel.

Sacrifices I would be willing to make if it were only to dispense with ordinary comforts and luxuries. These constitute but a small share of real happiness. The "rich love of an honest heart" joined to other qualities which I believe you possess and noble gifts with which you are endowed, would amply repay me for any such temporary privation. Though I've no ambitions for wealth and would not for one moment pospone our marriage from such motives so far as my own happiness is concerned -?- [on?] this account for I have too firm a reliance on your judgement and energy to doubt your ultimate success, yet I believe the best policy would be to wait until Spring. By which time subsequent developments may yield some insight into the destiny of our country, since upon the success or downfall of that, hangs all our hopes.

Though sanguine as to the final result it is uncertain how long this unholy devestating war will continue. Tom says we ought like him wait until peace and prosperity return to and bless our hand. He preceives such a project fully in the extreme now.

Do you think we will remain true to each other so long? If not our engagement will be broken. If ---?--- our happiness will be none the less sweet from being deferred.

. . . [remainder of letter missing] . . .

- - - - - - - - - - - - -

LETTER NO. 5
MARY E. BROWN TO JOHN R. NEAL

. . . [beginning of letter missing] . . .
admitted. I intended only to express a wish. That if such were your propensities or desires that while you had an opportunity you might gratify them; and it appears from your own confession that you did. But this is enough on this point.

Do you not find it rather dull turning from the uninterrupted enjoyment of social intercourse to the obstruse and intricate study of your law books?

July 21st– I am obliged to you for the love you sent me by Will M.– He has just been here and told me that you were coming over to Roane. I was not supprised to hear it for I expected you would be over soon. He saw me writing and asked if I was writing to you. I know you have not made him your confidant and I can not understand how come so wise.

I hope you are in a better and more cheerful humer, since you read this than when you read my last letter.

Mary Brown

- - - - - - - - - - - - -

BROWN REMINISCENCES

Amanda Melvina Brown (1848 - 1929), daughter of William Franklin and Amanda (Renfro) Brown, married William Moore Wilson (1830 - 1909) on 26 October 1871. They lived on a large farm about four miles northeast of Rhea Springs.

William served as a commissioned officer in the Confederate Army and was in Captain A.J. Cawood's Company (organized at Rhea Springs in October 1861). The group became Company B, 43rd Tennessee Regiment. After serving their 12-month enlistment, the men reenlisted for the duration of the war. William was elected First Lieutenant. Captain Cawood was mortally wounded during the siege of Vicksburg in 1863, and William became Captain of Company B, a position he retained until the close of the war.

The following reminiscences were found in the files of the Rhea County Historical and Genealogical Society.

REMINISCENCES OF AMANDA MELVINA BROWN

I was born in Roane County, Tennessee, in 1848, and during the early part of the war was sent by my parents to the Methodist female college at Ashville, North Carolina. Three of my brothers were off in the army, but the fourth went as an escort for Julia Reagon, Eliza Doss, my sister Rebecca, and myself.

There were no railroads through our part of the country so we took the stage coach which passed our house, running between Nashville and Knoxville, and were joined at Loudon by Julia Ragon, who lived at Sweetwater, then on to Greenville, where we spent the night, taking another stage the next day.

As we went up the mountain towards Ashville, the road was narrow and rough, which made travel very dangerous and at one point the stage turned over and almost rolled into the French Broad River and brother Tom lost his hat.

The school was run by Dr. Cummings, a Northern man, and we were fed so much light bread that we hated it, and almost starved. We were there five months and were not allowed to leave the building. One night, we were so hungry that we slipped out, pulled a paling off the garden fence and stole onions. We bribed the cook to bake us some corn bread, and were having a feast when Carrie Swain, one of the teachers, caught us.

The next morning, we had onions for breakfast, were tried and got off with a lecture. Dr. Cummings had a kind-hearted son named Perry, whom we hired to take a letter to the post office, and we got word to the home folks. Several of the girls ran away, but mother sent us money and we got home.

About a week after our return, our cousin, Victoria Brown, who lived at what is now Rockwood, was married to George Gillespie [*] of Kingston, who was in the Confederate army with a regiment that was at this time stationed at Kingston. It was quite an event, as the soldiers from Post Oak and Kingston attended and the military bands played patriotic tunes. George's present to his bride was a set of jewelry made from cuttings of his own hair mounted in gold. Jewelry of this style was very fashionable at that time. The wedding clothes of Victoria were all made by Mrs. ----, who lived in a small house on our place. [* George was the son of William Neilson and Sidna Ann (Leuty) Gillespie of Rhea County]

Sister Mary was married the same week at our house to Col. John R. Neal. There were several sick soldiers at our house at the time. Sister Mary went upstairs the morning before the wedding to see one and told him she wished that he could attend. He said that he felt better but was not able to get downstairs. While the wedding was taking place, he died, his twin brother watching over him. The bride and groom left the next morning on their bridal trip to the valley of Virginia where Col. Neal's regiment was stationed.

Mother was afraid for us girls to stay at home where so many soldiers were passing back and forth, so the same week we were sent to Macon, Georgia. Judge Swan, a cousin, and his wife had refugeed to that place, and we were put at Montpelier, fifteen miles from Macon, in the school. We boarded with Mrs. Oliver, a widow with two nice children. She owned a big plantation with a good many slaves. While I was there, I was taken down with an ulcer on my leg, and Mrs. Oliver sent for the old doctor and was like a mother to me. I have always wanted to go back and see her.

Fannie Tipton of Selma, Alabama, went to school at the same place we did, and when school was out took us home with her. Sister Mary (Mrs. Neal) had refugeed to Selma and had her first baby while staying there. Rebecca was taken sick, could not eat or sleep, mostly homesickness. Sister Mary wrote to our brother, Polk, and he got a furlough and took Rebecca and me to Atlanta.

Sherman had been there, and we saw the ruins from his visit, nothing but bricks and mortar. We had to stay several days trying to find a train that was leaving, as the tracks were torn up from Atlanta to Dalton. We had ridden in a box car from Selma to Atlanta. Polk got a team and the quartermaster let us have some food. We did not know how to cook. It tool us three weeks to make the trip to Dalton, fording creeks that were out of their banks.

Brother Polk had learned to cook in the army but did not always have food to cook. Polk was determined to get to a rebel home and when we came to a creek and started across, the mules began to swim and the water came up over our waists. The driver said that we were going to drown, but brother said "No we are not" and taking the lines, landed us safe on the other bank.

We drove on and at sundown came to an old house that was being used by bushwackers. Brother got permission to let us go in and dry our clothes. It was the first of March and the weather was cold. Brother made a fire and while we were drying our clothes, the men would bang on the door and call out for us to hurry and go to bed so that they could come in and warm. We went to bed in our wet clothes and brother, who had on an old blue uniform, spread his overcoat on the floor, his gun by his side, and lay down by the bed.

The next morning, he got an old ox team that was so poor, but it drew the wagon all day. As we got near to Dalton, we saw an officer coming toward us riding on a big gray stallion, and when he got near he called "Are you Frank Brown's children?" We told him we were. He was Capt. Rogers, and Polk had to leave us there as it was not safe for him to go on.

The man who was the driver took us on and in about half an hour, we met an Indiana regiment. Rebecca had on a Dixie bonnet, it was made of flowered calico and fitted in front with splits. While we were in Atlanta, I had bought a coarse straw hat trimmed in green, for which I had paid eighty dollars, and a purple calico dress with a scalloped ruffle trimming, which cost one hundred dollars. When the soldiers saw us, one called "Come out of that bonnet, we know you are in there." I told sister to put on her hat, she replied "That no yankee should see her face." I reached back and got my hat out of our trunk and put it on. Another soldier called "Little girl have you seen Johnnie Reb?"

We drove on and near Dalton one of the oxen fell dead from starvation. A fine looking man, the colonel of the Indiana regiment, rode up and said "Little girls where are you going?" We told him that we were refugees from Macon, Georgia, trying to get to our home in Tennessee. He said "I have daughters at home and I will take care of you." He sent to Dalton for an ambulance, took us to a house and gave us the best rooms. When he went to leave, he said "This evening I want to see you." After dark, there was a tap at the door, and there was a big negro man with a basket of food the colonel had sent us. I was almost starved, but Rebecca refused to take it, saying that she wouldn't eat Yankee food and for him to take it back. I said "Rebecca let me have some supper," but she said "No, no, take it back." The colonel sent for us and laughed at Rebecca's stubornness, which made her madder. She bought some food at the hotel, as we had about six hundred dollars in gold.

We stayed there several days and Rebecca ate the Yankee food before we left. The colonel gave us transportation to Chattanooga, and we made the trip in a box car with the soldiers. The colonel cautioned us not to look out of the doors as the rebels might shoot in.

Colonel Robert Byrd, a cousin of mothers, was at the train. He was from Kingston and was in the Federal army. When he saw us, he said "Howdy girls" and took us to the Crutchfield house. Before we could sit down in the reception room, a big fat negro woman grabbed and hugged us saying "These are my children."

Grandmother Rentfroe gave this woman to our mother when she married. Frances got so homesich for Riceville that mother let her go back there. I do not know how she knew us. She carried a big bunch of keys on her belt and was looking after the house while Mr. and Mrs. Crutchfield were on a trip to New York.

We stayed several days and Col. Byrd told us we would have to take the oath of allegiance. We felt that we would be disgraced and refused. He said if we did not take it, we would be sent to Camp Chase. He said "You will have to go with me to the provost marshall's office," so that afternoon he tramped us through the mud and when we arrived at the office, the marshall was gone and we had to tramp back through the same mud. The provost marshall came to the hotel and compelled us to take the oath. I told him I would take it but I would not keep it. He said if we did not take the oath, he would not let us go home.

We went with Colonel Byrd to Loudon. We stayed a day or two at the Julian Hotel kept by the Misses Huff, two sisters. Mr. John Gillespie came to our room and told us that he was in trouble as all his property had been taken away from him by the federals. The boat was overdue and Col. Byrd grew impatient and came and told us we would have to go home in a skiff.

Walt Robb, a federal soldier who had been with us in Chattanooga, went with us and it was anything but a pleasant trip. I steered the boat to Kingston to keep off the bank. It was a moonlight night, which was to our advantage, and we arrived at Kingston at two o'clock in the morning. Col. Byrd took us to the home of our cousin, Rachel Brown Coleman, where we stayed until the next day, when we took the ferry across to the Thomas Clarks. He sent word by a boy to mother that we were there.

As there were no horses or mules left on our place, mother sent an ox team for us, and we made the eight miles in the wagon back home, where we were gladly received but found little to eat. Mother could not borrow a horse from the neighbors, who were mostly union sympathizers, to go have her corn ground. She could have gotten more if she had had more diplomacy.

CLACK DIARY

William Raleigh Clack was born on 4 February 1839, the son of Micajah and Margaret (Kerr) Clack. He was married to Sabra Caroline Newport on 12 September 1865, and had six children, including Raleigh Micajah Clack. William died on 25 April 1919.

William Raleigh Clack was a member of Captain A.J. Cawood's Company that was organized at Rhea Springs in October 1861. The group became Company B of the 43rd Regiment Tennessee Volunteers (James W. Gillespie, Colonel).

THE PERSONAL DIARY OF THE SEIGE AND SURRENDER OF VICKSBURG, MISS., JULY 4, 1863

The heading continues: "kept by William Raliegh Clack, father of R.M. Clack of Spring City, Rt #l, Rhea Co., Tennessee. W.R. Clack, Private of Co. B, 43 Regt. Tenn. Vols– Aged 24 years 3 mo. and 19 days, This May 23, 1863."

Yesterday the enemy attempted to charge our breastwork but were repulsed with great slaughter sharp shooters firing this morning– sharp shooting and heavy cannonading continued all day.

May 24– Sharp shooting and cannonading as usual this morning– continued all day–

May 25– Dueling commenced early again this morning. 3 o'clock p.m.– A flag of truce asking for permission to bury their dead. It was granted. All is quiet now on our line.

May 26– The enemy opened fire at daylight this morning. We moved over to the river below town just before daylight and took a position in the trenches. 9 o'clock land batteries have commenced shelling town again and a number of gunboats in sight. The prospects for our success and deliverance seems to darken every day. Oh! May the God of heaven aid and deliver us from this unhappy state is the constant prayer of the writer– W.R.C.

May 27– Three gunboats come up opposite our line and shelled us rapidly for an hour but hurt none of our regt. One man just to our right had his head shot off and two others were wounded. In the meantime another boat attempted to pass down by our batteries which was sunk up at town. Sharp shooting and cannonading is going on along our back lines and a general engagement is expected daily. It is reported that Genl. Johnson has attacked the enemy in the rear. 4 o'clock– The Yankee picketts have come in sight of our lines.

May 28– Sharp shooters as usual opened fire at daylight. A few can be seen in sight of our line again this morning. The gun boats that attacked us yesterday are about two miles below on the opposite side of the river lying still. W.R. Clack

May 29– Firing commenced after day dawned again this morning. 8 o'clock a.m.– heavy cannonading going on along our back line and continued an hour or two. Twelve transports and two gun boats came down today and have anchored out in line of battle above Vicksburg. One boat came up and shelled us awhile today but done no damage to us. 3 o'clock p.m.– All appears quiet along our back lines at present. It has the appearance of rain this evening cloudy and thundering. Gun boat shelled us awhile tonight. W.R.C.

May 30– Day dawned and the sun rose in its undimmed splendor this morning and all is quiet and still around old Vicksburg– not even the firing of a gun can be heard around our line. Those boats spoken of yesterday are still in sight above town– anchored out. 7 o'clock p.m. Mortars shelling us from the other side of the river and the gunboat dropping a shell occasionally from below.

May 31– 3 o'clock a.m.– heavy cannonading going on along our line on the left. 4 o'clock a.m.– Gun boats shelling us. One man belonging to the battery was wounded last night by a shell from the mortar. 6 o'clock a.m.– All appears quiet on our lines at this hour. The Yankees threw shells at us occasionally all day. W.R.C.

June 1– Heavy cannonading was heard this morning just at daybreak on our left. It is supposed they were making a charge on our trenches. All appears quiet at 7 o'clock– From 8 o'clock a.m. cannonading continued in a mild manner all day long on front lines. W.R.C.

June 2– All appears tolerably quiet this morning– occasionaly a cannon can be heard. Lieut. Hopkins started home tonight. Moon is now shining bright and the Yankees are shelling town at 11 o'clock p.m. W.R.C.

June 3– All is quiet this morning. 3 o'clock p.m.– Gun boats are now shelling us. Charley Graves was wounded a few minutes ago by one of those shells. His leg will have to be amputated. 4 o'clock p.m.– Heavy cannonading at this hour on the back line– musketry can also be heard. It is reported that Johnson will attack the enemy on Friday the 5th. 8 o'clock p.m.– We left our trenches and moved up the line to the left, to support a weak point near the Houls Ferry road. Heavy cannonading is now going on at that point. 9 o'clock p.m.– The gunboats have now come up and are now shelling the bottoms in the direction of town reapidly. They continued an hour, then calmed down and we got to sleep a little. W.R.C.

June 4– We are now in Col. Brad rear on the Houls Ferry road sharp shooters opened fire at daylight this morning in our front. An attack is expected today. The minies and shells are now whistling over our heads. God speed the happy hour when we shall be delivered from this unhappy state. 5 o'clock p.m.– I have just now been informed that some La? troops went over the river and spiked those mortars opposite town last night. A negro boy had his head shot off with cannon ball in sight of us this morning and two other were wounded. He was in a house near the breastworks. 9 o'clock p.m.– firing has about ceased– occasionally we can hear a sharp report from the picketts. W.R.C.

June 5– Things are tolerable quiet this morning– some shooting going on as usual on our lines. We are still held as reserve at the same place. 7 o'clock p.m.– I feel very unwell and have been all day. 9 o'clock– all is quiet tonight. Oh! Lord watch over us while we sleep tonight. W.R.C.

June 6– The sharp shooters opened fire at daylight this morning but in a milder manner than common– continued all day. Night has come on and the firnament is again decked with the beautiful stars, while we lay us down again to sleep upon the rough ground of Vicksburg. I pray heaven's blessing to rest upon us. W.R.C.

June 7– Several cannons were fired during the night on our line commenced as usual at day dawn. 9 o'clock a.m. W. Adams was just now wounded (thought mortally) by a spent ball. The Feds have just commenced shelling town again after an intermission of two days. W.R.C.

June 8– Things are going on as usual this morning. An other man of Co. D was wounded this morning. 7 o'clock p.m. firing pretty rapid at this hour. We have received intelligence from Johnston and also from other points of a late date by the grapevine telegraph which is very cheering. It is said that an English fleet of boats have come over to our aid and are now in possession of New Orleans and General Lee has nearly destroyed the Yankee army in Virginia. Genl. Price has got Possession of ---?--- above here on the Mississippi river; also that Genl. Loring has retaken Snider's Bluff on the Yazoo. W.R.C.

June 9– Some shooting continued all last night. Firing going on as usual this morning. Night has come on again and the Yankees are shelling town rapidly from the opposite side of the river. W.R.C.

June 10– Sharp shooting as usual again today. 4 o'clock p.m.– We have had a fine rain today. 5 o'clock p.m.– cannonading pretty rapidly at this hour. Night has again come on. The wind is blowing hard and a dark cloud is rising, while the bright lightenings play across the heavens and the awful thunder appears to shake the whole earth. Oh! May Jehovah, he who rides upon every tempest protect me tonight. W.R.C.

June 11– Very cloudy and damp this morning. It rained very hard last night and our things or nearly all are wet– some sharp shooting going on today. We are liable to be struck with a ball any minute. We are in a position where they fall all around us and in our midst. J.L. Miller was struck with one today. The ball was well spent and didn't enter his flesh. It is reported that Genl. Grant has called for 100,000 more men to reinforce him. Genl. Price has taked --?-- and therefore cuts off his supplies. It is said we have in Vicksburg 31,380 men with 30 or 40 days rations. W.R.C.

June 12– Cannonading continued all night. Sharp shooters commenced operations early again this morning and continued all day. W.R.C.

June 13– Firing at intervals was kept up all last night. The sharp shooters as usual commenced their daily operations very early and in a little warmer manner than usual.

June 14– All around our lines was more quiet than usual last night, but we were awakened from our sleep early this morning by the sharp shooters. 12 o'clock– heavy cannonading to our left. It is supposed a charge is about being made upon our trenches. 7 o'clock p.m.– We have no news yet from the left. An other sabbathe has passed and we are still confined to this same unhappy place and almost without any ray of hope of deliverance. Oh! Lord how long shall we remain in this state? Deliver us at once Oh! Lord. W.R.C.

June 15– Sharp shooting as usual today. It has the appearance of rain this morning. All the conalesenus [sic] that are able have come out from the hospital by order of the Brig. surgeon. I judge from this that a heavy attack is expected upon our line. It is reported that the Yankees are receiving heavy reinforcements. 7 o'clock p.m.– this day passed off tolerably quiet. We wait impatiently for the hour of our deliverance. May God speed the hour. W.R.C.

June 16– Things are going on here this morning as usual. No change in anything as I can see. 7 o'clock p.m.– Warm firing has been kept up all day. I lie down again to rest with the ethereal blue for my covering, and pray the Lord to watch over me while I sleep. W.R. Clack

June 17– There was a right smart shooting during the last night. Firing as usual this morning. 6 o'clock p.m.– Co's B and G now starts out on picket in front of the trenches. 7 o'clock– we have arrived at the picket post. The bullets cut pretty close to us here. Speed– speed the hour that well deliver from this place. W.R.C.

June 18– Things passed off tolerably quiet last night. Sharp shooters opened fire early this morning. A Georgan belonging to our picket post was killed today. We were relieved from post at 6 o'clock p.m. by Co. K. and retired to our camp and ate supper and lay down to rest. I had just got to sleep and I was aroused from my slumber by the rattling of musketry. The enemy was attempting to drive in on our pickets and get possession of our post. The remainder of our regiment was ordered out and took a position in the trenches with Col. Barklelew. By this time the firing had pretty well ceased as our boys still occupied their post. We had one man wounded. W.R.C.

June 19– We left the trenches at daylight this morning and came back to our old position in the hollow. Things are tolerably quiet this morning– some sharp shooting going on. 7 o'clock p.m.– All passed off tolerably quiet today. We commened drawing flour today. W.R.C.

June 20– Heavy cannonading commenced at daylight this morning and continued until 11 o'clock– While the bombs bursted and the pieces fall all around us and among us but hit none of our regiment. Thanks be to high heaven for our protection. The evening passed off tolerably quiet. W.R.C.

June 21– Another Sabbath morning has rolled around and found us still confined to the neighboring hill of Vicksburg without any better prospects of our deliverance. It is reported that Johnson has attacked the enemy but I doubt it. Sharp shooters are pecking away as usual this morning. Warm firing was kept up all day. W.R.C.

June 22– At 12 o'clock last night Co. B and G and one Co. of 57 Ga. was ordered outside of our entrenchments to attack and drive the enemy from the ditches which was near our picket post. We succeeded in driving them from their first ditch. But we were forced by over whelming numbers to fall back as their ditch did not give us any protection from the enemies fire; which we did in good order. Lieut. Crookshauds was killed, Sargeant Denton and Gilbert Murray was wounded of Co. G– Capt. Cawood, Sargent Miller and Wm. Brady of Co. B was wounded. One of the Ga. was killed and two wounded. It was with great reluctance that I went into it, but I said nothing. I saw it could not profit us anything for we could not hold it when taken. I thank my God that we escaped as well as what we did. Sharp shooting going on as usual today. Oh Lord my heavenly Master deliver us from this unhappy state. Hear my prayer Oh! God and save us from the destruction of our enemies. W.R.C.

June 23– Another attempt was made last night to charge the enemy trenches by six Co's of our regiment and a squad of Georgians which was successful. We drove them back and filled up their ditch, but our regiment suffered severely. We had twenty one killed and wounded. George Day of Co. B was killed and Andy Hughes and Wm. Boles was wounded. Though it is said the Yankees occupy the same ground again today that they did yesterday. Andy Hughes died today. Loy was not killed instantly but died early this morning. W.R. Clack

June 24– The next regiment to our left charged the Yankee ditches in their front last night and drove them back, but the Yankees occupied their old position today. Sharp shooting as usual today and the Mortar battery is shelling town. W.R. Clack

June 25– Four companies of our regiment (Co. B was one of the four) was ordered out last night to reinforce Col. B. as a heavy attack was expected to be made last night. We remained there in the ditches until 11 or 12 o'clock when we were relieved by a regiment and received orders to move back to our old position on the river. Daylight has come and the sharp shooters are at work– as attack is expected here today. The Yankees appear to be pressing upon our lines. Major Guthre was wounded today by a ball from sharp shooters. We had heavy cannonading here on the lower end of our lines this evening. Night has come on and one third of us has to be on watch loer around Vicksburg. I pray Heaven's blessings to rest upon us and that the all seeing eye of Jehovah may watch over us and protect us from all danger and harm. W.R.C.

June 26– Sharp shooters firing away as usual this morning 4 o'clock p.m., we have received orders to move back to support Col. Bartlow. 7 o'clock we now start out to the trench.

June 27– We got to rest last night. Everything was more quiet all night than common. Firing commenced at daylight agin this morning. 9 o'clock a.m.– the mortars are dropping shells about us. They are throwing them about five miles. 7 o'clock p.m. We now start out to the trenches again. A young man by the name of Garghess belonging to the 3rd Tenn. Regt. was killed here in fifty yards of me this evening with a piece of shell. Oh! Lord I pray for thy protection. W.R. Clack

June 28– Another Sabbath has found me alive and well for which I feel very thankful and glorify my heavenly Master. Things were very quiet last night. I worked nearly all night painting a battery. Sharp shooters commenced operating as usual at daylight. Lieut. Clesser of Co. Eva [sic] was mortally wounded this morning. He was in the trenches. W.R.C.

June 29– Sharp shooting today as usual. Mathisas of Co. F died in the tenches this morning of cramp. He did not live more than ten minutes after he was taken. King Stalcup of the 31st Tenn. Regt. was killed last night by some of our own men. The Yankees made a charge on our right this evening but were repulsed. W.R.C.

June 30– Some picket fighting done last night to our right. Sharp shooting as usual today. 10 o'clock a.m.– pretty heavy cannonading to our right at this hour. We lie in the trenches every night. The sun has now set beneath the western horizon for the last time in June, '63 and we are still in possession of Vicksburg. W.R.C.

July 1– William Bowles of Co. P died last night about 10 o'clock. Things are moving along here about as usual today. W.R.C.

July 2– Firing was kept up all night from the mortar batteries on the opposite side of the river. Sharp shooting as usual this morning. The evening passed off tolerably quiet. W.R. Clack

July 3– Things are rocking along as usual this morning. 10 o'clock General Pemberton sent out a flag of truce requesting General Grant to cease firing on our hospital. All was quiet up until 1 o'clock p.m.– 3 o'clock p.m. Heavy cannonading along the river. 6 o'clock p.m.– Pemberton now sends out another flag of truce trying to make a compromise preparatory for a surrender. 7 o'clock we now go to the trenches. All is very quiet now. W.R.C.

July 4– All is very quiet this morning around Vicksburg. The boys and the Yanks are conversing together. 10 o' clock a.m.– Vicksburg is surrendering on account of our rations giving out. We marched to General Reynold's headquarters and stacked our arms and then came back to our old position where we expect to remain until we are paroled. The evening passed off very quiet. W.R.C.

July 5– Sabbath morning has again rolled around and I (with many others) as a prisoner. The Yankees visited us today and we conversed freely and friendly together. We are treated with great hospitality by them. Today has been unusually calm. W.R. Clack

July 8– Wm. Casy was seriously burnt this evening by foolishly setting powder on fire. We have not as yet received our paroles but expect to get them in the morning. W.R. Clack

July 9– We have just returned from town with our apparoles [sic]. W.R.C.

July 10– Wm Hill died last night. My friend --?-- died day before yesterday. We are expecting to leave here tomorrow morning. W.R.C.

July 12– Yesterday we drew six days rations preparatory for a trip to Jackson, Miss. and today we marched out at 7 o'clock a.m. and tonight we are camped 7½ miles from Vicksburg on the railroad. It has the appearance of rain tonight. W.R. Clack

July 13– We marched out this morning at 4 o'clock and struck camp at 6 o'clock p.m. in 8½ miles of Raymond– distance 15 miles. I had a pretty severe chill this evening with fever. W.R.C.

July 14– We marched out at 5 o'clock a.m. and came Via Raymond to Coopers Wells– distance 13½ miles Lieut. Pyott, J.H.C. Pyott and Thomas Roddy were left at Raymond in the hospital sick. W.R.C.

July 17– I am so unwell that I cannot keep up my journal any longer. We are moving along the best we can. A good many of the boys are chilling. W.R.C.

July 21– We have at last arrived at Enterprise, the place so long looked for. We are to take the train in the morning for Mobile at 7 o'clock. It is now raining hard, but we are under shelter. My health is improving. W.R.C.

July 24– We left Enterprise yesterday morning at 8 o'clock a.m. and arrived at Mobile at 8 o'clock p.m. and lay by through the night. 7 o'clock a.m. We are now passing up Tom Bigbee on the boat. W.R.C.

July 28– I arrived at home today.

COLVILLE LETTERS

Warner E. Colville (1818-1876), son of Young and Nutty (White) Colville, organized the first company of infantry from Rhea County (Company D, 19th Infantry, C.S.A.) and was elected Captain. His wife was Vesta Waterhouse, daughter of Richard Green Waterhouse. Warner and Vesta are buried in the old Mynatt Cemetery at Washington.

Young Colville, son of W.E. and Vesta, was a member of Captain W.P. Darwin's Company (Company C, 16th Tennessee Cavalry). [mentioned in Letter No. 4]

Richard W. Colville (12 March 1843 - 18 December 1923), also a son of W.E. and Vesta, was a member of his father's company, and was promoted to First Lieutenant after the battle of Murfreesboro.

After the war, Richard married Mary L. Paine, daughter of Orville and Elvira (Locke) Paine. Richard and Mary are buried in Hamilton County (White Oak Cemetery).

Both the Colville and Paine letters are presently the property of Eugene Colville of Chattanooa.

LETTER NO. 1
RICHARD W. COLVILLE TO WARNER E. COLVILLE

Camp near Dalton
April 29th 1864

Dear Father

Yours of the 23rd inst came to hand yesterday and I hasten to answer to let you know I am well. We have orders to be ready to march at a moments warning and it is reported that the enemy are advancing in force and probably before this reaches you we may be engaged in deadly strife with the enemy.

I have no fear about the results. I believe we are as certain to whip them as we fight, and if we once get them started back like we did at Chickamauga, Johnson will follow them up and drive them out of Tenn. The whole army is in better health and spirits than I ever saw them. Kennedy received a letter from Sam a week or two ago. He was still at Johnsons Island and was in good health.

We have 18 men present in our company now. I do not know why Col. Walker has not sent after Cy Henry and the rest of them. He has been threatening to send after them ever since we have been here. Lt. Caeny got a detail to go after them a while back, and I gave him their names and the command they were with, but he did not go. I have not time to write so I will close. Your Obedient Son,

R. W. Colville

\- - - - - - - - - - - -

LETTER NO. 2
R.W. COLVILLE TO CAPT. W.E. COLVILLE

Camp Near Etowah
May 22nd 1864

Dear Father

Having nothing to do today I thought I would write you a few lines to let you know my where abouts and that I am well. We have been continually marching and counter-marching for the last twelve of fifteen days. Our Regiment has had several skirmishes with the enemy, but I will in part give you the movements of our army since the enemy commenced advancing. They commenced advancing about the 1st of May. Our cavalry gradually fell back to our main line. On the 8th they made three assults on Dug Gap which was only defended by cavalry, and were repulsed each time. Our brigade was sent to reinforce them. We double quicked three miles and got there just as the cavalry repulsed them the last time, taking our flag and 18 prisoners. On the 9th the enemy made several assaults on Buzzard Creek Gap and were repulsed each time with slight loss on our side. From the 10th to the 12th there was nothing but skirmishing along the line. The enemy were sending all their forces in the direction of Resaca.

On the night of the 12th our forces moved down to Resaca. May 13th our brigade had heavy skirmishing 1½ miles from Resaca. Our Regt. lossed 7 wounded. Jim Renfro was wounded in my company.

May 14th enemy made several assaults on our right and were repulsed each time with heavy loss. Nothing but skirmishing along our part of the line. Mace Wright was wounded early in the morning in the head. His skull was broke and the Dr. had to take out a piece of the skull, but Dulany said he would get well.

May 15th enemy attacked our right several times during the day and were repulsed. In some instances our [men] leaped over our breastworks and charged them in turn driving them from their rifle pits. During the night our army fell back across the Oostanaula not because we were whiped for we whiped them in every engagement, but because they were flanking us.

May 17th our division engaged the enemy near Adairsville and held them in check until night. Our regt. lossed 2 killed and 9 wounded, none from our company.

On the 20th we arrived at this place where we have been resting every since. I do not know where Johnson intends to make a stand but I am certain of one thing that wherever we do make a stand we will whip them and that badly. It is reported that reinforcements are coming to us from Va. Nothing more at present. Excuse bad writing. Your Obedient Son

R. W. Colville

\- - - - - - - - - - - -

LETTER NO. 3
R.W. CALDWELL TO CAPT. W.E. COLVILLE

In line of Battle near Marietta
June 26th 1864

Dear Father

I received your letter of the 29th May the other day. I was sorry to hear that somebody had stolen your clothes. I myself have been tolerable bad off for clothing on this trip. I started from Dalton with only one suit of [clothing] and they are nearly worn out. I have got plenty of cloths with the wagons but they are near Atlanta. I wrote you later that long since giving you all the news since we left Dalton, but if you may not have received it I will repeat some of the particulars. Our Regt. has been in several skirmishes but in no general engagement. Jon Renfro and J.M. Wright were wounded at Resaca. Renfro was only wounded slightly in the eye and has since come back. Joshua Gentry was wounded in the shoulder at New Hope on the 28th of May. The regt has lost several men since, but none from our company. Last Thursday the Yankees opened a furious cannonade on our division for about an hour. When it ceased the Yankees charged and drove them back taking about 30 prisoners. Our Regt. had one man killed and one wounded by the shelling.

The Yankees are still trying to flank us. I am in hopes we can find some place where they can't flank us.

There are 17 men in our company present for duty. There has been less straggling in our company than any in our Regt.

Stevenson's division had a right smart fight on the left on the 22nd. Brown's brigade drove the enemy from two lines of breastworks and charged their main line but had to fall back. The 26th lost about 80 men killed and wounded.

I am anxious to hear the particulars of Jones late fight in Va. I know of nothing else to write at present. I do not expect you can read this letter for I had to write it in a hurry.

Your Obedient Son R. W. Colville

- - - - - - - - - - - - -

LETTER NO. 4
R.W. COLVILLE TO CAPT. W.E. COLVILLE

Blind School Hospital
Sept. 2nd 1864

Dear Father

I arrived here last night from Smithville where I have been on furlough for thirty days. I had a fine time down there. Had plenty of watermelons and peaches to eat. Had a horse and buggy to go where I pleased and when I offered to pay them, wouldn't take anything. My wound has almost healed up.

I received a letter from you of 2nd inst. It was the first I had got from you in sometime and I was glad to hear that you and Young [Colville] are well. It seems that you are unlucky in getting your clothes stolen. As it is the second time they have made a raid on you. All of my clothing is at the front with the baggage and it may be lost by this time. The last time I heard from the company they were doing very well. Ben Dyer was wounded on the 22nd and George Knox a few days afterwards in the back. Capt. McDermott was killed on the 22nd and Capt. Brabson severly wounded. Lt. Sharp was killed on picket. Col. Heiskel came back a few days ago. S.R. and Cy Henry came with them. They came back with the expectations of getting a transfer. Lt. Wallace is here with his guard. I was over at his camp today.

There has been no news from the front for two days. It is reported there has been hard fighting going on for two days but nothing reliable. It is also reported that Genl. Hood is killed.

I wrote you several letters while at Smithville, but I do not expect you received them as I did not direct them right. Wright Hackett was wounded about the 28th of July and died at Griffin. Nothing more at present, but remain

Your Affectionate Son R. W. Colville

- - - - - - - - - - - - -

LETTER NO. 5
R.W. COLVILLE TO CAPT. W.E. COLVILLE

Blind School Hospital
Sept. 7th 1864

Dear Father:

I am still at the hospital. I thought when I last wrote that I would have been with the Regt. by this time, but my [wound] is not much better than it was then. In another week I think it will be able for duty.

I cannot learn any of the particulars of the fight on the 31st, but it is generally conceded that our army met with a disaster and from what I can learn our troops are very much demoralized. They do not have that confidence in Hood that they had in Johnston. Although Johnston fell back a hundred miles the troops had as much confidence in him as they did before he evacuated Dalton, and if he had fell back to the Gulf they would have followed thinking it would all turn out right in the end. But they do not put that confidence in Hood and I understand they are deserting in large numbers. C.C. Major was wounded on the 31st and had his leg taken off. Ike Brown was also slightly wounded.

I have seen several persons that I knew since I have been here. I saw Dave Roddy the other day. There are more officers in Macon than I ever saw. I think there must be at least a brigade of officers. Gen. Hood has sent down an order to the Com. of the Post to find out the business of each officer and by whose authority they are here.

There was a fire in town last night. It looked beautiful from here. I do not know what damage was done. I have not heard any news from home for several months. I know nothing else to write so will close.
Your Obedient Son

R. W. Caldwell

- - - - - - - - - - - - - -

LETTER NO. 6
W.E. COLVILLE TO LT. R.W. COLVILLE

Bristol Ten Oct 23/64

Dear Dick

After a time I am back in Tennessee with a good prospect of once more getting home. Since I last wrote to you Genl Early met the Feds at Winchester, was worsted in the fight fell back to Strausburg made a stand was again driven back to Brown's Gap where we again made a stand in which we repulsed the Feds in an engagement with the cavalry at that point. John Robinson of Capt Darwins Co was killed in the engagement at Strausburg. Saml Robinson was captured as also John T Miller, Hugh Ferguson and Lt Armor. The two last were wounded. After the repulse of the Feds at Brown's Gap, Early advanced to Mt Szaney at which place the remainder of Vaughns Brig were ordered to join their command in E Tenn. We started back on the 4th Oct with about 125 men, the balance except what were killed wounded and captured had run away and gone back to Tenn. On the 6th we camped at Cedar Grove 8 miles from Lexington where Lt Hopkins ordnance officer killed Capt Day under the following circumstances. Day and Hopkins had a difficulty at Winchester some 5 weeks before in which Day abused Hopkins very much H– not resenting it. On the evening of the 6th after going into camp Day pulled off his coat and pistol picked up a bucket and started to the Spring passing a fire where H– was standing. On his return as he emerged from a cedar thicket H– steped out and remarked that the insult heretofore given had to be settled at the same time fired at Day but missed he fired again and missed. Day still advancing at the third fire, Day had advanced to within six feet of him when he fired the ball penetrating his heart about the time he was shot he called me the only word he spoke he died in less than a minute. I had him taken to Lexington and buried. H– was arrested and sent to Genl Vaughn who turned him loose. If he has not yet run off he will be re-arrested and dealt with.

I have charge of his private property and am winding it up. So soon as I am through if I cannot get home I am going south to winter. My health is not as good as usual, nothing serious. Will Allen is here, was in Rhea a short time since. Says your mother and family are all well and plenty to eat. Gamry staid in Va until ordered of him and Dick Thomason the only two of the Co left. He is in good health and wildest chap you ever saw. He has got so well up to stealing that he can steal the molasses out of a ginger cake and it buttoned up in your pocket.

Vaughn drove the Feds from Greenville through Bulls Gap to Bean Station. He attacked them there driving them from there. They retreated through Powder Spring Gap making for Cumberland Gap. The belief here is they are leaving East Tenn, is so I can get home in a few days. I start tomorrow for the front.

W. E. Colville

EVERETT LETTERS

John W. Everett (born 4 August 1839) served in Company B, 4th Tennessee Cavalry. He was captured, along with his brother Will, on 5 August 1863. They were transferred to Rock Island prison on 24 January 1864, where John died of consumption on 13 July 1864. He was buried on the island along with his brother who died prior to April 1864 (see letter number 2).

On 1 April 1858, in Rhea County, John married Elizabeth W. Barger. They had two daughters: Margaret Jane (born 1859, married Jacob M. Kelly) and Martha Ellen (born 1863, married John W. Clouse). The following two letters were submitted by Jane Moore.

LETTER NO. 1
J.W. EVERETT TO ELIZABETH EVERETT

Louden, Tenn., Feb 10th 1863

Dear Wife

I set my self to drop you a few lines to let you [know] that I am well at this time hoping these few lines may find You and the children in the same health. I have nothing of importance to rite. I rote to you last week and have not got my answer yet. I am at this place yet and dont know how long I will stay here. I hear no talk of having to leav here yet but I dont know how soon I may here it. I have not had any thing hardly to do sence I came back. I get a days work to do once in a while. I have ben well and harty ever since I came back. I begin to want to here from you. I would liked to here from you every week and I want you to rite to me and not neglect it for when you get out of paper and money I can Send more. I read(?) that old man was dead. Tell the boys to rite to me for I would be glad to hear from them. I heard that they was a going to run the conscript a gain in Rhea tell the boys if they had to go with the consceipt to join ---?--- Company.

Liz I would be glad to be with you but it is impossible for I am here and you are there but I hope there is a better day coming When we shall live a gain as we once did. I want you to pray for me that I may live at my post. I pray for you and my little babes often. I am trying to discharge my duty the best I can under the circumstances I am placed God forbid that I should do any thing contrary to his will. I now must bring my letter to a close I want you to rite to me as soon as you get this letter without fail and if I never see you any more I hope I will meet you in heaven. So remains your affectionate husband until death.

J.W. Everett

A few lines from A Cowin to wife
I take my pen in hand to let you know that I am well at this time hoping these few lines may find you in the Same. I have had a mighty bad carbuncle on my back but am getting beter now. I want you to write to me and let me know how you are a geting a long. You can rite a few lines in Mrs Everets letter.

- - - - - - - - - - - - -

LETTER NO. 2
J.W. EVERETT TO ELIZABETH EVERETT

State of Ill. Rock Island
April the 17th 1864

Dear Wife

It is with greate pleasure I take my pen in to hand to let you no that I am well at this time hoping these few lines may find you enjoying the same blessing. I received a letter from you on the 15th which gave me greate Satisfaction to hear from you that you was all well and doing well my health has not ben good ever since I have ben in prison I want to get home once more if their is any posible chance for it. I want you to tell your father and friends to get up a petition for my releas I donot intend to be exchanged and I think I have friends enough in that Country to get me out of prison. I have ben treated well every sence I have ben in prison but it is a disagreeable place to be I can get out by geting a petition from hom with the Governers name sined to it which I hope friends will do that mutch for me.

Bill is dead he died with the Small pox. I must bring my letter to a clos rite to me a gain and let [me] now what you can do for me I give my best respects to all my connection and friends So remains your husband till death

Direct your letter to Rock Island
J. W. Everett a prisoner of war
No of Barracks 65

FRAZIER REMINISCENCES

The following reminiscences were written by S. J. A. Frazier about 1901 and read before a meeting of the Daughters of the Confederacy at a meeting in Chattanooga. The presentation was published in a Chattanooga newspaper and a copy was included in a scrapbook kept by William G. Allen (now in the files of the Rhea County Historical and Genealogical Society).

Samuel Josiah Abner Frazier was born in Rhea County on 29 January 1840, the son of Samuel and Ruth (Clawson) Frazier. He served as a Captain in Company D, 19th Tennessee Infantry.

PRISON DAYS ON JOHNSON'S ISLAND IN LAKE ERIE

Daughters of the Confederacy— Upon the invitation of your committee, I will attempt to give you a history of our life on Johnson's Island as it comes to me after forty years.

I was there about nineteen months, and suffered more mentally and physically than all the balance of my life. I could scarcely talk above a whisper while there. My clothing was insufficient for the coldest weather ever known there.

A few weeks after I reached there I took chills and fever, a remnant of the Mississippi campaign. A companion of mine from South Carolina, who accompanied me to the island, delicate and refined, also took chills. He was taken to the hospital and died. We had one heating stove for forty men. There was dirt a foot thick on the floor, and ice six inches thick on the windowpanes. I had nothing to read. I could not hear from home nor companions. We had plenty to eat, but no place to cook except on a heater.

Two cases of smallpox developed and remained in the room several days after it appeared. There was no ray of sunshine that broke the dark cloud. These conditions were those of the first three months. Most of those who were there with me are gone. Col. Aiken, who resided in Chattanooga, alone is left. Frank Gardenhire, Warren Hooper, Dan Kennedy and others of Chattanooga; Hugh White, Lip Taylor and Frank Blair, of Knoxville, former schoolmates of mine, are all dead.

Some years ago Col. Aiken and myself met Mr. Gerido, of South Carolina, who preached for us in prison. We recalled together many incidents of the past. He, also, has crossed the river. In recalling the many actors who moved to and fro up and down that long walk in prison, then full of hope, life and strength, it seems like traveling in memory in a graveyard.

HOW SITUATED

Johnson Island is situated in Lake Erie, a few miles off the city of Sandusky. There was probably several hundred acres in the island, but the inclosure where the prisoners were kept embraced about sixteen acres. There were thirteen blocks, two stories high. They were situated in rows, and on a side about 100 feet between the rows of buildings. In that space was a long walk, graveled, on which the prisoners constantly paced to and fro, thinking and talking about things and events transpiring in their own southern homes. It was intended for officers only, and was the largest officers' prison in the north. Towards the last there were about 3,000 persons there.

The climate was extremely cold in winter and was hot in summer. The bullpen, as it was called, was inclosed by a plank fence twelve feet high, on top of which was a parapet four feet wide; and sentinels walked back and forth day and night, being relieved every two hours. There was a regiment of soldiers kept on the island for guard purposes, generally home guards. Sometimes old soldiers were sent there to rest up. We were always glad to see them, as they were much more liberal and would bring in most anything we wanted in their large overcoats.

Numerous vessels of all kinds sailed around the lake for business and pleasure.

GUARDED BY CANNON

Five cannon were kept at the entrance, trained on the prison, ready for instant use in the case of an uprising, which they constantly feared. They also kept paid informers in them to watch and report. Prisoners were searched on their arrival for money and arms. I gave them $10 in greenback, which was placed to my credit and afterwards checked out. In the sutler's tent I kept $200 in Confederate money, which I afterwards sold for $10 in greenback.

Whenever a fresh batch of prisoners came the cry of "fresh fish" was raised, and men of the whole prison flocked around them to see if there were any they knew from whom they could get information from the front and from their companions in arms and possibly from loved ones at home. They were eagerly questioned as to what was going on down south, as to who was killed and as to whether old "Bob" Lee and others were whipping those Yankees.

The best blood of the south was represented there, the soldiers being from every state and territory. They were highstrung and proud. Their demeanor was more like that of captors than prisoners. They would brook no insult even from armed guards, and they would strike even at the risk of life.

ALL AGES OF MEN

The prisoners were of all ages, from the youth of 21 to gray-beards of 50 years. They were mostly young and unmarried men, and in the vigor of youth. Those inside the lines, accessible to friends, were well dressed. Those outside were no so much so. Many wore their battle-stained uniforms of gray. The drum beat at 9 o'clock p.m. for lights out; no fires were allowed before daylight, and a violation of those orders brought a bullet from a sentry, so in those long winter nights we could only lie in bed on cots inside of the walls and dream of hog and hominy, big corndodgers and buttermilk away down at our homes in Dixie. We did our own cooking and washing, which most of us were not accustomed to doing. A negro boy Tom performed those duties before my capture.

As long as the sutler was allowed to sell provisions and boxes were allowed to come in from friends, provisions were abundant. Those who got boxes let their rations go to the others. But when all boxes containing provisions were cut off and the sutler was not allowed to sell anything to eat, then starvation commenced. This condition lasted about six months. It was not so at first or at last. I got a box in on a doctor's certificate. This was because I looked so pale and thin, caused only by want of nourishing food.

FOOD WAS INSUFFICIENT

We drew up petition after petition to the authorities, stating that our food was insufficient to sustain life. There was a gnawing sensation of hunger most of the time. We went to bed hungry and got up hungry. Our dreams were of the tables at home loaded down with food and a darky bringing in more. Pumpkin pies and potato custards would have been more acceptable to us than gold or silver. We could not buy except by bribing some one. Fat dogs, which usually followed the scavenger wagon, disappeared. Pet cats were seen no more. Sometimes gaunt, hungry-looking rebs were to be seen with bow and arrow, watching for the appearance of the warf rat. I learned that in other prisons the soldiers suffered much more than in ours. Many an emaciated Confederate succumbed to the cold winds of the north who might have lived if he had had sufficient food. I unwillingly recall those unpleasant memories that the truth of history may be vindicated and that it may be seen that the horrors of Andersonville were not confined to one side.

For convenience the prisoners were divided into messes of different sizes and each one took it week about cooking and drawing rations. In my mess was A.C. Smith, of upper East Tennessee, and a man by the name of Kennedy, from Louisiana, who was a reckless person and had been at West Point, and cared more for good eating than all other things. And when rations grew slimmer and scarcer he said he must get out. He could not stand it, and was always planning and trying to escape, until at last one dark, rainy night, when the lamplight could scarcely penetrate the falling rain, he dug under the wall with a caseknife, took an officers' boat, rowed to Sandusky, then took the train to Canada, and wrote back thanking the officer for the loan of the boat.

We concealed his escape for some three weeks or more in order to get his ration, and then did not have enough. At roll call I answered to my name, then passed down the line where Kennedy was accustomed to stand and answered to his name. Smith answered to his own name, stole into the barracks, was counted among the sick. Sometimes he had to use some extra groans to deceive the doctor. Then he stole back and was counted in his own place. We managed it so successfully that only a few of the prisoners knew of the deception. After a few weeks a spy informed the authorities that a man was missing. They sent in an extra sergeant to examine and report at roll call. We still deceived them. They said they were satisfied all were present or accounted for and that it was a mistake. After a little while the deception played spread and got outside. They sent a sufficient force to bring all in line, sick or well. Then we gave it up.

A week later the authorities sent in and arrested a Smith from Kentucky, for aiding in the escape of Kennedy. I wrote the best effort of my life to Col. Hill, telling him the correct Smith, and that there was no law of God or man requiring one prisoner to betray another; that the beasts of the forest and birds of the air pined for freedom and beat against their prison walls; that we were not under parole; that it was their duty to keep us and ours to get away if we could. They answered by sending in a guard and placing Smith, my messmate, in close confinement. He wrote me he was delighted with the change, for he had an abundance to eat and plenty to read. He even hired the guard to bring me some of his extra rations. But, as often happens, our greatest misfortunes are a blessing in disguise. He was exchanged soon afterwards under a general order exchanging all persons in close confinement. He engaged in the pension business after the war in the office of Judge Roderick Butler, and assisted his old foes to get pensions from the government. He died long ago.

KENNEDY IN A RAID

Mr. Kennedy, my other messmate, headed a raid that tried to burn New York City with phosphorous. He escaped back to Canada. He was not satisfied with his grub, as he said, and moved to the American side, was captured and hanged in New York City. Refusing the services of a Yankee chaplain, with an oath, he declared that he died a true rebel, true to the cause, and that was religion enough for him. His statement was published in northern papers as another instance of rebel depravity.

The prisoners made repeated efforts at escape, but were generally unsuccessful. In that cold January of 1864, the coldest ever known, the lake froze over. It was supposed that no southern man would venture out in such temperature. Over twenty prisoners scaled the walls, crossed over the ice to the mainland, but were compelled to go into farmhouses to warm. They were betrayed and recaptured.

On one occasion, when some work was being done in prison, wagons and workingmen were coming in and out constantly. One rebel exchanged clothes with one of the workmen and accompanied the wagon out. Soon as it got out among the prisoners, blue coats were in demand at any price. And during that day and the next, about fifty prisoners had passed out as workingmen. Only about two got off the island, by forging an order, with the post commander's name, to pass them on boats. The others wandered around the island until next night, when the discovery was made, and drums were beaten to arms, and soldiers called out amid great excitement, as if a regular battle was expected. The Confederates, who were playing cards with, and making themselves agreeable to, Yankee soldiers, snatched up muskets, fell in line, and led the pursuit of those terrible rebels, who were not discovered until next morning, when their southern features betrayed them.

Storms were numerous and violent. One of unusual severity blew the planks off of some of the barracks, and shingles were flying in the air like snowflakes. The wonder was none were killed. Some took refuge in a deep ditch. Whilst one was praying his comrad asked him to pray for him. He told him to pray the Lord's Prayer. He responded: "Oh, shucks, the Lord's Prayer is not worth a d--n in such a storm as this."

The prisoners passed their time reading and writing letters, condensed to one page, telling jokes, discussing the war, reviewing their campaigns, and making jewelry. The jewelry was the chief source of income. They talked of things transpiring down in their own sunny south. All kinds of jewelry was made, violins and all kinds of musical instruments. I had no mechanical skill whatever. But necessity is a great inventor. I learned to make finger rings out of guttapercha buttons, with silver sets, and sold them for 50 cents to Yankee soldiers. Hundreds of dollars were made in this way by some prisoners.

An enterprising genius from Baltimore had a lot of old books, sent him by a friend. He added to them and bought all the old books from prisoners he could, sent them by friends, and established a circulating library, at 50 cents per month. I studied an old Blackstone, printed in 1796 with long ss.

At night there was music of the finest kind. Amateur theatricals, plays, and dancing were in vogue. To the casual observer joy and gaity seemed to reign, but beneath it all was an aching heart, and a sad strain that was never absent. The forced effort to drown sorrow was evident to the close observer.

Oftentimes, when the snow was on the ground, they had mimic battles. One side represented the Gray, the other the Blue. They divided into regiments and companies, with a full set of officers, ambulance corps, skirmishers and all the equipments of war, and one negro on each side. We had two in prison who had stuck to their masters. They advanced and fought furiously, with snow-balls, fell back, reinforced, and advanced again. The wounded were carried off. The ordnance officers rushed snowballs to the front. The improvised flags were flying, the drums beat, fifes played and bugles sounded. Prisoners were captured and hurried to the rear.

Finally when a negro was captured a flag of truce was sent out to negotiate exchange of prisoners. They agreed on all terms, but the negro. One side declared they never would exchange a negro. The other they never would agree to an exchange unless the negro was embraced in it. Hundreds of spectators often lined the parapets from Sandusky city. When the battle was over, both sides joined in the rebel yell, just to keep in practice. When good news came from the front that yell was heard, causing the Yankees to rush to arms, fearing an uprising.

WAS WOUNDED

Pardon the digression, but when I lay wounded on the battlefield of Chickamauga before a fire of rails, our troops, Cheatham men I think, made a night attack in the dense woods, on the federal line just after dark, on Saturday night. For one hour they fought furiously at close range. The roar of musketry was continuous. Finally the Federal line was driven back a half mile and formed just in front of the hospital. For a few moments there was a dead calm. Not a sound was heard. Then there arose on that clear frosty air a yell so loud, so wild, so firm, so full of victory and defiance that I never heard anything like it, before or since, and never will. It was the sweetest music I ever heard.

REPORTED AS DEAD

For a long time I did not hear from my command. I was reported officially dead. At last I received a letter from Col. F. M. Walker, of my regiment, giving full details of the many changes that had taken place in my company and regiment. No braver, nobler man, no one who exemplified the highest type of Christian manhood, ever died on field of battle for his country than Col. Walker. Chattanooga may well be proud of him. You Daughters of the Confederacy do well to honor him.

I do not remember to have seen but one woman enter the prison, and that was a mother come to her dying boy. She reached the hospital in time to kiss him a last farewell as his soul was wafted into eternity. As she came sobbing from the hospital, on her way out, although it was snowing fast, many prisoners lined her way to catch sight of a southern woman once again. With heads uncovered, they silently watched her pass, and with moist eyes thought of their own dear ones down south.

When Gen. Morgan made his raid into Ohio the home guard regiment guarding us was sent to intercept him. They left with many a boast and brag that in two days' time they would bring him back, a prisoner. In two days' time they came back paroled prisoners. Morgan had captured them.

The old soldiers were as clever and good as they were allowed to be. Of the 3,000 officers on Johnson's Island in the bloom of youth, and just entering on the active duties of life, a large majority has passed away. The youngest of them are now old and gray and soon there will be few left to tell their experience of prison life.

- - - - - - - - - - - - -

S.J.A. Frazier died on 11 December 1921, and the following obituary appeared in a Chattanooga newspaper (from W.G. Allen scrapbook):

CAPT. FRAZIER PASSES BEYOND
BELOVED CITIZEN SUCCUMBS TO PNEUMONIA SUNDAY MORNING AT TAMPA

At 4 o'clock Sunday morning at Tampa, Fla., Capt. S.J.A. Frazier, native of Rhea county, one of the best known citizens of this entire section, and a gallant Confederate veteran, answered the final roll call.

. . . Funeral services, conducted by Dr. J.W. Bachman and Dr. J.A. Burrow, will be held from Capt. Frazier's late residence in North Chattanooga . . . The body will be laid to rest in the Confederate cemetery.

. . . Capt. Frazier received his education in the schools of the state and was valedictorian of his class at graduation from the University of Tennessee, then the "East Tennessee university." At the outbreak of the Civil war, he organized Company D, Nineteenth Tennessee Confederate cavalry and was commissioned a junior lieutenant. In 1862 came a promotion to a captaincy.

Capt. Frazier took part in all the engagements in which his command participated. In the battle of Chickamauga he was badly wounded and left upon the field for dead by his men. He revived, however, was taken prisoner and, on account of his condition, paroled pending his recovery. He was taken to the home of the late Dr. McCallie and was tenderly nursed by members of the family. When he had recovered sufficiently to travel, he was sent to Johnson Island prison, where he remained eighteen months.

Following his release he came back to Tennessee, read law under Judge Frazier, a kinsman, of Nashville, was admitted to the bar in 1866, and began the practice of his profession in his home county.

Elected attorney-general for the then Fourth circuit, Chattanooga district, four years later, Capt. Frazier continued in this important office for eight years, during which time he prosecuted and convicted Shade Westmoreland, one of the first men to be hanged in Hamilton county.

At the end of his term of office he retired from the active practice of law and devoted himself to farming until 1882, when he removed from Rhea to Hamilton county. He was elected president of a farmers' convention in Knoxville a number of years ago. Capt. Frazier's father was also attorney-general for many years, and his great-grandfather was one of the framers of the constitution of Tennessee.

Captain Frazier was one of the early settlers of North Chattanooga and a pioneer land owner there. At that time the section north of the river was unimproved, and he was an important factor in its development.

In 1884, a number of prominent families were living in the neighborhood, and in that year R.M. Barton Jr., now Judge Barton of the United States labor board, took up his residence in Hill City, purchasing the place later owned by Dan C. Wheeler. The river was crossed in a skiff, and as this was not a very satisfactory means of transportation Judge Barton, Capt. Frazier, C.E. Stivers and G.H. Jarnagin purchased a small steamer and established a steam ferry.

The subject of a county bridge was then agitated, and several years later the present Walnut street bridge was built. . . .

GANNAWAY POEM

The following poem and music (now in the possession of Cecil B. Smith) was written on 14 November 1869 by Mary Permelia Gannaway from a description given to her by a participant. On 12 August 1873, Mary was married to Isaac N. Broyles, but he was not at Shiloh. The poem has been copied exactly as written.

BEATTLE OF CHILO

1st Come all ye brave Soldiers a story I will tell
It is of a Noted battle I do remember well
Of this auwfull Strief and will cause your blood to chile
Twas of a famous battle that was fought on Chilo hill

2nd It was on the 8th of April Last at the brake of day
The drums and fifes were playing to march us all away
The feelings of that hour I do remember still
When first my feet were tramping the top of Chilo hill

3rd About the hour of Sunrise the battle did begin
Before that day had ended we fought there hand to hand
The honor of field did my heart with anguish fill
For the wounded and the dying that lay on Chilo hill

4th There were men from every nation lying on that battle field
There were fathers sons and brothers who were remembered with the slain
That has caused so many homeswith deep mourning to be filled
Was from the famous battle that was fought on Chilo hill

5th The wounded men were crying for help from every where
While others who lay dying were offering god their prayer
Protect my wife and children if consistent to thy will
This was the mournful praying I heard on Chilo hill

6th Early the next morning we were called to arms again
Unmindful of the wounded unmindful of the slain
The struggled was renewed and 10,000 men were killed
This was the 2nd conflict of the famous Chilo hill

7th Before that day had ended the battle ceased to roar
And 10,000 of brave soldier had fell to rise nomore
They left there vacant Camps for some other brave to fill
And now there mangled bodies are lying on Chilo hill

8th An now my Song is ended about those bloody plains
I hope the Sight by no other men will ever be seen again
I pray to god to save them if consistent to thy will
This was the mournful praying I heard on Chilo hill

Wrote by M P Gannaway Nov the 14th 1869

GUINN LETTERS

Guinn Letter No. 1 was among the Lillard Papers in the Tennessee State Archives, and Letter No. 2 was contributed by Mary Jane Erwin.

Allmon Guinn (1818 - 1895) was mustered into Confederate service on 1 November 1861 as a member of Captain Hodges Company (D), 43rd Tennessee Infantry Regiment (Col. George W. Gillespie commanding). Allmon was later promoted to 3rd Lieutenant. The company was captured at Vicksburg, paroled, and exchanged about 1 October 1863 in Decatur, Georgia. He was captured again at Rogersville in 1864 and sent to Johnsons Island, Ohio, until May of 1865.

An order for transportation and a pocket-sized ledger kept by Allmon Guinn has also been preserved (copies sent by Mary Jane Erwin). Two pages from the ledger and the order are reproduced on the following pages.

Allmon was married to Nancy S.A. Hamilton (1820 - 1908) about 1841, probably in Bradley County. Of their three children, Jesse Hamilton Guinn (1842 - 1914) served as First Corporal in Company I, Third Tennessee Infantry, but later transferred to his father's company. While in Company I, he participated in the first Battle of Manassas. He was captured at both Vicksburg and Rogersville, but after the latter was in prison at Camp Chase, Ohio, where he remained until the end of the war.

Joshua Guinn, brother of Allmon, married first Elizabeth Brooks about 1810. At least two of their sons, John Hamilton and Leonard B., were members of Company I, Third Tennessee Regiment.

Three sisters of Allmon and Joshua also are mentioned in some of the letters: Elizabeth (married John W. Blevins in 1830), Malinda H. (married William J. Abel in 1850), and Martha Lucindy (married Calvin C. Robeson in 1850). Letters from C.C. Robeson will be found in the Lillard Letters.

LETTER NO. 1
ALLMON GUINN TO JESSE H. GUINN AND OTHERS

Decatur
July 16th 1861

Dear Son

I now whilst it is Raining a nice gentle Shower Set down to write to you and I am glad that I can Say that we are all well and when I Say we I mean all the Relations and friends So fare as I have any knowledge Your Uncle Joshua Received a letter today from John H Guinn dated 9th & 10th which Stated that you ware well I have not Received a letter from you Since that dated 30th June I have written to you myself and Some of us Write every week but we lern that you do not get all we Send I want you to write, if you get the letters we send or not.

We had Speaking hear to day by Mr Welker of Chattanooga he is a Candidate for the Congress of the Confederate States. Mr George Bridges is a Candidate and Says he will go north to South and will take the Oath either way he has not made any Speech to us yet and he need not no use in his talking to us. Mr Hirst & Mr Jarnegan(?) of Polk County is Candidate for floter both on the same side in polaticks. Mr Lane and Mr Dun of Polk for Seventh no Excitement in Elections.

The Union party in E Tennessee has had a Strong movement of Rebellion and Say they intend to have protection from the North but thare is a greate change among them now I think one half of them would go with the Southern men now but conciderable Excitement yet I do not no how it will terminate yet. I must stop a little for Bill Adams and Old Man Binyon has had a fight down in town and I will go and See whitch Whip Swarpt(?) him.

Now the 18th. I am trying to get my oats halled in We made 4.20 doz in that field at Alfred Cates Corn looks fine generally Silking & tawseling I will say no more of these things now.

The male has come and I got your letter dated the 9th which I was glad to Receive and hear that you are well and that the Buoys are all getting Better of the Measles; also letters from J.E. Stewart & B.F. Taylor I was glad to hear that B.F. was in good health I would Write a line to all the company but I Believe that Every Body is Writing by B Frasheur and his male will be too heavy; your Mother Sends you two pare Socks by Mr Frasheur and if you have not got money to buy Clothes when you want them Write and I will Send it to you; or anything you want Write and I will do the best I can and if you set Sick go to Some house where you can be taken good Care of and if you cannot get Sutch place get N.J. Lillard or I.G. Cross to git it for you and I will pay the Damage; it is now Raining So hard I must Stop again.

Mr Rogers has bin gone 4 or 5 weeks to Missourie after Lizzy King and has Just got home he found her well and got back Safe he says that the Spirit of War is pretty high in Missouri and Arkansas McCullom of Texas has got to Missouri and had 1 Battle Lost 200 men on the Southern Side and killed 900 Yankeys and took 1400 prisoners. We se the Same in the papers. He is making things quake there if this be true.

Now the 19th. Mr Frasheur had meeting last knight at the baptist church and a very good time Van Stewart Shouted all over the house and a good many others and we want you all to be good Buoys.

Now a few lines to John H Guinn. We have heard that you have had the measels and your Aunt Nancy wants you to Write whether you have got better of that bad caugh B.F. Lillard Write that you had a very bad caugh and we have not heard whether you have got better or not. I want you to take the best Care of your self that you can and Write to me as often as you can.

Now a few lines to L. B. Guinn. I want you to take the best care of your Self that you can and Write to me often I would have Sent Letters to you and John H by Mr Frasheur but he is Loaded with letters Clothing &c.

A few lines to Pat Blevins. I Received A few lines from you I have nothing to Write that will interest you only the girls Say they do not intend to Marry till you Buoys Comes home they do not intend to have a home guard they Say Kill the Yankeys and come home and they are fer you Shore and they dont lye.

Now Wm Runyan. My Respects to you; all is well I think I have not saw your Mother for a few days but if anything was rong I think I would hear of it Soon. I have got your thirty Six dollars in my hands for her now and that I will hand to her Soon.

Now Stephen R. Baldwin. I will write you a few Lines your folks are all well your Mother was here to day and took dinner with us George is not doing mutch good he has bin gone 2 or 3 days and your mother does not no whare he is She thinks probably he has gone to Calhoun to Join a Company your wheat all in the Barn your oats Some halled in and Some is not. Write to me often S.R.B.

Mr N.J. Lillard My Respects to you I will not write to you now as many are Writing I will soon; I wish you all the good luck you may be assured Write to me.

Mr I.G. Cross I will write a line to you I was over at John Taylors a Sunday and Saw Mary and the children. they ware all well children playing & sciping about; times is hard here in the Money line Jerry McKenzie Resigned last Court as tax collector and J.H. Cate was Elected in his place I Spect he will get the tax he has now got Everetts Cow levied on for tax I will Say to you that Evrett is gone from town to the denton or Cox Settlement our oats is Safe in town and it is Said he is a Candidate for floter I mean Everett Isaac Write to me often as you Can.

Mr Wm A Smith My Respects to you your uncle J.R. and aunt Nancy is gone on a visit to ducktown and Maryann is Staying with the children I am sorry to hear that your arm is Crooked(?) Write to me Wm A Give my respects to all the Company as I cannot Write to all

Allmon Guinn

- - - - - - - - - - - - -

LETTER NO. 2
JESSE H. GUINN TO NANCY JANE GUINN

Camp Near Vicksburg March 10th/63

Dear Aunt N.J.

Yours of the 23rd Feb came to hand yesterday evening while I was out on picket. One of big Bill's brothers come along by and I asked him if he had been up to [3rd ?] Regt and whether or not Bill had come. He said he had. He then asked me if there was a Lieut. Smith in the 43rd. I told him there was. He said he had some letters for him. Pap was thar and he told him to give them to him. And upon looking at them we saw they wer marked to him insted of Smith.

We have not saw Bill yet but expect him to be down soon to see us. The letters found us in tolerble health. The health of the boys is generaly good in both Regts. Our duty here is verry heavy at present but I hope it will not be so long. Some think there will still be a fight at this place while others think never. I am not able

3 Office Acting Quarter Master
Knoxville, Oct 7th 1861
Superintendent Orange & Alexandria R R Co
Will please furnish transportation for
Allman Guinn and three Recruits for 3rd Tenn
Regt (Col J.C. Vaughn) from Lynchburg to
Fairfax Station and charge to Confederate
States —
C. B. Wallace
Agent Qr Mast Dept

to say. I think if thete is a fight at all at this place it will be soon. The river is still rising and if the Enemy does not move on us soon they will have to craw fish. It was rumored hear yesterday that there was a fight going on at Port Hudson. I will not vouch for the trouth of the rumor as there is always more or less afloat.

I would like to have been at that valintine drawing verry much and to have hope the boys to bear there heavy burthens. I know the boys had a powerful time. I was some what sorry for the three boys, especially Frank. I know he was crouded verry much; but I can only say to them be of good cheer. I am in hopes there is a better day coming. A day when you can be relieved to some extent of your burthens. I know boys that there are plenty round about Vicksburg to relieve you, and they are ready and willing to relieve you, if they was just reliced from the duty thst they are now at. But it may be that you do not wish to be relieved, and that it would not suit either party to be relieved. I hope the time may soon come that we can all see each other and fix this thing to the satisfaction of all.

In regard to that letter and to its contince I can only say that I was verry much astonished at the idiea that had ben formed from it. I was also at a loss to know what there was in it that could have led them to such belief or supposition. The letter was in relation to the death of Harrisson L. Miller which was a verry serious affair as it had happened. And I could not of cource write otherwise and tell the whole case as it realy was. I hope you will look in to the matter and see that there is no misunderstanding about this thing.

As night is drawing near and I have some cooking to do, and tomorrow is our day to go on Pickett again, I shall have to close. Asking you to pardon all errors and write when convenient. J.H.G.

- - - - - - - - - - - - -

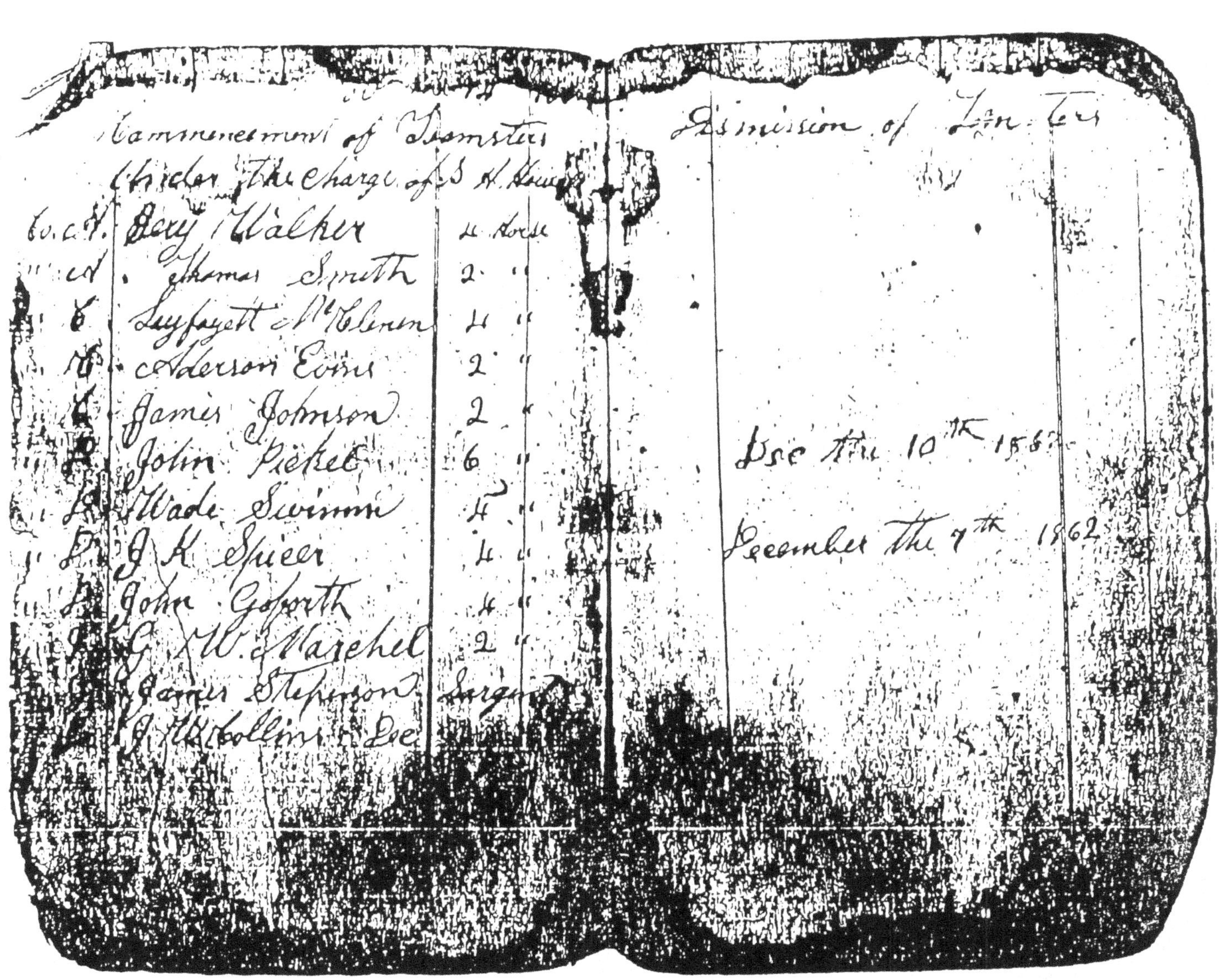

Commencement of Teamsters
Under the charge of S H. Guinn

Dismission of Teamsters

Co.	Name		Dismission
Co. H.	Berry Walker	4 horse	
" "	Thomas Smith	2 "	
"	Layfayett McClenan	4 "	
"	Anderson Evans	2 "	
"	James Johnson	2 "	
"	John Pickel	6 "	Dec the 10th 186[illegible]
"	Wade Swinnin	4 "	
"	J K Spicer	4 "	December the 7th 1862
"	John Goforth	4 "	
"	G W Marshel	2 "	
	James Stephenson	Surgeon	
	J McCollins	Doc	

PAGE FROM ALLMON GUINN'S LEDGER DATED 14 NOVEMBER 1862

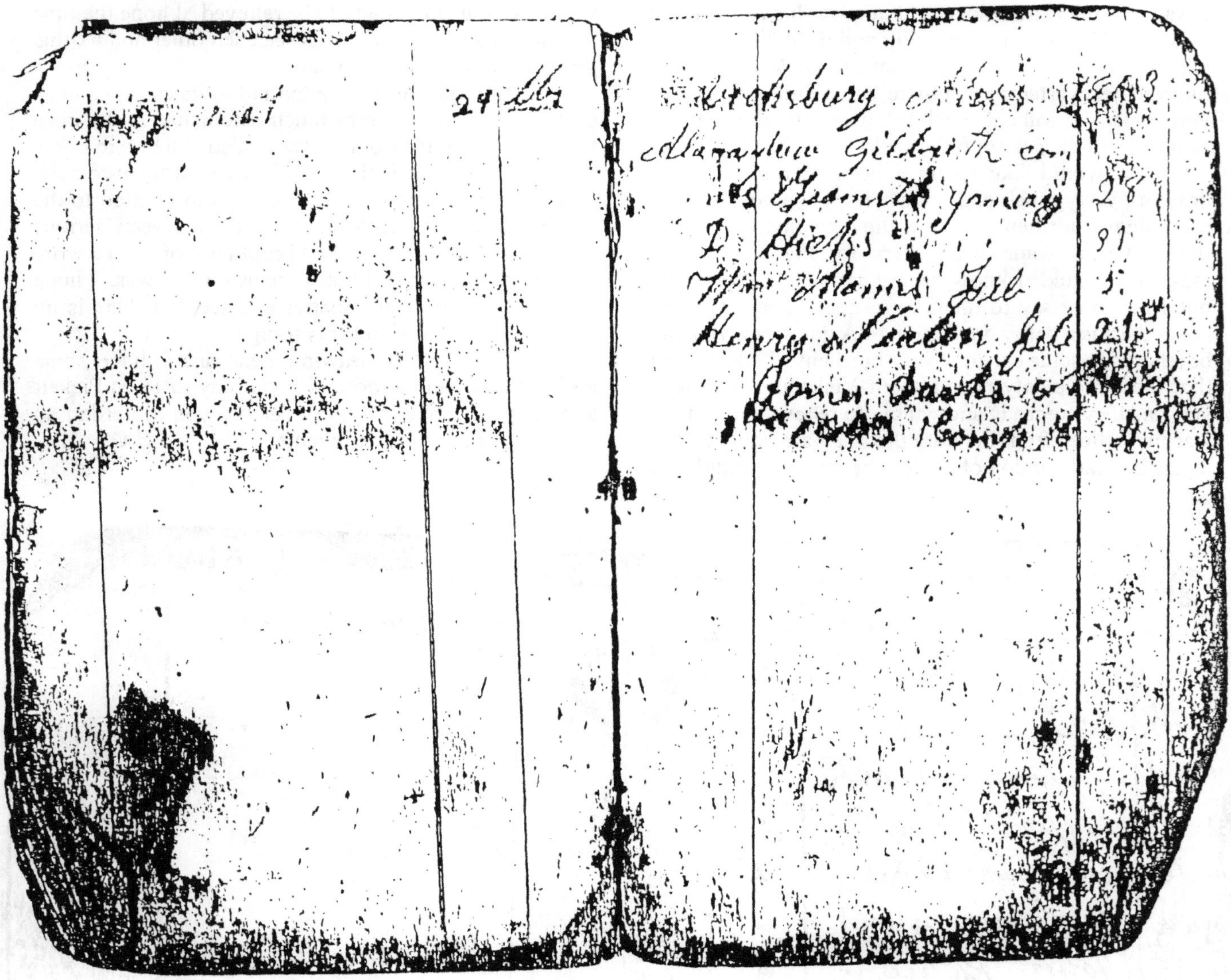

PAGE FROM ALLMON GUINN'S LEDGER DATED VICKSBURG, 1863

HOWELL DIARY

Joseph Anderson Howell (1832-1877) was a 2nd Lieutenant in Captain John Crawford's Company (E), 26th Tennessee Regiment (organized in 1861).

The following diary was transcribed from the original by Cathy Winkleman of Choctaw, Oklahoma. The small book is about two inches square and was "Bought at Camp Chase Ohio March 1862 price 25¢" according to a note written in the front. Another note states: "Joseph A. Howell Prisoner of War Kamp Chase. If I should die I wish my friends to send this to my wife at Decatur Meigs Tennessee."

The diary was kept from 1 January 1862 through 15 December 1862, although several days passed without an entry. Each entry was begun with the day of the week, date, month, and year. The year has been omitted below to save space, and the month and day has been reversed. The original was written as "January Wed. 1 1862." A few miscellaneous notes have been added in brackets to identify the individuals mentioned by Howell. The words that could not be deciphered are indicated by --?--.

Joseph married Venie [Vina] McCorkle on 10 April 1860 in Meigs County.

Wed., Jan. 1– At Bowling Green Ky. in Camps
Fri., Feb. 7– Prepared to start to Clarksville Tenn.
Sat., Feb. 8– Left Russleville Ky. for Clarksville Tenn. with the Wheeler command I was very sick.
Sun., Feb. 9– Was left at the National Hotel Clarksville Tenn. sick.
Mon., Feb. 10– R.C. Knight came to wait on me getting some better. [Richard C. Knight of Rhea County, son of Thomas, member of Co. E, 26th Tenn]
Tues., Feb. 11– Still at Clarksville improving.
Wed., Feb. 12– Improving soon be able to go on duty. Heard firing at Fort Donelson & Henery.
Thurs., Feb. 13– Left hotel went to the house of Thornburger to stay until better. Good place to stay I will ever remember the Lady's the way they treated me.
Fri., Feb. 14– Left Mr. Thornburgers for Fort Donelson at 2:oclock aren't Quite well, but think I can do some good arrived at Donelson at 12 night. Might lay down, air same, rain to sleet and it snowing.
Sat., Feb. 15– Got up at 3:oclock proceded to Regt. & marched out in line of battle made the attack at Day light was wounded on the left leg at 8:oclock am. Fought six hours.
Sun., Feb. 16– Advanced at 3:oclock am. for the purpose of cutting through after standing in line --?-- two hours was ordered back to camp and was surrendered and I ordered to stack arms Genl. Pollow & Floyad escaped, went on boat at night.
Mon., Feb. 17– Lay at Dover all day my leg very sore. General Ulysses S. Grant captured Joseph A. Howell. He became a prisoner around the 16th.
Tues., Feb. 18– Left Dover on the T.L. Magill for Cairo suffering with my wound had nothin to eat only had crackers and meat it does not get me by.
Wed., Feb. 19– Arrived at Cairo Ill. staid on the boat all day & night, leg partly sore getting better I think.
Thurs., Feb. 20– Left Cairo on the cars for Indianapolis Indiana Run all day & night with out anything to eat & but small quanity of water.
Fri., Feb. 21– Arrived at Indianapolis Indiana staid in train until 11:oclock without any thing to eat till morning we was quartered in the depot & hungry.
Sat., Feb. 22– Left the depot and was taken to quarters in large house on Washington street.
Sun., Feb. 23– Still in quarters on Washington St. Capt. Crawford sick, my leg considerably improved. [John Crawford of Rhea County]
Mon., Feb. 24– Still at Indianapolis Ind. nothing of interest transpired.
Tues., Feb. 25– Still at Indianapolis Ind. got orders to pack our baggage to start, and started and returned back to quarters for further orders.
Wed., Feb. 26– Started at 9½ o:clock am. for Columbus, Ohio. Left Capt. Crawford sick not able to travel arrived at C. at 94-Opm. and marched to camp Chase 4 miles --?-- --?-- --?--.
Thurs., Feb. 27– At Camp Chase fixing about our quarters & try to get somethin to eat having eaten nothin for the last 24 hours. I very sick can't eat any.
Fri., Feb. 28– I have got better of my sickness got a very bad cold.
Sat., Mar. 1– The balance of our Regt. arrived here from St. Louis Capt. Gorden, Lunt. Hunter, Graham, Rud, Brown, McElver, & Butler
Sun., Mar. 2– Nothing of intrest came up McBuffer pretty sick
Mon., Mar. 3– Nothing of interest transpired we have some hint that the field officers will be sent off.
Tues., Mar. 4– Col. [John M.] Lillard left at 12:oclock do not Know to what --?-- going taken a --?-- leg most well some man tried to make his escape.
Wed., Mar. 5– Nothing of any interest all improving in health commenced snowing pretty cold. Have a hint of fighting on the Patomac several prisoners arrived.
Thurs., Mar. 6– Nothing of importance all improving of our colds quit snowin had chicken soup for dinner.
Fri., Mar. 7– Nothing new turned up, reported that Andy Johnson is to be here. Did not. Rev. McBuffer & Big Sam sent to hospital sought some Hickory nuts & eat. [brother Sam in N.J. Lillard's Company]
Sat., Mar. 8– Nothing of interest commenced white washing the prison Andy Johnson past here tonight.
Sun., Mar. 9– All improving in health J.W. Easley released & started for home. Horace Maynard was here & Ethan. Say we will be moved to Sanducky hand(?) Checking

Mon., Mar. 10– Had Sacifras tea for dinner nothing transpired of intrest Rev. McBuffer came back from hospital improved in health.
Tues., Mar. 11– Nothing of interest a negro struck a white man he knocked him down with a piece of timber. Three prisoners escaped another tried.
Wed., Mar. 12– Whitewashing the prison & rearranging the bunks Dr. Talifono left the mess, Grahams be to see him I am well of my wound &c.
Thurs., Mar. 13– H. Paine sick --?-- had beef heart for dinner nothing of interest making for the prison. [3rd Lt. Hanibal Paine of Rhea County, son of Orville & Elvira Locke Paine]
Fri., Mar. 14– Capt. Burgess sick bay, Bill commenced to cook. Received some clothing from Ky. through Mag. Hayes I and Paine cooks for the day and had a fine time of it.
Sat., Mar. 15– Sick myself bowels running off taken salts Sam Returned from Hospital getting pretty stout goes to cooking.
Sun., Mar. 16– Capt. Welcker pretty sick Capt. Burgess improving went to prison #2 rain last night very muddy. A long day think a great deal of home. --?-- --?-- --?-- [Capt. Welker was from Roane County]
Mon., Mar. 17– Capt. Wilcker very sick nothing turned up, read a letter from Col. Lillard, he was well. Was very much relieved to hear from him.
Tues., Mar. 18– Nothing of importance, drew flour, had biscuits for supper the first we had my health is better than common.
Wed., Mar. 19– Nothing transpired of interest, Lunt. Mobly still very unwell I visited prison #2 all down in the mouth.
Thurs., Mar. 20– Working a fife half the day finished in the evening plaid Yankee until 11:oclock with Capt. Welcker, Lt. Foster & McElver.
Fri., Mar. 21– Nothing of interest transpired Major Cassady died at Columbus of Typhoid Pneaumonia only sick 48 hrs. cast a gloom over the camp.
Sat., Mar. 22– All improving of their sickness, read Johnsons proclamation to Tennesins Capt. McFarland, Lt. Willis, Gorba, & Owens arrived from St. Louis.
Sun., Mar. 23– Visiting prison #8 saw Eldridge Cash, brothern in law Cole(?) Was taken at Mill Springs got some clothing snowing some.

Abraham Lincoln	Cr.
1 pr socks - - - - - - - -	25¢
1 woolen shirt - - - - -	$ 1.50
1 pr pants blue - - - -	$ 3.00
1 wool hat - - - - - - -	$ 1.00

Mon., Mar. 24– Nothing new, pitching horseshoes around. First clear day in 10 All --?-- rained. I got a letter from Maynard saying he would try to release us.
Tues., Mar. 25– Nothing new Dr. Tulever went to town sick pitched quarters some had letter from Maynard.
Wed., Mar. 26– Nothing worth of note.
Thurs., Mar. 27– Nothing of note got a letter from Col. Lillard was well.
Fri., Mar. 28– Tried to Color our shirts myself & Lt. McElver I gave over mine.
Sat., Mar. 29– Iron my shirt for the first been raining all day.
Sun., Mar. 30– Nothing new only we had a pudding for dinner made by Lt. McElver. Written to Jake Mayers heard from Capt. Crawford he was mending (fine day).
Mon., Mar. 31– Connelly F. Triggs was here I suffer for the purpose of getting the prisoners to take the oath some one acting a fool. (Damn)
Tues., Ap. 1– No April fools all in good health have been fun.
Wed., Ap. 2– Nothing of interest all well except Mobly say some prisoners from Va.
Thurs., Ap. 3– Nothing doing all in health some talking of taking the oath Col. F. Trigg is here for that purpose. I hope none will take it had pudding for dinner.
Fri., Ap. 4– Fine day or morning Col. Trigg addressed the prisoners after he was done the prisoners gave three cheers for Jeff Davis & co. he was completely whip sum.
Sat., Ap. 5– Raining and windy nothing new all in tolerable health.
Sun., Ap. 6– Fine day I have got the blues some playing marbles pitching horse shoes preaching by Rev. Overton a prisoner I was more reckless than ever before.
Mon., Ap. 7– Nothing new raining too.
Tues., Ap. 8– Col. Triggs was here to see Lt. McElver, Maj. Hays was sent to some other prison.
Wed., Ap. 9– Heard of the battle at Pittsburge Tenn. all down in the mouth after a letter. Cheered By the news forgotten fight hope the Rebels have the day &c.
Thurs., Ap. 10– The KO. left this prison at 5:oclock am. I feel bad.
Fri., Ap. 11– No news to still have the accounts of the battle of Pittsburge have more confidence in the success of their cause (Rebel)
Sat., Ap. 12– Nothing new some excitement about Island #10 & Pittsburge Fine day.
Sun., Ap. 13– Cloudy and some rain.
Mon., Ap. 14– Regt. starts for Nashville
Tues., Ap. 15– Arrival from Island #10 Capt. Hennese & others Brownlaw tried to make a speech we growned him down.
Wed., Ap. 16– Building a kitchen by Lt. McElver, Gordan & others.
Thurs., Ap. 17– No letters from Col. Lillard feared he sick written to Uncle Jr. Howell. Raining.
Fri., Ap. 18– Heard of death of Capt. Crawford he died on the 11th at Indianapolis Ind. some news of fighting at Yorktown.
Sat., Ap. 19– Lt. Hunter seemed to be in a rather distructive condition Lt. Blair & others from Cummens Regt. came in today brings some news from Pittsburg.
Sun., Ap. 20– EASTER Had feeling no stupid eggs, dark day and raining
Mon., Ap. 21– Nothing new rained all day, cold
Tues., Ap. 22– Learned that we would be sent to Sandusky Island all the Comm. officers.

Wed., Ap. 23– Rained some preparation to go to Sandusky.

Thurs., Ap. 24– Burgess, Brown, Bumbling & Gordon started for Sandusky at 4:oclock am. the balance goes Sat. Had a big pudding for dinner.

Fri., Ap. 25– Making preparations to go to Sandusky Island.

Sat., Ap. 26– Left Camp Chase at 5 am. & got to Columbus at 8 am. started for Sandusky City at 9 am. change cars at Shelbyville & arrived at Sandusky at 2 pm. Travel to Johnson Island (Govener) (Columbus to Sandusky 20 miles) for the night 3 miles camp &c.

Sun., Ap. 27– Fine day everything looks pleasant read a letter from Col. Lillard. Nothing new.

Mon., Ap. 28– Nothing new not much to eat. Weeler home by(?) fits.(?) my(?) Norfork.

Tues., Ap. 29– I played bust some read a letter for Col. Lillard from his wife. I and Capt. Burgess opened and read. Was so glad to hear from home late 4 inst. all well forward to Col. Lillard at Fort Warren.

Wed., Ap. 30– Nothing new fine day cold wind blowing.

Thurs., May 1– Fine day not much sign of spring but few buds & the trees see some small vessels on the lake, lay back and enjoy life only for a shave.

Fri., May 2– Looks a little cloudy arrival of prisoners from Camp Chase Levi Hughes of Cleveland Tenn. Capt. McFarland 26th Tenn. Regt.

Sat., May 3– Raining Bringing of barges of prisoners that arrived got tired of dark day.

Sun., May 4– Fine day preaching by Rev. Hasten not much --?-- at 3 pm. again some excitement about Pittsburg fight. have no --?-- --?-- written to J.G. Spears fox man.

Mon., May 5– Mr. Waud died at 1½ am. with Regt. battles.

Tues. May 6– Got a letter from Col. Lillard he was well &c.

Wed., May 7– Written to Col. Lillard & G.J. Meyers Fine day everything looks beautiful preaching by Rev. Witherspoon of Ala.

Thurs., May 8– Preaching again this morning.

Fri., May 9– Preaching nothing.

Sat., May 10– Nothing

Sun., May 11– Nothing new went to preaching.

Mon., May 12– Heard some news of fight at West Point.

Tues., May 13– Heard of the surrender of Norfork & the blowing up of the Merrimack the prospect looks gloomy.

Wed., May 14– Nothing of interest no letters from anyone. Would like to have a letter from the boys, Oh when shall I get a letter from Home?

Thurs., May 15– Worked on horse half the day very tired. The Federals ran up the Stars & Stripes over the prison groaned at by the C.S.A. prisoners.

Fri., May 16– Lasted till dinner according to Davis proclamation very same from --?--.

Sat., May 17– Little sick diahrea. Learned or heard some news of --?-- being turned over to Gov. Johnson. I do not like the change as he is a Soundrel.

Sun., May 18– Went to church twice today had two very good sermons hear rumor of another fight at Corinth no particulars.

Mon., May 19– Very cold enough to snow, plaid bust some. No news of interest high winds large waves on the lake.

Tues., May 20– Cold had to have large fires all day Lt. Bowling improving hope he will [be] up soon. Large waves on the lake.

Wed., May 21– Raining this morning look dark & gloomy.

Thurs., May 22– Cook today I Capt. Burgess Lt. Battles pretty hard work. Washing isles. Capt. Burgess got a letter from Col. Lillard he was well, no news &c.

Fri., May 23– Fine morning Lt. Sikes has been exchanged got a letter from Genl. Wright saing he had not stold my money (I believe he lied)

Sat., May 24– Written a letter to send home by Lt. Sikes

Sun., May 25– Staid in my room all day did not go out to preaching written a letter to home to Vina. Capt. Welcker had a letter from Matt Allison.

Mon., May 26– Lt. Rheo [Rhea?] died this morning Lt. Foster & Evans sick.

Tues., May 27– Heard of the battle in Va. of Shanandoah some excitement.

Wed., May 28– Lt. Murry of Tenn. died this morning his remains sent out this everning. Some talk of exchange hope it is so been fine day.

Thurs., May 29– Nothing new Sandusky City had about excursion produce some excitement. Capt. Brinner was shot at night by centinal while going after water.

Fri., May 30– Raining this morning Heard of the defeat of Bank some particulars highly gratifing &c.

Sat., May 31– Cloudy and raining some. Been cooking all day tired &c. Nothing new heard Beureguarde had avacuation 9th are particular the Yankees astonished.

Sun., June 1– Dark day & muddy has been a very long day went to sleep and dreamed of home.

Mon., June 2– Mud and rain all day got a letter from Col. Lillard He was not well.

Tues., June 3– Rainy and muddy heard of the fight at Richmond thank we have had the best of the fight all in glad spirits no letter from home.

Wed., June 4– Raining hope it will be clear some time.

Thurs., June 5– Some anxiety about Corinth and Richmond News anything but good Written a letter to J.A. Cash & washed my close the first time. [James A. Cash, of Rhea County, was First Corporal of Company E, 26th Tennessee]

Fri., June 6– Nothing new all a little down about the news from Richmond.

Sat., June 7– Great excitement on the subject of exchange hope its so the Preachers and surgeons to be released without conditions or as noncombatants.

Sun., June 8– Fine morning oh how I wish I could see Vinna and Dixie and be with them today May Heaven bless them.

Mon., June 9– Got a letter from Col. Lillard no news.

Tues., June 10– Written a letter to Col. Lillard Heard of the taking of Chattanooa Lt. Sikes of Miss. started home. Had a fuss with Capt. Battles, I think he treated me badly, I do not like him.

Wed., June 11– Some disharden about exchange of prisoners. Lt. Blair got a letter from E.L. (Oh when shall I get a letter from my wife?)

Thurs., June 12– Fine day Lt. [Hanibal] Paine sick fear he will have a bad spell hope he will get up soon.

Fri., June 13– Fine Day & warm nothing new today heard of Shield & Jackson fight in Ala. Capt. James Matters of 1st Ala. Regt. shot by sentinel last night while going to --?--.

Sat., June 14– Moved Lt. Paine to hospital no better stayed all in Hospital Nothing new all quiet.

Sun., June 15– Cold day staid in Hospital with Lt. Paine all day he is better I think I been thinking Vinna & Dixie all day Oh when shall I see them May I some --?--.

Mon., June 16– Cold morning Lt. Paine better I think. No news from sent of Wa. nothing of exchange all believed Lt.

Tues., June 17– Look for a letter from home and Col. Lillard did not get either. Oh How I would like to hear from Vina I hope she has read some letters from do they miss me at home? [the following letter was written on this day] Johnson Island

June 17 1862

"To the Yankees generally I hereby express my hatred not for a moment but eternal for ever. I shall teach my children to hate you, I hope to keep it up. Will one of my kindred and name last? And when I and all my race is done on earth that the spirit will who haunt you. I intend to fight you while I live and be separated where I cannot see you."

Wed., June 18– Read a letter from Col. Lillard He was well & answered it more talk of exchange hope it is true but I have but little faith seems as tho I never will get a letter from home.

Thurs., June 19– Pretty morning Lt. Paine better rested well last night no general news all seems quite same talk of exchange hope it will be soon.

Fri., June 20– Fine Morning nothing new Lt. Paine Seems Better.

Sat., June 21– Some prisoners arrived from Gov. Island taken at Fort Pulaski & Hanover. C.H. fine looking set of men. Capt. Battles got a letter from home.

Sun., June 22– The surgeons was all unconditionally released. I wrote a letter by Dr. Tallafario to Veanna. I hope it will not be long before I am released.

Mon., June 23– Cooked all day it has rained most of the time no news of any kind Lt. Paine is better.

Tues., June 24– Nothing of interest had no news from any place Lt. Paine better.

Wed., June 25– No News all quiet

Thurs., June 26– Read a letter from Col. Lillard he was well Thought no exchange would take place till after the fight at Richmond. Went in bathing.

Fri., June 27– Gunboat landed &c. no news from any must write a letter to Col. Lillard not quite well head ache.

Sat., June 28– Red Gimms 83/100s dollars from Baltimore Capt. Hinson got a letter from E. Tenn. Nothing new there (Running excursions by the citizens of Sanducky & Boat)

Sun., June 29– Raining Oh how I wish I was there. No news all seems to be quiet I think we will have some stirring news before long.

Mon., June 30– Heard of the battle of Richmond great rejoicing by the Rebels We think our folks have gained a glorious victory. I hope it is and the fight is not closed.

Tues., July 1– Suffering with boil in wrist, getting some better. Heard of the death of Col. Lillards wife written to him about it what a great callamaity all well at home June 8/62

Wed., July 2– Excurrsion on boat no excitement no letters from anywhere good news for the Rebels from the fighting Richmond Say that Curtis is hard pressed by Hindman in Arkansas

Thurs., July 3– Still have the conframation of a Rebel Victory at Richmond arrival of prisoners from Camp Chase. Capt. Welcker & Lt. Hunter in the crowd. Some think we will be exchanged soon.

Fri., July 4– Warm morning and clear the Yankees fired 54 guns as salute. Two Boats pass with parties on pleasure trip. Some prisoners went to Camp Chase. Blevins & Grant & Stuart 12 months today since we left Washington for Knoxville.

[the following letter also was written on July 4th]

"Twelve months to the day since I left home to join the service of the confederates. I do not regret it tho, it has been one eventful year to me. All I have to regret is being separate from my wife and friends. But I hope it will turn out for the better, and that I may still live to see my country in peace and prosper again. And be permitted to live and enjoy life among my friends.

"But if I fall I hope to fall at my past and never let it be said one of name should be guilty of a dishonorable act that the family would be ashamed of in after grave my hope and prayers to God is for my country." Joseph A. Howell

Decatur Meigs Co. Tennessee

Sat., July 5– Still same news from Richmond which shows to be a victory for the Confederates. Written a letter home Lea nint got a letter from the Sanduskyites had excursion and music all night.

Sun., July 6– Fine morning very warm all day nothing new still same reports of the fight at Richmond. I spent the day thinking about home. I look all day for a letter from home did not get it.

Mon., July 7– Warm day nothing new rained in the evening cooled the air. Lt. Pearson died last night no letters from home or any place else.

Tues., July 8– Writen a letter to Col. Lillard & recived one. He seemed very much affected about the death of his wife. No news from [home], Oh when will I get a letter?

Wed., July 9– Some excitement about the fight at Richmond no news from home Lt. Morgan released some say he taken the oath. I do not know particulars now.

Thurs., July 10– Sanduskyites go on an excursion to Cleveland reported evacution of Huntsville by the Federals some think they are fighting in east Tenn. Washed

Fri., July 11– More encouraging news from Richmond some hint of exchange written a letter home read no letter from anywhere

Sat., July 12– News of exchanges hope its so. Grant debate in papers about the policies of the government no positive news as to the release but it is general belief the unmancipation.

Sun., July 13– Went to preaching service by Rev. Wilson. Long day Thought a great deal of being at home do not think it will be long before I have that --?--.

Mon., July 14– Cooked very tired heard of the fight at Murfasborrough hope our folks will all be up and I am. No news from home When shall I see Vinna?

Tues., July 15– Had glorious news from Murfasboro all feel much satisfied at pros. Think exchange is certain no letters from any are here some prisoners arrived from Columbus.

Wed., July 16– No news all in good spirits and in good health.

July 16, 1862

Abraham Lincoln	Dr.
20 Swords - - - - - - - - - -	$30.00
20 Saddles & Bridles - - -	25.00

Thurs., July 17– Heard of the fight of Murfasboro all rejoicing think our forces have gained a great victory.

Fri., July 18– Saw --?-- all day nothing of interest, cooked all day for Lt. Neil.

[NOTE: no entry for Saturday]

Sun., July 20– Received letter from home dated 3rd July all well I was so glad to hear from home. Went to church old crippled fellow preached pretty good.

Mon., July 21– Written letter home

Tues., July 22– Nothing new all talk about exchange

Wed., July 23– Cooked for Capt. Welcker, Lt. Crow died last night he was a son of Ben Crow of Tenn. He was from Arkansas.

Thurs., July 24– Cooked for Rev. Adams, Capt. Hodges of Memphis died this morning from sore leg caused by a wound Recd in Mexian War Written a letter to Col. Lillard

Fri., July 25– Washed this morning. Heard of the death of Jeff Crist no particulars all in good spirits about exchange.

Sat., July 26– Nothing new

Sun., July 27– All in fine spirits about exchange went to church Rev. Adams Preached

Mon., July 28– Cooked for Rud Brown. no letters from anybody

Tues., July 29– ----?---- for Capt. Burgess. Capt. McWhehter died this morning (MIP) and Burgess got a letter from home all well.

Wed., July 30– Cooked for Lt. Gidmarch rumor of England --?-- in the --?-- all the Rebel in great glee I think they will be exchanged in a few days.

Thurs., July 31– Read letter from Col. Lillard he was well speaks of an exchange as a fixed fact I think we will all be released soon.

Fri., Aug. 1– Warm day good news from the south arrival of 13 gunboats at Mobile.

Sat., Aug. 2– Nothing new very warm.

Sun., Aug. 3– Got a letter from Col. Lillard was starting for Dixie in fine spirits the chaplins is released unconditionaly today.

Mon., Aug. 4– Nothing new.

Tues., Aug. 5– Cooked all day very warm

Wed., Aug. 6– Some talk of exchange all in great anxiety to hear the news to go the --?-- for Dixie

Thurs., Aug. 7– The federals firing salute to the death of Martin Van Buren and man had his hand shot off.

Fri., Aug. 8– Cooked for Capt. McDonald, Lt. Gibson was shot & killed at 9:oclock pm. he belonged to an Arkansas C. Regt. It was a cold blooded Murder while he was going to --?--.

Sat., Aug. 9– No news several letters received from east Tenn. no general news

Sun., Aug. 10– Le asked for Lt. Neil

Mon., Aug. 11– Heard of the fight the --?-- & Jackson at Culpepper. C.H.D. think we have gained a great victory

Tues., Aug. 12– Sick to think it is only cold feel very bad. All in good spirits about exchange hope it will come soon

Wed., Aug. 13– Still think I am some Better.

Thurs., Aug. 14– Still sick not well yesterday I am suffering very much.

Fri., Aug. 15– Came to --?-- --?-- --?-- taken some much came --?--.

Sat., Aug. 16– Slept no last night thought I think I am & now me considerable easier.

Sun., Aug. 17– Did not sleep much But think I am getting along very well.

Mon., Aug. 18– Feel some better this morning at least I am not so much misery.

Tues., Aug. 19– Have become deaf head in road from Quinine can hear to do any good.

Wed., Aug. 20– Feel better this morning no pain in my back My hearing is the worst.

Thurs., Aug. 21– Do not feel quite as well as I did yesterday morning felt better in the evening.

Fri., Aug. 22– Rained last night I feel some considerable better think I will be up in a few days some excitement at starting

Sat., Aug. 23– I am improving too some. A little deaft. Cooler today than has been I walked about some over the room.

Sun., Aug. 24– Feel a great deal better this morning. Quite cool Think a great deal about getting home I do not think it will be long before I get a start that way.

Mon., Aug. 25– Better this morning fine day. Lt. Anderson of the 41st Tenn. Regt. died this morning at 5:oclock am.

Tues., Aug. 26– Still mending will be well in a few days. If I still improve. 330 prisoners arrived from Camp Martin. mostly --?-- prisoners from Kentucky.

Wed., Aug. 27– Rained this morning I feel very well. All excitement about getting off I will be going shortly.

Thurs., Aug. 28– I am improving think I will be all straight in a few days All think we will get off tomorrow. I fear we will not make it.

Fri., Aug. 29– Still improving disappointed by not getting started to Dixie this morning.

Sat., Aug. 30– All in fine spirits about getting Monday for Dixie rations has been sent in for us to cook for the Troops I am improving so I will be able to travel.

Sun., Aug. 31– All packed up and sending out our baggage all feel good.

Mon., Sep. 1– Left Johnson Island at 8:oclock am. left Sandusky at 2 pm. all in fine glee. Good can get some Watermelons & peaches & apples the feast --?--.

Tues., Sep. 2– At Sidney Oh. at day lite next place Union State Line Oh & Ind. got to Indianapolis Ind. at 1½:oclock pm. several friends came to see us.

Wed., Sep. 3– Still on the road to Cario, arrived at Cario at 11:oclock pm. put on the steamer Universe & anchored out I slept on top of the [boat] all night.

Thurs., Sep. 4– At Cairo anchored out in river hard times to get anything to eat. Hope we will get started soon I am suffering a great deal from pain in my side.

Fri., Sep. 5– Still suffering from my side cannot get any medicines left the Universe Boat at 8:oclock pm. & went on the Chateau & got a bed. I had been laying on the floor.

Sat., Sep. 6– Feel better this morning imp. I will be up soon.

Sun., Sep. 7– Still at Cairo I am Improving am almost well this has been one of the long days. So anxious to get away down in Dixie Raining all day.

Mon., Sep. 8– Left Cairo at 2½:oclock pm. past Columbus at 5½:oclock pm. Saw the Fort & Belmont Battle ground I feel almost all strait go to New Madrid tonight.

Tues., Sep. 9– Lay East at Island #10. Run all day without anything of interest happening. We got some cheers from women on the bank. Past Fort Pillow after night started at 1:oclock.

Wed., Sep. 10– Started from our anchored at 700 and got to Memphis at 900 am the place looks deserted been getting air cool all day they came to see us in great numbers all jublent

Thurs., Sep. 11– Lay all night at Memphis & still anchored and this (am) Left Memphis at 200 pm. I feel much better almost well.

Sept 11, 1862

"Left Sandusky City Sept 1st under the command of Capt. Tarletti & Lt. Evans of Hoffman Battalion. Had good passenger car to Indianapolis where we changed off into stock cars. Not cleaned out, very nasty place indeed. Went to Ciaro that way when we was put on the boat the Universe where we staid two days when we was changed to the Chateau a little cleaner much larger boat. But very much crowded 1200 of us all."

Fri., Sep. 12– Lay all night at Helena Arkansas 2 men died last night and rained this morning. We are all tired going J.A. Stone Curtis, forces is here looks like about 10,000.

Sat., Sep. 13– Still at Helena no signs of starting do hope we will start soon Left Helena at 4 pm. run on till 10 pm. & stopped above Napolean

Sun., Sep. 14– Started at sunrise past Napolean about 9 am. Saw some very pretty farms deserted. Run in 60 miles of Vicksburg met other boats from there that had taken prisoners down.

Mon., Sep. 15– Still anchored not moved this morning. Do not want the response for not staryed at 11 am. run near Vicksburg all in fine spirits.

Tues., Sep. 16– Near Vicksburg all waiting for the word to march. Commenced exchanging at 12 am. Got down to the city 4 pm. taken quarters at Washington Hall.

Wed., Sep. 17– Staid all night at Vicksburg, was very sick in the evening eat to much watermelon. Think it will wear off in a few days.

Thurs., Sep. 18– Better this morning but pretty sick. Started for Jackson at 12 noon arrived there at 4 pm. found most of the Regt. here some death sick.

[NOTE: no entries for September 19 through 26]

Sat., Sep. 27– Left Jackson for Chattanooga at 8:oclock am. arrived at Meridian at 5:oclock pm.

Sun., Sep. 28– Left Meridian 6 am. got to Mobile at 2 pm. Rained very hard lay on the train all night.

Mon., Sep. 29– Left Mobile Ala. 12 am got to Polland at 5 pm. Staid all night

Tues., Sep. 30– Left Pollard at 8 am. arrived at Montgomery Ala. 3 pm. Hanners McLanakan died at 5 pm. went to the fair gound to camp.

Wed., Oct. 1– Left Montgomery Ala. at 2 pm. arrived at West Point at 11 pm.

Thurs., Oct. 2– Left West Point 2 pm. arrived at Atlanta 8 pm left Atlanta at 11 pm.

Fri., Oct. 3– Arrived at Chattanooga at 2 pm. drew rations went to Tenn. Station and pitched tents

[NOTE: no entry for October 4th and 5th]

Mon., Oct. 6– Left Tenn. Station at 1 am went W. Athens met Vinna staid all night.

Tues., Dec. 9– Deth of Van(?) Lux(?) April 4, 1862

Mon., Dec. 15– J.L.H. Dr. D.C. Howell

Tobacco	10¢
Tobcco	15¢
	$5.15

Tues., Dec. 16–

Apples	5¢
Tobcco	15¢
Apples	5¢

A Memorandum at the end of the Diary contains a list of the "Comm. & Staff Officers of the 26th Tenn. Regt. Volenteers" who evidently were taken prisoner with J.A. Howell.

Linville Hunter, 1st Lt., Jamesboro, Tenn.
I. R. Gabo, 2nd Lt., Jamesboro, Tenn
Sam W. Battles, 3rd Lt., Braglesville, Tenn.
[probably Broylesville, Tenn.]
A. C. Hicky, 1st Lt., Newfond --?--, Tenn.
J. W. McNoble, 2nd Lt., Newfond, Tenn.
A. S. Saggerty, 3rd Lt., Right, Tenn.
W. C. Blines, 1st Lt., Washington, Tenn.
[probably Dr. A.C. Blevins]
Hanabull Paine, [3rd Lt.] Washington, Tenn.
R. M. Soffle [Saffles], 1st Lt.
H. W. Graham, 2nd Lt.
J. L. Butler, 2nd Lt.
A. H. Foster, 1st Lt., Ringgold, Ga.
L. C. Reid, 2nd Lt., Ringgold, Ga.
J. W. Nillis, 3rd Lt. Ringgold, Ga.
W. P. Gordon, 1st Lt., Ringgold, Ga. - Gainsville, Tex
B. Hendrix, 2nd Lt. Ringgold, Ga.
C. W. Owings, 3rd Lt., Ringgold, Ga.
Thomas B. Brown, 1st Lt., Ala.
Thomas J. Brown, 2nd Lt., Post Oak Springs, Tenn.
W. E. McElver, 2nd Lt., Post Oak Springs, Tenn.
W. B. Coniar, 1st Lt., Bluntville, Tenn.
C. L. Franzier, 2nd Lt., Bristal, Tenn.
C. R. Monsill, 3rd Lt., Bristal, Tenn.
John M. Lillard, Col., Decatur, Meigs Co., Tenn.
James J. Odell, Lt. Col., Bristal, Tenn.
Thomas M. McConnell, Major, Rutledge, Grainger Co., Tenn.
George Stewart & S.C.W., Newport, Tenn.
Tolbot Green, D.M.G., Jamesboro, Tenn.
J. A. Cash, D.D.S., Washington, Tenn.
E. T. Taliafero, Surgeon, Pikeville, Tenn.
?. W. Eanis, Assist. Surgeon, Ringgold, Ga.

NOTE: the following three officers were listed separately and may not have been members of the 26th Tennessee:

Henery C. Evans, 1st Lt., Thornhill, Tenn.
Livi Mobly, 2nd Lt., Thornhill, Tenn.
J. W. Easly, 2nd Lt., Thornhill, Tenn.

"Lt. Hicks says he was not with the compny when the attact at Fort Donelson (McConnel claims to have commanded Capt. Allens Co.)"

KING REMINISCENCES

The following article was found in the scrapbook belonging to William G. Allen. Letters written by several of the individuls mentioned in the article will be found elsewhere in this publication. The source of the article (newspaper and date of publication) is unknown, but the type of print eliminates a Chattanooga or Rhea County paper.

CONFEDERATE SHARP-SHOOTER.

REMINISCENCES OF WAR TOLD BY 'SQUIRE KING

The confederate picket line was established at the base of the hill parallel to the federal lines about 400 yards distant. Our regiment was kept on duty here for several days, and firing and yelling between the pickets never ceased or abated up to the time we were relieved. At this point the federals used balloons for making observations. They were held in position by ropes.

A few days after we were relieved at Munson's hill, we were ordered on picket at Mason's Hill, which belonged to the same range about two miles south of Munson's. Our picket line here was a considerable distance in advance of our water, and the weather was intensely hot. Between our line and the federal line, in a beautiful grove of trees, was a deserted farm house.

Being exceedingly thirsty, and believing that there was a spring in the grove, I determined to explore it. So creeping through the underbrush, to avoid being seen by the federals, I soon entered the grove and directly came to a beautiful bubbling spring.

Immediately prostrating myself by its side I was proceeding in the primitive way, to quaff pure refreshing water, when a little noise attracted my attention. Looking up there stood a man apparently about eight feet high, with the biggest pistol I ever saw.

His salutation was, "How are you Reb?" Rising slowly up I replied: "I am pretty well thank you. How-how-how-did-you leave your folks?" He was a good natured fellow and seeing my embarassment, promptly relieved me by saying, "Reb, I don't think either your capture or mine would materially influence the course of events and I will not follow up my advantage." Says I "Old fellow, them's my sentiments, give me your hand."

After shaking hands we sat down in the shade and had a long pleasant talk. As we separated he gave me a copy of Harper's Illustrated Weekly which contained a cut of Munson's Hill showing the earth-works, the piece of artillery mounted there, (stove-pipe) and a long detailed account of its capture, etc., which was as near the truth as any army reporter ever got to the front.

By agreement, we met there again the next morning. I took William G. Swan with me, and he had a lieutenant of his company with him. The lieutenant was very polite, but was not very communicative. He kept a close watch on the private and seemed to be seeking information, and not very much inclined to give any. However by a little strategy, Swan obtained from the private several newspapers which he had concealed on his person. We then shook hands and separated.

MET GEN. JOHNSON

That evening we were relieved by another regiment and returned to camp at Fairfax court house. Soon after this we moved to Fairfax station, and the Third Tennessee regiment was camped immediately beside Gen. Joseph E. Johnson's headquarters. His quarter guard was detailed from the company to which I belonged. I was often about his quarters, and had frequent opportunities to observe him. He was a plain, simple-mannered man, who seemed to recognize no superiority among the soldiers, save rank, necessary to enforce discipline.

I was told by those of his camp at that time, that he was never known to have a detail made to do any work for him about his quarters. If he wanted anything done he would commence it himself, and there were always volunteers who would go to his relief. His name and fame will live as long as history, an honor to the cause he espoused and to the country which gave him birth. I bow respectfully before so great a theme and shall leave it to more eloquent pens to rear monuments to his memory.

SEES STONEWALL JACKSON

From Fairfax station the whole army fell back to Centerville. At that point Gen. Stonewall Jackson was ordered to the Valley of Virginia. I remember distinctly seeing him as we rode out of camps at the head of that gallant band, whose subsequent valor and glorious deeds will make a triumphant march through all time beside which the laurels of all who confront him will fade away and finally be forgotten.

About this time William G. Swan received news of his election to the confederate congress having beaten Col. John Baxter. I felt his loss as a friend and companion severely. His place, however, was soon filled by gallant Thomas O'Connor, who one morning came striding into our camp from the First Georgia regiment.

This regiment, he with Robert Ramsey, John Hope, John McAffery, James Mitchell, and few others from our city, joined in the city of Atlanta on April 18, 1861, six days after the firing upon Fort Sumter, and were among the first enlistments from Tennessee in the confederate army. Tom liked the appearance of things in our camp, and by consent of the colonels of the respective regiments, he effected an exchange with a member of Col. Bill Parker's company by paying a difference of $50 and became one of us.

Cold weather then coming on, the army went into winter quarters at Manassa Junction. During all this time a chair picket line of regiments was kept up several miles in our advance. We were cautioned to use the greatest vigilance and every pass was guarded. Some ladies of that section who aspired to military honors were used by the respective armies in gaining information and the greatest caution was observed to prevent them as well as men from passing through the lines.

One night about 3 o'clock, I was sent out a quarter of a mile or more in advance of the regiment to relieve a vedet. It was in a lonely desolate place upon an old road where the undergrowth had encroached on either side until it had become a mere path but little used. A videt station is the prayer-ground of the soldier where the scriptural injunction, watch and pray, is fully complied with.

After walking my lonely beat for an hour or more mentally going over my little "Lay Me Down to Sleep," counting the stars and thinking of home, mother, friends and sweetheart, who perhaps I would never see again, I was aroused from my reverly by a slight noise in the path immediately in front of me. It sounded like some one stealthily creeping up on me through the brush. I gave the command "Halt! who come there?"

Receiving no reply and finding I was not obeyed I repeated it twice without effect, and then fired. There was a slight moan and all was still. The regiment being aroused by my firing stood up on their arms until day. As soon as it was light enough to see, the captain and I went to the front and there upon the side of the road about thirty paces from where I stood, with the blood oozing from a face wound, lay the dead body of Mrs. John Nolen's old sow. She like all her progeny, had given her life to the southern cause.

It is proper, however, to say that she had the sympathy of all who viewed her remains; and in extenuation of this unfortunate event, her body received that kind and considerate attention, which was customary to be bestowed by a Christian soldiery.

And in consideration of gallantry displayed on that occasion I was promptly brevetted "pork-picket."

GETS HONORABLE DISCHARGE

After the army had been quartered at Manassas about a month, Tom O'Conner and I both became seriously afflicted. The surgeon who diagnosed our cases pronounced it ennui, a fearful French malady, but he feared it would not pass muster in our camp. He was a kind-hearted, good man, however, and in consideration of his friendship for us he gave the disease some different name. Certified to our disability, which went up through the proper channel, and in about a week thereafter we received an honorable discharge, procured in an honorable way from the Third Tennessee regiment and returned home.

Tom joined the artillery and I joined a cavalry company which was being raised by John R. Neal, Rube Mastin, and my brother, W.N. King, in McMinn county. The company was soon complete, and went into camp at Post Oak Springs, Roane county, Tennessee. It organized by electing John R. Neal captain, Rube Mastin first lieutenant, W.N. King second lieutenant and Dora Vaughn third lieutenant.

It was the nucleus of what afterwards became the Sixteenth battalion of cavalry. Other companies were ordered to Post Oak Springs, but before the field officers were elected, Col. Rucker was ordered to take command of the battalion. The duties of this battalion were to guard the passes, and scout the mountains which were infested with bushwhackers. We made frequent excursions across the mountains as far as McMinnville on the west, and Kentucky on the north. These trips were usually uneventful, save from an occasional shot from some mountain crag, the only effect of which was to keep the boys in line and prevent straggling.

At one time we even ventured to invade the dominions of Tinker Dave Beatty, the hero of the Calf-Killer.

During the early part of the war, it was a very common custom for the captains, when a fight was imminent or even apprehended, to make long-winded speeches to their companies, in which they reminded them of their lineage, and even appealed to their pride and patrotism. It was on this last trip, and on the soil of Kentucky, that the best and most effective speech I heard during the war was delivered by Captain Tom Brown, of Roane county.

Early one morning we received orders to mount and be ready to move at the sound of the bugle. There was something in the manner in which the order was given, and our location, which caused us to believe that the enemy was upon us. Capt. Tom rode to the front of his company, straightened himself in his stirrups, unsheathed his sword, and delivered himself as follows:

"Here we are, fellow soldiers, mounted upon our barb steeds. With the armor of death buckled around us. Looking for all the world, for all the world, for all the world like a passel of fox-hunters. Right face steady in ranks, and the first d---d man that makes a noise I will kill him on the spot."

The perporation was too much for the boys; it broke their risible strings and such a shout never went forth from so many throats on the soil of Kentucky. If there was any enemy in the neighborhood they immediately decamped, for after the most diligent search we were unable to find any.

Returning from this trip, we went into camps at Kingston, where we remained until October 20, when we were ordered to Knoxville to enforce the conscript law.

This we did in a most effective manner. We drove across the mountains, and into the federal ranks more soldiers in two weeks than forty federal recruiting officers could have enlisted in six months, and that too without adding a dozen good men to our army. Having performed this patriotic duty, we were ordered to Rogersville. At this place the Twelfth battalion perfected its organization by electing John R. Neal lieutenant-colonel, and Capt. Payne [Flavius J. Paine], major. The election of Capt. Neal colonel made a vacancy in our company, and I was elected third lieutenant. There had been one vacancy prior to this, by the resignation of W.N. King, which was filled by the election of Doc Hudson. We were here joined by the Twelfth Tennessee battalion, under the command of Major Day. The two battalions united constituted what was known as Rucker's legion and were attached to Pegram's brigade. This brigade was composed of Col. Ashby's Second Tennessee regiment, First Georgia regiment under Col. Morrison, First Louisiana under Col. Scott, Twelfth and Sixteenth battalions.

RAID INTO KENTUCKY

Gen. Pegram made a raid into Kentucky in March, 1863. We struck the enemy at Danville, and after a brisk fight we took the place and drove them toward Camp Dick Robinson. Gen. Pegram undertook by a byroad to cut them off from Camp Dick Robinson but on account of a heavy rain the march was retarded and night came before we reached the pike; and when we did it was so dark that part of our brigade fell in with, and marched side by side with the federals for a mile or more before the mistake was discovered. Neither side could boast of advantage gained by this dilemma. We got a good many prisoners, and I suppose they did the same, all of which were paroled.

The brigade remained in camp at Dick Robinson three or four days, during which time details were sent out for cattle. We then fell back through Lancaster, keeping our booty in front of us. On the retreat I had command of the rear guard, and orders to burn the bridges as I passed. This I found to be a very necessary precaution, as we were very closely pressed, and at Somerset were overtaken by a superior number, who took occasion to assert their superiority in a very unfeeling manner. We, that is the most of us, however, crossed the Cumberland river with the cattle; what became of them I know not.

LILLARD LETTERS

A large collection of letters and documents from the Lillard family was donated to the Tennessee State Archives in 1961. A few of the letters were published in 1975 by Stewart Lillard in his book ***Meigs County, Tennessee*** (reprinted 1982). All of the collection was microfilmed by the Archives so that it could be used for re-search purposes. The letters included here were transcribed from the microfilm.

An attempt has been made to identify the authors and some of the individuals mentioned in the letters. One of the problems has been that everyone is referred to as Brother or Sister when they actually were Brothers-in-Law or Sisters-in-Law.

John Mason Lillard and Newton Jasper Lillard were sons of James Lillard III and Mary (Sandusky) Lillard.

Col. John M. Lillard (1827 - 1863) was married in 1856 to Jennie Thomas of Ashe County, North Carolina. John served with the 26th Tennessee Regiment and participated in several battles, including Fort Donalson (wounded and taken prisoner), Murfreesboro, and Chickamauga, where he was mortally wounded.

Newton J. Lillard (1832 - 1905) was a Captain in the first company organized in Meigs County. They became Company I of Vaughn's Third Tennessee Regiment and took part in the first Battle of Manassas (21 July 1861). At the re-organization in 1862, Newton was elected Lt. Col. After the promotion of Col. Vaughn to Brigadier General, Newton became Colonel and commander of the Regiment, which was surrendered on 8 May 1865 in Washington, Georgia.

J. S. V. Lillard (1829 - 1908), another brother, also was a member of the 3rd Tennessee Regiment. Another brother of John M. and Newton, William, and his wife Julia were mentioned in several letters.

Crate Lillard (also referred to as Evie) wrote many letters to her brothers John and Newton. Other sisters mentioned were Mary E., wife of J.B. Boggess; Louisa E., wife of the Rev. Beriah Frazier; and Texannah (Tex), wife of William Stewart [see Stewart Letters].

William Lillard (Letter No. 15), a brother of James III, married Nancy Elder in 1820. Two of their sons, Francis and John M., were members of Company I, Third Tennessee Regiment. On 1 January 1861, John M. married Martha Martin.

Amanda C. Lillard and Elmira Lillard were daughters of William W. and Lucretia (Blevins-Thomas) Lillard. William W. was the son of John Lillard (another brother of James III) and Elizabeth Taylor Lillard (daughter of Robert and Catherine Sevier Taylor and sister of Peach Taylor). William W. Lillard was Captain of Company I, McKenzie's Fifth Tennessee Cavalry.

Lizzie King (Letter No. 49) was the daughter of Aaron and Martha Jane (Lillard) King.

William C. Rogers (Letter No. 55) probably was the son of William and Mary (Lillard) Rogers. Mary was the sister of James Lillard III. W. C. was a private in Company I.

Kate Leuty, daughter of Thomas and Esther (Eaves) Leuty, is discussed in the introduction to the Taylor, Cross, and Blevins Letters.

B. F. Taylor (Letter No. 9) was the son of Peach and Mary (Blevins) Taylor, and Isaac G. Cross was his brother-in-law (married to Mary Taylor). Both of them are discussed in the Taylor, Cross, and Blevins Letters.

David M. Blevins (Letter No. 4) was the son of James and Ruth (Rockhold) Blevins. He served throughout the war in the Third Tennessee Regiment, initially as 2nd Lieutenant and, after 1862, as Adjutant. Hugh T. Blevins, 2nd Sargeant in Company I, was a brother of David M., as was Alfred Blevins. He served 12 months as a Lieutenant in the 26th Tennessee Regiment and was then appointed Surgeon of the Third Tennessee Regiment by Colonel J.C. Vaughn.

William L. McKinley (Letter No. 10) was the son of John and Susanna (Locke) McKinley. He evidently did not join the army, but continued to serve as acting County Court Clerk throughout the war. His comments in the minute book are rather humerous, as there evidently were several times when he was the only one in Court.

Calvin C. Robeson (Letter No. 14), a school teacher, was married to Martha L. Guinn in 1850.

Mary E. Russell (Letter No. 72) was the daughter of William S. and Susan (Blevins) Russell. Three of her brothers served in Lillard's Company: Thomas J., Felix Grundy, and John T. Russell.

Samuel M. Cox, a private in Company I, was the son of Abraham and Celia (Collins) Cox.

LETTER NO. 1
A. COX TO SAM COX

Athens, Tenn
6th May 1861

Dear Sam

I write you from this place to ask you to see Thos Riggins whether he will come home or not. he intended as he told me yesterday that he woukd come on the train with me. he has not done so I want to know Whether he is comming or not. See him on the Subject and write me if he does not come home. I will send the papers he must Counsell that Land trade before he leaves, he said to me he would do so ask Nute to pass him or have it done on the road. I expect he has not the Money to pay passage and that accounts for him not coming write by retrurn Mail. Your Father, A Cox

- - - - - - - - - - - - -

LETTER NO. 2
JOHN M. LILLARD TO "SIR"

May the 10th 1861

Dear Sir

We received a letter from Tish & one from Callie in the last few days in which we learned all was well as usual at North Fork. We was very glad to hear it. Jennie is uneasy unless she gets a letter often. We are all well in this Country. I have been nearly laid up with a cold I have been exposed some helping Brother Newton off with his Company he is now at Knoxville with his Company of 80 men Nute is Captain, Sheriff Cross 1st Lt, D M Blevins 2nd Lt, Benj F Taylor 3rd Lt, S R Baldwin 1st Sgt, Frank Lillard 2nd Sgt. &c &c it is the finest Company I ever saw. to give you an idea of what kind of Material it is made of I will mention a few of the private and they are nearly all as of the same sort of material to wit, Rev B Frazier, Dr Galleher, J F Russell, Tom Russell, Frank McCorkle, Dick & Buck Stewart, J M & J B Boggess, Sam Cox, J S V Lillard, J M Lillard Jr, Jos Buckner Jr, Tom Sharp, Jo Moore &c &c in part. It is made up of the sons of our best families. They will organize a Regment at Knoxville and go to Virginia as is supposed. We will have 2 or 3 more Companies from this County if Necessary.

Well Tennessee legislature has formed a military League with the Confederate States, also declared her independence of the Lincoln government & addopted the constitution of the Southern Confederacy–the two last to be voted on by the people on the 8th day of June which will be ratified by the people by a large majority in fact in Middle & West Tennessee is now almost unanimous, here in East Tennessee there will [be] some opposition to it Andy Johnson is going round wherever they will let him speak defending the Lincoln government We can account for him & Maynard for if reports be true they both have sons in the service of the Lincoln government; I received by Tri Weekly paper from Nashville yesterday with all the proceeding & notes of our legislature on the subject and would send it to you but the only one here and every body anxious to see it I am glad to see the old North State [North Carolina] taking her true position. and I think if the whole south had done so at the first war would have been avoided but now it is impossible and it is fight or submit and we know what all true southerners will do in that event. My paper also has a telegram from Arkansas which is reliable that the Convention has passed an unconditional ordinance cutting loose from Lincoln & joining the south so old Abe will find somebody will be hurt if he Continues his plans of coercion & subjugation.

Well Crop look well wheat very promising corn coming up fine. Weather rather rainy & cool yet. I said all was well but Fathers health is very feeble again and left alone without son or son in law except me & Mr Stewart. I hope you will rite soon & often. Tish is waiting for her ant to come but she dont talk much like unless ma was to get worse or I go to the war.

We have a company called the home guard formed of old men Wm M Rogers Capt, Joseph McCorkle 1st Lt & R M McKenzie 2nd Lt who will attend to the Negroes and white men that take the Lincoln side in the struggle they furnish themselves at their own expense there will be about 3 such companies in the county give my love to all Yours truly Jno M. Lillard

- - - - - - - - - - - - -

LETTER NO. 3
SAM [COX ?] TO COL. LILLARD

Clinton, Tenn
May 13th [1861?]

Col. Lillard

Dick has been delayed in taking your things but will start this morning. Official vote Capt Boyd Co

Vaughn	88	
May	1	Col
Boyd	82	
Morgan	5	Lt Col
Lillard	4	
Morelock	81	
Haskins	7	Maj
McKamy	3	

There is no news here at all. All your boys are with the Regt excep two or three that are here caring for the Baggage in camps. The Conscription is suspended so says the Provost M By Order of Genl E K Smith He is Notifying the people of the fact has it placed on the door of his Office. I Created quite a sensation among the boys here and I expect it will do as much in Camps. I understand they will be dischargedible 6th June though I have it from no official authorities. Dr. McKenzie just from Knoxville says so. There is a very fine Georgia Regt of One Thousand men come here in the last few days. Morgan and his Cavalry are said to be on their road to this point part of his men are now in Knoxville I learn from passes. Yours as Ever Sam

- - - - - - - - - - - - -

LETTER NO. 4
D. M. BLEVINS TO N. J. LILLARD

Union, Tenn
May 14th 1861

Capt N.J. Lillard

Dear Sir I recd a few lines from I G Cross which informed me that Our redgement would not move for Some time we came here with the intention of not returning to Camps but armed to get on the Train at Union. One other thing the furlow that you Gave to us did us no good we had to pay $4.75 each for our passage here. We wish you to make some arrangement for us to Get to Camps without paying so much Money. Write to me by return mail and let me know what we should do.

Your True friend
D M Blevins

- - - - - - - - - - - - -

LETTER NO. 5
ISAAC G. CROSS TO JOHN M. LILLARD

Camp Cumming
May 19th 1861

Dr John M Lillard

Dear Sir I have arrived safe in Camp and found all the Boys well I had the pleasure of Capt F M Walkers Company from Athens up he was very glad to meet me and I was very glad to see him you may depend. He and J D Powell are both here with fine Companies. There is 15 companies here now 7 complete, viz, Ours Walkers, Powels, Matheus, Snaffle, Dills, Vaughns. I cannot tell when we will organizie I have seen Capt Powell since I came and also Vaughn & Key, they say that we will organize Tuesday next Powell Walker the Knoxville Guards and the Hawkins Boys have gone into Quarters to themselves, but I think the thing will be compromised and all of Lower E Tenn will go into one regiment and elect Walker Col. Vaughn told me since I came that he would give way to Walker and take the chances for Lieut Col I cannot say who will run for Maj I am told old Gus set Chattanooga in a blaze Foot and House are to Speak in Knoxville to morrow VanDike and Will Lowery spoke at Mouse Creek Yesteday it is said they did Some good. Write to me if you dont come up

Yours truly I G Cross

[the following letter was on the back of the Cross letter]

NEWTON LILLARD TO JOHN LILLARD

Dear Bro. I would have writtem you sooner but be assured all my time has been employed in seeing to the equipment of my Company and have almost got the same complete that is we are much ahead of all the others in that Respect. I has written you the proble Turn affairs will take here. I am quite east Let them go at the maj, if Either Cumming Vaughn or Walker is elected I would be glad all the Company from Lower east Tennessee would all be in one Regiment.

We are getting More Character every Day we remain here, from the fact that we are independent asking nothing only to be let a lone in our affairs and as far as military affaits we know about as much as any of them the Boy are all well most all want to come home & you cannot tell what anoyance it give me. Some of them go however come as soon as you can get your company made up use all your energy in the Matter make an effort and be here soon.

N. J. Lillard

P.S. May the 20th I forgot to correct the mistake in relation to the little Boy that got hurt here before the dificulty between Morgan & Douglas two men fell out, one threw a rock at the other and missed and hit the Boy that is the way the Boys tell me the Boy that caused the fuss was Morgans little Boy hollowing for Jeff Davis Mayberres House was burned here last night about 12 or 1 oclock. Suppose to be the work of an incendiary I taken a pile of men but got there two late to to render any assistance he saved all his plunder there is divers conjecture as to the firing of his house.

Yours &c I G Cross

- - - - - - - - - - - - -

LETTER NO. 6
JESSE MARTIN TO N. J. LILLARD

Goodfield, Tenn
May 24th 1861

Capt N J Lillard

Dear Sir I write to let you know Thos Riggins could not get his business setled in time to get back to Knoxville Sunday next he request me to write you he Could not Reach Knoxville before Tuesday or Wednesday next his business is of Importance.

Yours Respectfully Jesse Martin

P S We went to everone in the 2nd District to organize another Volunteer Company J M

- - - - - - - - - - - - -

LETTER NO. 7
AMANDA C. LILLARD TO N.J. LILLARD

At home
May the 28th 1861

Brave and Gallant Cousin

I resume my pen in han this morning to respond with your ever welcomed letter. But think it exceedingly doubtful whether or not I shall make it worth your attentions For my mind is as wandering as I imagin the mind of and Arab in the Desert of Arabia. I received your letter the 27th which I read with great pleasure. Was glad to her that you and company was in good health. I have attended Sabbath School ever Sabbath since you left Meigs. We meet at eight O clock and read untill ten O c. Which afterwards spend an hour or so in praremeeting praying for peace to be restored again to our once happy Country. I honestly believe if ever ther was a company saved without the loss of a man by the prayers of the people it will be the Gallant little band that left Decatur. I was over at Decatur yesterday found all the people as well as common. But very loansum. The girls looks like boiled cracklings. We have had one wedding since you left. Miss J Wood to her William Smith. But I dont expect we will have another shortly. For all that the girls try to get in an old split bonnet the oldest one they can find and it pulled down over their eyes. Poor girls what boys are left here the girls are quarling which will have them for their beau. So luck would have it I caught a beau the other day he is smart and a good looking youth. I asshure you I tried to treat him like a Lord to get him to com back again. I was down on Goodfield the other day found John and family well. Went from Johns to the Coxs. There I met Dr Gilbert, Dr Everett, and Mr Abe Denton. They were blazing away about the Election to a great extent. Abe Denton said they had pestered him so much that he didnot know Calico from Muslin. Mr Cox is still for the Union as strong as ever. James Martin landed home last Thursday he says ther is a grate excitement in Texas. John Martin is married he married a young Lady by the name of Fisher. Her weight is one hundred and 65 lbs. Brother Hugh writes that he and Rices girls were at the wedding had quite a glorious time.

Newt I am a fraid that we will have to confine Miss Mollie Russell when she heard what you wrote back in Tenn McCorkles letter concerning herself. She went out of one spell in to another So Says reports. I have enjoyed my self only tolerable for the last three or four weeks Indeed I have not heard a young Lady laugh a bove their breath in three weeks. I slept in a room with a number of young Ladies the other night and ever onceed and a while I could her one talking in her sleep about her Sweet heart it was discerting to listen at her. I was happy to her that the young Ladies of Knoxville presented you a flag and supplied you all with Testaments and the most of you with nice boquets. But I knowed the Decatur jents would attract the attention of any young Ladys that the grate King of the day ever Dawned on. I am sorry to inform you that we are a bout to loos one of our Meigs County boys. Mr Andrew McKenzie is lying at the point of death the Doctor think it improbable for him to recover.

I saw Dear Tenney Mc last week I tell you she looks cacy. Newt you must quit dreaming of your Lady Love for if it --?-- you like it does me when I dream a bout my Spence you do not feel very eaty next morning. Donot let any husband lay out in the rain and get rusty for he looks bad enough at his best. Give my love to Vern, John and Frank Lillard. Pinch Jessee Guinn, J. A. Love and S. M. Cox for me. Give my love to all enquiring friends if I have any. Write me who you are messing with. Write soon give me all the news if you have time. I will take delight in answering your letters. The best I can [ink blob] shal not promas to interest you in either of them unless something strange takes place. Tell each and every one to be good boys. Mary N. sends her love to you and Sam Cox. Tell Mr Edward Hodges that Miss M D Blevins is still on the carpet. As ever your unflinching Cousin

Amanda C. Lillard

P.S. I am tickeled at this time A young Lady past along the road I tell you she looked Picturesque, all but what it lacks.

- - - - - - - - - - - - -

LETTER NO. 8
S. M. COX TO NEWTON J. LILLARD

Clinton Tenn
May 28 [1861?]

Col Neut J Lillard

Dear Friend There is no news here more than you have already heard. Jackson has taken Winchester with 4000 prisoners Hurt(?) & Marshal was repulsed in green Briar Co with a loss of 39 men Jackson got all Any supplies at W.

My health has been very bad for several days I have been suffering from the piles in fact I can hardly walk at all and have leav for a week hope I will get better soon. Bot Allen killed Smith Hutton and has run off Dont put out your Reward for me as I am here under orders of Smith. All well at home Your Friend

S. M. Cox

The Conscript has suspended without Specification and it is a question whether we will be kept in service or not. I think we will if they can possibly. The appointment time has run out for Conscripting and no State has taken any step that I can learn to enforce it I fear it will cause some desturbance before it ends Harris proposes to Receive 12 month troops as Many as will Offer. I Cant understand the figureing in this matter There is no one here but Dick and Zek Massengil and they are neither of them fit for duty you can tell Capt Cross so he May know how to Make his report on 31st and there will have to be two men here or all the things will be stolen S. M. C.

- - - - - - - - - - - - -

LETTER NO. 9
B F TAYLOR TO ESTEEMED FRIEND

Linchburg,
June 6th 1861

Esteemed friend

With much pleasure I this morning avail myself of the opportunity of drafting you a few lines to let you know that we have landed safely in Linchburg. We got to camps about 6 O Clock yesterday morning found all the boys in tolerable health and a comfortable place to stay; each mess has a small house to stay in and a poarch extending from one to the other. We are much better situated than we were in Knoxville with the exception of something to cook in. I suppose you have already learned that the redgement left Knoxville on Sabbath at 10 O Clock which gave them one day the start of us that left Decatur last Sabbath evening. We lacked but one hour of catching them at Bristol as they had some bad luck on the road about 30 or 40 miles above Knoxville, none of the Decatur Guards were hurt they all belonged to Vaughns Company I believe.

I learned this morning that 2 or 3 of them were dead. The boys that were with me at home laid over at Bristol from 6 O clock Monday evening until half past 7 next morning. We came through without any accident hapening to any of us and I believe it is because we are more civil and moral than the rest of the company. The Decatur Guards have always tried to be as moral as posible and hope we will remain so.

I do not know when we will leave this place perhaps in 1 or 2 days, we were mustered into the service of the Condeferate States this morning for 12 months unless sooner discharged. We will start to Manases Junction between now and next Monday the place of the last reported fight that you had received when we were at home, we have a report since I have been writing of a fight at 2 or 3 points yesterday and the day before, the particulars of the fight we have not received. We will receive them tomorrow and I will write to some one in Decatur. I will not write any more at present and write more the next time. Nute and the boys are all well except bad colds. Tell the girls houd for me and give them my best love. I remain as ever;

Your best friend

B F Taylor

P S I conversed with a man from Texas last Tuesday that knew your brother William he had seen him a few days ago he was well the gentleman came on the trane with us from Bristol to Abingdon. We have also learned that Stephen A Douglas died last Monday. You need not write to me until I write to some one in Meigs and let you know where to write to; then want you to write immediately.

Your Schoolmate B F

\- - - - - - - - - - - - -

LETTER NO. 10
W. L. McKINLEY TO N. J. LILLARD

Decatur, Tenn
June 10th 1861

Capt N J Lillard & Co

Dear Friend I answered Lieut Cross letter and directed it by his request to Richmond Virginia by return mail But believing that he intended Lynchburg instead of Richmond I again write seeing that you will remain some time perhaps at the former place before leaving for the latter. This leaves us generally well so far as I know with some slight exceptions and slight indispositions. In my Letter to Cross I stated the death of Andrew J McKenzie which you will all doubtless see in due time. You will also learn from said letter many facts which remain unchanged, And I will now give you some other Items not therein Contained. On last saturday our State Election passed off and quietly too. Our majority is 245 votes for separation & nearly the same for Representation, A few less. I have the Poll from all but the 1st District and have a verbal report from it which I consider reliable although I would fair believe it otherwise. Here is the Vote

	Dist 1	2	3	4	5	6	7	8	
Separation	15	72	68	128	54	72	57	23	485
Representation	15	71	68	126	54	72	51	23	
No Separation	125	44	47	3	00	17	1	16	253
No Representation	125	44	47	4	00	17	1	16	___
									736

This statement is from the Poll Books except as to the 1st Dist, which on Report as above stated. Rhea County I am informed will separate by nearly 200 votes. I have no other news only from 3 Districts in Roane which gave secession majorities in the County will go for the Lincoln Union. The 3rd (Thomas) District in McMinn went for session by 8 votes & in February last was 23 against. About the action of our County Court &c you will learn fully from my letter to Cross.

Mr Jasper W Lillard furnished the House of S M Cox & Co with one Keg Powder which we attached and appropriated to the use of the Home Guards. We also served Messers Howell & McCorkle in like manner as to Lead. Capt A F Boggess' Company have arranged to leave here on Thursday next. The Rhea County Company is not yet Organized but they will be soon no doubt. Dr Blevins tells me that Jno Crawford or Jeffrey West will probably be Capt of the Company. Captain Jesse Martin is Making no movements that I know of to leave now. Capt R S Baldwins Cavalry Company will likely not leave until late in the summer or fall but about that I do not know.

We will now anxiously await the returns of our late Election and the action of our Legislature which will meet on next Monday (17th). We have no doubt the state by her vote is virtually now in the Southern Confederacy; but do not know the fact. Should she possibly have acted otherwise we are a ruined people in Tennessee and when you return you need not expect to see me here. Abel, Everett & Jno Ingle were the 3 who voted for the Lincoln Union in our District. In the 2nd, 3rd, 4th & 7th there were registers kept showing who voted for separation &c & who the Contrary Col Abraham Cox stands promnent Amongst the Lincoln Sympathisers in the 3rd District. I mention him because I am advised that he is writing you to the effect that he is as good a Southern man as any &c, which is false. In making this statement I expressly reserve the feelings of my young & patriotic Friend S.M. Cox now one of us and every has been. And I would further remark that the time now is when we must ignore Consanguinity and affinity so far as this war is concerned and recognize only Southern Rights men as our Relatives. They are My Brothers.

I think the state will go out of this unholy Union by from 30,000 to 50,000 votes. I hope more but it may be less. Business here is dull and Money scarce. We also elected John Gourley J.P. in this District over I.S. Binyon that leaves the Town without a Justice of the Peace. Tell Jno T. Russell that I have issd 1 Marriage License since 2nd May last for Wm H. Wilson to marry Elizabeth Tankersley. Write "abody" and let me know the points as you see them "sticking out"

Very Truly Yours
W. L. McKinley

- - - - - - - - - - - - -

LETTER NO. 11
CRATE LILLARD TO N. J. LILLARD

Meadow Springs
June 16th 1861

Dear Bro,

I received your very welcome letter which gave me much pleasure to learn that were well. Bro. John started to Knoxville last Thursday. Miss Kate Lock presented them with a flag. Jennie took it very hard about his leaving. A suppose they had 72 mustered into Service. Jennie Peak stayed here last Wednesday night all her conversation is about politics. Sister Mary is down here going to stay two or three weeks.

Bro Jasper left here Yesterday morning Says he expects he will start to Charleston this week. Uncle William Rogers started after Lizzie Sunday. We have not received any letter from her since yours came.

Jennie is staying here now, she expects to go to N. C. in a few weeks.

Papa has finished harvesting, says the wheat is very good. Papa's health is tolerable. we succeeded in keeping him out of the field. Cal S. Peak didnot go in Boggess Company. He & Dr. Galaher are trying to make up another company the Dr aiming to be Capt & Cal 1st Leut wouldn't you like to have the Dr for a Capt. The family are all well, there has been a little sickness in Decatur.

I suppose you have heard that Andrew McKenzie is dead. The churches have prayer meetings for the Vols. I have not time to write more although I would like to. Buck has written to Bill and is waiting to take the letter to the P. C. May God bless and protect thee my dearly loved Bro. With many heartfelt wishes for your future success I remain as ever

Your loving Sis
Crate

P.S. All the family sends love give mine to Vern Frazier & Boggess relatives & friends. Crate

- - - - - - - - - - - - -

LETTER NO. 12
JOHN M. LILLARD TO JENNIE LILLARD

Camp Cummings
July 3rd 1861

My dear wife

I have delayed writing a few days so I could write you fully— Well we are now fully in the service, with a Company of 80 and more coming. We will I think have 100 by the time our Regment is full— efforts still making to raise Companies in Meigs but will not succeede. Jessee Martin made a fail and told his men to come with me if they wanted to 3 or 4 of them come with me I went home immediately after I got back and others went home too and we brought up and mustered in 21 more men, others will be in in a day or two the Rhea County Company set tomorrow to start I fear they will not get here with a full Company as they are riding in Meigs all the time to get men. I hope they will get a Company if they would get it from their own County but I dont want anymore men from Meigs County, as we now have two Companies from Meigs and furnished some men for 3 other companies.

Capt Boggess & myself are both run down getting up our Company, arming equipping uniforming it &c as it is such a hard matter here to get what we have to have. Camps, Camp equipage, Clothing, uniforms, arms &c &c. We are not complete yet, but are in a condition to live while we remain in quarters but not prepared to march yet but will be ready by the time our Regment is organized. The 2nd Regment is gone to Cumberland Gap to cut off the supply of arms that Andy Johnson is sending through Kentucky. I understand they left the Ohio River by way of Lexington for Cumberland Gap. Where we will go to is not known if the Lincoln men attact anything as they threaten we will doubtless be kept in E Tenn for a time.

I found all well at home. Liz King had not got home, all well at Fathers they all sent their love to you & Tom— tell Tom he must not forget Pa give my love to Ma and all the rest I had hoped to get a letter from you by this time so I would know whether the mail is running or not. I will enclose this to Tish, our Company is all well except a few cases of measels. My health is good as usual only tired—

Blevins had moved I took dinner there Sunday Viney put the big pot in the little one Mose went down & brought Lize and the children up to Fathers. I do hope you will take care of yourself & Tom. Until my time is out you will have Ma to see too which will occupy your time and keep off the blues— be sure and write me often if the mail is running, as you know how anxious I will be to hear from you— Write where Rews(?) Company is and what other companies are gone or going. hoping to hear from you soon. I am as ever your own dear Husband until death

Jno M Lillard

- - - - - - - - - - - - -

LETTER NO. 13
JOHN M LILLARD TO CAPT N.J. LILLARD

Camp Cummings
July 5th 1861

Dear Bro

I hope you will pardon me for not writing more often. We have been so busy as you know that I have not had hardly time to sleep or eat we are now nearly complete equipped got part of our uniforms, and our arms our company now numbers 82 and likely to be 100 in a few days. The companies here are Capt Boggess from Meigs, Capt Allen from Cocke, Capt McCounel from Gainger, Capt McClung from Knox, Capt Battles Mustered in at Johnston Station & be here probably to day. Capt Crawford from Rhea is looked for to day, Capt Bridgman Cavalry looked for from Bledsoe, Capt Gillespie infantry from Hamilton looked for soon, and I forget. it is thought our Regt will fill very soon

I was down home few day ago, all well Thos Blevins has moved to our place & cut the wheat & clover, & I rented him the place for 2 years hope the arrangement will suit you— Fathers health is better, wheat good corn looks promising— I took Jennie & Tom to N C tell all the boys their folks are are well in Meigs Give my Complements to all the Company tell them We hope to be with you Soon if Andy Johnson dont get us into a fight in E Tennessee We have a game Company, but 4 with me out of the 3rd district, 2 McClenahan, Bishop & John Poplin. We have a game Company, all good companys & large in number except McClung of Knox between 50 & 60, it seems Jordan is a hard read in Knox, Capt Boggess send his Compliments to all of you. Jesse Martin failed to get a Company ful & told them all to come that wanted to 4 of them come up with me. Dr Gillespie tells me just now several other Companies are looked for to Day or tomorrow. the Second Regt & 3 companies of Cavalry gone to Cumberland Gap and Wheelers Gap— to intercept arms said to be on their way from Cincinnati to Union Men of East Tennessee = I will write again in a few days please write me ---?--- Give my Compliments to all

Your Affect Bro
John M Lillard

- - - - - - - - - - - - -

LETTER NO. 14
C. C. ROBESON TO N. J. LILLARD

Decatur, Tenn
July the 7th 1861

Mr N. J. Lillard

Dear Friend Your favor of the 30th June came to hand yesterday, and I assure you, was read with no small degree of interest. It finds us all in good health But sorry to know that so many of our boys were sick with Measles and as supposed by your Dr. two cases of Billious Fever. I hope they will all soon recover and be restored to their true position; as defenders of our Common Country and common Liberties. While you are toiling and laboring, and suffering in the defence of our Country; let the thought that you have the best wishes and good feelings of all your friends you have left behind inspire you with much zeal and patience to forego all the dificulties and hardships of which of necessity always accompany Camp life. Dont think I would impose these things upon you of choice or desire; be that far from me; but on the contrary; were it possible to do so, I would carry you through your whole Campaign, on downy beds; but these things are impossible Then as I and you know, these hardships must be born. I know you will bear them like good soldiers as Representatives on the Battlefield of a brave and free people.

The Union men in McMinn Co. are also opposed to the Secession of E Tenn except G W Bridges, McGaughey and a few to contemptable, Abolitionists. Some, I learn are taking Strong ground against it. I think the Union Shriekers will soon explode, and I dont want to be close by for there will be a bad stink certain. We hear some pretty bad news from some of the boys. They complain of the fair and clothing and the impression here is that they are almost suffering for something to eat and what they have is bad. Now N.J. I am sorry to hear that Sort of News and I have no doubt but that they give the best information they can but I think I can account for that. I expect that such might be the case when they were on forced marches perhaps or that by some disappointments your provisions had not come in time or been delayed. That is the construction I put on it for the benefit of the women here who are taking on considerably about it. If it is so that forced marches or delays have prevented your provisions from comming on you would render great comfort to the good women and men too to write us and let us know it. Tell the boys all about it. But this not all the bad effect it is likely to produce here. I fear it will have the effect to keep some from Volunteering who would otherwise go. Report says the Southern Army is suffering for provisions and clothing. I hope it is no so and I hope the evil will soon be remedied. N.J. tell them to bear their afflictions patiently and be assured there are warm hearts here for you. They no doubt suffer but suffering must necessarily accompany a Camp life. If necessary require it Meigs can send some Flouer Meal and Bacon and they will do it too, nothing surer. N.J. I speak of these things so that you may know the effect such reports are likely to have here. Your quick perception will enable you to see it at a glance. You see I must close and will write to J H G & others. Write me often. I am as ever your affectionate friend C. C. Robeson

- - - - - - - - - - - - -

LETTER NO. 15
WILLIAM LILLARD TO F LILLARD, JOHN M. LILLARD, AND N.J. LILLARD

Decatur, Meigs Cty
July the 8th 1861

Dear Sons & Neffew

I received your kind & affectionate Letter dated July the 2nd & we received it on the 6th of the same inst. We was all glad to hear from you & to learn that you & all the boys from Meigs was a live & none dead. We are all well at this time Except my self I have been sick for the last three weeks first took the Disintary then the piles cant Set to write this letter with out a pillow under me But getting better all of your conection is well.

Nothing strange has happened since you left here only Decatur is one of the lonsomest little town that you ever seen all buisness stoped or nearly so except the Mail days all those that have friends with you or in the army will attend on mail days to get the News. We are all anctious to hear from you & all the boys. I want you Capt Nute, B F & John all write often you dont now how much good it Does the old men & old ladies to hear from you Single boys but I dont here the young Ladies say or Inquire much a bout you.

Dr John M Lillard & A Boggess is at Knoxville with ther Company. John has been at home since he & the Company Went to Knoxville all well he expects to be with you as soon as the nature of the case will permit. After John & Boggess went to Knoxville with the company some days after there went on from Here or our Men to Knoxville to Join Boggess Company & Johns— John Martin, Henry Lankford, Chub Baker, John Robinson, & perhaps others I dont recolect all that went & more talks of going.

Dr Galleher & Maj Peak is trying to make up a Company in which they have got a part of one. George W. McKenzie & Robert S. Baldwin Is trying to make up a Company to follow on But I think they will succeed in making one Them sort of Men is getting scarce in Meigs I mean men that will be receved in the redgment. Crawford Capt of Rhea Cty left with his company From Lockes Ferry by steam boat bound for Knoxville on the 4th of July this is a day that will be recollected by generations to come as well as the present one.

Her I will give you some admonition you have left Home to mantain this libterty that our forefathers Bled for and I want you Capt Lillard & My sons & Neighbours one and all to maintain this freedom That was garanteed to us in the year 1776.

I do not want to hear of one of the Meigs boys a being shot in the back, tho I am not affrade of that. Franklin & John & John in perticular Obey them that have the rule over you and Thereby you will fare better in Camps & your Captain will feel proud of your acts.

The wheat crops is harvested some time ago they were not as good as was expected but a good average crop eary(?) the same Oats good Corn crops at this time looks very promising but the dry time Is yet to come. I have some oats yet to cut but I expect to get done to morrow or next day.

No hands to hire & when you come a cross a man That will hire you Must pay him $1.50 per day, I have cut part of my rye & all of the oats my self & sick all the time but had to do it or loose my Grain. My Ear has not run any matter hardly Sence you left & therefour has not pained me much. Lane of McMinn Hurst of McMinn Dunn of Polk all candidates composed of McMinn Polk & Meigs. I understand that this man Dunn is uncle to the one that run for aturney general.

We are not done laying by corn yet, but Nearly so. No thrasher gone out yet & therfour No buiscuit to et got corn bread a plenty. Boys your aunt Avy Cate sends her best respects to you & all the boys she was acquainted with also Wests wife Adiline & Mrs McCorkle all present while I am trying to write to you.

John your wife is still living with me and is Satisfied to live with me as far as I know But appears to be uneasy about your wellfar & says She wants to see you the worst kind And wants you to come home but I think that Is a bad chance till you are discharged.

Marthey sends her best love to you & Frank Your Mothers health is a bout the same as when you left. She says if she was a man she would be with you to help slay the lincolnites.

Capt Nute Frank & John take good care of your Selves & dont expose your selves nomore than you can help Your uncle Dock & aunt polly(?) Sends their best respects & love to you.

Nothing more at this time but remain your Affectionate Father & Mother & wife. Farewell I will write.

Wm Lillard, Nancy Lillard, Martha Lillard

- - - - - - - - - - - - -

LETTER NO. 16
JOHN M. LILLARD TO JAMES LILLARD

Camp McGennis,
Fentress County, Tenn
July 12th 1861

Dear Father

I avail Myself of the opportunity to drop you a line by the man that brought Capt Lowry out from Athens. We are entirely cut off from Mails here and have only to send by chance. There is 4 Companies here to wit Capt Lowry of McMinn, Capt Rowan Cavelry from Monroe, Capt Allen from Cocke & Capt Boggess from Meigs. We are here to guard the passage of arms or amunition through the gap to the Lincoln men. They are verry mad about it and threaten to fight we came verry near having a verry fuss with them at Montgomery Allens Company & ours were together & Rowan & Lowrys a few days ahead of us they say no other troops shall pass, and we may have trouble yet I feel very much mortified that we have to be stuck out here to guard against danger from our own Citizens, instead of going to Virginia but so it is— We had a very serious march from Knoxville 91 miles in 5 days our Company stood it well 5 took the measels on the way but are getting well— Say to their folks that McClanahan Bishop Poplin J M Atchley Daniel Atchley Chub Baker Henry Lankford Jacob Smith John C Martin Hugh Tillery Prior Atchley Mart Ward all in my region are well. Jacob Smith & Chub Baker took the measels but are getting about again. I stood my tramp tolerable well I give out one evening in my left heel string how long we will stay here I cant say but hope to be releved soon by Middle Tennessee troops. We have fine water good shad &c. We are on the 3 forks of Wolf about half way from Imitown(?) to Uncle Emanuel Sanduskys I learn all of our kin in Wayne are Union but I dont know whether to go to see them or not it is only 9 or 10 miles— it is given up that our company can out march any company in the service and am proud to say we have less trouble with them than any company I ever saw so far. I do not know whether it is worth wile for you to write or not unless you have a chance. tell May Boggess to write if any of the stock drivers pass as it will be the only chance. I know of no mails here. I will try and keep you informed of our moves. please write Bro Nute or enclose this letter to him as I have no chance to write to him. Remember me to all

Your afft son
Jno M Lillard

- - - - - - - - - - - - -

LETTER NO. 17
AMANDA C. LILLARD TO N. J. LILLARD

Cold Water
July 18th 1861

Loving Cousin

I have just been cheered by the arrival of the precious little messenger which you so kindly commissioned a few days ago, To bear to me the endearing truth that I was still remembered by the absent one. And as a proof of the welcome reception it met with. Yep Cous. Your letters are dear visitors since they seem to add new life to my being and lift in to sum extent out of trouble. Your letter were received cordially by all of our little household. Yours came to hand a few hours ago, which found are all in tolerable good health. I can say to you that I am as well to day as heart can wish, hoping I may continue so while the war question is kept up as sichness and trouble is more than I can well bare.

We have some two or three cases of sickness that I know of in Meigs; which is Aunt Ann Blevins and Mr William Eves two children which is and has been bad and very bad at that. I have not heard from either of them to day it may be –?– of them are dead by this time as the Dr had almost gave them up to die yesterday; with these exceptions the people are well in her --?-- go so far as I am able to hear from. I was over at Decatur last Saturday and Sunday went with the expectation of seeing Mr Frazier but didnt see him as he and wife had gone to Rhea Co which I regret very much as I wanted to talk with him conserning the time you have had since you left Tennessee. But I reckon I shall not have the opportunity of so doing as it is raining and a bad looking day. Your Father is or was in better health last Sabbath than common but Looks very bad, he was able to attend meeting on Saturday and Sunday which was held by the baptist; had very good preeching. A man by the name of Holt preeched two Sermons. A man I no nothing of. The girls of Decatur seem very lonesome; Indeed it is a dreary looking place to what it once was. And I fear it will ever continue so. Know merry voice is heard there now. Decatur reminds me very much of geardens I have saw without flowers a bower without a bird and a bird without a song. I assure you fun her is down below zero all seem to have lost their laughfing faculties. I wish it could be otherwise as it is a task for me to live without Laughfing and a very heavy one at that. Cousin I can give you some encouragement in regard to Miss R. I suppose Sallie Russell has ent her out captivated Mr Abe by some means or other why this is so I cannot tell. I guess your few words which you send back to her has filled ever crevis in her heart. On hearing them I expect she discarded the above mentioned Gent. My dear Lizzie had not arrived home Sunday evening though I hope she has come by this time as they were Looking for and expecting her home this week. Tell her Sweethearts I will kiss her as many times as they want me to for them. I will kiss Little Mollie as you requested for she is very dear to me. I do think she has made the best remark a bout Lincoln I ever herd I liked to have split my side laughfing at it; I wish I could tell you the joke as I know it would amuse you very much. I asshure you the death of J A Love is very much lamented I learned from Miss Kate Leuty that his Sister was taking his death very heard, and for my part I esteemed him highly as a gentleman and School mate. Though the soil of Va has made his bed far from home I do humbly trust peace is his pillow, Heaven his home. I was very sorry to hear so many of your Company has been sick but hope that they will get over their sickness without the loss of another man. I was glad to hear of your bravry with Gen Patterson. Us girls can and will bost of our Southern boys having such noble hearts, think to much of us to place us in front of battle. I suppose the Northern troops are going to place the women and children in front when tha go to fight our gallant Southern Soldiers; and well they may for I think they will need all the force they can get and then not win the prize. May the God of battle guard and protect all who arm themselves in defending our Suny South. O I do wish I could see you to day in company with all of my dear cousins, how can I pass off twelve mounths without seeing you. And in all probability not then; as death is a brod in our land but hope it will not over take you while you are far from home. Though I am in a Tennessee Elevated land and deep water separates us far apart to day my heart and prays are with you all. I must close for the present as I have all ready arrayed your patients with such trifling stuff. Say howdy to all the connection. Tell Frank and Vern Lillard I would like to have a few words from them. Out of 18 cousins I donot get letters from but two,which is yourself and Cousin Frank Taylor and I have written to nearly every one of them. It may be that they have never received them. Tell my cousins not to be a feared to write me if I cannot get many no other way. I will get me a bunch of ax handles as did Bowlin, But if they were all to write none would I esteem more than you and Frank Taylors. Kiss Dave and Hugh Blevins for me. I intend writing to them once more and see if they will answer my letters. I shalnot render no excuse for this letter as you can easly see my vocabulary was drained to the dregs before commencing to write. My Love to all the boys for I love them dearly. Write me when ever you have good time so as to write long letters. I have got 65 cts yet and when that gives out I will try to get more as I Love to get and write Letters. I would have sent this by mail but Frazier can take it much safer. Rest assured that I am Your cousin and friend. Amanda C. Lillard

- - - - - - - - - - - - -

LETTER NO. 18
JOHN M. LILLARD TO N. J. LILLARD

Camp McGennis
July 24th 1861

Capt N J Lillard

Dear Bro I drop you a line in Atchley. I am well and all our Company except Measels, had about 20 cases lost none yet— Our Company Numbers 94, still coming in. We have a fine Company and We are now pretty well drilled. We will have fighting here I think Kentucky I fear will be another Maryland I had hoped to go to Virginia to fight side by side with you but duty calls and we must obey I will write you fully soon if any chance to do so I have had no letter from you or from Decatur since we left Knoxville over 3 weeks ago this is an important Gap & will be hotly contested if Kentucky fights for Lincoln but thank God Kentucky is now for making fighting men for us & will furnish as many for the South as for the north in any event Col Hudleston of Overton County who was raising a Company in Overton was shot on the road 12 miles from here yesterday. We bury him to day with Military honor. This may commence the fight and we will have a hot time— only a --- [line too dim to read]--- Cant you drop me a line to father & perhaps they can send it to me. My love to all your Company. Your Afft Bro

Jno M Lillard

P S My friends are runing my name for Colonel & I believe they are going to elect me. I do not Care Much As I am attached to my position & Company J M L

- - - - - - - - - - - - -

LETTER NO. 19
JENNIE LILLARD TO NEWTON J. LILLARD

North Fork
August 8th '61

My Dear Brother

Your very welcome letter of 9th July was received a few days ago, it had been a long time coming but was very gladly received nevertheless.

I thought when I left home I would write to you frequently but I have had so much trouble & been confined to a sick room so much I know if you had known the circumstances you would not have expected me to write.

My dear Mother is gone Nute, gone to be with the angels in heaven. She was very low when we got home and only lived two weeks died on the 11th July her last words were those of confidence & rejoicing that her sufferings were over. Our home is very Sad & lonely now home only in name to me not in reality it seems like joy or gladness never can came to it anymore.

Sister Lizzie Worth & sister Mira my Brothers wife have bothe been sick for some time, but are mending slowly & I trust will be well soon again.

I get very few letters from the Dr & they are a long time coming he was in Fentress [County, Tenn.] the last time I heard from him & well, but not very well pleased at the idea of having to stay there he wants to go to Va where all the soldiers want to go now. Were you in the Great battle at Manassas. I read the papers with their lists of killed & wounded for a few days with a beating heart for hear I would find familiar names.

I had several relations from Grayson county Va killed & wounded Capt Hale for one was killed. I was not much acquainted with any of them. I have noticed in the papers that Gen Johnson did not take all his command to Manassas & I have imagined you were among what was left at Winchester however if you were there I trust you & your brave boys escaped injury. I was distressed to hear you had lost two of your company from sickness.

I have only had one letter from Decatur since I left, there were two or three weeks here that we only had two or three mails, the contractors were Union men E Tennesseans & contrary & mean as those men always are

they would stop a week occasionally when they thought people wanted the news right bad We are only six miles from the Tenn line here consequently close to the tory hot bed, though there are some true southern folks there as lives in the land. You probably noticed about the Taylorsville folks shooting the confederate flag off the Virginia stage this summer, a few days after that hapened I had a cousin coming home from Abingdon where she had been at school, on the same stage that the flag had been shot from, she wore a flag in her hat & when she got out on the post office steps she called their attention to it & said she had heard they were fond of shooting confederate flags there & told them to shoot that if they dared. These same Johnson folks threaten to come over here & shoot the flag here, we all send them word to come on they shall have a warm reception. I hear all the little boys that were large enough to go to the election voted in E Tenn last week. Tom is well & growing fast has better health this summer than he has ever had. . . .
[remainder of letter missing] [Jennie Lillard?]

- - - - - - - - - - - - -

LETTER NO. 20
N. J. LILLARD TO SISTER

Fairfax C H Va
August 10th 1861

Dear Sis, et al

I again write you Knowing you would be anxious to hear how bro was. I taken him to Manassas on the 7th Inst to the Medical bord but could not get a discharge for him he is much better to Day. I am enclined to think that homesickness is the greatest ailment. You know how low spirited he gets when sick. I do not think he is dangerous or has ever been, but he cannot hear well and is not fit for guard duty, of right. If he get worse I will write you. We have find times here if it was not for such hard guard & Pickett duty But notwithstanding the health of the Co is improving we now have only four men on the sick list, and none of them with anything Serious. I cannot tell how long or how Soon we may Stay or have to move, If we remain here, we have good Camp Ground, good water & Enough to eat, But hard Drill & heavy guard duty, yet we do not complain for we expected to encounter them before we left home, Yet we did not think or emagine that Civil War would be in E T I had thought so I should never have Left, yet if they do rebel I hope that we may be sent home to service. I should have regretted to have fought them three months ago But how If they open the fight which I consider they virtually have, and there is no doubt that our regment would be more effective than any other troops that could be sent there, why dont you write me every week I know Vern Frazure & myself write you each once a week I would write something about the battle but you have accounts over and again and it would only be repitition. I have written a great many Letters; this is 3rd one to neight and still I am behind six or seven Letters.

Well Sis we are at Fair Fax Court House If you will turn to the Revolution history and see how & when this place was layed off and who by, and what movement engagements and being once the Home of the Great Washington you then Can imagine with what interest I stroll over town looking Up all these places of note, & intrest So never tire of asking questions &c. the Country is level for miles presenting a pleasing appearance on either side of Montain Rang distance Six or seven mile yet destruction meet us on every hand where the Yankees have been it was no doubt their whole aim was to plunder or steal rapen & distruction worse if Possible than the Wild Indians or the Uncivilized Arab. Yet we have men in our midst (I mean in Tenn) who sympathyse who would give aid & protection to such vandals & fiends. I cannot give any allowance to them for I must Confess that every thing proven to me that it is not an error of the heart But the wickedness that has long existed therein and it must have some place to oos out. Yet I had rather they would go into the army of the corrupt government now dictating to the world what is most proper and right for to be done. I like manliness in all things let them come out and declare what they want and what they intend doing in the event their demands are not granted, or by volunteering or enlisting in the army of their glorious union, supporting their principal with firmness, promptness & boldness, Nay they prefer to work in the dark and it may be well enough for I greatly fear that when they kick off their mortal Call that they will still have to work in the same dingy atmosphere.

We meet with universal kindness from the Ladies of Va they despence hospitalities with great grace and tenderness healing Soldiers with Care & kindness, seeming never to tire doing for them. Those who Bro is boarding with are very kind endeed I almost regret having him from the fact they will spoil him, I have not heard from Miss Hallie Morrison I presume she got home when the northern troops made their advance to Manassas how did you spend your visit to Cleveland I hope it was one of pleasure did you see my Sweetheart while on your visit., what is Mahala Elder doing I think she might write me a Letter, and tell me whether she still is Loving J D yet or not. When you see Sue Davis tell her she must not forget me in my absence for well She would marry if she was not ashamed to bring suffering. Tell Tech & Bill Stewart I wrote them a few lines several days ago would be glad to hear from them Just now say to Lee I Recd few lines will try write her soon say to her to Kiss Jenny for me have you heard from Sister Jennie since she has gone do you get any Letters from Bro Bill & Sister Julia if so are they still at Victoria.

Tell Aunt Racheal Howdy say to her bill has been an excellent boy as he ever has been & I cannot see how I can get along without him I will send him home to see them about Christmas if Possible, Tell all the servants

Howdy, would be glad to see them all & I know they are taking good care of Pa & Ma & G Ma as they promised to do, when I left. Write often, Your Bro aff

N. J. Lillard

Father. I wrote you a few days ago will write should Bro get worse though I believe he will get well with attention Bro John & Frazier are well, Say to Mrs Baldwin that stu is well and doing his duty with great proptness Frank & John Jim & Slick Buckmen are both well so is Crains Frank & Laffayette McCorkle & E Hodge S M Cox. I have you an over coat I could meet with an opertunity to send it to him if Jasper or Almon Guinns come up Tell them to bring a large trunk with them and we will fill it up with many things we have which we want to send home. If they do come bring two lbs of Soda a good ham or so Say Howdy to enquiring friends I would like very much to write them all but I have not the time to do so it is now 12 Oc at night I must be up by day light so I dont get much sleep. Your Son aff N. J. Lillard

- - - - - - - - - - - - -

LETTER NO. 21
JOHN M. LILLARD TO JENNIE LILLARD

August 13th 1861

My Dear Wife

I have just received your letter dated July 31st and although I wrote you 2 days ago Yet I have an oppertunity and gladly embrace it to answer yours as it is the second one I have received from you since I left you. I was so glad to hear from you and that you and Tom were well though I am very sorry to hear of Lizzies misfortune and bad health, she has been so kind and good to us You must act the part of a sister in full towards her in her sickness. Well I thought I had nothing to write more than to say I was well but Camp life daily afords items. to day we buried a member of our company Mr J C Mathers one of our Corporals he died yesterday of fever, he done duty in the rain & refused to go to the hospital until he got down & poor fellow never got up his father arrived here this morning with a waggon to take him home but alas we were fixing to bury him I commanded the burial service to day and it done the old man good to see him buried with military honor. We have only one more sick he had measels & caught cold.

On last thursday we were to leave for Knoxville but Col McNairy was ordered to Knoxville with his 5 companies of Middle Tennessee Cavalry to go to Virginia, leaving only our 3 Companies of infantry & 1 of Cavalry to stay till Middle Tennessee furnished troops to come here. A regiment is organizing at Kingston 30 miles from her to come here but it seems they are verry slow. We would like to be relieved of our suspense and know certainly whether we stay in this section or not for a state of uncertainty in camps is very annoying. the program is still for us to go Knoxville & organize our Regment but I now prepared to hear them countermanded at any time.

Well Col McNairy to the illustrous Genl George W Bridges from our Camp with him to Knoxville prisoners as I wrote you before he had played Lincoln and run to Kentucky & left his wife & children to get through as best they could. Our commander detained Bridges family & sent scouts to all the papers for fifty miles & the squad under Capt Lowry of Athens caught him he had been 8 miles further towards our camp & had sent men on to see about his family we detained them and he finally came himself he had been out at Monticello making speeches to a Lincoln Company and expected his wife every night. I helped Mrs Bridges & the little ones into the Hack this morning and I was truly sorry for her & the children. They all went to Knoxville started today Maynard made good his escape as I learn but they got Tom Nelson as we learn. Bridges proposed before he left here to take an oath and join the Southern Army if they would give him a position that would support his family he is evidently alarmed although he says he was not going to Washington City but only going over to Kentucky to practice law as he was broke up in Tennessee.

Paul McDermott that I wrote you was wounded & missing 48 hours on a scout has got in and is getting well there was 4 Lincolnites attacked him and left him for dead it has given our men a warning and will keep them from trotting around so much. A few more such cases and I hope we will be allowed to pay them back. our plan has been to treat them too well and they are growing bolder, and will have to be dealth with as their traitorous schemes deserve. a great change has taken place among the people here in favor of the south since we came here. It has been raining here for a week but this evening it is cool and I am at our camp fire writing and the fire feels verry comfortable. the climate here is something like Ashe though the Water is not quite so good or cold.

Your letter was a god send as I had only had one from you and none from any of papas folks except 4 lines from Jasper from Athens wanting me if elected Col to appoint a Knoxville gentleman to a office at the bottom he said in great haste.

My spells that I usually had this time of year are only light and of short duration my health better though I have lost 10 to 20 pounds of flesh and wish I could loose 20 more. the letter I got to day came from Alympus. Mr Fooshee was her a few days ago said he was at Decatur just before he left and said they had a letter from you to send but Dr Blevins took it up to Knoxville and I have never got it I hope when I get to Knoxville I will have enough to keep me reading all day. Give my love To all Kiss Tom for Pa & keep writing.

Your affectionate Husband

Jno M Lillard

2 Months of our time out tomorrow

- - - - - - - - - - - - -

LETTER NO. 22
SAM M. COX TO N. J. LILLARD

Fairfax Station
August 19th 1861

Dear Friend

Long Long ago I received your letter but hard service and fatigue I offer you as an excuse for not writing sooner which I hope will be satisfactory for not writing sooner I have been sick for several days past but am now very near well again by good care will be up again for hard service For the last few weeks we have enjoyed a quiet rest which was very exceptable to us as we was nearly worn down with fatigue and hard service Since the fight we have had nothing of great interest we are awaiting the approval of the enemy for another fight there are many Conjectures here as to what will be in the future My Opinion is that we will have to fight them some time this fall then I think the fight will close till spring as this Country is very cold and almost impossible to stand the snow and cold North wind.

We are in good health as a general thing Vern is getting better Mr Frazier has had the Meezels but to day is nearly well. the rest of our Company is in good health. We are going to have a band in our Company if we can get it Mr Swan of Cleveland starts to day for Richmond to buy it. I suppose we will have Music then so do some good. We was a little confused about the rebellion in E Tenn for several days but latter news has made us believe that all will work off with out a fight The Election went off much better than we expected I hope you will all be blest with peace and plenty while we are gone. We often think of home and the dear friends there I dreamed last Knight of seeing you in Decatur and when I awoke and found Myself lying on a pallet of straw I was nearly mad Tell Your Ma & Grandma that I was glad to know I had their prayers and hope I may have them an still give them My kindest love and best wishes for their affections for me I would rather have the good will of the aged than any other class of people in the world I also like to have the good wishes of the Young ladies which I hope I may so love as to deserve How are you all passing off your time.

What is Bill Rogers doing also J D Blevins. You must write me a long letter give me all the news at Decatur. Yours

Sam M. Cox

- - - - - - - - - - - - -

LETTER NO. 23
P.M. McCLUNG TO LT. COL. J.L. REESE

Campbells Station
Aug 26, 1861

Lieut Col J. L. Reese

Dear Sir My wife has been applied to by a Mrs Cates for information of her son George Cates belonging to Capt Lillards Company. She is in destitute circumstances and has need of a part of his pay to live. Will you be kind enough to give through me the necessary information?

I will also see that she gets the benefit of any money sent to me. I of course have kept up with your Regiment through the press and glory in your achievements. Truly yours P. M. McClung

- - - - - - - - - - - - -

LETTER NO. 24
E. M. FRAZIER TO BROTHER

Meadow Spring near Decatur
August 31st 1861

Dear Brother

This morning I write you a few lines as we have a chance of sending by hand, which is a much more certain way of sending letters. I know that you dont get all the letters that we send we generally write twice a week. I write every week to Mr Frazier, and oftener sometimes we would all be glad to hear from you all this morning. The health of the family is tolerably good. Pappas health is as usual. Vern is improveing some. Seems to be very low spirited. Crate had a letter from Jennie last week her and Tommie is well. I have not heard from Bro Bill since Mr Frazier was at home. The health of the country is tolerably good.

I suppose John will be at Knoxville next week, some volunteers from Capt Crawfords Company stayed here a few nights ago. They said that they would be there Sunday or Monday, but they have been expecting to go every week for a month. Jo Howell is at Decatur but I have not seen him since he came.

I was dreaming about you all last night. I thought Peace was made and that all had got back. I dreamed of seeing you and talking so plainly that when I woke I thought it must be a reality. How much I do wish you all could come home. I have nothing New to write you I will close

Your Sister, E M Frazier

- - - - - - - - - - - - -

LETTER NO. 25
JAMES LILLARD TO SONS

Medow Spring near Decatur
August 31st 1861

Dear Sons

I feel like wrightin you a few lines Jointly to all. Tho I have nothing particular to wright all Seams to be peac hear so far tho I do not now how long it will be so. thare has several Cavalry Companies from Knoxville Gon down beloe hear Meigs Bradley Hamilton and Rhea Countys to regulate Matters, Some thinks the union men will quite down. John thinks some of them will resist but

I think they have more sense tho I under stand some say thay will die before tha will submitt. It matters not how soon them sort dies that we mite not be troubles with them any longer. E M has written all that we no a Bout Bill & John I want you all to do the Very best you can take good ceare of yourselves act onestly and morally, be kind one to another and if thare is any fighting to do I want you to dooit and dooit well.

We had J E and J M Lillards wives with us yesterday thay wer well tho J E has chills once in a while we had Mary Boggess and Suse Davis a day and night. Suse is good lucking, and if you was a boy Nute and gits back I wold say go up to bobs tent. I will have to close I have got so nervis I can hardly form a letter and Little Jim is nocking me with a stick, Jim ---[ink blob]--- much pa and Ma in him it maks him a bad boy he pesters me a bout my stick wants to eat up all my musk Drink up all my bitters— not so with Marys Boy. I have no trouble with him a greate diffirance in children, as it is so different for me to wright I want this to answer for all F and J Lillard

James Lillard

- - - - - - - - - - - - -

LETTER NO. 26
J. T. V. LILLARD TO N. J. LILLARD

Meadow Spring near Decatur
August 31st 1861

Dear Brother

I write you few Lines. I reached home Saturday night I stayd over one day at Lynchburg it was covered by a slide in the road between Lynchburg & Bristol I got home with fourteen dollars my health improes verry slow my hearing is no better I have the piles verry bad yet, I cannot get anything don for them if it was not for them. I would get well verry quick. it has been raining ever since I com home I will get that Sertificate for you & send it by mail I think I am needed here although I would like to be with you verry well papas health is tolerably good. I am now wanted very bad get me a discharg(?) if you can if you cannot get --?-- Write to me soon. I saw Jasper at Knoxville he went with me to Athens. Jasper wants me to stay at home. I must close.

Your affect Brother
J T V Lillard

- - - - - - - - - - - - -

LETTER NO. 27
CRATE LILLARD TO N. J. LILLARD

Meadow Spring
Sept 3rd 1861

Dear Bro

I received your precious letter week or so since, & would have answered sooner but circumstances prevented. I am very glad to hear that the health of the Co is improving, for you are all so far from us it would be one greate consolation to know that you were all enjoying good health. Bro Vern came home last Saturday was a week. we were all very glad to see him indeed; there was such a crowd here Sunday that that we could hardly turn round, all seemed disappointed when they found that he had no letters for them. I received yours. You may know that we are very anxious to hear from you, every day if we could, the day between mailday seems like a week, them if we donot get a letter we are sadly disappointed. Vern is greatly changed. I am so sorry that his hearing is no greatly impared, but hope will get better. no I think his health is improving, daily—

Sis called me to help her eat a nice melon. I wish you was here to help us eat it, ever time I eat any thing nice I think of you and wish you had some. It has rained here for several weeks, but for the last three days we have had good weather. I pity you brave soldiers when it would be raining so hard at night I would lay down on a nice bed, I think that perhaps a blanket would be all you would have. It makes me feel very sad.

I am glad to inform you that the Union men are not rebeling I hope they will see the folly of any longer crying for the Union, and submit as rationable men ought to do. It makes my blood to hear men bemoaning the Southern Volunteers when I have dear relation in the Southern army, and proud that I have such noble and patriotic ones, the Union men are sinking in the estimation of the people they have sunk are called traitors and will be called such all their lives, and generations after them. Oh! they will repent when it is too late.

I spent a very plesant week at Athens & one at Cleveland, while there I could see the brave soldiers going up by thousands. I spent most of my time waving my handkercheif and making boquets for them, there were several Union men bradly I hated to look at them for it would make me mad to see them. I dont know wether I seen your sweetheart arnot, far I donot know who she is, I expect I did tho for I seen several very nice & patriotic ladies; Bro beware lest some of those Virginia ladies steals that noble heart of yours, for there are a greate many young ladies in Ten who claims you for a sweetheart. Sou Davis said she was not going to marry untill you come back, told me to tell you every thing that was good for her so you can accept any thing you please. Haly Elder(?) has been spending some four or five weeks in Athens but has returned she sends her love & says she does not love J. D. B. bestow her love on a more nobler subject

I suppose Bill Lillard & George McKenzie has made up a Co. 90 men, Jim & Dave Blevins have joined, donot know when they will leave. Joe Howell is home from Knoxville go back to day. I suppose Bro John & Co will be at Knoxville to day or tomorrow to organize the Reg. He cannot get any letters we write to him, we have received several letters from Jennie, she & Tommie are well she says she cannot hear any thing from you and scarcely any from John.

Lizzie is visiting Minerva Frazure I suppose Minerva & Ann Gillespie are coming with her, there is not a young man left Washington, Mr. Bean has join Capt Gass Co, his Co & Snows went down in Bradly through X Roads I suppose to see wether the Union are preparing for Rebellion hope they will settle them for I think have been let alone long enough Casey Thomas is here says you are sending word to all the girls but her says She hasnot forgotten you if you have her, sends her love and says she is just the same as she was that night Sam & Gass went out Doctering. Tell John B Mary was here Friday look very well all sends their love to all.

Mr Cox & Pa says they want you to take good care of yourself and do the best you can Frank has brought letters. Oh! we were so grieved to hear of Vans death. his mother didnot think he would get back he was so sickly, Oh those Yankees there is no word in the english language that can express their meanness if it had not been for them we might all been living peacefully and happily together & there is men in E. T. who sympathise with those who are the cause of all of this trouble. They will recive their punishment I hope, for the many homes they have made desolate in the South because some familiar voice is missing. I will close untill in the morning

Sept 4th

All are well. I suppose Mrs. Stewart took it very hard about Vans death. Cousin Will, R & I went over to Riceville to send some things to you. Mr. Owans was just starting to Vir we sent them by him. These were a pair of boots socks & gloves for John Boggess & pair gloves for Simon McGins(?) & a pair of gloves & two lb of soda for you.

All the sevants sent their respects to you thir love to Will and tell him to take good care of himself. Tell Billy Smith Jane Smith was here Sunday very well. Mr. Crain family is well & all the boys relations as far as I know. Jimmie sends his love; Mother says do try and take good care of yourself, all sends much love. My respects to all Accept the best love of

Your loving Sister
Crate Lillard

P.S. Almon Guinn is speaking of starting to Vir next Friday. Tell James Buckner his fathers family are all well. I have learned to shoot a pistol and gun. I think if a Yankee was to pass by I could shoot him all the Girls in town are well we are all wearing secession aprons. Tell Frank Taylor his mother was in town yesterday is well. May the God of battle protect you all

Your aff Sis C. E. Lillard

[the following names were written on the bottom of the last letter] G. W. Allen Sargt, T. J. Russell, E. L. Hodge, Lafayette McCorkle, J. K. P. Slaughter, Frank Sharp, J. C. Moore

\- - - - - - - - - - - - -

LETTER NO. 28
C.C. ROBESON TO N.J. LILLARD AND OTHERS

Decatur Tenn
Sept 22nd 1861

Messers N J Lillard, Cross & others

Gents and friends I received your very kind and interesting letters some days ago but have not answered until the present for the very good reason of having nothing which I thought would be interesting to you, Nor am I able at present to Command much. No doubt you have all the news from this Country from those who are more able than myself to give correct information, So if I should give incorrect statements I hope to be pardoned and the cause attributed to the proper source, Ignorance We have very many reports here of what is going in the Army but half may be incorrect. We have news of the fight in Western Va how glad we are we cannot tell. We have some news of a skirmish that took place in Kentucky between some Lincoln men and Gen Zollicoffer. Report says they the Lincoln men find once and new Guns & took 600 stand of Arms. No doubt Ky will be a bloody field soon. The Union party in E Tenn have all submitted and promise acquancence with the south soon all our Troops will be in Ky I recon not knowing where they will go.

Col J M Lillards Regiment are now enrout for Camp Trousdale in West Tenn near the Ky line you heard no doubt Gens Polk & Pillow being at Hickman and Columbus Ky. Gen Albert S Johnson who has Command of the Western division of the army is reported within 16 miles of Louisville Ky a day or two ago. Surly Kentucky will fight when she is interested. We have no more war news. I believe here at present.

Well Boys I will try to give you a few domestic Concerns and then will have to quit for the present. We are all toterably well some cases of chills and fever in the County none dangerous perhaps a few cases of Typhoid fever. Margaret Blevins has been sick a long while and died today about 12 O Clock Sunday (Saml Blevins Daughter). In the Midst of life we are in death. I hope she will reap her better reward in Eternity. Things are all quiet here. Unity of sentiment seems to be gaining ground here. Tell all our boys their Relatives & friends here are all well so far as I know. We have rather a cool time now a North East wind has been blowing ever since yesterday and I should not be surprised if we have frost tonight Surely you will.

I am still teaching at Goodfield. Have a large school doing all the good I can. We will have a plentiful harvest of every thing here corn is excellent. Pork will be very high here. It is now worth about 7 cts gross and cant be bought at that. In fact I dont know of a single hog to sell. Hog Chollery has killed a great many. I think there will be plenty of Beef and Mutton to suply the deficiency. We have had plenty of rain and pastures have been good and Cattle are in fine order. Coffee is cheaper to some of us than it has ever been. My Coffee only costs about $100 per Bu. Cate sells at 40 cts per lb but I buy by the Bushel and get it cheaper by wholesale you know mine is of a superior quality too. The real Rye A little whiskey along will make it up you know. I am willing on my part to make any sacrifice for the good of my Country. No doubt it will be better for us all We can do better without coffee and many other things we have been accustomed to than with them. I must close soon. I have written several letters not answered or I have not received the answer. Jesse H, John H, L B Guinn, S.M. Cox have not answered. If you have not time to write much write a little and send all in a bunch R Chambers Pat Blevins also, and all the boys read when I write unless marked private at the Caption. Write soon one and all accept my best wishes and respect to one and all. I remain yours &c

C. C. Robeson

My wife requests to be remembered to you all and especially N.J. Lillard because a Similar respect was paid her in his letters to me. Women will have ways peculiar to their Sex. C. C. R.
Jo and the Children sends their respects to all and say Howdy for all.

[letter addressed to Capt N.J. Lillard or I.G. Cross, Fairfax Station, 3rd Reg Tennessee Vol Commanded by Col Vaughn, To be forwarded if necessary]

- - - - - - - - - - - - -

LETTER NO. 29
CRATE LILLARD TO N. J. LILLARD

Meadow Spring
October 5th 1861

Dear Bro:

We received your letter by Dr Gilbert. I was truly glad to learn that you were well, also the Co. were very anxious to hear from you; hence you may know that we were truly glad to get all news from the boys. We are all enjoying ourselves as best we can considering the circumstances. Suffering from anxiety more than anything else I have had a tolerable sore throat but was well enough for me to go to town today. The ladies met and formed a Ladies Soldiers aid society in Decatur & vicinity. I will sent you a copy of the proceedings when it is published. We all met at Mrs Leutys, Mother & Mrs. Russell were among the No. kniting away. We have heard from Bro. John today. he is at Bolingreen Ky. Says the citizens there are very kind & willing to do anything for them. Those that are for the Union are as big a coward as the Yankees just lay down their arms & run. Jennie came with John, when he was ordered to Ky, he didnot have time to come by home & see us, which we all regretted very much as it had been along time since we seen him.

I suppose you want to hear about the elections for Supreme Judge. Cooper got 75, Ridley 3, Marchbank 1. I suppose McKenzies Company organized Monday. Noah Cate & Jemmie belong.

Mother says tell you she will have Jack at you cloths next week she is weaving you some of the prettiest you ever saw, and will try and send them with other things she has for you, by Mr. Nute King. Lizzie, Sis, & I have knit you some long warm socks will send them with this letter by Almon Guin if he will take them. Vincent is going to make you a pair of boots.

Jesse Martin has sold out to Mr. Dave Neil of Mouse Creek, he has been moving his plunder this week. While the soldiers were stationed at X Roads I went over to see them. I had not imagined the hardships of camp life to be half so trying as they really are there are such greate temptations. Some were playing cards, some dancing & some using proface language. It greived me to see them, instanty the thought of the Decatur Guards, wether they participated in such but I couldnot even think for a moment that they did. I havenot seen Sue Davis since I received your letter. There is a big meeting on Sewee today would like to go and see Jennie P. but mother willnot let me go says I am not well enough. Ten Mc [Tennessee McCorkle] told me to tell you "lots" of good things for her. Kate Leuty is here & sends her love. Pa has not been in very good health for the last to or three days, but think is better, mother suffers from anxiety sometimes. Bro Jasper has been very sich but is so he can sit up, is at Athens. All sends love write soon & often to; Your loving sister,

Crate

Tell Bill Aunt Rachael can walk a little

Your Sis

- - - - - - - - - - - - -

LETTER NO. 30
JENNIE LILLARD TO NEWTON J. LILLARD

Scapeover [Meigs Co]
Oct 6th– '61

Dear Brother

I hope you will excuse me for neglecting to answer your very welcome letter for so long a time. I intended answering it this day. Dr Lillard came to North Fork & after he came I was so busy I didnt have time to write. I was bothered a good deal about letters up there. I scarcely ever get a letter see it was three or four weeks old occasionally one would come direct but they were few & far between.

I had a few lines from Dr Lillard yesterday the only time I have heard from him since we parted, he was well but I didn't think he was in very good spirits I imagine he has a very trying position for one of his disposition he is too sensitive.

Mr Howel [*] writes to Viny three times a week so I suppose I will hear pretty often whether the Dr writes often or not. You may thank your stars that you have no wife these troubelsome times to be grieving about you. [* see J.A. Howell Diary]

I was much obliged to you for offering to come by North Fork & bring me home if you come maybe you may have the pleasure of taking me back. I had to rather promise to go back before they would consent for me to come Dr was ancious for me to come home though possibly if I was here he would get to come & see us this winter some time or if I should want to go to see him I would be so much nearer. Father looks a good deal better than he did last summer when I left here & seems to be a gooddeal stronger.

Vern & Lizzie are gone to Sewee to preaching to day. Mrs Moors funeral is to be preached today and some other ladies funeral, I forget her name. Vern is looking tolerably well but his hearing seams to be considerably worsted. I was surprised to see Mr Boggess here when I got back. I scarcely knew whether it was him or his gost, he was suffering very severely with his head when I came but he got better in a few days & went home. I have not heard from him and suppose he is improving.

Mr. Frazure came from Washington yesterday says Mr Parks(?) is very sick again.

I sent a bundle to the Dr the other day by express consisting in part of a splendid blanket coverlet & comfort & various articles of wearing cloths & etc.

Dear Nute I hope you will have good health & spirits & that you may soon whip the Yankees off Southern soil. You must come home if you can this winter. We would all be so glad to see you. I tease Mother & the girls some times & tell them I am jealous that they never think of the Dr its just Nute the darling child all the while. Write to us often.

Very affectionately,
Your Sister
Jennie Lillard

- - - - - - - - - - - - -

LETTER NO. 31
F.M. LAYTON TO NEWTON LILLARD

Centerville
Oct 25th 1861

Capt. Newton Lillard

Dear Sir having lerned fact as I left the Camp for home that there was a gentleman of the name above mentioned. I there fore take the liberty to write to you thinking you are a relation of mine. My name is Fountain M. Layton, a son of Richard Layton from the County of Madison NC My Mother was Milly Lillard before her Marriage her Fathers Name was James Lillard & his Mothers Name was Frazier. I should have been glad to have seen you if you are Relation of Mine or other wise as you are from Tennessee if from what I have Stated above you are a relation please write to Rockingham County Va Port Reputie(?)

Yours truly
F. M. Layton

I have a son in the 10 Va Regiment [letter is torn] is John R. Layton.

- - - - - - - - - - - - -

LETTER NO. 32
JOHN M. LILLARD TO N. J. LILLARD

Camp near Bowling Green Ky
Nov 9th 1861

Capt N J Lillard

Dear Brother I have been looking for a letter from you some time but have received none lately and I suppose you are so heavily engaged watching the Yankees you have no appertunity to write we have been looking anciously for news from the Manassas region lately and although we have never doubted the result of the conflict if you had a general engagement yet to tell the truth we have dreaded to hear of a fight for so many Gallant and brave ones have to fall when the battle rages. I cannot undertake to give you the news generally as you doubtless get it by the papers long before my letter.

Brother William is here in a Texas Cavalry Regiment for during the war he is now at my tent staying all night with me it is thought we will make a move in some direction soon. The fortifications here are in a forward State and for the last 2 week the army here has been very busy about half at work on the works and the other half on drill daily. So you see we eat no idle bread.

We have been 2 weeks in Brigade Drill and have no doubt if you could see our Regment on Drill or Revew you would be Surprised. I never saw men learn as fast in my life. We stand our hand respectably in Brigade Drill. Genl Buckner is our General and the 14th Missippi & Our Regt Constitute Brigade Commanded by Col Baldwin of the 14th Missippi. I prefered to be in a Tennessee Brigade but I think Baldwin a good officer.

The rumor of East Tennessee being invaded reach us occasionally & if it proves true I want us to get permission to return & defend it and I think I will make application if it proves true & I have no doubt Col Vaughn will do the same, in fact a rumor has reached us that your Regt is ordered to East Tennessee in support of Zollicoffer. the health of the army here is tolerable good this evening it was reported to us that Nashville may be the general Hospital for the sich of this --?-- and all not able for duty or who would not be in the next week to be sent to Nashville & I supposed by this that we might be ordered to move in a short time, though your own experience teaches you that these things are uncertain. Bro Wm C intends to visit Decatur soon as he can get a furlow.

I received a letter from Coz J M L from Fairfax the other day. tell him I will write him soon. I wish you to give my complements to all the boys tell them I would like to be side by side with you all if we meet the yankees, for I now their pluck. I think I have as good fighters as any body and will make their mark if we get a chance— do you count on coming home this winter if so at what time so I can try to meet you. Write me often as you can & believe me as ever Your affect Bro

Jno M. Lillard

- - - - - - - - - - - - -

LETTER NO. 33
CRATE LILLARD TO N. J. LILLARD

Scrapeover
Nov 18th 1861

Dear Bro;

After being wrought to such a high pitch of excitement, I have at last composed my self enough to write a half of a letter. Old Meigs has been excited more last week than I can remember of ever seeing her. the Union men or rather tories collected at Sale Creek camp ground, all armed ready for any mean, lowlife, cowardly acts that their leaders should command them to do after burning the bridges. I suppose they intended to do all the mischeif they could, they threatened to burn up Washington, and the secesh men came over in Meigs post hast after men sent runners to adjoining countys to Knoxville after troops 300 Cavalry companies went; crossed the river above here, and 3 infantry companies two came through Decatur an Alabama Co. and an E. Tenn Co, the ladies gave them supper and breakfast. they slept in the Academy everyone was talking about them being such moral nice gentlemanly behaved men, persons say they reminded them of your co. they were so civil. you ought to have seen them flying around the girls, said they were so surprised when they were so kindly treated, said they thought all E. Tenn were Union people, we told them that they neednot think all E. Tenn is wrong for there are a great many as noble patriotic people here as any where else. they said there were the cleverest people in Decatur they ever came across and more pretty girls & they would come back through here if they had to stay over in Rhea again and go fifty miles out of their way they left one sick man with fever at Col McKinlys, Liz, Sallie Mc, and I went to see him last evening, he is very bad poor fellow I am so sorry for him away from his friends. When the Alabamians was passing through they told the girls they would not come back this way if they didnot get some prisoners. one said he would bring Jake Zeigler to us. I suppose they have some thirty prisoners. they arrested one who was carrying dispatches to Dan Trewit which read as follows; "Help now or never" I recon old Clift thought this was the last dying struggle they had about 15 hundred collected in arms and the secesh had about 17 hundred and Alabamas Regt came up the river from Chattanooga, the malitia went from Meigs Old Squire Boggess went over with his men. Capt McKenzie & Capt Hodge with their Co. the men said when the Alabama Regt came up the river our picketts thought they were union men and when they hollowed at they ran to give the alarm the Alabamians fired at them, scraping ones heel & ones shoulder, when the picketts gave the alarm they all formed themselves in battle array expecting to have a big battle, which they didnot as all the union men hid out as the saying is some Alabamians are going to Knoxville today to take some of their union prisoners they cought man in the act of burning Mcdonalds house they are after old Clift they think they will be certain to get him, I suppose the soldiers will stay in Rhea untill they clear out the Country of its plague, I have not time to write any more now but will write you a long letter when I hear more definite news. family all well but Pa his health is very feeble excuse my writing with a pencil and all mistakes. I recon Vern is with you by this time. donot be uneasy about us, give love to all the boys, all Send love Write soon and often to your loving Sis

Crate

- - - - - - - - - - - - -

LETTER NO. 34
JORDAN HORRID TO CAPT. N.J. LILLARD

General Hospital
Richmond Va
November 19th 1861

Dear Sir

I am in great need of money & clothing You will Confer a Great favor by Sending me my "Descriptive list" in order that I may receive my pay here in the City. I have the Honor to be very Respectfully ---?---

Jordan Horrid
Private 3rd Tenn Reg Comp I

- - - - - - - - - - - - -

LETTER NO. 35
W. B. RUNYAN TO N. J. LILLARD

Goodfield Ten
Nov 22nd 1861

Capt. N. J. Lillard

Dear Sir Isaac arrived this morning very unexpected to me finding we were unwell but improving & will be able to return in a few days. I started Ike alleten(?) the 18th of this month requesting him if he would reather stay out their I would Join McKenzies Company as we could not recruit them I would not change my Company for now one I want now transfer it was not because I wanted to leave but for his benifit knowing he had agularkes(?) to take cear of & my survis was neaded very bad at home. I have had now rest untill I tuck sich & do not want any as long as I am neaded give my best respect to all the boys look for me ever mail the clothing was sent to Knoxville against orders the reason I do not know if I ove take them I will come with them all they may I supose they will not go any further now telling

Respectifully yours
W. B. Runyan

- - - - - - - - - - - - -

[The following interesting list of purchases were made in November of 1861 by Captain N. J. Lillard. The drawing at the end of the list is one type of candle holder used by the soldiers.]

CAPT. N. J. LILLARD & LIEUTS Dr TO WILLIAM E. SNEAD A.C.S.

Nov	1	9½ lbs	Canvass Ham	@ 22½¢	2.14
	2	12 lbs	Do Do	22½	2.70
	8	25 lbs	Flour	2¾	.68¾
		8 lbs	Canvass Ham	22½	1.80
	9	4 lbs	Sugar	10	.40
	10	2¾ lbs	Coffee	35	.96½
	12	1 lb	Soap		.12½
		3 lbs	Sugar	8	.24
		13 lbs	Canvass Ham	22½	2.92½
		19 lbs	Flour	2¾	.51¾
	14	1 lb	Candles (Tallow)		.20
	15	5 lbs	Sugar	8	.40
	16	12½ lbs	Canvass Ham	22½	2.81¼
		1	Candle		.05
	17	26 lbs	Corn Meal	1¾	.45½
		½ lb	Candle (tallow) pr Cross		.10
	18		Bal on Oct Acct		.24
	20	11 lbs	Canvass Ham	22½	2.47½
	21	4 lbs	Sugar	8	.32
		2 lbs	Coffee	35	.70
	23	14½ lbs	Canvass Ham	25	3.62½
		5 lbs	Sugar	8	.40
		1/6 lb	Candles (Star)	40	.07
	24	36 lbs	Flour	2¾	.99
		2 lbs	Coffee	35	.70
	26	5 lbs	Sugar	8	.40
	28	14½ lbs	Canvass Ham	25	3.62½
	30	1	Candle Star		.07
					$ 30.13¼

Recd payment Wm E. Snead A.C.S.
3rd Tenn Vols

- - - - - - - - - - - - -

LETTER NO. 36
CRATE LILLARD TO N. J. LILLARD

Scrapeover
December 1st 1861

Dear Brother;

Again has my heart been gladden by the receipt of your letter, if you could witness the pleasure it gave us to receive a letter from you and how disappointed we are when we donot get any. I know you would write to us oftener anyhow. What has become of Vern? he hasnot wrote to us since he left home, I recon he has forgotten us.

Jennie received a letter from John, he and Bill were both well, John said Bill had the premise of a furlough to come home the 20th of this month, if all our brothers could come home would not we have a happy christmas, Oh what a big Christmas dinner we would have, I know it would be the happiest day ever I saw; do try and come.

Yesterday another company left Meigs it didnot seem possible that so many men could be mustered up in Meigs as to form a company, but Dr.Hodge has quite a fine looking company. Mr. Goforth formerly a Union man has joined Hodges Co. several of the Union men that they took prisoners in Rhea joined also, Mr. Joe Pain & Tom Allen took 8 prisoners to Knoxville by here, they were the meanest looking pieces of creation I ever saw some were nearly naked, I heard the men laughing about one man, I suppose after their little fight was over they saw him lying on the ground they went to him and asked him where he was hurt "I am hurt all over" said he, and there was nothing the matter with him only fright. I recon the poor deluded wretches ought to be pitied, but when one thinks of our dear relatives leaving their homes and those that love them, to endure so much hardships and privations of life how much they have to suffer. it seems like a person cannot have much much pity for them when they sympathise with those that causes all this suffering.

Dr. Hodge went to river and got on the boat with his company, several of us ladies went out to the river to bid them a last farewell. Major Holt and James Martin were taking several prisoners to Knoville from X Roads on the boat, they were rough looking customers. Tenn McCorkle wore a mineno(?) riding skirt out to the river, one of the Vol. took it aboard and I suppose it landed at Knoxville. you can imagine her discomfiture, riding home without any when she had on her "new calicer." We made Capt Hodge a very nice flag and Kate Leuty presented it at our request. Mr. Dick Bynion is a very fine looking officer. The women seem to give up there bands tolerably well, some tho took it very hard cousin Adaline is very despondent but I recon she will cheer up and do the best she can like the rest us we will all greatly miss Dr. Hodge, we have been so accustomed to see him riding round. Men are so scarce we see are we feel like shaking hands with him, it is such a rare occurance. I suppose Messers Moore, Boggess &c didnot suceed in making up their Co. I think everbody wanted to be Capt & busted up the Co. Cousin Bill Rogers ate dinner with us today his Co are at Smiths X Roads occasionally scouting around the country and over the mountain hunting the remnants of Clifts army and taking the Union mens arms from them. Bill seems to like camp life very well James Lillard was elected 3rd Sergeant, makes a very good soldier. Rod Blevins didnot get any office at last. Old Esqr. Goldly is running for Ordly Sergeant in Hodges Co. I suppose nearly all are running for that office. Sam Cox arrived in town yesterday evening you can imagine our surprise on seeing him, it looks to me like every one can come home but you of course we are very glad to see any of the Co. but we would much rather see you. I got little Mary a dress. I tried to get Martha to get it, but she wouldnot. There is a sick soldier in town at Colonel McKinlys belongs to that Alabama company that passed through Decatur going to X Roads he was sich and they left him, he is now convalescent, they citizens are taking very good care of him. Sam Blevin's Willie has bought Dr. Hodges horse and is going over to join McKenzies Co. Col Genno then will be the only young man town if he will not go to the war I recon we will have to send him female garments. Mr. Abe Denton comes to town occasionally but he looks like he was afraid all the time being among so many women. Dr. Gilbert went in Hodges Co. yesterday, he makes a very fine looking little soldier. George Hale joined also and was mustered into service so now I recon he will have to serve his time out. Mr John Baldwin lives where C. C. Roberson used to live & Mr. R. has moved out in the country. We have two very nice additions to our society. Mrs. Bell and Mrs. Moore the circuit riders wife both very nice ladies I think. The girls dress very plain just so they are dressed neatly they dont care wether fine or not most all are making or have made southern confederacy dresses (cotton). Kate had on a cotton dress when she presented Dr. flag looked very indepentent. I know you would be amused if you could be standing in some secluded corner, where several girls are assembled, all they talk about is "our boys" Hugh Blevins says he believes that is all we ever think or talk about.

I havenot had the pleasure of seeing Sue since I wrote you last. I suppose you have heard of her professing religion. Sue is a clever girl.

Hugh Blevins starts for Bowling Green, Ky this morning to see Alferd. havenot got to converse with Sam Cox yet, but am very anxious to ask him how you all are doing was rejoiced to hear that you enjoyed such good health hope will continue so. Pa's health has been very feeble for some time but is little better now, mother says seems like you have been gone five years. she dont know how long it will appear if you have to stay away till your time expires, all her boys gone and Pa's health so feeble. Oh! you must not think of staying away if there is any possible chance of getting to come home, you cannot imagine how badly we want to see you. I donot think we need apprehend any danger from the Union men now. I suppose Pleas Miller offered to join Hodges Co. but he was to old they would not have him. The neighborhood are generally well. their family are well but Pa & grandma their health is tolerably feeble grandma says she is very sorry you didnot come home with Sam Cox. All send love to you and Vern with hope that we will see you Christmas. I will close do come we will all be sadly greived if you donot. love to all;

Your loving Sis,
Crate Lillard

- - - - - - - - - - - - -

LETTER NO. 37
H. T. BLEVINS TO N. J. LILLARD

Decatur Tenn
December 1st [1861]

Capt. N.J. Lillard

Dear friend I write in answer to your very kind letter which I received on yesterday by politeness of S.M. Cox. I was proud to hear from you & to learn that you was enjoying good health & your company was in a like condition. This leaves me in a condition to be restored to purfect health in a short time, which will enable me to return to my respective command.

The health of the people is generaly good your folks are well. I am limited as to time & news of interest to write. The cry of rebellion is known more that party whose damnable deeds are so corrupt & who is so wanted in pressciable(?) are reduced to silence & are made to trimble & ask what shal I do to be saved, but little quarters are shown to them some of them are purmited to volunteer they are all more than willing to Join the confederate army but only the best are taken. I hope we will get rid of them soon. McKenzies company is in Rhea yet & doing great work. they have not caught Clift yet but swear they will have him, he is in that section somewhere.

County Court meets here tomorrow but little business to transact. A W Hodges Company left hear for Knoxville yesterday he had a fine company. A beautiful banner was presented to said company on their departure by the Ladies of this section. Being the fourth flag that has been fited up & presented in stile by the Good & patriotic Ladies of Meigs. The We should be encouraged while exposed to the pelting storms of winter when we reflect upon the nobility & generosity of those who are well wishers for us at home.

I received a letter from Bowling Green a day or two ago which stated that health was good there. my letter was from Alfred. he stated that he wanted me to come to bowling Green without fail if my health would admit I have concented to go. The ladies have some boxes of clothing I am going to take them. I am going to take your fathers bay Mare to Col J M Lillard allso some clothing for him. I will start tomorrow will be gone but

few days. I will come to Virginia as soon as I return if my health will admit. Capt confide in me for I will be with you ere it is long. Give my love to all the boys tell Steve to pitch under I will help him before long. I will desist for the present. let me hear from you soon.
Your friend H. T. Blevins

P.S. The Gals are all right, talk of nothing but the Decatur Guards.

- - - - - - - - - - - - -

LETTER NO. 38
JAMES K.P. GIDDENS TO J. M. LILLARD

Calhoun Tenn
Jan 5th 1862

Col Lillard

I send down a number of my men to the company and will be down myself in about 15 days. I am as yet very weak and not able for duty. I will get up the ballance of my men as soon as I can and send them on. I have ordered Capt Carmack, provost Marshall, to send me a Hack down from Athens. He shot himself through the hand and did it intentionally. I want you to have him Court martialed and shot, ought to have been shot long since. I do not want you to approve of any enlistment in my Co. unless the substitute is as capable of doing duty as the one for whom he is taken. If you would send me an order I could probably get up absentees of campaigns. I send you a permit outlining certificate of my disability. There is no army surgeon was here, also three other certificates which will answer until I came down as there is no army surgeons near here. I shall expect to hear from you soon. Direct to Calhoun Tenn

Yours as ever
James K.P. Gddens
Calhoun
McMinn County, East Tennessee

- - - - - - - - - - - - -

LETTER NO. 39
A. W. HODGE TO N. J. LILLARD

Decatur, Tennessee
January 15th 1862

I hereby certify that Capt N J Lillard Third Regiment Tenn Volunteers, Col Vaughn commanding, now at home on furlough, is unable to return to his Company, on account of severe indisposition he is laboring under an attack of Tonsillitis and after a careful examination, I would deem it very imprudent for him to go to camps and be exposed under thirty days or longer if the winter proves very inclement, and his duties should be of an active nature. A W Hodge M.D.

- - - - - - - - - - - - -

LETTER NO. 40
JOHN M. LILLARD TO JENNIE LILLARD

Clarksville, Tenn
Feb 9th 1862

My Dear Wife

As you will observ I am in old Tenmnessee once again I arrived here with my Regment tonight at 8 oclock and will leave here as I understand by steam boat for Fort Donnelson down the River in the Morning as soon as we can embark. Floyds & Buckners Brigades are all here & some of them gone on down the River. We anticipate some warm work from now on. You have doubtless heard all the news in regard to the Lincoln opperation on Cumberland & Tennessee River and much better informed than I am as now days We do not leave camps and hardly get any papers or letters. This is 3 days & nights since we got orders to be in readiness to come here and consequently I have had no rest or sleep hardly and am now when I finish this letter going to take a pallet in the Hotel to get a nap by day light then up to see that we get provisions or the boys will not have any for Breakfast until it is procured & it could not be done to night. I am well though I have had one of the worst colds lately I ever had and Col Baldwin being absent I have had command of the Brigade as well as my own Regment and am very tired but getting pretty well over my cold. We had to leave some of our Regt at Russelville with the mumps. Lieut Hoyl & several others are still at Bowling Green with most of our Baggage. I have nothing here with me only what I had with me at home, & do not know when I will see it again.

The Federals have been cutting up feriousally(?) it seems lately, but I do not know the particulars but you will get them in the paper in the mean time I will write every chance. Give my love to all & write soon & often to me. direct to Clarksville, Tenn to be ford.

Your one true Husband
Jno M. Lillard

- - - - - - - - - - - - -

[The following report was written by Col. John M. Lillard after the fall of Fort Donelson. It is important because several of the men included in the report were letter-writers or were mentioned in one or more of the letters. The handwriting is very difficult to read, and there was almost no punctuation. A few periods and commas have been added for clarity.]

26th TENNESSEE REGIMENT

To Col. W E Baldwin Col
Commd Brigade

Report of the killed, wounded &c &c, 26th Tenn Regment in the engagement of Fort Donaldson, Feb 15th 1862, also the Number engaged in the Battle.

Field & Staff that went on the Field with Casualties &c. Jno M Lillard Col wounded slightly in the shoulder, James J Odell Lt Col wounded slightly in the arm, Lt Jas A Howell adjutant wounded slightly in thigh, Geo Stewart QM, E T Taliafero Surgeon, Henry T Welker Commissary, Jas A Cash Ordenance Sergeant, Jeffrey West Colour Sergeant wounded slightly in thigh.

Co (A) A F Boggess Capt in command. Went into action with Lt Lea Neil, T B Bowling 6 non com officers & 37 privates total 46, killed none, wounded H Stephens in shoulder, H Sails in Bowels, N Deathridge in side, S Duckworth in Hip, L H Harmon in shoulder, P J Cade in arm, W Deathridge in arm, W Rhodes in side, Ed Hutson in side, Jas Johnson in Hand. total 10

Co (B) Jas L Battles Capt in command. Went into Action with Lt Gaba 3 non com officers & 23 privates, total 28. Killed Joshua Collins, wounded Danl Justice in thigh, Isaac Justice in arm, Sgt W M Bayless in arm.

Co (C) A C Hickey in Command. Went into action with Lt McNabb & Leut Swaggerty, 3 non com officers, 40 privates, total 46. Killed Private John Hensley, Wounded Lt A Swaggerty through lungs, Lt McNabb in ear, Sgt A M Griffin slightly, Geo Brotherton severely, T T Baldwin severely, Alex Gray in shoulder, J A Hicks in thigh, Geo McMahan shoulder, John A Sample in shoulder, F M Jinkins in hand.

Co (D) Leut Easley in Command. Went into action with Leut Mobley, 4 non com officers & 33 privates, total 39, one killed, T D Nash. Wounded S Hammrick(?) --?--, R Stratton severely, J Williams in arm, R Brooks seriously, J T Satterfield slightly, J P Godwin slightly, H D Godwin slightly, A Hepsher in arm.

Co (E) Capt Crawford in command. Went into action with Lt. Blevins & Lt H Paine, 6 non com officers, 40 Privates, total 48. Sergt J Flemming killed and Private James Childress killed. Wounded A M Johns(?) in lungs, J T Mondy in knee, Sergt J P Godsey in thigh, A S Bacon in leg, Corp Cunningham in arm, D Moore in knee, John Mundy in thigh.

Co (F) Capt Hu L McClung in command. Went into action with Leut Saffell, Leut Graham & Leut Butler, 4 non com officers & 26 Privates, total 34. Killed Private C Graham, Wounded Capt McClung in Epegastric(?) Region thought to be mortally, Leut Butler slightly, Sergt Bruce slightly, Sergt J B McCallum slightly, F Cloud slightly, W M Evans mortally, H L Evans slightly, J McDade slightly, J Rothchild slightly, W Hensley slightly, W Parton slightly, L Lea slightly, J Wright slightly, J L Foust slightly.

Co (G) Capt C D McFarland in command. Went into action with Leut Foster, Lt Reid, 6 non com officers, 27 [privates], total 36. Killed Capt Hancock. Wounded Private G W Guire in arm.

Co (F) Capt J C Gordon in command. Went into action with Lt Gordon, Lt Hendrix & Lt Owings, 7 non com officers, 38 Privates, total 49. Killed Geo Cross(?), J R Young & W Philips. Wounded B A Jones, J Carter, G W Kelley, J M Myers, J Brock, J W Davis.

Co (I) B F Welker, Capt in command. Went into action with Leut Brown & Lt McElwee, 7 non com officers & 36 privates, total 46. Killed Private F M Moss. Wounded Sergt H L White in Head, Private F M Gilliland in foot, H H Goin in head, S D Hembree in shoulder, A J Kincade in arm, J W Hendrix in side, J K Kincade in hand, P F Kenedy in leg, G W Morrison in arm, Wm Netherley in head, J H Odom in shoulder, Wm Warick slightly, A J Deathridge in leg, Roland Hudson in leg, John Cates in neck, A East slightly.

Co (K) J R Morrell Capt in command. Went into action with 5 non com officers, 23 privates, total 29. None killed. Wounded L D S Richards supposed mortally, W Alford supposed mortally, J Green slightly, Walker McCrary slightly, Ben Emmet slightly, John George slightly.

REMARKS

To Recapitulate, the 26th Tennessee went into the action with 400 Four Hundred including officers, Field & Staff &c &c. There was 11 Eleven killed & 85 Eighty Five wounded, inclusive, making in killed & Wounded (96) Ninety Six.

The Regment was second in the columns(?) of attack on our left in the morning the 26th miss(?) being in front and at the time action commenced the 26th Miss(?) was deployed to our right leaving the Regt in the Road from then until the enemy was driven from the Crest of the Hill was the hardest part of the fight and where this Regt lost nearly all the killed and wounded after the enemy was driven from the top of the Hill they were next routed from their encampment, and from there to the center the enemy was driven back on their right wing by a succession of charges, the enemy making many stands on the various hills. We drove them over in the road leading from the enbemies center to their extreme left was a Battery of the enemy said to be Taylors which they had started to the assistance of their right but finding their forces flying in confusion they attempted to retreat with it failed the Regt taking 2 of the guns & the 26th Miss(?) 2 as my observation was 2 of them being in one road & 2 in another each in the course the Regment were charging there guns were taken inside of our works as my men helped do & I saw one of the pieces going inside of the Works before I went in with my Regt & was not recaptured by the enemy until we were surrendered next day.

To undertake to particularize the deeds of daring & bravery of each officer or men on the occasion would be a pleasing task but time & space forbids. Suffice it to say all done their duty and done it well and it is left to the Brigade commander to say how the Regment behaved itself generally. It is probably proper to say Leut W A Wash of Kentucky, who was assigned command of Co K was drill master for the Regment & Capt Morrell being unwell in Dover ---?--- ---?--- ---?--- before the fight began Leut Wash fought bravely until he was wounded & taken to the Hospital. Capt Morrell came up with his Company & took command of it driving the rest of the ---?---. The Regment was in the fight firing & charging without ---?--- 56 hours from between 5 & 6 oclock to between 11 & 12 oclock. When we were ordered to remain in charge of the enemy --?-- until further ordered & until —?— be pro--?-- & subsequently marched to the —?— of our Works & then to one place in the Regt --?-- [impossible to read meny words in this portion of report and last two lines] Respectfully Submitted

Jno M Lillard Col
26th Tennessee To

N.B. One Regtal Coler & one Company Colers captured.

- - - - - - - - - - - - -

LETTER NO. 41
ELMIRA LILLARD TO N. J. LILLARD

Decatur Tennessee
March 30th 1862

Capt. N. J. Lillard

Dear Cousin; You surprised me so when you mentioned my name in Mandas letter that I could not forebare, but must write you a line. I have just been waiting to see if you would serve your twelve months out and never drop me a line. I am ever ready to confess my inability to interest any with whom I should chance to corespond, But will do the very best that I can on all occasions whatever. You know my disposition is to be Sivil and say nothing, for I had as soon not talk at al as to not talk to purpos, for which reason I say that I never was able to interest with the pen, or conversing verbally. But I suppos the reason you chose to corespond with Manda, was because I was never able to post in reference to the White house, and tell you so many funny things that hapened around about. You will also See from the length of my letters that I do not love to write long ones, but it pleases me powerfuly to get long ones.

I will have to quit for Manda & Lizzie is cutting up so I can not write. I would like to get a whole volume from you before many days. As Ed is going up this evening or in the morning. We will send our letters by him. Take good care of my Spark, O, I didnot go to say that, of course he can tak care of his self yet a while. I meant to tell you to Spark him for me every Leasure time you have, do that Strange as it may appear, give my doubled and twisted love to Co and reserve the Same Sort to yourself, nomore, this time.

Your Cousin Affectionately
Elmira Lillard

Cousin Sallie Blevins sends her love to you.

- - - - - - - - - - - - -

LETTER NO. 42
KATE LEUTY TO [N. J. ?] LILLARD

Decatur, Tenn
April 2nd 1862

Dear Friend

I drop you a few lines this morning in reply to yours of March 31st which came to hand yesterday evening. After returning home yesterday I was told there was a letter in the office for me but supposed it was not a letter being the 1st April I was rather expecting your gal to send me an April fool if she had so intended to give her particular fits. But So soom as looking at the envelope I knew the hand writing.

Crate Lillard Will Rogers and myself have been to the factory this week visiting had quite a pleasant time while we were there, but Oh coming back was the worst I know you would have laughed to saw us we each one had two bails of thread to carry and how tired we were you can guess.

We made the acquaintance of the two Miss Kings (not Kate) Miss Blizzard and Miss Atley also Mrs Arwine a nice widow, they are all nice ladies.

There was a very hard storm last Sunday evening about sun down blew a great many fences to the ground and the pailings but they have them put up again if they had not I dont know what Tommie would do for a resting place you know it is very tiresome to walk so often from his fathers to the store and back with out visiting and is a very easy place to rest now especially when there is such attraction just inside in the door or window.

You asked if any one was sparking your gal I wouldnt be surprised from appearances if there wasnt I heard him say he was there last Saturday night and roasted potatoes but you kneed not suffer any uneasiness when you get so much better treatment. When you get cake wine preserves and so on I have not made her acquaintance yet you know we are strangers have been expecting her to call on me though recon I will have to wait untill you come home to introduce her for no one else will. Some of the boys have been making their brags they were going to take her to Cuba to pick cotton as soon as the war is over. I shouldent blame you to kick up a fuss. I see the black critter coming in town with the young lieutenant.

Be sure take good care of that Cleveland Bug as you call him have no idea how it grives me to hear of him being sick dont let him run in the cold and rain if he dont watch he will die then what will become of me there is no telling. How many fish did you catch next time send me a mess or give that bug some will do as well.

Aunt Shaver says she is going to give you and Sam Cox bringer when she sees you for not going down while you were at home. I will close I know you will never want to see another such a peace [*] that --?-- place [*]

Your friend truly
Kate Leuty

P S Ask Frank Taylor when he thinks he will put up at the tavern again. K L
[* ink blob over several words in two lines]

- - - - - - - - - - - - -

LETTER NO. 43
JENNIE LILLARD TO JOHN M. LILLARD
[AT FORT WARREN, BOSTON HARBOR]

Decatur Tenn April 23d 1862

My Dear Husband

Your letter of 6th came by yesterday mail; & I heard from you also through Maj Brown of Mi [Mississippi]. I was truly thankful to hear your health was so good & that you were as comfortably situated as what you are. We are all very anxious to see you home again, but while we cannot it is a great comfort to know you are well, & to some extent comfortable. The family & friends are all well & we are all getting along about as usual. We had letters from Bro Willian & Nute both yesterday they were both well & in good spirits. I hear from N. Fork [Ashe County, N.C.] most every week but I shall not go up there til you get back which I trust will not be a great while. I have not been down to the farm in a good while though I believe Mr Blevins is getting along very well. We have had a great deal of rain the last month. What was left of your Regt was gathered to gether & are down below some where at Chattanooga probably. Lieut. Blevins was at home some time sick; he told me your bagage was all burnt [following the surrender at Fort Donelson], suppose it was so as I never heard of any of it.

The family all send their love. Tommie says he will soon be large enough to go after you, if you dont come. he is growing so fast you will hardly know him when you get back.

May God bless & protect you, & bring you safe home to your ever devored Wife   Jennie Lillard

- - - - - - - - - - - - -

LETTER NO. 44
JOHN F. WHITE TO J. DEMINICKS

Fort Warren, Boston Harbour
25 May 1862

Col(?) J. Deminicks

I am expecting some letters Containing funds which I have requested My friends to direct to me to this place to your care. You will confer a favour by turning over all my mail matter and any monies that may come for me to Col John M Lillard while he remains at Ft Warren, should any monies come to me after he should leave please send it to me pr Express to Chickamauga, Hamilton County E Tenn & oblige. Your Friend

Jno F. White, Lt Col 1st Tenn Cav

- - - - - - - - - - - - -

The following notice appeared in ***The Athens Post*** of 23 May 1862:

"Died at Decatur, May 17th after a short illness, Mrs. M.J. Lillard, in the 30th year of her age, wife of Col. John M. Lillard, now prisoner of war at Fort Warren, Boston, Mass."

- - - - - - - - - - - - -

LETTER NO. 45
AMANDA C. LILLARD TO N.J. LILLARD

Coldwater, Tennessee
June 10th 1862

My Loving Cousin

You donot know the gladness and joy with which I answer you as it had been so long since I was cheered by rival of one of your kind letters. Yours of 16th and 18th of Apr came to hand 8th inst; which was last Sabbath. Mr. Cooley has had possession of it a long time as I suppose you placed it in his care. Though a long time on the road, rest assured that it was none the less welcomed; But while this is so, I am sorrow that I have not been the receipt of many such Letters as your last during the long period of silence I had thought many times you had forgoten me through the excitement, and busy time of war; but I didnot think the least heard; not withstanding, a line would have unsaded me greatly; as I have many times been cast down.

I still I have a host of things to write you; but think I will have to abandon many from the past. I am just from the cornfield; have been working so very hard that I feel to tired to write long; Spining howing and thining corn has been my occupation for several days past & how long it will contnue to be my lot, I am unable to say, but hope it will end soon; as I donot have a fance for the trade.

I was at Decatur Sunday found all well except Aunt Rogers, but was all more excited than I ever saw them since November; the place was full of Soldiers all day a passing from one place to another; so much so that some expected the Federals in in a few days I donot know what sort of feelings I will have when I see them acoming; but one thing is; I am not scared yet. War breezes has become so common that I fail to scare at ever one that over takes me. Your Bro Bill arrived home Sunday well except his ancle which was hurt by a hors. He says that he and many more was cut off 4 weeks by the Federls had not other chance only do cut their weigh through their lines loosing some few men killed.

The victory at Richmond is somewhat cheering to Southern people; Yet blood flowed freely from the brave sons of the South and today many a Mother & Sister ar bowed down on account of their loss. I saw a Yankey last Sunday. I assure you he is a casey looking bird. Many of the Girls says they will not have any of the Feds; that is if they donot look better than this one

Prisoner. I saw Thos Russell as he passed through Town. I was quite sorrow to see him return sick; but hope he will be up very soon.

Mollie & Sallie R. [Russell] stayed with [us] last Saturday night week. We passed the time off plesently; talking about you all. I promised Mollie that I would stay with her on next saturday and Sunday, which I intend working up to if possible. Your idea appears to be, that I joake --?-- to far about you but I denigh the charge it is her teasing me about her chance. I havenot saw my spark yet, which you spoke of returning soon with such a bright countenance; some thing surely has happened the fellow in his travail, who was it, Gorge Atchley or John Thomas, pleas inform me in your next.

Do you have any idea when you will be at home; if possible come against the 12th & 18 of July.

The 6th of June passed off, which time many of us has joyfully looked to for a happy meeting of Relation and friend, who has been absent so long but no such bliss. I know the joy would have been grate yes to grate to talk about. When I next see Amanda T. I shall return your love to her. Aunt Taylor [Mary Blevins Taylor] is grieving herself terable about Frank, but indeed he was a prize worthy to grieve after.

I am truly sorrow for you, that you are so old and ugley & not maried yet, but I never was in favor of children matches; just now thinking that you willnot be by yourself; that many more of us is travling the same road; one consoaling thing is should you not mary for 10 more years you will not have to live so long with a troublesom Woman. The ruler of the W H is all right so far as I know. I have spent the 2 last Sabbaths with L. she appeared to have on a plesant face all the while. I contrered(?) her in an inch of her life about yourself & John, S.R. You ought to have heard us, though I expect she will be mad the next time I meet her. I reckon I must close for this time believing I have already tired you with such stuff. Your Fathers folks is well as common. Give compliments to all. Say howdy to I.G. Cross for me, Tell him I still live in the range of Coldwater. Write when you have the chance. Look over such bad scribling for I am writing with an Lincolnites pens. Your --?-- --?--
Cousin Amanda C. Lillard

- - - - - - - - - - - - -

The following letter was written to Jennie before John learned of his wife's death.

LETTER NO. 46
JOHN M. LILLARD TO JENNIE LILLARD

Fort Warren, Boston Harbor, Mass
June 16th 1862

My Dear Wife

It seems as though letters had ceased to pass the lines, for I have received none from you written since April do my letters come to hand on yesterday a letter came to Col White from Tom Faw, which reced Col White when he left here gave me an order for all his mail the letter was dated the 24th May from his home, it had nothing but family news in it Tom sent his regards to me but did not say anything about the folk, at Taylorsville tho he stated he had just come from there, no doubt Col White has been to see you before now if he has got home he was paroled and started home and was as far as Murfresboro last account, he said he would take Mat & go & see you & tell you all about our prison life &c, many things I cannot write you. Though our life is so monotonous that that I can not add anything new in such successive letter but I am glad to be able to say I am still in good health so are nearly all the prisoners here no one dangerously sick and but one died since we have been here. (Col Dandson of Miss) & he came here sick, Well it is four months to day since we men surrendered at Donelson, 4 months of Prison life & some are chafing & grumbling & censuring-- but I must say that I do not consider them entitled to any more credit than many who are quietly enduring there their imprisonment, in fact when we consider what our government has on its hands the large number of our soldiers wounded to care for the enemy pressing in on all sides and in view of our Capital with their immense legions if for the present we are not exchanged or if we are somewhat overlooked can we grumble! there is only one desire that could prompt us to be extremely anxious now for release I mean but one unselfish desire & that is to mingle with those who are so bravely strugling for our independence, but those most anxious to get released I fear have their own comfort & enjoyment than our cause at heart but these instances are verry rare and arises more from a restless disposition and an aversion to inactivity than any want of Patriotism. I have never calculated on anything being done for a general exchange or parole until after the strugle was over at Richmond I get letters regularly from Capt Boggess

Leuts Howell & Neil all well Leut Bowling has been sick but is up again. I have never had but one letter from Camp Moreton [Morton] near Indianapolis, Ia. [Indiana] there the non commissioned officers and Privates they are not allowed to write only on business. I was verry much in hopes all the non com officers & privates would have been paroled & sent home till exchanged even if they did keep us poor officers in confinement as our government has paroled their privates, but patience is a great virtue and I suppose we will have to cultivate it. [J.M. Lillard]

- - - - - - - - - - - - -

RETURNED
The Athens Post, 3 August 1862

"Our friend, John M. Lillard, 26th Tennessee, captured at Fort Donelson, reached this place on Tuesday, on his way to his home in Meigs County. He has been confined in Fort Warren. During his captivity death invaded his household and plucked away the dearest flower, to bloom in a better land. Hundreds of true hearts welcome his return, but the face that would have beamed brightest is not here. Thy ways are just, O God, but unsearchable."

On 22 August 1862, ***The Athens Post*** reported "The rank and file of the Fort Donelson prisoners, as well as officers, have all been liberated and will probably reach their homes in a few days."

- - - - - - - - - - - - -

LETTER NO.47
LIZZIE KING TO N. J. LILLARD

At Home
Aug 1862

Dearest Uncle.

It is with the greatest pleasure that I write you a few lines this evening knowing your anziety to hear from all at home. We are all in tolerable good health at present. Cousin Amanda left hear a few moments ago looking as well as yousial. Uncle Jhon came home day before yesterday he is looking tolerable well he says that he has had tolerble good health. We was all so rejoysed to see him get home once more though it was joy mingled with sorrow. him and Uncle William was boath here last night. O! how mutch I wish you could have been hear two. Uncle W redgement was to cross the river this morning at pinhook he suposed that they was going to start over the mountain. Their is about 16,000 Yankees reported to be at Macminvil destroying every thing as they go couting down the corn an killing up the stock it looks like if that is the way they are doing they intend to leave thare. I hope those that have started over in that direction will meet up with them and pay them back for they way they have been doing over there.

Mr Frazier and Uncle Jhon started to Chattenary this eaving. Uncle sead that he did not know whither he would have to go and meet his redgment or what he would do untill he got down thare.

They have had a meeting that helt a week down at loer Goodfield their was a good many profesions Cousin Amanda and Melisia Blevins is two and I dont know who the others was as I was not there. I will have to quit writing as granma is caling me to eat some watermelons. I have been down and got som very nice milion. I fear you wont get to seat out in the poarch and eat thou I hope you will get to come yet before they are all gone. Their was a nefew of Uncle Rodgers hear this weak he belongs to the Texas rangers he was a very nice looking man and I think him to be a gentleman. I will have to bring my letter to a close as Sue Davis, Sallie and Mollie Neil has come. Write soon and write a long letter to your loving neic

Lizzie King

Dear Nute. I would like very much to see you. I thought of you often, sence I have been here wishing you could be with us, I hope you will continue to have good health and come safe back to us before very long. Give my love to Frank & John Lillard and George Allen.

Your Sister E. Frazier

- - - - - - - - - - - - -

LETTER NO. 48
AUGUSTUS HILTON TO CRATE LILLARD

Camp near Chattanooga
Aug 15th 1862

Dear Cousin.

I this morning take the pleasure of informing you that I & Bro Abe is in tolerable good health at present hoping these fiew lines may find you enjoying the same Blessing. I have nothing of much intrest to write times is pretty hard in Camps at this time. Wee have not Beean at this place But a few days and dont expect wee will stay here very long But I want you Cousin to Write to me in haste and give mee all the news that you can I see in the paper that Cos John has Been exchanged and got Back to the Confederacy again.

I want you to write to me whare Cos Neute is so I can Write to him. Wee are about 12 miles from Chattanooga on the Knoxville RR I cant hear of any Yankies about I think wee will make another move shortly But cant tell Whare too I am looking for a discharge now But wont get off in 2 or 3 weeks I said that I and Abe was in tolerable good health so we are But the wound that I got at Shilo will give me a discharge I havent don any duty since the Battle. I would like to come to see you all when I get my papers fixed up if I could get there for the enemy if there is any earthly chance I will come I have Been in West Tenn and am now in East Tenn But I want to see the middle My desire is to see that fair young lady Which you have chosen for me I must come to a close give my love & Best respects to all the family and connection Also excuse my Bad Written letter for I have no place to write and this Confederate paper is Bad nothing more at present But remain your friend until Death.

Augustus Hilton

- - - - - - - - - - - - -

LETTER NO. 49
MOLLIE GATHERS TO N.J. LILLARD (?)

Schoolroom,
Aug 22, 1862

Much esteemed friend

Tis noon and I have Seated myself amid the Shouts of childish laughter, to respond to your kind favor of the 9th which came to hand this morning and was perused with no small degree of pleasure But if I Should fail to write a connected letter you will attribute it in part at least to the confusion and noise in which I write. Many thanks to you for your congratulations at finding me still in "Dixie"

How I or --?-- --?-- came to be So well posted you Say is hard for you to tell. Not very Strange to me. Who ever heard of Such a thing being kept a Secret not I. You hate an engageement do you where one or both the parties know nothing about it So do I but I have no reason to think that that is your desperate condition. So just out with the truth and tell me all about it and give me time and I will wish you a nice pair of Slippers.

You wish me to be a little more definite So that you can defend yourself affirm or deny poor fellow your cause is in a precarious condition. I did not know that when a person was accused of being a conspirator in a Secret plot that the name of his accomplice had to be given before he could assent his own innocence or admit his guilt. Besides that is not my part of the game.

It was you that Started out to interpret my meaning and I am sure that I was much more explicit in my list(?) than what you construed into a threat at your Bachelorship which contruction forced me to try to vindicate my character, Which I did by telling you the light in which I had Seen best to regard you for Some time past And now you flare up again and are ready to take my old head off make a powerful act as though you were going to --?-- the whole affair and then finely wind up by saying out with it you can not be hurt. Not only that Since you are undoubtedly about to take your leave of the State of Single wrechedness and enter into that of double blesssedness I must content myself with Sticking pins in you every now & then. I admit that it is poor consolation But it is a fact that has long Since been demonstrated that it is a predomment(?) characteristic of our nature to try to bring every body down on a level with ourselves. So if I am doomed to a State of eternal celibacy I am determined to render the last days of those that are emegrating to that "happy land" just as miserable as I possibly can. But enough of Such nonsence. If your patience are not exhausted they must be equal to old friend Jobes.

Well the mails are started up again So you can direct to Smiths X Roads. If you could have Seen me this morning when I received your letter you would have Seen one of the mad girls I had like not to have read it at all for all the news was read out of it before I got it. George W Calahan had taken the liberty to read it before I got it and then put a note in it asking my pardon. He Stated that he thought it was from Brothers and that he could take the news to Pa to Camps. I will be compelled to give him a little advice when I get to See him.

There is a great deal of excitement in this vicinity just now. There is a Com about four miles below here that are arresting all the prominent old Union men. The most of the men that have been arrested are old grey headed men. They nearly all have Sons in the Northern army and it is Said have been harboring Lincoln Spies. I know nothing about it though it may all be a false accusation. I am getting along finely with my School. I have 41 Students & am as blith as a bird Still hoping for the best. If the 4 Ten Reget is Still near you please hunt up my little brother and find out why he is not discharged. He is not 18. He wants to join your Reget. We never hear from through his own letters I Sometimes [think] his officers stops his letters to us. They know that he is under age. I am more than willing for him to be in the Service but I am not willing for him to stay where he is. Please give me all the information that you can. I Shall Start about the sixt of next month to See about him.

As ever a true friend

Mollie Gathers

Write Soon

- - - - - - - - - - - - -

LETTER NO. 50
NEWTON J. LILLARD TO SISTER

Camp Before Cumberland Gap
August 24th 1862

Dear Sister

This Sabbath evening being on pickett and every thing being dull & still & I have a sheet of paper I thought I would write a few lines though nothing to write. We have a pickett line Drawn around the Gap about three miles from the forts & occasionally we received a shot or fire from them. We do not reply in any shape whatever they have not done us much Damage wounded one man from Ga & killed one in Kincades Co while we have picked several of theirs off & Taken 10 or 12 prisoners. How long we will continue here I suppose depends upon what Genl Smith does over the mountain. We have a Camp rumor that he is over at Cumberland ford and has been there several days, Making for Lexington with a part of his force. We can hold our position here against odds should the Yankees Conclude to fight us on this side of the Mountain.

Uncle Bill & Dr Buckner is here, been here three days say they are agoing to stay untill a fight comes off. James Lillard was over to see us to day Looks pretty well says Bill Rogers is at their Camps and is pretty well. Sent me word that he would come over to see me in a few days. Tell Aunt I dont think she need to be uneasy about him. I thank you for the Collars & Shirts, they come in very good time also the pants. Tell Bill Stewart I should like very much to come home but Suppose there is no chance during our active operation as a General cleaning from Tennessee of the Feds seems to be the move, and I hope we will succeed in driving them Out of the State entirely for I think Tennessee has suffered enough for One year though the fates of War is very unceretain indeed.

I am truly Glad the Col has arrived home. I hope he will not be so unfortunate again I know his men will hail their deliverance with Joy. I know Bro feels like a new man. I shall look for him out here on his return home, If he can possibly spare the time. If we get over into Ky we will have Level land over there no doubt. I see Morgan is striking them again about Gallitan Tenn where he was recruited with two Companies of Ky there was one Co come through Pound Gap yesterday they are now at Tazwell Old Abes draft will run a many men off over here, and the thought of the Conscript is making of the E.T. get Out. I wish they were all gone then we would not have to leave guards behind us. Give me all the news you have at home. Tell Bro I will write him if he does not come by. Give Love to all I will answer Lizzie & Amandas letters soon. Your Bro

Nute

- - - - - - - - - - -

LETTER NO. 51
ABSALUM C. HILTON TO CRATE LILLARD

Camp Near Tennessee River
Aug 26, 1862

Miss Crate Lillard
Dear Cousin I was handed a letter yesterday adressed to Brother Augustus and he having ben left behind at Sick Camp near Chattanooga I taken the liberty of Breaking the Seal and reading the Contents and I this morning attempt an answer. Brother Gus was not left behind Sich but he had not Recovered from his wound yet Susficently to march any distance and the Presumption is that he will be discharged in a Short time as he has made application and I think there will be no great difficulty. Cousin you insist in your letter on Gus and me visiting you soon if Gus gets his discharge I will insist on him visiting you but my chanch is a bad one and I will make no Promises as I have ben in the Service now nearly 12 months and I never had a furlough to go home yet.

I hope this letter will Secure your further good words in my favor to that pretty Black eyed Girl you Spoke of for I think if any body in the World is entitled to a pretty and good wife it is a Southern Soldier who has bin fighting for his Country. I would like very much to be with you to eat peaches and apples as we have to walk about five or six miles when we get any peaches and have to pay a Price for them at that or we Buy them from Union men. I would like very much to come up and be with you at that meeting you Speak of But I Guess I had Better Stay with the Boys. I would say however Should I not Get there at your usual hour of Starting to Church that you need not wait for me, As I Guess there is Some nice young man in the Country who will See you Safe to and from Church if they have not all gone to the War. I would like very much to know who that is that you expect to marry soon. I Sepct it youself. This leaves me hoping To hear from you Soon. I Remain your affectionate Cousin

Absalum C. Hilton

- - - - - - - - - - - -

LETTER NO. 52
NEWTON J. LILLARD TO SISTER

Camp before Cumberland Gap
August 28th 1862

I had first intended to send this by mail But did not get it off & then I should have sent it by Uncle Witt(?) I was on out post duty when he started Everything is usualy quit yesterday. This morning the feds are burning all the houses along the foot of the Mountain before the Gap What will be the result is hard to surmise But I am of the opinion that we will Starve them Out in a few days more It is said that Genl Smith is on the other side of them drawing his lines closer every day.

We have been here ten days and will remain Longer from the signs of the times. Our Boys are in pretty good health But very durty not having a change of clothing, and no opertunity to wash what they have got. I have been looking for Bro Vern & John have given then Both out we are expecting an other hard Battle at or near Mannasseth we have no news from Beuls Army or Bragg. I will wrtite if anything occurs.

Your Bro

N. J. Lillard

- - - - - - - - - - - -

LETTER NO. 53
AMANDA LILLARD TO N. J. LILLARD

Decatur Tennessee
Sept 22nd 1862

Dear Cousin;

With pleasure I write you anothe line, as Hugh [Thomas] failed to start on last week, not as I feel able to interest you, but only to send you a fresh line. I com over here yesterday morning, & am now at Uncle Rogers have been entertained all the while with good preaching & good company. Meeting closed last night until to night. L.R. Blevins, J. O. Taylor, Bro John & several others are Moarners, to my great supprise.. We had the glorious news on yesterday evening that the Federals had all left the Gap Without the loss of a man. Whether this is so I cannot say, but hope it is true.

We received a letter from Pa Saturday he is in Kentucky, well & doing well so says letter. Well I knohed(?) Frank for a beau yesteday evening. he sill has those charming features about him. Abe was with Miss Sallie Neal yesterday looked fine as usual.

Sallie Russell is here in the room with says to tell you is as pretty as ever sends you her love. Mollie is not here. Buck Stewart is sparking her. --?-- Roberts is sparking all the girls, but ---?--- [two lines too dim to read] I must close as Hugh is going to start. Give love to all. As ever ---?--- your affectionate Cousin,

Amanda

- - - - - - - - - - - -

LETTER NO. 54
CALLIE LILLARD TO NEWTON LILLARD

Phildo(?) Tenn
Nov 5, 1862

Cousin Neut;

I hastin to answer you, for it is so hard to keep up with there Army movement. When once started from A point it is difficult to find you any more. I am so sorrow for you Soldiers. I know you see hardships enough, so worn out, and taxed beyond human strength. Would to heavens this war would Stop! For it has caused so much suffering everywhere.

Murrell has not come yet, But looking for him every day. Jno Wash would have gone up there sooner, But we still kept looking for him. I cant imagine why he does not write or come home if he is sick. I wish you could both come down and rest awhile. You need not care for being dirty, that is A natural consequence with Soldiers. I can enjoy your company amidst all that. And besides I'll furnish you some clean clothes. Do come home with Wash tomorrow. I do think the Soldiers are treated right mean, that their Commanders will not let them go home (Stationed where you are) and prepare for the winter, and take some rest after so fatiguing a march. But of cours they ought to know best.

Julia and I have almost been tempted to go up and bring Nyrl(?) home any how, but knew it was no place for us, and would have been presumtion in me to think so. I hope you will not have to take another such A march soon.

No news of interest down this way, or at least to tedious to write at present as I am going to Write to Murrell again without receiving any answer. Come when you can, for you know we are always glad to see you.

Ever your Cousin
M. Callie Lillard

- - - - - - - - - - - - -

LETTER NO. 55
WILLIAM C. ROGERS TO COUSIN

Decatur, Tenn
Nov 23rd 1862

Dear Cousin

I send you a Line though have nothing of interest to write you. The Business that I promist to do for you I have not had the chance to attend to it for I have had to stay close at home ever since you left hear I spose that you hav heard of the death of my Dear Father I am very Sorry to hav to tell you of it he sufford very much for several days the Doctor seem to do all he could for him Capt Sandusky & Snider have been home since you left. Sandusky left to day Snider is not going for days he is unwell those Mulasses cannot be Bought at the figures that we wer Speeking of they are asking $123 to 150 per Gal ther is So many of them Maid that I do not think that ther is much mony in them strange if you say by them at that I will do it well --?-- as it is I will hafto act as a man for I have to see to my Mother Write me soon an give me all news.

Your Coz
Wm C. Rogers

- - - - - - - - - - - - -

LETTER NO. 56
JOHN M. LILLARD TO SISTER

Murfresboro, Tenn
Decr 21st 1862

My Dear Sister

As every body is asleep I thought I would drop you a line before I went to bed. I have no news. good health generally I am very well I went to Church in town to day and heard a good Campbellite sermon. Col Wm B Lillard & family were there they all belong to that Church but dont like to be Called Campbellites but say it is the Christian Church, the Chaplin of our Regt preached in camp this evening. I was at the Courthouse the other night at a party given by Breckenridges Division. Genl Bragg, Polk, Johnson & Morgan & his new wife were all present besides all the other little Generals, and quite a number of little Col Lt Col Majors Captains & Leutenants the ladies seem to enjoy themselves verry much they feel so releived since the Yankeys left. We are still busy trying to get in good fighting trim we drill dailey but it seems like I never will get my Regement as well drilled as before having new companies & new men in the other Companies. Your acquaintances in the Regt are all well. Maj Sharp & Dr Clementson left Yesterday morning they only staid with us one day. I was verry sorry Mr Thomas could not come out I wanted to see him very much. I was so glad to hear from Tommie. I had heard nothing so long I have had no letter from Callie since I was at home when you answered her letter for me. I feared she was sick & gone home you nor Mr Thomas neither say anything about her in your letters is she at Abingdon yet or gone home. I hoped to hear from Tommie often through her letters and cannot account for her silence in fact if it was not for you I would get but few letters & I hope you will still write often & long leters to me and I will write often if it is only to say I am well.

I have promised to spend Christmas Eave night at Col W B Lillards and it is close at hand but no telling what a day may bring forth and we may be on a march or on Pickett, but I hope not. Cousin Lizzie & Julia W Bs two grown daughters are very nice girls but do not look much like sisters. They are half sisters. Lizzie is large & fleshey & Julia is slender & delicate & very pretty black hair & eyes. Lizzie will weigh as much as I do but is very good looking & is so good & kind. They want to see you verry much. Write me all the news from home give my love to all & be sure to write often to Your Affect Bro

Jno M Lillard

- - - - - - - - - - - - -

LETTER NO. 57
W.P.W. ALEXANDER TO J.M. LILLARD

Athens, Tenn
Jan 6th 1863

This may certify that in April 1862 I was professionally called to attend Martin Shook a private in Co -- Capt Giddings 3rd Regt & Ten Bat Col Lillard commanding I found Mr Shook suffering from a severe attack of influenza accompanied with a billious diarhea wh[ich] had greatly prostrated him. At the time I waited on him I made a written statement as to his disability and recom-mended that "sick leave of absence" be granted him for thirty days, if I remember correctly, wh[ich] was duly ford [forwarded] to his command, and wh[ich] his family now understands did not reach its destination.

Subsequently on Dec 23d I was again summoned to visit Mr Shook who I found suffering from a gunshot wound in the hand. The bullet (from a minnie rifle) having entered the --?-- surface and penetrated the hand in its course shattering the second and third Metacarpal bones a statement of wh[ich] has already been ford [forwarded] to his regiment --?-- and as I have learned by the Provost Marshall of this post Capt J W Carmack.

Respectfully, W P W Alexander MD

- - - - - - - - - - - - -

LETTER NO. 58
STEPHEN THOMAS TO J. M. LILLARD

North Fork
Jan the 6th 1863

Col Lillard

Dear Sir Your very welcome letter Duly came to hand Last Saturday we was truly glad to heare from you and to heare that you was well this will enform you that we are all well as Common Little Tommy is Still in fine helth growing very fast looks better than I Ever Saw him talks a good deal a bout his Pa. Mrs Worth has had a fine Son a few days a go and a pearse to be doing very well when I was out in Tennessee I did not think that I would bring Eliza a way, til the night before I Started home She a peared so antious to Come to North Carolina I thought I would Let her come and as I had promised here when she went to Tennessee to Let her come back at Som convenant time and She thought that if She did not Come now She never would get to Come and I thought in as much as She had beean very good to Pinny I would let her Come and now when Even you want them to go back they Can go at Eny time &c well Wiley has gone in to the Servis in Capt Browns Co Capt Falks Battalion they now are Stationed neear Johnsons Depo I suppose Wiley has the Second Lewtenants offise I think they promist him the quartermasters ofice but faild by Some reasons I under Stand theare is a good manny wants him yet for quartermaster & you mention in your letter a bout his Comming(?) to you I would a Liked vary much for him to have Come to your Redgment if you Could have maid it Suet.

Well as the mail will be on in a few minets I must Come to a Close please write as often as Convenant for I am very antious to hear as I hear thare had beean fiting going on at Murphysboro So nothing more by Remain yours Truly Stephen Thomas

At Home, Jan 17th 1863

My Dear Brother:

I write a few lines on the back of Mr Thomas letter to let you know we are all well as usual sister Ell has been over this week, she and mother are on a visit to sister Mary, isen't that a wonder.

Jasper was over this week for the first time since you left, doesent he treat me badly he looks rather thin, I believe I have written you two or three letters since Mr Thomas was here, Callie is going to school at Abingdon, Peiss at Jefferson.

I don't believe I wrote of sis Tex affliction her little boy just lived one day it was a beautiful child, it died New Years night Tex is almost well. We have not had letters from Col Nute or Wm since they were at Meridian, neither have we received any from Jos, we were very unesy -------?------ Jon didnot write to me, we heard that you are safe we cannot hear any of the casualities of the 26th brother write to us ever --?-- far we know how we suffer from anxiety. accept the best love and wishes of your loving sister,

C E Lillard

- - - - - - - - - - - - -

LETTER NO. 59
J. M. COX TO NEWTON J. LILLARD

Goodfield
Jan 13th 1863

Col Neut

Dear Friend Through my prolonged sickness I am induced to ask a favor of you if it be in your power. I wish you to give me a discharge from the service. I am not able to come to the Regt to see to the matter myself and I think you and the Dr Parshal can as a favor and as a due to a friend arrange the matter for me I have been laying here at home two months and done nothing and Dr Gilbert thinks my health will not sufficiently improve soon to return to the service and my men at Knoxville keep writing me to know when I am coming back to duty and feeling bound up in the service as I am I am pestered to be called upon to do a thing that I am not able to do. I fully believe I am intitled to a discharge and if I was with you I could have got it before now. If it was otherwise I would not ask such a thing and I feel no backwardness in coming to you and asking such a favor or a favor of any kind at any time Dr G sends letter to Dr Parchal which will set him right. Capt Buckner will do all that is necessary in the cure I think I do not wish to involve any one if there be any danger of that. Write me upon the subject. Your Friend

S. M. Cox

- - - - - - - - - - - - -

LETTER NO. 60
JOSEPH A. HOWELL TO N. J. LILLARD

Tullahoma Tenn
January 20th 1863

Col N.J. Lillard 3rd Tenn
Vicksburg, Miss
Dear Nute

I received yours of 8th inst was glad to hear from and your good health & seaming good spirits. I have nothing of any special intrest we are here after our Skiddalle from Murfreesboro in the mud this is one of the mudyest places I have seen I do not know how long we will be here (I hope not long) every thing is very hard to get & our Regt is very ready having not been able to get much. Our Regt was in the fight and suffered pretty severally 13 killed & 74 wounded. Capt Allen of Cocke County was among the killed. Capt Cash of Rhea is supposed to be killed. Col John had his horse killed under him. Lt Col Battles and Major Saffles were both wounded. John was not hurt. The Regt was in line of battle 7 days and nights liked to wore them out they were in the charge on the last day of the fight it was a dreadfull affair. I think Breckenridge undertaken to do to much with the men he had without support, but I do not think we have lost much by falling back now that the forage that was in the county we got all the Stores away with us the Country is to level to defend without we had a very large force for ther is no advantage to be taken in position any way.

Col John started for Chattanooga this morning he is sick or has been since the fight but better he goes there to recruit his health I suppose he will go on up home he has his old deseased billious or Jaundice I think will be all right soon.

You asked is we had any thing to drink well we had a few quarts of County made we had quite a dry time Christmas but hope to do better the next one as we was too buisy to enjoy the holladays as Mr Yanky was uncomfortably near and Kepted disturbing us now and then in our --?--. I hope we will not have the same luck again and hope we may all be at home next Christmas at old D. when all things is quiet & peace rains and then we will have a big bust (hope so)

I am geting along with my business pretty well I have got along very well I find it pretty troublesome to please every body I have learned not to try to please them much every thing in my line is very scarce.

The last letter I had from home said Sam Cox was very bad supposed he would not live. I am very sorry I wish he could have lived through the War so he could have deviled old Abe, he will have nothing to hold him on to the Southern army after this. Gilbert has resigned and gone home I understand I do not think he was much Southern.

I do wish we could all get into the same brigade then we could be together more but I suppose ther is no chance for that now. I fear your healths will not be so good long as I think that climate will not suit Tennesseans it will be pleasant through the winter I reccon. Tell Sam & John to write to me I have writen them several times and get no answer.

My regards to all my health is not good I think I will go home tomorrow write soon &c Yours truly

Joseph A. Howell

- - - - - - - - - - - - -

LETTER NO. 61
HENRY B. LATROBE TO N. J. LILLARD

Col. N. J. Lillard
3rd Regt. Tenn Vols.

Tellico Plains
24th Jany 1863

Dear Sir

I am engaged in starting the Tellico Furnace, to manufacture iron for the Government. I am anxious to obtain the services of three members of your Regt, viz: Wm Coppinger, David Sylvester, and Wm Queen, belonging to Capt Morlocks Co.

The two first are experienced boat hands & I can find no others who understand the navigation of Tellico River. Queen is an old ore digger, & I need him much to mine for me. All three of them are now at home on furlough, & if you can possibly detail them to work for me at the Furnace, you will not only confer a great obligation upon me personally, but materially promote the interest of the service, by enabling me to have their assistance in the manufacture of iron. I send this note by Sylvester, one of the men named. Very respectfully

Henry B. Latrobe

- - - - - - - - - - - - -

LETTER NO. 62
UNIDENTIFIED
[SISTER TO NEWTON LILLARD]

At Home
Jan 31st 1863

[NOTE: square torn from corner of paper removed portions of several lines (indicated as . . .) and there apparently was a third page that is missing. The letter is not signed.] . . . I received your letter pr Capt Allen . . . welcome indeed. I am glad that . . . health down South. brother John came home last Tuesday was a week his health was very bad, he had the camp fever after the battle, he improved fast after he came home &

got fried chicken to eat, which you know is his favorite dish. he started back today, he had to go to Cleveland to report to the surgeon, perhaps he will come back home if he doesnt feel better. Mr Joe Howell & Henry Crawford eate dinner here yesterday en route for home. Jasper, Mr Boggess & Mary came yesterday Capt Allen has just come from a quilting or rather party at Mr Russels. he gives a glowing duscription of the fun they had. I suppose they had a delightful time. bro John being here we didnot attend. I have not been to a social party or quilting this winter, nor do I wish to be a good reason Lizzie & Emma has gone over to Dr Buckmers with Learge(?) to get their teeth worked on. I hope your coat will please you, we could have had you pants made, but the cloth was striped. We regretted it very much because it was so nice.

Sunday morning Ugh! what a . . . soldiers who have to be out in such . . . Mr Boggess and I went down to . . . he looks so badly. I was very sorry . . . such bad health, he is still able . . . little yet but is very week. I saw . . . looked very neat. Papa has sold his . . . & I. Benson got two hundred and . . . Pa's head has rize (?) and --?-- he suffers a great deal with his head and finger nute he is a greate deal better; Tex is improving, hope she will be well soon. brother I wish you was here to whip Mary. She is reading my letter & making fun of it. isnot that to bad. Dr Buckner & Crate was over last week both hearty. Bill Harbison is at home looking bad. I donot know whether I ought to tell it or not (but you know I have a proclivity to tell everything I know) Capt Learge has been breaking into your arangments. I thought it my duty (being your sister & loving you dearly) to inform you of the fact.

John informed me that my sweetheart came through safely at Murfs Can't you rejoice with me 'oh! me if mother was to see that !! Yes we heard that the State was going to be married Christmas & sincerely hoped it was true, not that I wish her any harm, but thinking it is her desire & would be the realization of a hope for many years. I suppose Lt H.B. is flying around the tother.

- - - - - - - - - - - - -

LETTER NO. 63
MINERVA [FRAZIER?] TO N.J. LILLARD

Washington
Feb 2, 1863

Dear Friend

I had no thought you would ever receive my last letter so I sent a short one by George Allen, but will write again. Some persons do not believe in dreams and I can say I do not, but sometimes they come to pass the Night before I received your last I dreamed Jennie and I both received one from you Jennies 10 or 12 pages long and mine a very short one but what a disapointment to her I was very sorry to hear of your illness but hope you will soon recover. I was sorry to hear the Small Pox had found its way to Col Gillespies Regt for it is a terrible disease. Mississippi is a hard place to live in and very disagreable in the Summer season every one says that has tried it if the Citizens treat you as well as they did the 19 Regt while they sojourned in the Paradise of that State you may consider yourselves blesed 20 & 25 cts for a glass of Water but enough for that portion of this Confederacy. Last Night which was Fryday the little Girls and Boys had a Candy Stew at the Academy and gave the grown Girls an invitation. I tell you we had quite an interesting time and a single young Gentleman there. Mollie Kelly and I had Possey(?) King for a gallant. I enjoyed myself finely dont you wish we could have Peace again and all enjoy ourselves as in days of old. if I could I would send you some of the Candy.

You say you are better posted about Miss Tennies affairs far off as you are than some of us at home no boubt you are for I am not atall but hope it will come off soon. Kate and I gave you some advise but we were ignorant of it at the time. I have often thought of that night and did feel somewhat ashamed but do nor care now. I was sorry that we had said anything that would break up that march. Ann Gillespie was so anxious to know whether they were married or not she had to ask Mr McCorkle if John was married.

Henry Crawford came home yesterday and is going to stay untill spring so Ann an him will have quite a nice time I should think.

If I had any news from the 26 Regt or 19 I would give you but I have not had a letter from Cousin Sam since soon after the Fight. I suppose Henry might tell me something concerning the 26 if a boddy could get to see him. Capt Neal sent some word to all of us Girls but we have not yet received it but hope to soon. Your Brother John just left home for Cleveland Fryday morning he has been sick.

I would have thought hard of you if you had not explained what you did but think you a good friend which I always considered you or you would have done as some do never mentioned anything about it to me I was very much surprised when I learned what they were. Col Bean never mentioned such a thing as that he ever thought you was courting one in his life for he knew better and when I asked him what he had said he did not know unless it was something he had said in a conversation with you. What if we had been corresponding that was no reason or sign but one cannot correspond with a Friend but they are going to marry if that was the case I would have been married long ago and to a good many. He did not want an explanation but will give it when convenient but persons must have fun you know sometimes but I am glad you do not & will not have it at the expense of as good a friend of yours as I am. I read Jennie what you said about her She said Tell you she was in as good earnest as you and if it would please the Lord to spare you through the next fight at Vicksburg She expects to see you whether the War closes or not She thinks you might have called to see her when in W but I told her She must ecuse you and the reasons why you did not. Emma says she would love to see you and often thinks of you accept her best bishes for your safety and welfare.

Aunt Ell & Uncle Bee [Frazier] I suppose will answer your Letter soon all well, my respect to Capt F-?-- also yourself accept the kindest regards of your

Sincere Friend,
Minerva

- - - - - - - - - - - - -

LETTER NO. 64
JOHN M. LILLARD TO SISTER

Tullahoma, Tenn
Feb 4th 1863

Dear Sis

I arrived here safely on last evening and feel very well am still improving it is bitter cold here and I am not on duty yet and will not be until the matter moderates found all presently well everything quiet here Genl Joseph E Johnson is here and the army is in fine spirits. I have seen more of our relations from near Murfresboro since I returned but understand the Yankeys are destroying everything in that section. I have heard nothing from our wounded men left at Murfresboro since got to camps. Our boys have all got wooden chimneys to their tents and can keep warm in them. We can do well all to wet weather we can protect ourselves against cold but rain & mud is hard to get along in.

I have nothing to fill up a letter with to day but will rite you often. I hope you will rite me often fill a sheet with something as every thing from home is interesting. I hope Teck is up by this time tell her not to get too smart all at once. I shall expect a letter from her occasionally. My love to all.

Write soon to your affect Bro
Jno M Lillard

No body has asked me anything about you & Tex & Liz—

- - - - - - - - - - - - -

LETTER NO. 65
STEPHEN THOMAS TO DOCT. LILLARD

North Fork
Feb 6th 1863

Doct Lillard

Dear Sir I Recd your very welcome letter Baring 28 of January we was truly glad to heare from you and to heare that you had once more escaped the dangers of bulets and shell in such a Bloddy battle we field that we Can never bee thankfull nough for the kind protection of an over ruling providence hoo has shealded our heads sc far. We are well Except one of your little Black girls Linda has been Compainen a good deal and is right bad off yet I think she is a little better this morning. Tommy Looks well and harty Elizabeth Worth has had another heir a boy and is growing very fast and doing well So far &c We have no news of interest at present only times is gooing worse very fast I never once drew an Idea that we should have the defeculty with East Tenesee Toryes and Sum in our County a Long neear the State Line they are Robing Stealing and plundering almost all the time and shooting at Southern men when Ever they can get a Sly Chance I have been Looking for them to give me a --?-- Every night they have taken nearly all the guns in neighboor hood a bove me the Torys takes Every thing they Can carry off they take Corn & bacon Clothing thread and Even the womens Clothing &c Holks Battallion was at or neear Johnsons Depo the Cold Some of them Back and they have had several atacks the Toryes way Lays them and keepe conceald in the Bresh and shoot and then ran Capt Brown the Company that Wiley belongs too sent out a Squad to take Some fellows that had beean Shooting and Stealing and they taken three at one house and left a guarde with the three they had taken and went on to a northern house and theane they found four Stout big men and Wiley was ofeser and had Comand he Calld at the dore an the Toryes told them to go off but nocked the dore open and Toryes fired Several guns at them one ball jest Cut the top of Wiley head and a barrel Wiley knocke the gun up and took Close holt and and the fellow was a big Stout fellow and he throwd Wiley and nocked his pistol out of his hand but in making an Effort to rise he accidently threw his hand on his pistol and he jest turned it up and shot the fellow off of him self the Torys shot one of Holks men and kild him and wounded Several others I think that we will have peace a nuff to Sabdue them in a few days if the mishes(?) will doo their duty I want them to Shoot and hang them as fast as they can get holt of them I Should Like very much if Wiley Could be Transfeerd to your Command but I Expect it Could not be Convenantly done please write to me often as Conveant as I must Come to a close for my pen is So bad I do not Expect you Can read what I hav wrote please giv my Love and respects to all the Famly So I Remain yours Truly

Stephen Thomas

- - - - - - - - - - - - -

LETTER NO. 66
NEWTON J. LILLARD TO CRATE LILLARD

Vicksburg Miss
March 13th 1863

Dear Crate

I have delayed answering your letter a few days thinking I would have something of interest to write you but have waited in vain. We are all well as usual no cases of sickness in the Regt that is dangerous. Co (I) has usual good health. I believe Posy Marshall is Complaining and not able for duty. I would have much rather they had let him remain at home, he never will be able to do us any good. Frank John Bro & Bill Rogers are all Stirring around I think this Climate will suit Bill pretty well. I recd a Letter from Jno dated the 20th of Feby he was well at that date. We are eagerly listning for the Roar of Cannon in that direction. We know a battle cannot be delayed much longer unless there be a falling back Somewhere, and great result depends upon how the conflict goes. We also have been expecting a fight at Port Hudson, the accept opinion & believe is that the great Reb fleet that has been threatning Charleston S C Will no come up the Miss River if so we will have our hands full to over flowing we will try and manage them However. So far the fight at this point all hands dispair of an engagement soon. The Yankies are still here but all indications are that they will not attack us soon. Indeed it will take a tremendous force to accomplish anything here we are well fortified, and If we are fully provisioned we can hold out for a long time, our rations have been very scant but now they are full & we are receiving heavy supplys from Texas and if the Feds do not stop our Channel it is said Texas alone can fed the Confederate army 6 months.

I would like to send you a diagram of the City and fortifications but they are so complicated & extensive that I have failed to draw anything that would gave you an idea. I will still continue to try and may be after while I can accomplish something. Sam Crain arrived yesterday. Say he is agoing to stick with 3rd untill the matter is settled. We have still escaped the small pox and I think we will not have any of it among us all having been vaccinated. The river is still Rising and will soon be at high water Mark. When The Mississippi Bottoms will be entirely over overflowed It gave the gunboat a fair chance to do something & no doubt aid the Yankees in making their Canal navegable we will be ready for them even should they suceed The road down the Miss river is agoing to be a hard road to hold so much so probably as the road to Richmond.

What has become of Jasper. I have done everything I could to provoke him to write me but he still keep sullen silence well I dont Much care I shall write him pretty often & let him pay the postage.

I am truely glad bro Vern was allowed to remain with you though If it were possible to restore his facuties I had much rather see him in service of the army. I hope the government will not loose anything by the exemption. he surely will be industrious in doing what he Can to raise something to Clothe & Feed them for much of our success depends upon the supply of rations & clothing for the army. I know the women (God Bless them) understand this point and are exerting all their energies to relive these wants, but the men are bent upon speculation even if it cost them their own destruction with still greater loss of the Liberty of the South.

I hope Fathers hand is getting well & he more Careful next time of the danger of Duml(?) trite(?) Teeth. It must have pained very much. how is he getting along farming have the season been unusually bad for plowing. Farmers here have their foreord corn planted & have commenced plowing it over we will have green corn soon. It would supprise Tennesseans to see what quantities of Corn planters raise Some as high as 20 thousand Bb to Farm.

I am truly sorry for Jim Cox & Jane but the needseseties of war are stubborn things and most all except the favored few gave to bend to them and I suppose they will have to bare it the best they can It is very cheering to hear the young ladies have so good health I hope they will bear in mind that we are to return Home after the war closes, & I hope we will not be to old to marry when we do return. The Ladies of Miss are very fine indeed the are pictures of health Many of them blooming Young widows.

I have heard nothing from Amanda lately. What has become of her, has she been conscripted recently. how is S.M.C. is he improving I hope he will be restored to health I should like very much to have an old Tennessee dinner but you know it does more harm than good to think of these things (impossible one) Tell Aunt Rachel that Bill is [in] good health give them all a Howdy.

Tell Ma I am trying [to] be a good boy & taking care of myself as well as possible I would be glad to see you all. how is Grand Mas health this winter is she still knitting away except the wish of your Bro

Affectionately

N J Lillard

P.C. dont be scared about the Money

- - - - - - - - - - - - -

LETTER NO. 67
JOHN M. LILLARD TO E.C. LILLARD, LIZZIE LILLARD, SALLIE McLEAN, AND JULIA LILLARD

Camp 5 Miles from War Trace Te
May 8th 1863

Dear Sis & Cousins

I arrived safe last evening and found all well in fine health & spirits everything quiet no prospect of an immediate fight what may turn up yet I cannot tell. I saw Cousin Ben just now he sends his love to all he got Lizzies letter and had answered it and desires to hear from them often. Cousin Sally in particular I deliverd the letter and package to Col Butler & Capt Crokett & Lizzie Sallie & Julias message to Col Palmer & the other young Gentlemen they [too faint to read] pleased to hear from them. Col Palmer is going to make application for leave of absence to go to East Tennessee. Where must I advise him to go if he gets his leave. The boys from Meigs are all well— asked how all the young ladies were.

Tell Cousin Lizzie I delivered her love to Adjt Hickey and he was much pleased, but scolded me for showing his letter. I should not be surprised if he & Capt Neil has an altercation though I told Hickey that I did not think Neil done any damage while at home as he did not have time to be with the Ladies but very little. I have not heard from Col N J Lillard he has never been to the Regt yet but I will look for him every day now as he knows about the time I would get back to camps as he will need his saddle bags & cloths. Capt Neil says he is willing to give them cloths but intends to try and get a pledge from some one and think the best chance is from the old man as he has so many rivals with the young ladies.

It has rained ever since I left home an is verry cool, is still raining some, log fires are verry fine all except the smoke the ground is damp & hard to sleep on after sleeping in beds, but I think I can now stand if any will. Cousin Ben tells me that they have his brother Tom in the Penitentary at Nashville. Uncle Ben is at home though the Yanks have burned all the rails and cut all the timber on his lands— this is a rich rolling Country & will be fine Camping ground in warm weather. It is muddy now but it is muddy everywhere. The boys were all glad to see me and crowded around the old Col to welcome his return with hearty greetings.

I have not time to wright much as it is five miles to War Trace & the mail is ready to be sent to War Trace. We send out every day. I want you & Cousin Lizzie to write me long letters on large paper. Give my love to all and write soon. Afft your Bro

Jno M. Lillard

- - - - - - - - - - - - -

LETTER NO. 68
JASPER LILLARD TO SISTER

Athens, Tenn
June 1st [1863]

Dear Sis

The news from Vicksburg is good Bro Nutes Regt did not Suffer but little he did not get hurt nor any of our particular acquaintances. Kyrt(?) & myself go to Cleveland to day will be over the last of the week Kyrt(?) is Sober now Hope you all have a sweet tooth left yet love to all. Jasper

- - - - - - - - - - - - -

LETTER NO. 69
WILLIAM BUSTER TO E. C. & LIZZIE LILLARD, LIZZIE & EMMA KING, AND SALLIE McCLAIN

Knoxville, Tenn
June 4th 1863

My Dear Young Ladies

It pains me very much to learn from our brave Soldiers at Vicksburg who are now bravely defending the beautiful valley of the Miss from the Ruthless invader of our Soil. to be informed by them that you had deprived them of their rations Such as Sweet bread, more commonly called Ginger Cakes, which was prepared for them by their wives mothers and sisters. It is with regret that I shall and do order you one and all to appear before me at these kind Quarters to answer the charge made against you viz: Sweet bread riot there by trying to make yourselves Sweet at the expense of the Poor Soldier—

Specifications

1st for eating said ginger bread without butter
2nd for taking to large mouth fulls
3rd for Eating as much as 2 rations each with out water
4th for consuming the whole 10 Sacks and asking for more

Maj Gen S B Buckner
Commander Dept East Tenn
Geo H Gainer, A ACT G C S

- - - - - - - - - - - - -

LETTER NO. 70
W. W. SHIELDS TO N. J. LILLARD

Benton Tenn
Aug 20th 1863

Col Lillard

Yours of the 18 inst is at hand and I embrace the earliest opportunity of answering it.

We had a very nice time last Thursday. I would have been glad if you could have been here to take dinner with us. I was very sorry to hear that you had been chilling. I am mending as fast as could be expected. I can walk on one crutch now. I don't think my knee joint is injured any the swelling is all gone out of my knee. I would like very much to be able to return to camps with the 3rd. We are going to have a nice ball in Benton tonight. When you get back to camps write and tell me your whereabouts for I am going back to camps when I eat up all of Ma's beans potatoes & chickens.

Your sincere friend
W. W. Shields

[NOTE: All the extra space on this letter was taken up by short messages to Newton from sisters and cousins. There was no order to the notes, but they are included below in the order written. Most were signed]

Lieut Frank Lillard and Will Boggess has been to see Cousin Sallie twice since you left. What a poor letter this man ---?--- wites!! Evie

McLean scribbled all over this letter. Some body else scribbled too. Love to Brother Jasper. Unkle I know you are disgusted with Evies & Sallies scribblings so I will not scribble on your letters. Come home if it is but one days visit. Lizzie L.

Please Come & qualify Sallie McLean

Mr. Janalt(?) returned this morning, havent seen him yet. Seems to be "hearty" I hear him asking questions spec he's scared too like Sallie McLean

We received a note from Capt Vaughn this morning, but instead of directing the letter to --?-- it was directed to Cousin Evie. Oh I am so jealous! Julie

Who was the S. you sent your love to, dont think I am jealous S. M.

We know who it was there isnt any use of repeating the name anymore. Lizzie and Sallie are eating apples and such mouthfuls!! it would make you open your big eyes. I was not up here when those Evil children were writing this foolishness. I had to prevail on them not to send it. Julia

If the Yanks come we will strike out for Athens making brother Jaspers Headquarters. ---?---

We all want to go to the dinner in McMinn next Friday. My Respects to Capt. Lizz L.

Cousin Sallie talked about you in her sleep last night. Julia

Col I begged Evie not to break this letter open. Evie received a letter from Capt VanDyke & Mr Cates. Lizzie received one but she will not let us see it, and I didnt receive any. Yes she did from a young gentleman. She begged me to read the letter, but I was too honorable I declare she read it. I was too honorable to hear it read, left the room, but came back in time to hear the latter part of it. I know it was some thing about beans and irish potatoes. You know I do not possess any share of womans curiousity. ---?---

- - - - - - - - - - - - -

LETTER NO. 71
EVIE LILLARD TO NEWTON J. LILLARD

Decatur
August 24th 1863

My own dear precious brother, and Sallies sweetheart;

Tis once more my indescribable pleasure to write a letter to you. it has been a long time since I have cimmuned with you through letters. Oh how I missed them they were like sunbeams flitting across my pathway. We were all so sorry you didnot come home. We all think you could, as we cannot see why you are obliged to stay there, when there are none of the Regt. Miss Sallie says you must come. You requested me to keep you posted well. Miss Sallie received a letter from Lieut. Whitfield I donot think there was anything of a suspicious nature in it, anyway I donot think you need entertain any fears from that source, so you must not give up, but try the harder remember "faint heart never win fair lady" Sallie says "Evie make him come" I know a sisters influence should be greate over a brother but if mine is, I cannot wish to influence mine to leave his duty, although it is such greate happiness to have our brothers with us. Sallie says her selfishness (but I think love) overcomes her patriotism.

Brother Neut we were all very much alarmed last night 12 oclock some drunken soldiers stopped at the gate, and were gabbering cursing &c it awaken us all, we thought the Yanks had come sure. They stayed there a long time at last uncle Lillard gave them some fire to light their pipe and told them there was a sick woman in the house they left then. It is enough. It makes ones heart ache to see the way they do, just go in squads to Ham Cate after whiskey, all come back drunk & canteens swung round them. Are these the defenders of our Sunny South if as alas! for her, but how it gladdens our hearts to think of those brave gallant soldiers who have endured & suffered so much for their country this makes us feel confident of our success. Genl. Armstrong has head quarters in town. I suppose he is staying [in] your old storeroom. There is one company in town his body guard who are always getting drunk I think there ought to be something done with Old Ham Cate I sent the gray goods by Capt James Wallace today.

Willie has just come with the mail. we are all excited over our letters. have you seen Lieut Butler and Vandyke give them our love. Pa's health has been quite feeble for two or three days but am glad to say he is better this morning. Heard from brother John he is well, Frank (Coz) has been here twice. Will Rogers once!! give our love to Jasper & brother Wm tell Jasper cousin Julia is well and sweet as ever. Mary didnot rest so well yesterday and last night. The yanks were very plenty in Washington yesterday evening they carried off Capt Colvilles negroes & stock, broke into Mr. Parks store. all the male citizens are on this side of the river scared to death . Miss Mary Mcdonald was compelled to run from the Yanks on a blind horse through the woods.

We all feel mighty lively as we had buscuit this morning. How is Jasper getting along housekeeping tell him I am learning to play the music he brought me, I am making my dress. Do come over won't you? We all want to see you so badly. May the flowers of happiness forever bloom on the guarden of yours and Sallie's destiny.

Ever will be (Unafraid)
Evie Lillard

Please don't let any one see this.

- - - - - - - - - - - - -

[The emblem on top of the stationary used by Mary E. Russell for Letter No. 72 is reproduced at the end of the letter]

LETTER NO. 72
M. E. RUSSELL TO NEWTON LILLARD

Locust Grove
Aug 27th 1863

Friend Neut

After long silence I am blessed with the privilege of answering a line from you, be assured the contents of your letters were perused time & again with interest. I did not deem it imprudent in you sending your letter by a friend in the least.

As to the news that is afloat in this section, I suppose Maj A. will post you in what was going on when he was here, we got news from Rhea almost constantly through the day. of which none is good. The Yankees pickets have been shooting across the river Today they have taken Mr. Howell prisoner, had anything wrong I will report but do not think will, as to how me & Mr Sherman is getting along, I can say that I am doing only tolerable, & I have not seen him since the Morning after the partie, hope he is doing well, if he has not gone home perhaps he is at Sallie Neils house please give me some advise concerning how to do should the Yankees cross. Tell Maj A. that Fannie is here yet & that she heard from home today. I will close hoping to hear from you soon. Your Friend

M. E. Russell

P.S. Excuse bad composition for I cannot keep my mind on any thing one minute at a time

- - - - - - - - - - - - -

LETTER NO. 73
J.K.P. SIDDENS TO NEWTON J. LILLARD

Wood Lawn, Ga
Sept 14, 1863

Dear Col Lillard

I am as yet very sick have been sick ever since I came home, not able to set up, and am reduced to a mere skeleton. I dont know whether I am on the mend any or not. I am entirely without money or any thing to get what I need.

There is about $500.00 due me in the Regt. If Ben can collect it, will you be so kind as to allow him to bring it to me. He will return as soon or when ever you say for him to. It is very possible that we will have to move again. If such should be the case I will need money very much. My Dr Bills are all to pay. I have no clothes and futher cant buy what I need. If Maj G W Allen will send me pay for Sept it will --?--. Ben is authorized to sign my name to any papers requiring my signature.

Please tell Maj Allen to do the best he can for am in the way of money. If Ben cannot return, I will expect a reply to this and direct as below

J. K. P. Siddens
Wood Lawn, Ga

- - - - - - - - - - - - -

LETTER NO. 74
-----?----- TO NEWTON J. LILLARD

Campbellton, Georgia
Sept 28th 1863

Col N. J. Lillard

Sir I this morning try to write you a short letter. I am at a lost how to address you under the present circumstances. I will assine the cause why I have not done my duty to report with my command I been with father geting his property away from danger of any damage. I

[remainder of letter too faint to read]

[letter below was on back of the above letter]

- - - - - - - - - - - - -

LETTER NO. 75
J. B. BOGGESS TO NEWTON J. LILLARD

Col N J Lillard, dear Brother

As to us Righting I will work some --?-- all well But . . . [handwriting too bad to read on 3 lines] . . . rest have not come yet we cant get corn in --?-- --?-- land When we do we pay $3 pr Bus I dont no wheare we wold go to from here We have no news from home I would give anay thing to hear from home. My wife is in Such a bad fix Her health is so very Bad. We have not heard nothing Reliable from Col Sellers & Capt Boggess un till Maury Collins got your letter we first lerned they Boathe was kild. This is Bad nuse to me this you know. Col John Lillard is as near to me as my oun Brothers if you get anney nuse from home let me hear it & all you heare I have not got A . . .

[remainder of letter impossible to read]

I remain your Brother

J. B. Boggess

- - - - - - - - - - - - -

LETTER NO. 76
W. J. HUGHES TO COL. LILLARD

Cleveland
Oct 3rd 1863

Dear Sir

Some time in September a young man by the name of Blevins who is Adjudent of your Rdg left my house to Join you in Atlanta he was sick I gave him a bout $2500 to hande to J B Hoyl & Mr Hoyl says Blevins has not joined the command if you know any thing of him pleas inform me I suppose he is sick between here & Dalton. Yours &c

W. J. Hughes

- - - - - - - - - - - - -

LETTER NO. 77
M. S. L--?-- TO NEWTON J. LILLARD

Camp Bellton Georgia
October 11th 1863

Col N J Lillard

My dear old friend Nute I received your kind missive some few days ago and would of responded but you know the fate of a poor School Girl had to wait until Saturday or write in the night and I had to study of a night. I have not got any thing that will interest you much at this time.

I am so very sorry to hear of Col John being killed, he was such a noble man and soldier. I have not heard from brother Carter yet and Uncle Bige directly more than you wrote me. That battle was so destructive, so many nice men killed, I do sympathize so much with the poor Soldier that have to go threw such a battle.

I fear our loss are very heavy. I have not heard one word from any of the boys yet, I hope they came out safe; but some ones have to be killed and as apt to be my friends as any persons else. Nute I fear you will find me a very dull correspondent as I am not in the habit of writing to old folks like you, I mostly write to young gents when I write. You asked me for a description of that Sweetheart that I gave you to. I am a poor hand to describe any thing at all, but this young lady is so perfect I cannot say too much for her. She is very intelligent indeed would be admired by any young gentleman but I do not know about an old one but think the same. She is about twenty one years old. That will suit you, and has blue eyes and light complected, and very funny. that will do for it would not be right to have a wife that never talked any for old Newton. She is our teacher (or music teacher). I must tell you her name, Miss Rosa Wood. She is a Virginian, and has one of the nicest "brothers" I always did want to be some kin to Uncle Nute. Miss Rosa received your respects and returns them and says she hopes to see you ere long. I will tell you when I see you the description I gave of you when I see you, I will assure you I flattered you as much as possible; but you know quite well I could not do that, enough about Miss Rosa this time. Our teachers do not allow us to even think of the "boys" (he never says any thing about the old gentleman). It makes me think the more about them. I hope you will excuse me for writing so much nonsence.

Brother Tom and Uncle John, Grand Father and Father all came here last week. They are very anxious to get back home again as the Georgians do not like the idea of Tennesseans coming in here much, but they are doing better than I thought they could do. I received a letter from Aunt Tex Boggass a few days ago and she wrote me that she heard the Yankees was all in McMinn and Meigs and said the Lincolnites was giving them dinner and having a fine time indeed.

O! my Nute I get to thinking about the

[last page is missing but the following note was written upside down on the top of the first page]

P.S. Give my respects to the Capt and Maj George if he is ingaged. Write soon. M.S.L.

- - - - - - - - - - - - -

LETTER NO. 78
N. J. LILLARD TO EVIE LILLARD

Hd Q past Charleston Tennessee
Oct 24th 1863

Dear Evie,

I hasten to write you a line I will be releived in the morning by Genl Wright. I am ordered to Cleveland with 100 men to garrison that point, the Ballance of my men go up to the point. You know I had much rather go up too, but Genl Jackson insist that I shall go to Cleveland. I suppose I have no choice in the matter. I have news from Dalton Mose is getting well. We are expecting some fighting up at Loudon every thing bid fair for our cause in E.T. I am pretty well worn down with work(?). Think I will get some rest at Cleveland. Cant you Manage to write me oftner I have no direct news from home since Jasper left.

I shall make an effort to come home When I can be spared from the service. I --?-- to duty at present it seems that I am --?-- for home directly, The mountains & hills look quite familear Indeed. I have no news from Uncle Lillard Since I last Wrote you. I suppose they are at Rome yet. Give Love to all. How is father getting I hope he has his usual health, Many E.T. refugees are returning home. We permit very few to go North of the Tennessee river. Ever Your Affectionate Bro

N. J. Lillard

- - - - - - - - - - - - -

LETTER NO. 79
GENERAL ORDERS

Head Quarters Near Beans Station
December 6th 1863

General Orders
No 11

The following extracts of a letter captured in the skirmish of the 14th inst and written by one of the enemy are published for the information of the soldiers of this army.

"Perhapse you would lend me your attention for a few moments and let me recount the adventures &

moves & draws of this "Left wing Army of the Ohio" we the 117 Regt Indiana Vol Inf six months men have lead a checkered life for the past two & one half months, we've seen the olephant in a shape that few Indeana soldier have seen him. We had seen fighting some of us. Our Col was in all the Vicksburg fights as Maj of the 8th but fighting of the soldering by a long shot as you are well aware. In the last ten weeks we have marched nearly 500 miles and for the past two months have never drawn full rations. When we got to Morristown we were put on quarter rations. We went to Greenville 65 miles N.E. of Cumberland Gap and drew no rations for three days, then drew meal and 3/4 rations of fresh beef without salt. Corn has been issued to us as rations and we have had for days at a time absolutely nothing but parched corn and beef. Forty round of parched corn in your Haversack was an order from Sergt Berry to his squad about a month ago, and it has passed into the Regt as a general order for every march. We retreated from Greenville on a run to Bulls Gap which we commenced fortifying and the --?-- --?-- our position as impregnible.

"Before the telegraph had given publicity to the news our impregnible position was evacuated and we are skedaddling for Cumberland Gap. We had nothing to eat then for several days except a little and once or twice some parched corn. Our Brigade goes among the troops by the name of the Parched Corn Brigade Wilcoxs running Tigers & the Lank Expectant Hoosier. We have been four times in hearing of several sharp little fights one in sight, but we never get in a skirmish. Were marched & countermarched advanced and retreated and have killed a good many good men by foolish running and unnecessary starvation. We went beyond Cumberland Gap into Ky & then we went two days with nothing to eat save parched corn & meat which we foraged for. We drew some flour there that just lammed(?) it to any thing you ever saw. If you would take the screenings from a flouering mill & to one bushel add a peck of oats & another peck of dirt & grind it all & you have a bushel & a half of the kind of flour that was issued to us on Yallow Creek Ky. I have a specimen of the bread & will save it until we the 117th Regt Ind Vols Inf d - d Six months (thats our title, the swearing is not mine) are mustered out exhibited it in Indiana & then send it to Barnum for his celebrated museum. Strady hast.

"Quick Marching orders: We left Clinch river on the 10th and advanced to the top of this Mountain six miles from old camps. We are encamped right square in the gap where the wind whistles & moans & cuts our cloths off our backs. It is awful cold here. When at the base of the Mountain it is as warm as summer. Rebs left here the day before we got here. They had several thousand at Beans Station"

The publication of the forgoing letter has been suggested by the knowledge of your own hardships & perils & that you might compare them with those of the enemy and fin[d] that they too have their privation which according to the writer of this letter far exceeds our own.

If those who come upon our soil to invade us with the avowed purpose of subjugation can carry out their work under such trials & with such gayety & Cheerfulness as this letter exhibits far much more of that endurance patience & hope should you have who are resisting tyrany and are fighting for your honor, your homes & your liberty. Let it not be said that the heart of the invader is stronger & stouter than the determination of you who fight for your all.

Your wants are known to your Gen and every effort has been made to relieve them. Supplies of clothing & shoes have been ordered and are daily expected. Until they arrive you are called upon to support the rigors of a severe and trying Campaign with the Same manly fortitude & patience that has always been So honorable to you. By Command of Lt Gen Longstreet

G W Sorrell A A Gen

Brig Gen J. C. Vaughn
Comdr Brigd

- - - - - - - - - - - - -

LETTER NO. 80
I. R. BINYON TO N. J. LILLARD

Hd In Brigade
Near Rogersville, Tenn
Decr 20th 1863

Special Order
Col N J Lillard of the 3rd Tenn Regt will Arest and place in close confinement all officers of My Brigade that Deserted My Command at Louden Tenn or Since we left there. By order of Brig Genl Vaughn

I R Binyon, Capt
Act Insp Genl

- - - - - - - - - - - - -

LETTER NO. 81
J. C. VAUGHN TO N. J. LILLARD

Headquarers Regt
Near Rogersville, Tenn
Decr 20th 1863

Special Order
Col Lillard You will proceed at once to the --?-- Counties of East Tenn, Bradley, Monroe, McMinn, Polk, Meigs & others and arrest and bring to these Headquarters all Soldiers belonging to the Seven(?) regiments of the Brigade, whether commissioned or not, if absent without proper authority. All officers who are absent detached from this Brigade are ordered to report to him and be subject to his orders.

He is authorized to draw and receipt for 2 Mi Stores --?-- equipment of the Brig. He will await orders from these Hd Qs after completing the execution of this order. Brig Gen J C Vaughn

- - - - - - - - - - - - -

LETTER NO. 82
J. G. PARSHELL TO N. J. LILLARD

Bristol Tenn
March 29th 1864

Col Lillard

I was detained at Greenville until Monday morning at which time I could not go to the Junction. Col Sorrell advised me to come to this place since my arrival I have been unable to learn the whereabouts of the command. I shall remain here until I find where to go. should you stop to remain a day or two before you arrive here, please send my horse to me.

There is no news here no person knows where the army is going or what is to be come Longstreet has them all in the dark --?-- [hole in paper]

Please say to Col Gillespie that Capt Wm McKamy of his old regiment is here & wishes to go to the command & if possible to send him a horse at the time mine is sent. Your early complience will much oblige. Your friend J. G. Parshell

- - - - - - - - - - - - -

LETTER NO. 83
I. A. RHEA TO N. J. LILLARD

Hd Qrs 2nd Cav Brigade
Kingsport April 11th 1864

Col

The General directs that you return as soon as possible with your Command as the larger portion of the Brigade has been ordered to the rear. Col Humes near this point can give you directions as to our route.

Very Respectfully,
I. A. Rhea, a a s(?)

- - - - - - - - - - - - -

LETTER NO. 84
J. C. VAUGHN TO N. J. LILLARD

Brigade Hd Qrs
Bristol May 27th 1864

Col N.J. Lillard

In regard to your picketting below at the mouth of the Wautoga, I think it best for you to keep a small picket there. I will relieve you any time you may desire, but I allowed while you were on the front you would stand a better chance to capture horses for your men that are dismounted. You must picket So as not to be Surprised. All quiet no news of Importance from Va. last news from Genl Johnston, he had fallen back to Marietta. I hope he will whip & soon drive Sherman back to Chattanooga. Your obt Svt

J. C. Vaughn, Comd Brigade

- - - - - - - - - - - - -

LETTER NO. 85
J. C. VAUGHN TO N. J. LILLARD

Near Leasburg, Va
July 15th 1864

My Dear Col

One line this morning as I have a chance to send it by hand to Charlotsville. I have no Special News to write you Only we are all well & in good spirits. Our Campaign has been a perfect Success Since we defeated Hunter at Lynchburg. We have had Several Heavy Skirmishes & one hand fight, it was near Fredric MD. We killed over 400, took 600 prisoners. We were Skirmishing two days around Washington within three miles of the Capitol. I feel Certain we Could have taken the City on our arrival then but Genl Early Should know better than I. the Supply Captured & destroyed have been Emence.

We destroyed the Baltimore & Washington Rail Road between the city badly also the Baltimore & Ohio Rail Road badly for near one hundred miles. the Canal we have damaged badly also. this has been the greatest raid of the War. Our Infantry Force is not over - - - I will not Say as this letter may be Captured. We have brought out four or five thousand head fine Cattle about three or four thousand fine draft horses. If Col Carter had Come up with our horses I would have discharged them for good ones, but I hope to have a chance yet Soon. Our horses are now at Winchester. We will get there tomorrow night. Our boys are in fine health. I am sorry the old Third was not with me but I could not help it. Many live now that would have fell at Peadmont, as they would have been put in the thickest of the fight.

I cannot Speak of our next movements. the Enemy is now within three miles of our Rear. Only a Mounted force I think Our Cavalry under Genl Bradly Johnston was within two miles of Baltimore. I hope Grant has started a large force after us. have no news from any quarter for five days. I hope all is well with you. I will write again soon the Stage runs now to Winchester. Write me amadely tell Capt Allen & others to do So. pleas Order Dr. Parshall to report to me for duty Amediatly, under the new staff Bill I give him a position if he desirs it, tell him to write or come amedeatly. Keep every thing well up. Collect all our men of the Brigade. Genl Early Says I shall return very Soon to my old position give me all the news, Send all the mail by Parshall let him come on Rail Road to Stanton & then Stage to Winchester. if we change our position he will here of it & I will write him to Stanton.

My best respects to all of the boys & all friends. I have not lost any men, only by Stagling & sick who had to be left.

Your Devoted friend
J C Vaughn

- - - - - - - - - - - - -

LETTER NO. 86
RESHY BRADFORD TO N. J. LILLARD

Bristol
July 24th 1864

Dear Col:

Private

I have just recd a telegram from Genl Breckenridge, ordering me, with all of Vaughns Brigade under my command & all others, except 3rd Ten under you, to report to Winchester Va . I have sent to Morgan for instructions, as soon as I know what to do, will answer and notify you. Say nothing about it, for I understand perhaps that Capt Giddens represented that I refused to obey the former order –a mistake–and it is likely this may have brought about the order.

Reshy Bradford

- - - - - - - - - - - - -

LETTER NO. 87
-----?----- TO FATHER & MOTHER

Prisoner Camp Elmira N.Y.
Oct the 5th 1864

Dear father & mother.

I am hapy to in form you that I am well trully hoping these few lines will reach & find you all well & so . . . [remainder of letter missing]

- - - - - - - - - - - - -

LETTER NO. 88
J. C. VAUGHN TO N. J. LILLARD

Bristol Tenn
20th Jany 1865

Col

Thinking you might be willing to go round with the recruiting officers, I Send you Authority to do So. You now have one officer or more from Blount, Monroe, Polk & Meigs you may take one more officer from your Regt. No men must go.

If Col Gilaspie wishes to Send Any one from his or the 31st Tenn Regt, He can make the delaites & you are Authorized to approve the detail and Sign my name I think Capt Tonken could do good in the Duck Town Country. Maj Paine & all the others have gone to Jefferson N.C. & then will turn for Ashville or Col Thomas' Camp. where you and your Squad Can join them.

If you go keep the strictest decipline and dont allow the men to stragle off home, as they would be certain to be picked up. But alltogether you can whip any force they have mounted below Knoxville. Genl Breckenridge talks of Sending me down Soon with a portion if not all my Command. Yours truly

J. C Vaughn

[the following was written on back of the above letter]

Every soldier who runs off and follows you arrest & put him in nearest Jail. You will find many men among Thomas Palmers Command belonging to our command. Tell Col Love to let me hear from his Scout as soon as he gets any facts. tell him to do his best pick up Bowers & other Bushwhackers. There is some 40 Encamped So Wilbur Carter says on --?-- Bob Mill road they are at the Gap every day or so.

Yours J C Vaughn

- - - - - - - - - - - - -

LETTER NO. 89
JOHN C. VAUGHN TO N. J. LILLARD

Washington Ga
May 10th 1865

Col

I have Just returned from Augusta Ga where I accomplished everything that we desired, finding that the command had moved several miles from Town and being very much fatigued I will not come out. This I regret as it would have given me pleasure to have again met you and the members of my command. You will please give my sincere thanks to both the officers and men of my command who have followed me this far. I shall ever remember with pride and gratitude the --?-- men who have proven themselves true to the last. Again you and the entire command accept my heart felt wishes for your future prosperity and happiness.

I am very Respectfully Your Obt Servt
John C. Vaughn,
Brig Genl

P.S. Col Please Write me fully and often directing to John H. Parker, Lewnosville S C as I do not want parties in E.T. to Know where I am I expect to come to E.T. whenever you say its safe. J.C.V.

- - - - - - - - - - - - -

LOCKE LETTER

Although Thomas J. Locke and his son, David Leuty Locke, were both in the 16th Battalion (Capt. W.P. Darwin's Company), only one letter has survived. This is undoubtedly the worst spelling and handwriting of all the Civil War letters and is copied exactly as written, with all the misspelled words and lack of punctuation.

David was born on 8 November 1845, the son of Thomas J. and Nancy Harris (Leuty) Locke. He died on 24 November 1864 of smallpox and was buried at Panther Springs, Tennessee.

LETTER
DAVID LOCKE TO T.J. LOCKE

At home Meigs Co Tenn Aug 26/63

Dear father I Seat my self to let you know that I arived home tuesday eavning found all well a gential(?) of ecitement all of the rhea co men over(?) and some of the women the men is camped out the capt is here sick and his family here to = there is several troops in meigs now Jeneral armstrongs head qrs is at decatur now they herd cannon some where below here yesterday the yanks came to the fery and fired at our pickets and ours returned the fire and they soon withdrew tell Jim(?) peaterson that I have done as he requested of me and sent the letters across to washington tell boys(?) they had a scift at our cribs but there is a picket there now tell E D pierce(?) that I best not send his corsp(?) across but will as soon as I get a good chance as I told him when I Started I got home with out mutch troble I had to go back up to the ford and cross then to the point to cross Tenn the troops was crossing So I had to stay until about 3 oclock at which time got across and rode to ten mile that night then came home about 3 oclock that eavning and some how lifted the mash that night and we have looked every where me to cottenport Garpa(?) to the fery J. to Decature and no mash. I have Just come from the river and herd cannon while I was there ther has bin no more fiering across the river– Biron Locke is here uncle and James Locke is with the 3rd Arkasaw regiment the armstrong(?) boys is all at home yet So I beleave that is all mother said she would not write as I was writing So no more Give my best respects to Co (C) so remaining your son David I will leav the other side for you

- - - - - - - - - - - - -

CONFEDERATE LINE OF BATTLE IN THE CHICKAMAUGA WOODS.

[**NOTE**: This page was left for a letter from another family that did not arrive in time to be included in this publication. Since the index had already been prepared, it was not feasible to move all of the letters and articles that follow.

Battles and Leaders of the Civil War

MORGAN LETTERS

Federal Soldier

Although members of the Morgan family were from Rhea County, they left the area early in the war to enlist in the Northern Army.

The records show that Henry Sampson Morgan enlisted on 5 November 1861 at London, Kentucky, in Company G, 2nd Regiment East Tennessee Infantry (later Company G, 2nd Regimemt Tennessee Infantry).

Henry S. Morgan, the son of Charles and Emeretta (Riddle) Morgan, was born 7 December 1841 and died on 18 May 1864, at Andersonville Prison.

Three other sons of Charles and Emeretta also served: Franklin Robert (born 5 October 1843), William Barcla (born 14 June 1845), and Thomas Calvin (born 25 February 1848).

Milo S. Riddle was a son of Joshua I. and Martha Riddle and the brother of Emeretta, wife of Charles Morgan.

When the following letters were copied, they were in the possession of Tom Morgan of Morgan Springs, Rhea County. Some of the handwriting was very difficult to read (indicated by ---?---), and it has been impossible to identify all of the individuls mentioned in the letters.

LETTER NO. 1
F.R. MORGAN TO W.B. MORGAN

Stanford, Lincoln Co., Ky.
9 Aug 1862

Dear Brother

I take my pen in hand to let you know that I am well hoping those few lines will find you Well and not in the hands of the Rebels. I Fell into the hands of The Se Rapaeians & Villains at Crabb Orchard But this was nothin But Fun. I Would have been tickled this time though But --?-- T, and others were thinking ------?------ Shooting at them. I --?-- for them --?-- they done --?-- I stood my ground. They --?-- and left there Bad Scared. I have ---?--- any more than ---?--- F.M. Morgan in Which --?-- that Boys was all Well at Carthage.

The Boys are all well here that you are acquainted with. Sam is well and as fleshy as ever. Tell Mother to give George plenty of milk and mash potatoes Tell pap to give him plenty of venison. I want him To be big anuff To go out Squirl hunting with us When we Come back if we Should Be So lucky. tell the Children To feed my Pet. Hiram is here but i havent saw him atall he is well

I have met with many of my friends in Kentucky. I must come to a close. Give my Respects to all aspecialy the girls. tell them i am in A land of the free But i yet Remember my Native Tennessee. Kenticky is quite lucky But i am Coming Back To Tennessee To Kill Another turkey.

Tell all my Tennessee friends that I to them my Respects lend. Bill you and Cal must have a party muster up the girls and Send for your humble Servant Give my Respects to esqr Bill and family also to every Body else this To M.J.J. Carvey To W.B. Morgan, F.R. Morgan
it To her please

- - - - - - - - - - - - -

LETTER NO. 2
H.S. MORGAN TO F.R. MORGAN

August the 11th 1862
Headquarters Camp, Cumberland Gap
2 Reg't E Tennessee Volunteer Comp

dear brother it is 1862 & with much pleasure that i tke my pen in hand to let you know that I am well at present i hope that these few lines will find you in good health I havent any thing of much importents to rite to you, F.R. Morgan it has been Sometime Since We have been to gether though I hope not the last time We will meet to gether and have our liberties enjoy our selves as We wonce did I want you to rite to me and let me know how you are getting along and how you have been i would like to know how times has yoused you since i left you i am im--?-- you are all doing well an in good health

We are in good Spirits aplenty to eat drink an ware nothing to do if i could see you i could tell you ahundred times more than i can rite i want you to tell my friends to excuse me fore not riting to them for i have a bad chantay to Send a letter in Rhea I supose it has been the case with you i could rite but Sending the letter is the mischiefe tell my friends ther i would like to See them tell them howday for me.

now I will tell you of a friends death. thomas Jonson got drowned in cumberland river i felt that i had lost afriend he was a clever man. So nothing more at present i yet remain your friend until death

give my best respects to all William piercin James B green the too been boys Marien donkn three housers boys and others all well as far as i know So nothing more as it is dark an my hand trembling

- - - - - - - - - - - - -

LETTER NO. 3
H.S. MORGAN TO M.S. RIDDLE

Lancaster, ky,
March the 31, 1863

dear Cousin it is with great plesure that I Seat my Self to drop you a few lines to let you no where we are & what We are doing I am well At present & hope that when this comes to hand it Will find you in good health.

I wish you had a come with us We had a fine time avery plesent trip came up on the Jacobs teader to louisville took the train & went to Lexington from there to Micklesville & advanced to the kentucky bridge & their Skirmisht with the rebels a day or too captured several prisners & among them was Decator beils [*] adjutant Joseph paine & too of the Walker boys & others too teages to mention a man from hamilton is right from home he Sais there is no rebels there people is at work in Rhea & hamilton he seen pierson & they was well. I do not no where we will go from hear I supos we will go to somerit though i do not no

R.D. Morgan is with us at this time he is doing a good deal of work & seems to be very well satisfied.

The first redgement Staied at Lexington I havent heard from them since I left thiss is the best part of kentucky i have ever been in I am afraid if I stay heare that I will fall in love with some of these prety girles heare.

I have seen more prety ladies since I left Murfresboro tell W.J. pierson & J.M. geinse they ought have been with us at louisville & Lexington if he had abeen with me I would have detailed him for picket but I do not no whether I have releived him as soon as he releived me I would have staid to get my Shoe mending i do not no I never refuse tell Swan hunter I saw William Woods at Lexington he is well tell him to rite to me soon & let me no how he is getting along I would be better satisfied if you was with us

if I get to heare from home any time I will rite to Some of you boys perhaps I will Stand a better chants to heare you will & I want you to do the Same rite to me soon tell all of the boys to rite So nothing more at present give my best respects to all

H.S. Morgan
Very respectfully in Camp

\- - - - - - - - - - - - -

[* NOTE: This is Sanders Decatur Broyles, Flavius Joseph Paine (see PAINE LETTERS), and the Walkers who were members of Captain W.P. Darwin's Company from Rhea County]

\- - - - - - - - - - - - -

LETTER NO. 4
H.S. MORGAN TO MILO RIDDLE

Camp Near Sommersett, Ky
May the 8, 1863

dear cousin I received yours of the 18 on the 4 inst & was glad to hear that you was well & doing well We was at Mountacillo When I received your letter 20 miles South of the Cumberland river but was compeled to fall back across the river on the account of subsistance Will I havent any thing of much importants to rite only that we are heare & all well. I heard from home the other day passon Jordan & George Gears(?) has moved there familys to kentucky they are in 8 miles of thiss place it has been 30 days sinc they left home our folks is Well a bad accident happend yesterday as we was crossing the river the boat turned over near the current of the river & drowned 15 men of the 27 New Jersey regiment you said to tell R.L. to rite he is at Stamford at thiss time I am looking for him to come up evry hour He stayed with J.H. Everett he was taken sick the day we started from Stamford. J.R. Everett has ben sick but He is getting better. John Barger is heare with his family

I rote a letter & started it home but I do not have much Ide of its ever getting home I have rote so often I cant rite with much satis faction it is gitting so dark that I can scarcely see what I have rote you must excuse my short letter I will try to do better next time

So nothing more at present I yet remain your true Cosin untill death

H.S. Morgan Very Respectfuly in Camp
rite soon tell all of the boys to rite

\- - - - - - - - - - - - -

LETTER NO. 5
H.S. MORGAN TO
MRS. MARY EMERITTA MORGAN

June the 30, 1863
Headquarters Camp Near Sommersett

Dear Mother I received your kind letter or letters I disremember the date I read them with great satisfaction I was glad to head that you was well & all of you well it found me well & doing as well as could be expected I very well satisfied. Well Mother I now you would not understand me the mistak I made put & old letter in & envelop & directed it I never did such a trick before nor since well Mother I havent any thing of mutch importance to rite not any thing Strange. F.R. Morgan & Isac riddle arived hear Safe the 26, 1863 there appearance was very acceptable in my sight & that is not all that was glad to see them they havent a frend a miss heare without they wist seeing them

R.L. Morgan & ---?--- has returned Safe. Mother I would like to see you all very well & tell you a fiew Stories concerning a Solders life it makes me think of Some of daniel boones adventures to Ky

Mother if ---?--- moves aunt Jane to ky tell him to come to Sommersett & see me I would be very glad to See him I would be glad to see all of my frends though we are fore a fight thoug I still live in hopes of meeting you all again in thiss troublesome world

Mother I will send you my photograph it is not a very good one I dont like it be cause I think I am mutch the best looking So I must close by asking you to rite give my best respects to all of my inquiring friends give my respects to father & all of my beloved brothers & sisters give uncle J.I. Riddle & family my best respects & all & espesily to your Self I yet have the honor to bee your Dear beloved son untill Death true to His Country So no more at present I Still remine respectfully

H.S. Morgan

rite your letter to Co J 2 reg Vol M inf

- - - - - - - - - - - - -

Stationary used for Letter No. 6

LETTER NO. 6
F.R. MORGAN TO
CHARLES & EMERITA MORGAN

Camp Nelson, Jesseeman Co, K.Y.
July 16th 1863

Dear Mother

I take my pen in hand to let you know that I am in the land of living I am well at this time i hope those few lines will find you all in good health I have had the pleasure of meeting with many of my friends. Wee arived at Somerset on the 27th of June the 2and Tenn was Camped [at] this place I found H.S. M---- in good health also W.B. B-----, John Everet, hue chumly, W. Birely and all the Boys except James Everett. Was a little unwell I saw him the 14th of this month at Danville, K.Y. he was well

Stan Hogue was at Somerset he belongs to a Batery he was well J.W. Hogue furnishes me pen & ink Joel is Well Elex Hickman is well William Hickman & Co arived a few days since James Kelly Came with us from Somerset to the Hickman Bridge R.S. Green, W.L. Humpry, G.T. Morgan are all well Wee hapened with Bad luck on the 12th evening of July at Crab orchard K.Y. Wee was with a train of wagons ---ing at $30 a month wee ---d stuck up Camps wee hadnt ---- [been?] thare But a Short time ---ll The Poor wreched Blind & Naked Rebels Came Charging through an old field ordering us to surender G.T. Morgan fritts & Gery Coffy one Negro man tried to make their escape But failed they Shot 3 times at each one of them No Damage done the next thin after Surendering Was hall your money packet knives hats Boots &c Gid & Humpry Saved their mony they took a hat from mee that cost $3.86 pare Boots from Baly green they fired our waganss Which was all heavy loaded 2 with amunitian one with guns Some of them loaded While Burning fired into the croud the flames of amunition was roll like under a white cloud --- arising they taken us out about half amile wee taken the oath to Never take up arms against the Confederate States untill we was legally exchanged they Never ast us our Names at all When you take Such an oath as that and Violates it you are gave up for 90 days I am out of Business at the presant time James Kelly William Hickman and me expects to atend to horses at $3 a month Sam, Bill & Hue Chumly are With Wolford after old Mosier(?) he was Near Cincinnata Ohio the last heard from -----n and John everet was in the —ht at Manlieelo(?) Sam Said all he lacked Being perfectly Sarisfied was knowing that you was all doing Well I havent heard from ---------(?) F.R. Morgan

- - - - - - - - - - - - -

LETTER NO. 7
H.S. MORGAN TO MR. M.S. RIDDLE

July the 21, 1863
Camp Jackson Ohio

Mr M.S. Riddle Sir

I Seat my Self thiss eavening to drop you a few lines to let you know that I am well at present & I hope thiss will come to hand in due time & find you in good health Well M.S. I will tell you something of our Morgan Chase

We lefft Somersett July the 5 & crost the Ohio river at Braninsburg ky in pursuit of him golowed him to Salem(?) indianni & from ther to Ohio ----ling(?) he burnes evry bridge & depot he comes to & Mill & town or makes the citizens pay a very helthy tax one man paid Six thousand dollars for his Mills the general in Command of our force is arested he is a cused of being a traiter Col Wolford is in Comm the train arived hear one hour ago from parts North with the malisia 6,000 to guard the Town of Jackson & Cincinatti railroad the report is that Wolford has over taken them & whippt them & taken 2000 thousand of them prosoners & they are Coming in thiss direction though very ----(?) as i have rode our horses & one mule to death I am heare a foot I have misst the fright on account of it but ther is still a chance for old ------(?) the dispatch is that they are fighting 12 miles from thiss place they are on a retreat & will soon be in to me about six inches if I dont be be Smart the lady wanted to patch my coat & told her no I did not know as I would need it excuse my Scribeling it is the best I Can do under the present surcumstances give my best respect to all so no more at present & espesealy to your Self I still remain your the Cosin in till death H.S. Morgan

\- - - - - - - - - - - - -

LETTER NO. 8
H.S. MORGAN TO R.D. MORGAN

July the 29 1863
Hamilton Cty, Ohio

Mr. R.D. Morgan Sir

I take the present opportunity of riting to you to let you know that I am well at thiss time & I hope thiss will come to hand in due time & find you well & doing well after along & hard march through kentucky indianni & Ohio the terrable Horse thieff was Captured with his entire Comand more than 3 boat loads of priseners arived thiss Citty the 25 I also arived the 25 & I am yet hear waiting for the Command aportion of Hobsons Com came in thiss morning I supose the 2 will be heare to day Well perhaps you would like to know what I am doing I am doing as I please altogether I rode too Horses down & was Compelled to stop. We went as Far as Winstchestel more than one hundred miles above thiss place I reported to Jackson to the Millitary Committee & got a pas Came to Ports mouth & from there I -------?----- from the regiament than ever -----?----- I was on duty -----?-----

Gen John Morgan arived hear the 27 I havent seen him yet I was at a union meeting night before last. W.G. brownlow addresst the people John broughman Canidate for gov I must close give my respects to all of my inquiring friends. I remain your friend untill death. I remain Respectfully H.S. Morgan

\- - - - - - - - - - - - -

LETTER NO. 9
F.R. MORGAN TO CHARLES MORGAN

Hickman Bridge, Jesseman County, Ky
Aug 2, 1863

Dear Mother & Father

I accept of the presant oportunity of writing you a few lines to let you know that I am not very well at this time i havent been well since the 24 of last month But I am mending I think i will be able to work in a few days. I am boarding at A private house at $2.00 a week. I have made $20 since I arived in Ky I saw George

was all well i havent saw Hiram Sims(?) atall i heard from him yesterday he was well the 2ond Tenn hasent arived from Ohio we are looking for them every hour John everett received A letter from Sam While at danville about 10 days ago he was well he left Somerset about the first of July after Morgan they Captured him in Ohio. I wrote you a letter in July i doubt your receiving it for this reason i know not what to write i have seen Sam which was much Satisfaction to me i seen John Jordan and press Hogue a few days ago was both well Wash Everett also they belong to the first Tenn Batery William & E Hickman, Joel Hogue, Jim Kely, John & dave Durwick, Jim Bataly, 3 Shadericks are all well, W.T. Humphy(?) and R.D. Morgan was here the other day they started to Somerset their folks have arived

R.S. Green is here he is well Gid T. Morgan was well the other day Brownlow Captain & Elias Morgan are all Well. We are all Boarding at the Same place Brownlow said that Gid was clerking for the Sutler of the 2 Ten Ace & luke Been are here & carpenter Can make 2 dolars a day at this place I would advise pap and William to stay thare till the last of this month Mother I think it would Be best for you and the children to stay thare While you can get plenty to eat, Compare Tennessee with Kentucky Ky is the best in one respect the land is good corn looks fine i have saw meddows from 10 to 25 acres Timothy mostly, But Where is the good Water it is Back in good old E Tennessee. I Saw our speaker Doss yesterday from indiania & Ohio had been looking round to Buy a farm he Said he expected to Setle in Sequatchee

i know you are tired of reading my Nonsense Wrote With a pensil Write to me and let me know how you are all geting along also my pet excuse my Bad Writing please, Pap tell Jim, Jack Able i have the honor to be very respectfuly long lost H.R. Morgan

\- - - - - - - - - - - - -

LETTER NO. 10
H.R. MORGAN "TO EVERY BODY"

August the 3, 1863

I Seat my Self to let you know that the 2ond Reg. has arived at this place they Came in last night Sam is well & hearty W.B. Benson hasent Come in yet he well be here this morning he is well Bill and Sams horses give out upon an average the Regiment Artillary is low (?) 4 horses each before they caught Morgan hue Chumly is well they are going on to Danville to Day I am going into the 2ond if i Can Be discharged When the Regmant is Sam Says i can he is offerd 400 dolars bounty to go for 3 years longer and his time gos on from now and get pay for the other 2 years I will have to Come to a Close tell Margaret Benson to wright to me tell every Body to wright it would Be much Satisfaction to me to Receive leters from my friends in old Rhea give my Best Respects to all please excuse my Bad Composed leter, Signed H.R. Morgan

- - - - - - - - - - - - -

LETTER NO. 11
H.S. MORGAN TO R.D. MORGAN

Camp Near Danvill ky
August the 5, 1863

Mr. R.D. Morgan Dear uncle Sir

I seat myself to drop you a few lines to let you know that I am well at present & hope thiss will come to hand in due time & find you & your family well I under stand that Coather is hear & if he is if he got a Pasport to move your family to ky Tell him if he is going back to wait ntill I get to see him though I supose he doesnt aim to try to go back home

I received a letter from Father & Mother yesterday & was glad to hear that they was well & doing well I tried to get Permision to come to see him though in vain I could have come but I never hav left my post without Leave & do not want too I think we will be ordered to Somersett in a few days F.R. Morgan is at hickman bridge he has been sick though is getting well

So I must close as I havent time to rite I will come out as soon as I can Posable can get off give my best respects to all off my friends & espesuly to your self I still remaine your true friend until death

H.S. Morgan

there is two letters here for you one from Morgan & one from Wm E. Cuningham I would send them to you I dont know as it would worth while I will bring them as soon if you see my sweet heart tell her I am all right excuse my bad hand & Spelling

- - - - - - - - - - - - -

LETTER NO. 12
H.S. MORGAN TO MRS. E. MORGAN

August the 9, 1863
Head quarters Camp near Stanford, Ky

Dear Mother

I received your kind & affectionate letter of the 3 ins which give me great Satusfaction to hear that you was all well & enjoying a reasonable portion of health & satisfaction I am well at thiss time & I hope thiss will com to hand in due time & find you all well & doing well.

F.R. Morgan is heare & well. Elias Morgan is at th Kentucky Bridge & is going to Morrow I recieved a letter from F.M. Morgan He is Still at Cartheage Tennessee th boys is all well in the 5 rege E. Tennessee Vol it is not worth my while for me to mension every ones name for you know the boys that belongs to the 5 rege tell all of their folks they are all well & very well Satisfied as well as could be expected no more on thiss subject

I will give you a small detail of my trails through the State of indianni & Ohio wee left Somersett ky on the 4 of July & after Som 20 hard days march Captured John H. Morgan & his entire Command the miserable Horse Thief rebel of ky indianni & Ohio is the most Loyal States to the government of the United States the most clever people that I most ever seen I was almost attemted to Say that I would go there to Marry when Peace is made

R.D. Morgans family is at Sommerssett I al so heard that father was there but havent heard for sertain & So I must close by asking you to rite you must excuse me for not riting offner that I do I could rite often though I could not get it taken rite Soon give my best respects to all & especialy to your self I shall remain your true Son untill Death

H.S. Morgan

- - - - - - - - - - - - -

LETTER NO. 13
H.S. MORGAN TO MISS M.S. BENSON

August the 9, 1863
Headquarters Camp near Stanford, Ky

Miss M.S. benson Dear Cosin

it is with mutch plesure that I take the present opportunity of riting to you to let you know that I am well at thiss time & I hope when thiss comes to hand it will find you well & enjoying good health & Satusfaction W.B. is well & enjoying himself with the ky girles as to my self I do not Pestir them a grat deale the boys is well as far as I know I received a letter from F.M. Morgan dated Aug th 1, 1863

if yours & V Levia(?) Riddle sweet hearts is in the federal army they are well & I hope all will be right soon

Nothing more write soon as you get thiss give my best respects to all inquiring Friends except aportion to your self your true Cosin untill death give my respects to uncle J.I. & tell them to rite

H.S. Morgan

no respects to rebs what ever from thiss Lad

- - - - - - - - - - - - -

LETTER NO. 14
H.S. MORGAN TO MRS. EMERETTA MORGAN

November the 1, 1863
Camp near Rogerville,
Hawkins County

Dear Mother

I except of the Present opportunity of writing to you to let you know that I am well at Present & Hope these few lines will come to Hand in due time & find you all well. I got a letter from F.R. Morgan last knight dated Oct the 11 He was well at that time I am sorry to inform you that R.D. Morgan is dead He died Oct the 9 Aunt Jane is going back home Frank is going to move Her F.R. Said to tell you He would bring you a pair of shoes & W.B. & C.A. Morgan he would bring them Some fiddle Strings.

Mother I havent mutch news to write that would be of mutch intrust to you I expect to get a fourlough Shortly & come to see you I would have wrote to you before now but I thought it youselous I did not know whether the Mail was open or not & I dont have mutch chance to write for running after the rebs wee havent stoppt 3 days at no place Since the 4 of July when wee Started in Persuit of John H Morgan

I have been in Several skirmishes in E. Tennessee at Blountville Co G 2ond reg E. Tennessee Vol with Co B 5 ind reg fought 2000 rebs drove them 2 miles the rebs Played there artillery on us -----?----- when the 2ond ill Batterry Opened on the rebs & drew there attention Wee made a charge on them they moved there Batterry on double quick time 1/2 mile beyond the Town wee advanced untill they moved a gain our 2d Lieut was killed & W.D. frances was wounded in the ancle I discharged 24 rounds of Cartrages at them I Captured one of them & so I have the advantage of them one that I know of

Frank said for me to tell father to write to Edward F. daun(?) at Cleveland & Tell him That his brother has been Sick ever Since June & wants him To come after him he is about 9 miles from Somersett on the Stanford road I want you to rite to me Soon & let me know how you are all getting a long.

Tell Paw I would have wrote to him though I did not think it a Safe plan So I must close by asking you to write give my respects to friends tell W.B. to Stay at Home & do the best He can I remain your affectionate Son untill Death

H.S. Morgan

Direct your letters to Knoxvill E.T. Co G 2ond reg E.T. Vol M.D. inf in care of E.B. Jones Com Co G

- - - - - - - - - - - - -

LETTER NO. 15
F.R. MORGAN TO FATHER & MOTHER

Bunemon(?) Pulaski Co., Ky
Feb the 8th 1864

Dear Mother

I take my pen in hand To let you know that wee are well at this time Hooping those few lines may find you all well enjoying life in peace & harmony We arived at Mr. Humphrys the 24th after leaving our Briges & Mountains of ice. We expected this Day To Be at Home But havent But one oxen and No gears to work Him with. our off oxen died 4 or 5 days after we got here he was fed in the morning eat Hearty and at knight Was about we hunted for him about 2 days thought he had got out of the paster But we found him in the field dead. So we must Come Home A foot.

Buck Tell Jane I am Sory the case is So But we have done the Best we could posibly Do for her. So weare Compelled To Sell the Oxen and cart as Best we can we are Boarding at Richard Jordans and going To St writing Scool we work for Him to pay our Board we can get $1 per Day for work we are Coming Home as soon as we can Sell our things the Scool will Be on in 6 days I think we can sell them in that time

-?. & Mrs. Humphry was Truly glad to see us come they are all well Parson Jordan & family are all well. He expects to Make A crop in Ky. Times are hard in this part of the Country Corn $1 wheat the same Bacon 10 cts Goods plenty We Heard that the 2ond Tennessee was Exchanged I hope it is So

If this leter should come in Diew time Wright to us I expect it will Be the last of the month before we get Home So I will Bring my leter to a close as play time is over Nothing more only give my Respects To all inquiring Friends I Remain Truly Yours,

F.R. Morgan

- - - - - - - - - - - - -

LETTER NO. 16
W.B. MORGAN TO EMERITA MORGAN

Dalas April the 26, 1864

Dier Mother

I take My pen in hand to Drop you a few lions to let you no that I am well at present hoping thes few lions will com to hand & find you all well I am Doing very well at I am tending to Som ---?--- which is a very esy task I am geting 35 dolars per month wee hierd for one month I expect I will com home when My tim is out our forc is taking of moving 35 milds up the river in a few Days I Saw frank the other day he is well I want you to rite to me & let me how you all did this is a very good place to Stay I haent any news to rite to you So I must Come to a Close for the a it is bed time So nothing more at present only remaning Yours truly Son until Deth

W.B. Morgan

Direct Your letters to Chattanooga Care of Lut Drak agnt forward Dalas WBM

- - - - - - - - - - - - -

LETTER NO. 17
W.B. MORGAN TO CHARLES MORGAN

Camp Dalton, Georgia
Aprile 4th 1865

Dear father & mother

it is with much plasure that I take my pen in hand to drop you a few lions to let you no that weat well hoping these few lions will find you all well I havent any thing of much intrest to right to you wear very well sadesfid hear wea hav very good quarters & very good water part of the regment is out on a scout wea herd from them the other day they was fiting then wea havent herd from them since tho wear loking for them in wear expecting a fight at this place the rebls sent in a flag of truce for a surender of the town but wea cant see the point if they cum wea will soon tell them whether wea will or not. The teligraph dispatch cam yesterday that Richmond was taken they sent word from Nashvil to send all of the recruites home that is not musterd into the surves that they dont want no more solders musterd in to the surves they say that piece is a bout made

So I must close for the presant excuse my bad righting & mistakes for I am in a hury --?-- John Morgan is well & said tell you all to right no more at presant only remains your truly untill deth.

W.B. Morgan

- - - - - - - - - - - - -

LETTER NO. 18
THOMAS C. MORGAN TO F.R. MORGAN

Dalton, Ga
May the 14th 1865

Mr F.R. Morgan Dear brother

I again seat myself to let you now that I am well at the present time and I hope when these fiew lines cum to hand they may find you the same We have got Several letters from you since we have bin hear and we have rote several but we dont now whether you have got them or not I am allways glad to hear from home and the people in general W.F. Morgan has got back and he is noe Capt he looks like a new man Since he got on the uniform we got a letter from you the other day and was glad to hear from you and to hear that you was well at that you can tell Father that me and Bill are both well at this time tell all of the boys to rite to me and I will answer them John D. Morgan and all of the boys are well except Som of them have got the mumps and mesals I have bin a riding ever day sence I Came to this place we have made Several Scouts.

I shall be at home in five or six months if nothing hapens to prevent it on yesterday the Rebel General Wofford surrendered 4000 men and him self at Kingston, Ga Sum of our boys has got in from store(?) tell C.A. Morgan to rite to me and if he cant I shall make him go up the ---?--- tell Morgan that we are all well and tell him to rite to me as son as he can I shall bring my letter to a close for the present time rite soon yours as ever

Thomas C. Morgan

- - - - - - - - - - - - -

[The edge of Letter No. 19 is badly damaged; missing portions are indicated by . . .]

LETTER NO. 19
W.B. MORGAN TO MRS. EMERITA MORGAN

Dalton, Georgia
May the 25 1865

Dear Mother

it is with much plasur that I take my pen in hand to drop you a few lions to let you no that wear well hoping these few lions Will com to hand & find you all well I havent much news to write you weare doing very well down hear I am very well sadesfied hear . . . . .

I wold like to sea . . . . Will get to see you a . . . . Pice is close at hand . . . forces has captured --?-- . . . I jus cam in last eav . . . from Atlanta I Just got thire alitle too late to Sea old Jef they taken him thugh Atlanta the day before I got thire I went down with the male I hav ben ariding 6 days & part of the knights So you may no that I am not in very good toan(?) for writing the regment is in very good helth except a few cases of the smallpocks which has ben very light they are geting well T.C. is well tell father . . . wold like to bea at home . . . some of them cold . . . that is in the . . . I havent herd from . . . far sum time I recived . . . leters from Frank . . . ar three weks ago that said you was all well I was glad to her from you tho I havent herd . . . that I want you to writ tell father to write So I must close for the present exhuse my bad writing & mastakes for I am in a hury it is all most Dark give my best respects to all of my friends no more at present only Remains your truly Son untill deth

W.B. Morgan

- - - - - - - - - - - - -

LETTER NO. 20
W.B. MORGAN TO F.R. MORGAN

Resaca Georgia
June 7th 1865

Dear brother I Seat my Self to inform you that I am well hoping these few lions will find you all well I havent eny news To write as I am in geat hast for the bugel has Sounded to go to bed & I Will hav to go directly & I hav writen you 2 or 3 leters Sinc I recvd eny from you tho I herd from you the other John D. Morgan has arivd hee Said you was all well which was good news to mee

T.C. is not very well this eavning he has had a pane In his Sid tho is geting Beter the rest of the boys is well & in fine Spierts I am very well Sadsfied here I hav ben fishing all day I Caught one as long asa 6 inch pole thire is Some of the Boys going home in the morning all the boys has got back that went home C.P. Duncan & John arivd day before yesterday all write you can tell there folks If you see them I dont no When we will get to Com home I am not coming Untill I can cum ----?----

I want you to write evry chanc & tell evry body elce to write that Wants too if thire is eny tho I dont think thire is many that wants too tho I can exhuse them for I no they havent eny chanc to write I will close for the presant exkuse my bad Writing & mistakes for my eys is about Rundown(?) give my best Respects to all of my friends & tell them to write no more at presant But remains yours truly Brother untill deth Write Soon

W.B. Morgan
F.R. Morgan

- - - - - - - - - - - - -

LETTER NO. 21
F.R. MORGAN TO CHARLES MORGAN

Jackson, Madison Co West Tenn
July the 8th 1867

Dear Father & Mother

I now write you a few lines to let you know that I am well hoping this may come to hand in due time and find all well and going well. Times are very good at this time, we had very exciting times there Saturday last at Speaking. Two niggers from nashville Spoke. The Rebels with one voice called for Dyre a rebel nigger to answer them, he Spoke untill he Said the Yankees would all Steal our Yankees told him to come down Whil the Rebs told him to Say on but he Soon consented to obey the Command.

They have been threatening us very strong but they know better than to raise a riot. For we can in 2 days have 5,000 troops here there is enuff rebs in this county to overpower our company, but we could hold at bay 4 times our number, and us in the Courthouse. We Will Stay in the Courthouse unless we get tents. I have a good time in Camps. I do not have to expose myself half So much as if I was at war.

We draw plenty flour, Bacon, Sugar, Coffee, and rice. Clothing plenty. We can go to meeting S when we please. We go to Sabbath Scool. D.C. Belvin and me are about all that goes to meeting often. We went to meeting over night for over a week after we arrived at this place. I have wrote 3 or 4 letters to W.B. & T.C. But hanen Received but one letter from home yet. It would be much pleasure to hear from you. I will close by asking all to write. Give my best respects to all inquiring Friends. I am truly yours Son till death.

F.R. Morgan

Ps. I Send you a Speech of Col Vailbe(?) delivered at Nashville. the Best Speech I ever read, read it and hand it to the next door neighbor if he is a rebel

- - - - - - - - - - - - -

LETTER NO. 22
F.R. MORGAN TO W.B. MORGAN
(Smiths X Roads, Tenn)

Jackson, West Tenn
July 12th 1867

Dear Brother

I write you a line to let you know that I am well I hope this will find you the Same with all your acquaintance. This leaves times very good in this part. I have nothing of interest to write to you at present. I only write this to you to inform you that Capt Clingan will be at Cleveland the 18th recruting we want about 40 more men in our Company. If you choose to Join us and will be at Cleveland in time to Start back the 18th you can get transpertation. But bear in mind that I dont persuade you to come by no means in the wold. Use your own pleasure as I did and hear the voice of no man on earth that says go or stay listen not even to me, perhaps you can make more there than you could in the Service. I know if I was out of the Service here I could make double what I am making, But I am perfectly Satisfied where I am. That is what I came out for. If you dont receive this in time to get to Cleveland to come with Clingan and wants to come, write to me and I will send you Transportation. I have wrote you Severel letters since P -?- left Home & havent recd but one from you.

I hope it is not your fault. We are going to have great excitement here on the day of the election. Some think we will have abattle, But I profes i different from that. The Rebs think a great deal more of us since we made this nigger come down from the Stump for Saying the Yankees would Steal. I will close by asking you to write Give my respects to the family tell them to write also to Captain Bill and family, Lewis and family Give my respects to all most especialy the girls.

I am truly yours Brother & well wisher excuse bad writing mistakes &c direct your letters to Co D, 1st Tenn State Guards

F.R. Morgan

- - - - - - - - - - - - -

LETTER NO. 23
F.R. MORGAN TO W.B. MORGAN
(Smiths X Roads, Tenn)

Franklin, Midle Tenn
August the 28th 1867

Dear Brother

Yours of the 8th & also the 15th now lays before me. I received them Sunday the 26th our 2ond Liut brought the one of the 8 from Jackson, the other came to Nashville. In each of them I learned that all was well. This is very good news to me I hope all will be well when this comes to hand Should it ever come This leaves me not very well. The Co left Nashville the 25, I was left there with 8 more that was not able to come. I came down Sunday the 26th. I havent been past going about am mending very fair now. You Said in yours of the 8 that you had got to be an old Batchler. I hope girls is not that Scarce that wants to marry. Why dont you Step over & See Rachel. I am Sure She would accept a good offer Never Stop trying– perhaps you can get that one. you cripled at infair. You Said you had a fine time at the wedding & infair. I think if I had have had been there I would have wounded one worse than you did about like the one that didnt give us a dram, no more of this.

In the 8 you Said also that Brownlows ticket carried the day at Smiths X Roads by a large majority. I am glad to hear that. I want you to give them of that voted for Etheridge Opossom tail Soup to eat for days to come & learn them to be the right kind of Democrats.

You Said in yours of the 15th that you had first got my viol & trunk. I Suposed you was a good fidler by this time but if this is the case you have got to learn. If I had have knowed that I was coming out here when I Started, I would have brought my trunk & fidle. I cant keep any thing without a trunk.

You also Said that T.C. Morgan was Married. This was nothing unexpected to me. For he promised to ask me to the Wedding. I Supose he got tired waiting on me to come back.

The long looked for has come at last. The above named marriage has come to ---?--- May they live a long & happy life As Loving husband & Darling wife. You never Said whether any body was oposed to it or not, Any body mad, Or any body glad. I guess Somebodys gal was mad because She didn't get him. Or at least Several would have been mad, if it had have been me & I guess he is as good as Iam. You can tell him & every body else that I was not oposed to them Marying. For I will do as he did. Take who I please, Or who I can get. I Should have Said Ask no one to choose for you --?-- the --?-- I hope they may find Married life to be mutch hapier than Single. I wish them mutch good luck & great fortunes. I will be there perhaps before long to Sirenade them. You tell me of a weding in almost every letter. You write So I dont care how often you write So you dont tell me of my girl being Married. I expect to hear of yours next Which will it be, Rachel or the Mountain girl.

Again you Said that Meliss Hall Said She had write 2 letters to me one to Jackson & one to Trenton. I wrote to the P.M. at Jackson while I was at Trenton to Send my letters to that place, But I only Stayed there 6 days So did not get either of them. I will now write to Tremton for them perhaps I will Stay here 4 or 5 days, if no longer. So I can excuse Melissa. I thought She had told me a fib when She Said She would write to me.

Again you talk as if you was going to make all the corn. I am glad to hear that crops is good in that County. I am in hopes I will make a Sifter full.

Tell Sarah I accept her Compliment with mutch pleasure. Tell her I will Come on to E. Tenn returning by the time her boy gets big enuff to make a Soldier. Give My respects to her & W.F. You Said you & W.F. was going to Ga & was going bye I.M. Riddles. You must do as you Said write to me how our barn looks, & write whether They has got a letter from me or not. I have wrote 9 to him. I will look for a letter from W.H. Morgan. W.F. Said he would write But I havent Seen any yet. I think I will be at home in time to take care of my crop, but it is very uncertain.

We was ordered to Nashville to be discharged Stayed there untill the papers was all fixed up & our discharges made out and then was ordered to Franklin. So I cannot tell when I will be at home. Some think we will be discharged after the City elections is over. I know one thing I voluntered for 3 years & I will Stay till they get ready to let me go. I will not do like Several of our Company has done, Desert the Co and in dishonor go home. I now report 26 deserters from this Company, 2 left after we had come to Nashville to be discharged.

We are now Camped at Franklin. I like this place better than any place we have been yet Franklin is 8 ms South east of Nashville. This is a very beautiful town. We have very good water to drink. This is more than we have had generaly. If we remain in the Service we will be paid of the 1st of next month I will Send or bring you Some blue grass Seeds as Soon as I can for you to try on the Mountain.

Hoping to hear from you Soon I will Close also hoping to have Something interesting to write next time. I am under many obligations to you for writing to me. I have red 1 letter that did not have your name Signed to it. Give my Respects to Father, Mother, Brothers & Sisters, and to all my friends. Tell all to write it is no harm to ask them. I am well Satisfied in Camp. Excuse bad writing & Mistakes &c.

I am truly yours
F.R. Morgan

- - - - - - - - - - - - -

LETTER NO. 24
F.R. MORGAN TO W.B. MORGAN
(Smiths X Roads)

Franklin, Tenn
August 29th 1867

Dear Brother

Though I wrote you yesterday I will proceed to write again this morning, As I learn this morning that our Captain is Coming to East Tenn Recruting & I dont want you nor any body else that is any thing to me to come with him For Several diferent reasons. First is this it is the General opinion of the Company that he done all he could to keep the Company in the Service When there was no use for us any where all was quiet in West Tenn Where we was Stationed & that was Certainly the worst part of the State for out laws & more than this.

After we Came to Nashville to be discharged one of our boys Said he told him that he was going to do all he Could against the Company, that before this there was not a man in his Company that did not like him, But now there is not many that does like him. Now the election is over There is not one particle of --?-- for us in the Service. It is only Ruining the State to a useless expense. And the union man pays as mutch of it as the Rebel. But I Say it was right to call out troops to guard the polls for in West Tenn not a Single union man would have been allowed the priviledge of voting for Brownlow But he is now elected by a Majority of 5000 & there is no use of a State quarel But if they See Cause to keep us in It is all right with me I came out for 3 years & I expect to Stay untill I am favorably discharged.

I will give you another reason why I did not want you to come. That is I think you or me one ought to be there to See to improving that mountain place. Another is that there is Some pers[ons] in this co that does no duty. havent Scarcely any Since we came out But the officers never have mustered me yet. I never have ast to go any where yet and they ---?--- I went to meeting last night I am mending very much

In conclusion I will Say for you to Stay where you are & this is one time I want you to do as I tell you Yes I am doing well, Well Satisfied making 16 dollars a month & more for I did not take up what clothing I was allowed by Several dollars. do not make this a public letter only tell them that wants to came they need not come, they just wait(?) it give my respects to all my friends tell them to write to me in Franklin I am truly yours

F.R. Morgan

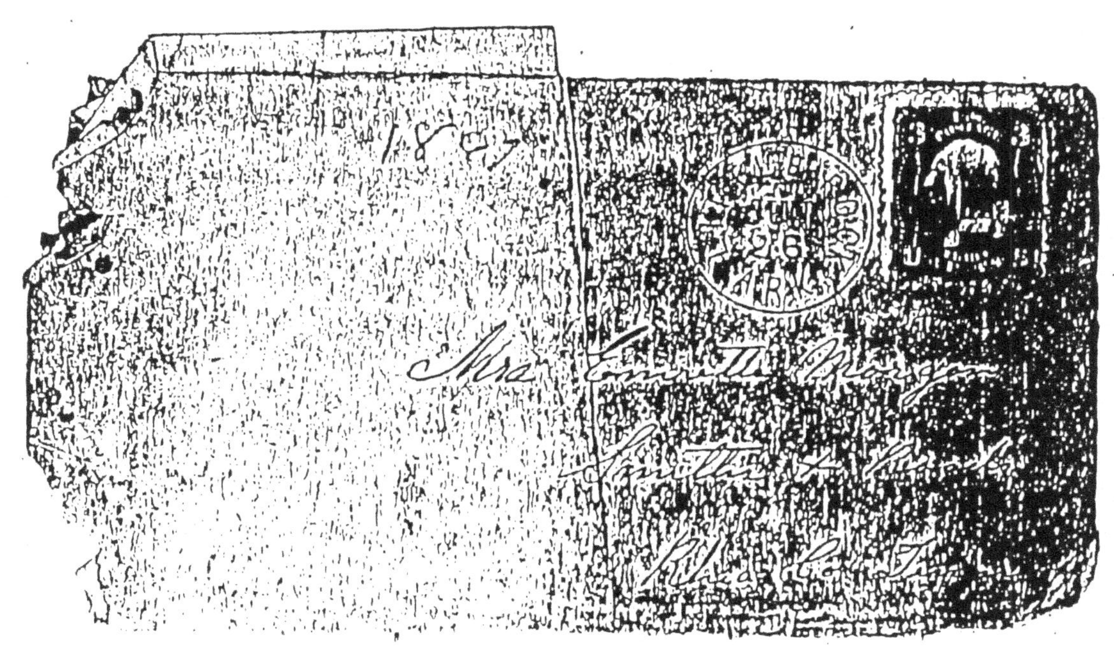

Envelope mailed to Mrs. Emeretta Morgan from Little Rock, Arkansas, on 26 June [1867?]

PAINE LETTERS

Mary L. Paine, Hanibal Paine, and Flavius Joseph Paine were children of Orville and Elvira (Locke) Paine. The family lived on a large farm east of present-day Evensville in Rhea County.

Hanibal Paine (1839-1867) joined Captain John Crawford's Company (26th Tennessee Regiment) and was elected Lieutenant. After the reorganization, James A. Cash was Captain of Company E. Hanibal was never married and probably was buried in the Paine Cemetery (no headstone).

Flavius Joseph Paine (12 May 1832 - 9 October 1893) entered Company C (16th Battalion Cavalry) in 1861 as a First Lieutenant, but was later promoted to Major. He returned home in May 1865. On 22 January 1867, in McMinn County, he married Amanda Caroline Latham. The couple made their home near Evensville and are both buried in the Paine Cemetery.

Mary Louisa Paine (1842-1896) did her part by becoming a member of the Girls Company that was organized in the latter part of the war. She married Dr. Richard W. Colville on 21 October 1869. A descendant, Eugene Colville, furnished copies of the Paine and Colville letters for this publication.

The other children of Orville and Elvira mentioned in the following letters included Alfred "Buck" Paine, Ann Paine, and Jane Paine.

LETTER NO. 1
HANIBAL PAINE TO FLAVIUS J. PAINE

Johnsons Island, Ohio
Aug 12th 1862

Via
Fortress Monroe and City Point
Care Genl John A Dix
Dear Brother

I have written to you some two or three times in the last two months past but having received no letter from you since the 3rd June I write you again today in hopes that if you have not received former letters that you may at least receive this. I can write nothing of interest except that I am in tolerable health. My health is rather delicate but I am still able to keep up my locomotion. I learn from the papers that there is an exchange of prisoners going on, and I hope that the exchange may soon reach this corner of "Uncle Sam's tater patch" and that we may all soon be on the road to "Dixie" though you know more of that than I do. It is my unpleasant task to announce to you the death of Jeff West of our company. He died sometime in July past. I suppose you have heard of the death of Capt. Crawford for I have written it frequently. He died 10th April. If you receive this before you hear intelligence of my release answer it immediately. Lt J Howell is well as are also all the officers of the 26th Tenn. I send you my receipt to enable you to make settlement as administrator.

Your Bro.
H. Paine

- - - - - - - - - - - - -

LETTER NO. 2
F. J. PAINE TO MARY L. PAINE

Knoxville, Tenn,
Sept. 29th [1862]

Dear Sister

I drop you a line again that you may know where I am &c. We are still in Knoxville just as we were when I wrote you last, and have not learned certainly where we will be assigned. I have no news more than you have had in the papers, more than I have seen a man or two who were prisoners at Johnsons Island and they say that the 26th Regt is exchanged and will either be at Chattanooga or this place in a day or two. I have heard nothing further.

I have not heard a word from home since I left, though I have not been looking for a letter until the last day or two. I am in good health except a bad cold which I hope will soon pass off. The boys are generally well, two or three of them chilling a little but keep able to go. We have not got our arms yet, and I do not know when we will.

Genl McCowan did not start to Ky with his force last week but is to start this morning. I suppose he will have 8 or 10 thousand to take with him and perhaps more. We will not go, as we are not armed. I think likely we will be kept in E. Tenn for some time, but can't tell certainly anything about it.

We get plenty to eat here such as Bread Bacon Rice Sugar & Coffee. We officers are allowed Coffee & Sugar by buying it, and they get it at government prices which is 50¢ for coffee and 20 for sugar. But they are not allowed to buy any more than they use themselves. We have been living very well since we came here but anything in the way of fruit or vegetables are very scarce and high. You must write to me as soon as you get this. I will write again in a few days. Give my love to all and believe me as ever.

Your Brother
F. J. Paine

- - - - - - - - - - - - -

LETTER NO. 3
F.J. PAINE TO MARY L. PAINE
WASHINGTON, TENNESSEE,
CARE OF H.C. COLLINS

Camp on Hiwassee,
Nov 29th 1862

Dear Sister

I drop you a line this morning as I have an opportunity of sending it by hand. We are moving on in the direction of Chattanooga slowly. We only go ten or twelve miles a day and are getting our horses shod up and re-crusted. I think our mission down there is to enforce the conscript law and arrest all straglers who belong to the army and send them up to their command. I am in good health and getting along very well.

The Capt is now at home and has been for a few days. If he had been here this morning I could have got off to come home a few days on business but as the Capt is not here, I have to sent Lt Collins. We have arrangements to take a few men with our company and that is what I sent Collins back for. I want to get enough to raise the Co to 100.

I have no news. We get no war news in this part of the world. I had quite a pleasant time while we were at Camp Davis. We stayed there 7 days and I saw my sweetheart several times while there. I learned that the 26th has gone down the road.

I have not heard from Hab [Hanibal] since I was at home. You must all do the best you can. I do not know when I will be at home, but will come the first opportunity.

Write me when you get this and leave it at Aults and tell him to send it by the first one that is passing. My love to all and tell Buck [younger brother of Flavius] to be a good boy and get along the best he can with the work. I will write again the first opportunity.

Your Brother,
F. J. Paine

- - - - - - - - - - - -

LETTER NO. 4
F. J. PAINE TO MARY L. PAINE

Head Quarters 16th Battalion
near Monticello, Ky, Jan 3rd 1863

Dear Sister

I drop you a line to say to you that I am now in tolerable good health. I thought when I wrote you last I would get off home in a few days for the purpose of getting up the absentees, but I do not know now whether I shall get off soon or not.

We are looking for a fight every day as the Yanks are threatening to cross at two different points and in pretty strong force. And if they come against us in much force we will have to retreat as we now have but one Brigade here. But I am told Morgan is in below us with his command, and if that is true we may be able to hold them in check. Our command has made three raids on the other side of the river and on each occasion routed the forces they found and captured more or less on every trip. I cannot now give you the particulars, but suffice it to say we have been gaining some credit for our command.

It was reported yesterday morning that the Yanks were crossing the river and we were ordered up to meet them, but on arriving at the place learned it was a false alarm. And we were called out this morning in the same way but I do not think it will be many days before they do cross. I sent a horse by Lt Collins. Tell Ann she must take good care of him as he is a Yankee horse captured. I also sent by him one hundred dollars which he was to leave with you or F. Locke. I wrote in my other letter that I sent $300 dollars but I bought a horse as he was starting and got part of it back from him so he only had $100.

If I do not get off home soon and we are not driven out of Ky, I will write again soon. Give my regards to my friends and particularly to Miss Janice. Write to me if you see any one coming to the command.

Your Brother,
F. J. Paine

- - - - - - - - - - - -

LETTER NO. 5
HANIBAL PAINE TO MARY PAINE

Camp near Tullahoma Tenn
January 10th 1863

Dear Sister

I well know how anxious you all are to hear from me and would have written sooner, but this is the first opportunity that I have had for many days. Since I have written last to you, I have participated in a great battle, and God through his divine wisdom and mercy has seen cause to spare me. I was struck by a ball on the leg, also had a finger glanced but escaped unhurt. For eight days and nights we stood in line of battle, in all kinds of weather, with no covering or tents save the heavens above us, and although we were not engaged fighting ourselves all the time, still there was not a day passed but what we were more or less exposed to the enemy's shells.

I shall not attempt to give you a history of the fight for you can get a more accurate account of it from the papers than I could write myself. I will tell you what Brigade and Division our Regiment belongs to, and then from the newspapers you can find out what part we acted in the bloody drama. Our Regiment belongs to the Second Brigade of General Breckinridge's Division. We were in the memorable charge made on Friday the 2nd January. We took the enemy position and drove them half a mile, but their batteries poured such a murderous and destructive fire upon us that we were compelled to retreat. I was afraid in the retreat that they would get many of us prisoners, still, they got but few. I really thought your humble servant as the boys say would go up a spout. We had to march back for half a mile through an open corn field and many were so much exhausted that they could not go faster than a slow walk. The enemy all the while were pouring in a murderous fire of shells, grape, canister shot and minni balls upon our retreating column. I thought once I was so much exhausted that I would not be able to get back across the field, but I staggered slowly on and reached the woods on the other side where our forces rallied and held the enemy in check.

Our Regiment went into the fight with about three hundred men and officers and lost ninety six killed wounded and missing. Our Company went into the fight with twenty three men and officers, and lost seven killed wounded and missing. Capt Jas A. Cash is missing, supposed to be killed or wounded and in the hands of the enemy. Seagt W.L. Rice is sevierly wounded and taken prisoner. Henry Hughes is missing and supposed to be killed. Stephen Spence is sevierly wounded and a prisoner. William R. Singleton was slightly wounded in the right hip and F.M. Loftis slightly in the face. The three last mentioned were merely scratched and are with us safe and well.

The Yankees got possession of the battle field before we could get our wounded off was the way they came to fall into the enemy's hands. It was the only portion of the battle field but what we held. That night we took our original position and staid there until the next night. About twelve o'clock when we commenced our retreat, we trudged on through mud knee deep that night and by sun rise next morning were ten miles away from Murfreesboro on the road towards Manchester. Our retreat was conducted quite orderly and quietly. We passed through Manchester which is on the McMinnville Rail Road and from thence to Arazona on the Nashville and Chattanooga Rail Road and from thence to Tullahoma, which is distance from Murfreesboro about forty miles.

In the charge we made upon the yankees on the 2nd January we lost two thousand men killed wounded and missing in thirty minutes and the yankees must have lost three to four thousand, for I am satisfied that where I went over the battle field we killed and wounded two or three of theirs to where they killed or wounded one of ours. I know it is generally the cry that we kill more of them than they do of our men, but I know it was certainly the case there for I saw how it was with my own eyes.

I expect that you have heard that I was wounded and suffered much uneasiness on that account. H. A. Crawford from what I can learn wrote that several were wounded who were not. That was because he was not in the fight and knew nothing about it, consequently he had no right to write anything about it. Him and Riley were neither of them in it. They were five miles distant with the waggons. Riley was waggon master and Henry don't belong to the army, but he has been with us all the time. He was letting on to be sick. Either of them might have had the best chance in the world to have fought if they had only had a willing inclination to have done so. But I phophecy that if the war lasts two years that they will neither of them ever be in a fight. So if you ever hear them telling what they did in the Battle of Murfreesboro you can tell them that they were not in it. We lost our Regimental Flag in the fight, but captured one from the Yankees, so we made a set off in the flag line.

Many of the boys lost all their clothes and blankets. I lost my quilt and blankets in the charge and am now without any bed clothing. But I am doing fine and am truly thankful that I escaped with my life. Perhaps I may be able to procure some more blankets. If you have any opportunity you can send me one, but put yourselves to no unnecessary trouble, for I am old enough and have seen enough of the world to shift pretty well for myself.

Tell Ann and Jane [Hanibal's sisters] that I have received some letters from them but could write nothing more at present than I have written to you. So I intend this as a general letter to you all. Tell them they must write to me again and then I will write to them. The probabilities are that we may have another battle ere long. Bragg I think intends giving them battle if they advance somewhere about Tullahoma. If they don't advance likely he will advance again towards Murfreesboro.

Tell Uncle Green that I saw his son James Mathis a few days before the fight. He belongs to Savages 16th Tenn Regiment, Donaldsons Brigade and Cheathams Division. I have not seen or heard from him since, for aught I know he may be killed or wounded in the fight. In the fight altho we have retreated we have lost nothing except that many brave men killed, and have come out winners at last. It is estimated that we have taken

Five thousand prisoners	5,000
Sixty one piees artillery	61
Small arms seven thousand five hundred	7,500
Destroyed nine hundred and fifty wagons	950
Killed and wounded the enemy	9,000
Our losses killed	1,000
Our loss wounded	3,500
Recapitulation	
Federals killed	3,000
Federals wounded	6,000
Federals captured	5,000
Amount	14,000
Our loss	4,500
Balance	9,500

I shall send this letter by Mr William Roddy, brother to G.P. Roddy who is a Lieut in our company. If he calls and stays all night or gets his dinner, don't charge him his bill. I also send by him, two hundred and thirty dollars $230.00 which I want you to put away and keep until I come home or if Jo comes home before I do, give it to him and tell him to give me credit for it on our books. I send my letter by him because it will be apt to reach you as soon that way as by mail, and then I wanted to send my money.

I want you to write to me as soon as you get this letter and let me know whether my money arrived safe or not. Direct your letter to Tullahoma, Tenn. I have no more news of interest to write. The army is in good health considering the hard times we have seen. I hope you all had a Merry Christmas and Happy New Years. Present my kind regards to all enquiring friends, and tell them I am still in good health, and ready to meet the invader and his hosts. All of the soil that Rosencrans gains now is going to cost him blood. The Yankees are sacrificing their lives for nothing, we ours for home and country, that is the difference. Several of them will have to die yet before they get possession of all of Tennessee.

Write soon Your Brother

H. Paine

- - - - - - - - - - - - -

LETTER NO. 6
HANIBAL PAINE TO MARY L. PAINE

Miss Mary L Paine, at Home, East Tennessee
Urbanity of Lieut R.C. Knight

Tullahoma, Jan 19th 1863

Dear Sister

I received a letter from you the 17th, and having no news I have not been in a hurry to write. I have detailed today Lieut R.C. Knight to go home to Rhea and Meigs counties to bring clothing, blankets, and other necessaries for our company. Since I wrote to you before I have been so lucky as to buy me a good blanket. I would like for you to send me by him another blanket if you have one. Don't send one of those fine bed blankets. I would rather do without than to have you send one of them. Send me some old blanket if you have one. If not perhaps I can get a chance to buy another. I would like if you can to make me another pair of pants and send them as I have but one pair. You may also send me one or two pair socks.

I would also like for you to send me something to eat. Send me some sausages, some green apples if you have any a little fried fruit, some sweet potatoes, and small quantity of any thing you may think of. Don't try to send too much. You can pack my things in a box and mark the box to Lt H. Paine, Co E 26th Regt Tenn Vols, Tullahoma. I would like to have some apple butter if you can fix it up so as to send it.

Lieut Knight will call and deliver this letter. He can tell you where and when to send the box so that he can take charge of them. If the boats are running the river he can tell you what landing to send it to. If they are not you will have to send it to Athens. I would say again don't try to send too much.

I send to Buck [Hanibal's brother] by Lieut Knight about 40 Yankee cartridges. In your next letter write to me whether Buck got them or not. I have no news to write. We had a considerable fall of snow the other day but it has melted off and the weather has somewhat moderated. We have been having a hard time of it lately. I forgot to tell you I would like for you to send me a few onions.

I can't tell how long we will stay here. We may stay some time and we may leave in a few days. I recd a letter from Jo the same day that yours came to hand. I will answer it in a few days and send it to Greenville, Tenn. Tell Uncle Green that I have written about three letters to him and never received an answer. I think he should write to me before I write to him again.

My eyes are so near smoked out that I can scarcely see to write, so excuse the imperfections. I can think of nothing else. Encourge John McDaniel to come to the company he is now absent without leave.

Your Bro. H. Paine

Jan 22nd 1863

When I wrote my letter I expected Lt Knight would get off sooner, but I never got his papers fixed up until today. So I have extended my letter a little. I have but little more news. I see in an extract in the Mobile Register taken from a Nashville paper the names of several Rebel officers taken in the fight before Murfreesboro. Among them appears the name of J.A. Cash, Capt 26th Tennessee Regt, so he is not killed, but a prisoner. I hope he may soon be exchanged or paroled and returns to his friends in "Dixie". I think we will be likely to stay here two or three months, until towards spring. We are in no condition to advance on the Yankees and they can't advance on us. I would like much to see you all but have no hopes of getting off on furlough anytime soon. I believe I have given you a list of all the articles I need and more too. Send me some of them if you have them, if not I can do without them. Put yourselves to no unnecessary trouble. Invoking Heavens Blessing upon you all, I remain

Your brother

H. Paine

- - - - - - - - - - - - -

LETTER NO. 7
F.J. PAINE TO MARY L. PAINE

Washington College, Tenn
January 28th 1863

My Dear Sister

I drop you a line again as I am stopping at this place for a few days and have a tolerable chance to write. I wrote to Jane from camp near Greenville the morning we left that place and since then we came to Broylesville, a small town in the southern part of this county, and from there we marched south into the eastern corner of Greene Co, crossing Chucky River and there an eastern direction along the base of the Chilhowee Mountains until we came to where Chucky runs along the foot of the mountains, and then crossing into this county again. We crossed Chucky River again at one of the roughest fords I have crossed any river at, but we all got over safe and camped just on this side. We had a pretty rough trip up to that time but made it very well.

Monday night it began to rain and we had a good deal of rain that night and Tuesday morning it began to snow, so we remained in camp until about 12 o'clock and as it got no better I was satisfied it was going to be a rough time, so I determined to move up to this place, a distance of some five or six miles. We arrived here and found the college vacant and the boys all have quarters now in the college in good comfortable rooms, that all have good fire places and notwithstanding the inclemency of the weather we are all getting along comfortably.

I selected a very genteel cottage near the college where I have made my quarters. It is a very neat room and a good fire place large enough to have a fire that soon warms up the room. So upon the whole we are quite comfortably situated considering the kind of weather we are having and I think I shall remain here and not try to do any duty until the weather gets better.

I told you it commenced snowing on Tuesday morning so it snowed on all that day and melted as fast as it fell, and about night it began to lay on the ground in places and this morning the snow was some four inches deep and it has been snowing all day and is still falling fast as ever and it is now about three o'clock in the evening and the snow is now some 6 or 7 inches deep.

When we first came here while we were traveling along the foot of the mountain, before this last rain commenced we could look up towards the tops of the mountains and see that all of the high peaks were covered with snow and white. It fell at the same time that you had a skiff of snow while I was at home.

I am about through with what we came here to do so I will return to Greenville as soon as the weather moderates so we can travel without suffering too much from cold. I have been improving since I left home and am now stout as usual. There are several of the boys left back at camp near Greenville sick but none of them I think very bad. Bill Mathis is down again, but not seriously sick or dangerous as he is uncomplaining as he was while at home before. Tell Wesley to tell Mrs. Shelton that Jim is well and hardy.

I have no news of interest to write for I have seen no papers nor had any chance to get any news for several days. If you have written to me at Greenville any of you since I left you need not write any more until you hear from me again. I will write again in a few days.

As ever your Brother, F. J. Paine

January 29th 1863

The snow ceased to fall last night and the sun is shining forth this morning in all its brightness and every thing looks gay and cheerful after such days as the two last. And it really looks pleasant out of doors over head, but the ground is buried in snow. I have enjoyed the last two nights sleep as I have had a good feather bed to sleep in and I met with a man here who lives close to where I am staying in my shanty, and he would agree to nothing but that I should eat and sleep with him while we run around here and as it suited me very well I at once agreed to do so, and am faring finely as they are nice folks and live well. They are very kind and accommodating.

The citizens of this county are a majority of them Southern and treat us very clever and some disposed to accommodate us in any way they can but there are some Tories here to. The Headquarters of the Battalion are down near Greenville and as we are only here on a scout, we will return in a few days to that place. Perhaps you had better write to me at Greenville as soon as you get this as we may be in that neighborhood for some time. I must close and start my letters to the office.

Ever your Brother, F. J. Paine

- - - - - - - - - - - - -

LETTER NO. 8
MARY L. PAINE TO LT. HANIBAL PAINE

Near Washington, Jan 29/63

Dear Brother

I received your letter sent by Lieut Knight on last Tuesday. He came over and took dinner and staid about two hours with us. He said that he would come back and see us again before he went off if he had time. The ammunition you sent to Buck all came safe, also a package of letters. Buck was much pleased to get it for ammunition is very scarce and hard to get about here. We will send you the articles you speak of wanting.

We received a letter from Joe dated the 25th. He was at Greenville when the letter was written. The election had not come off. He said that the company was going to start to Washington County on a scout and would be gone about six days enforcing the conscript. Lt Col Bean is still in Washington. He has not been out to see us yet. I do not care if he does not come atall for I think he is a coward and managed to keep out of the battle. He says he never wanted to be in a hard battle.

But I must tell you about the candy stew that they had at Uncle Frank's [Franklin Locke] last Friday night. Miss Jennie and Manurva had been up above town on a visit and came back there and asked if they might have one there. She told them she did not care if Uncle Frank was willing. She said she had no idea that he would be, so they waited until he came home and then they begged him until he agreed that they might have one there. So they went on home and came back that night with several other girls and had a fine time they say. But I will tell you who was there and then you can guess what a time they had. There was Miss Jennie, Manurva Sharp(?), Ann Gillespe, Jane Locke, Mollie Kelly, and Isabel Cunnyngham. Bean was the only young gentleman that was there.

Mother and Ann went over the next morning. Ann said she had a long conversation with Bean and enjoyed herself finely. The girls all left soon after they got there and Bean stayed until after dinner and then went down to town. He said the commander of that Brigade of cavalry had gone to Knoxville to get them all furloughed for thirty days. I think they had better disband at once and come home for there is some of them always at home. I do not believe that they will ever do much fighting. I think they have several cowards among them.

There was a man here last Saturday that said he was very well acquainted with you. That he saw you while you were in Prison at Johnsons Island and that he would like very much to see you. He had been wounded badly in the face also in the arm and the first finger on his right hand was off. He said that he was wounded and taken prisoner at Shilo. We prepared him some dinner and he eat and seemed very thankful to get it. He said his name was Chomley and that he was in search of employment. He said he wanted to work on the farm. He went on towards Knoxville from here.

I wrote you in my last letter that there was a courier here, but it was a mistake, it was one of Seats men. He was so drunk that he did not know what he was telling. He said he was a courier and that he was going to stay 15 weeks. He also said that the man that was with him was wounded but he too was only drunk. They staid all night and left the next morning and I was not sorry of it for I had got tired out with the cavalry.

There was one of Capt Robinsons men of Bledsoe staid with us last night. There is also two of Morgans men here tonight. They have been up about Sweet Water on some business they say.

We have sent John McDaniel word that he had better go to his company. I expect he is able to go if he was anxious to get back. But I believe I have written you all that I can think of. We are all well and in fine spirits. We would be glad if you could get off to come home. I hope that you will have a chance to come before long. Some of us will write again in a few days. Write soon.

As ever your Sister,
Mary

- - - - - - - - - - - - -

LETTER NO. 9
HANIBAL PAINE TO MARY L. PAINE

Tullahoma,
Feb 4th 1863

Dear Sister

Yours came to hand a few days since informing me of the arrival of Lieut Knight and safe delivery of my letters and ammunition. I can't say much for his personal appearance or shrewdness, but I presume you found him sociable and communicative according to the extent of his knowledge. Upon the whole as it was not convenient for me to take the trip myself, I judged him to be the best selection I could make in our company, and hope he will perform the task alloted him satisfactorially to all concerned.

As for the candy stew, I had a brief sketch of it from one who said they were present in person on that festive occasion. They represented it as a brilliant affair, rather on a small scale. Said tho that they had quite a merry time of it. I hope myself they enjoyed themselves well, "for whatever fate betide me" I always wish the virtuous and good prosperous and happy.

As for Bean, like yourself I always have a contemptable opinion of all such persons. I well knew before the fact was written from home that he was not in the battle, I learned that he was sick and went to the waggon yard beyond the reach of danger the day before the fight began. I never saw him myself, but some of my men saw him the day he rode out there and was telling me what he said, but you had better think when the retreat commenced he was able again to get himself out of harms way. I saw him myself on the retreat, he passed our Regiment about noon the first day riding his roan horse. At the time I was trudging along in the ranks through mud almost knee deep. I perceived that he never saw me and so I let him pass without calling him to attention, for I would not at that time have stepped one step out of my way to have shaken hands with Jeff Davis. I am of opinion that he thinks himself about as high as it possible for him to climb (and I have no doubt but what he ranks higher than he deserves) and he now wants to live in glorious ease, and reflect the honor and glory of our brave soldiers without sharing their toils, privations, and dangers, though for aught I know he may be really sick and bad off, and I can at the same time allege nothing disreputable against him, I merely write what I do to make you think and to let you know that I take slight notice of events transpiring around me. And take notice at the same time that I want the contents of this letter not to go beyond the family circle.

[NOTE: Col. Onslow Bean, born 11 February 1831, was the son of Edmond and Lucretia (Locke) Bean. He was a Methodist minister and was never married. One Regimental History states that "Col. Onslow Bean, of the Sixteenth Tennessee Battalion, as senior officer, commanded Vaughn's brigade. This was during a very active part of the campaign, and Col. Bean proved himself to be an officer of great resources. Brave, prudent, vigilant, he handled his little brigade with consummate skill and ability. This gallant officer was killed at the head of his battalion at Marion, Va., in December, 1864, while resisting an overwhelming number of the enemy." J.N. Aiken, ***Military Annals of Tennessee, Regimental Histories and Memorial Rolls***, 1866: 525]

And there is another nice man just returned home, Mr. H.A. Crawford who has never been the least advantage to the cause since the war began. Can you tell me how him and Miss Ann [Frazier] are making it? I am of opinion his star is waning. I understand he says Mr Jasper Lillard is all the man he fears (is Martha Frazier at Washington now?). I think from what I can learn that Jasper has been making his life quite an uneasy and unhappy one of late. He used to write to Ann and Mollie both and used to say he could easily get Mollie. I reckon he thinks if he can't get the one now he will not be choice and so will take the other. But I would not be suprised if he fails yet in the end to get either of them.

Well I have almost consumed my space, and given you but little current news. But at the same time I can say that I have but little to write. A few days since I heard cannon in the direction of Shelbyville, and it has been reported that the Yankees are advancing by that pike, but I don't believe one word of it. So allow yourself to suffer no uneasiness on that account. General Johnston is here now, and I suppose will assume command.

We have some cold bad weather now and occasionally some snow. Why don't Jane write to me, I have been expecting a letter from her for some time, that is the reason I have not written to her before now. I must close by bidding you good night.

H. Paine

- - - - - - - - - - - - -

LETTER NO. 10
HANIBAL PAINE TO MARY L. PAINE

Tullahoma,
Feby 24th 1863

Dear Sister

I recd a letter from you a few days since and would have responded sooner, but I have been out of postage stamps and have been waiting until I could get some. Where there are so many thousand to write it is a difficult matter to keep all supplied in stamps. Tullahoma is to my notion decidely a dull place. There is but little of interest transpiring to note. Bragg, occasionally to break the tedious monotony of a dull camp life, has a soldier for some unbecoming conduct shot. There have been several shot since we have been at this place both officers and privates. It was mostly for misbehavior or cowardice before the enemy in the late battle before Murfreesboro. So far there have been none shot in our Brigade, and I have never yet witnessed such an execution. I might have saw some hung and shot both but I have never been curious to see such sights.

We also have small pox here, but then we have all become used to that, so we have but little dread of it. Don't understand me that we have it in camp, for we have had no case of it amongst us since we have been here. The cases of it that are here are confined in some houses off to themselves and a guard kept round them to prevent any persons going near them. I have a few times passed in sight of the houses in a hundred yards or such a matter, but have never cared to be closer and have never tarried while that close.

There is no fighting going on and all seems to be quiet. We are having some very bad weather now and quite a chance of rain which will certainly make the waters very high. I have answered Jane's and Ann's letters that I received by Lieut Knight. I have nothing more at present to write that would interest you. Remember me to all

Your Brother,
H. Paine

- - - - - - - - - - - - -

LETTER NO. 11
HANIBAL PAINE TO MARY L. PAINE

Camp Fairfield, Tenn,
April 24th/63

Dear Sister

I recd your letter some days since, but as we were just on the eve of a move, I have had no chance to write until at the present time. We left Tullahoma at daylight on the morning of the 22nd, that is our whole Brigade left there, and started in persuit of some Yankees who were making their way toward the McMinnville Rail Road. We marched that day as far as Manchester where we encamped for the night and there we learned that the Yankees had beat a hasty retreat.

So that changed our purpose somewhat, and at eight o'clock next morning we set out again for Beach Grove in the direction of Murfreesboro, and only distant some seventeen miles from that place, at Beach Grove, we turned to the left and struck in the direction of War Trace, and are encamped now five miles north of that place on the north fork of Duck River. There is no town, mail route, or anything of the kind here. We are just out in the country. War Trace is our nearest Post Office, so I shall send my letter there to have it mailed the first oppertunity.

How long we will stay here I can't tell. I am of the opinion we will move in a few days down to War Trace. I don't know certainly, but I am of opinion that our whole army will leave Tullahoma and establish our lines this much nearer the Yankees. We have had no fighting, nor have we saw any Yankees, yet, but we were expecting a brush all along the road. The citizens would tell us all the way that they were only two or three miles ahead, but I don't believe there are any nearer than Murfreesboro, except it be some scouts.

I have no further news to write, it may be that in marching round that I will get so far from any main route that I will have no chance to write. If you fail to get letters you may know that such is the case. Direct your next letter to War Trace, Tennessee. Present my best wishes to all and accept for yourself the kind regards of your Brother,

H. Paine

April 25th 1863

I failed to get a chance to send my letter to the office yesterday, but will send it to War Trace this morning. I have no further news to write. H. Paine

- - - - - - - - - - - - -

LETTER NO. 12
HANIBAL PAINE TO MARY L. PAINE

Camp Near Fairfield, Tenn,
May 27, 1863

Dear Sister

I recd a kind communication from you some days since and would have written sooner but for some days past I have been continually on the march and have had no opportunity to write sooner.

On Saturday night the 23rd of May we received orders at three o'clock. It was to cook one days rations and be ready to march at daylight so we made ready at the appointed time and set out at break of day for Hoover's Gap about eight miles from this place and on the road leading from Murfreesboro to Manchester. Hoover's Gap is nothing but the continuation of a long hollow with a high hill closing in on either side, and is considered to be a strong defensable position.

Well upon Sunday our Regiment was placed out upon picket duty in some ten or twelve miles of Murfreesboro and remined ther until morning. Early the next morning we were relieved and marched back in a half a mile of our former camp ground. Our Regiment was halted there, and our company was thrown out as skirmishers about three miles in front. We were out there on the lookout all day but saw no Yankees while we were out on picket.

Our general learned that a force of Yanks were advancing out from Murfreesboro toward McMinnville and they concluded to cut them off and make a capture. So Monday evening late our Brigade and General Bushrod Johnson's Brigade from Major General Claburne's Division were set in motion for that purpose. They marched that night some five miles more since as I have told you before out on picket and by the neglect of somebody we were not relieved until about eleven o'clock at night.

We then had to march about ten miles that night to overtake our Regiment. We marched within about a mile of where they encamped that night and then spread down our blankets under some trees and slept about an hour. We then arose and started again and caught up with our regiment at day break as they were preparing to renew the march. We filed into line with them and went ahead all marching at quick time.

We marched on to Bradysville passed through that place, halted about a half a mile beyond and as I thought were going immediately to have a battle, but things turned out quite differently. When we were halted an "Infirmiry Corps" was detailed to carry off the wounded and a Regiment was deployed as skirmishers and I expected a battle would immediately open. But after marching about an hour I learned that the Yankees that we were trying to capture had in some way learned of our approach and "double quicked" it back to Murfreesboro thereby saving their scalps and very possibly a few of our own.

So after marching about an hour as I said before we received orders to about face and had to march all the way back. The day was very warm and I never saw men so fatigued. A great many gave out by the way and it is reported that no less than seven died on the march from fatigue and heat and drinking too much water.

We got back Tuesday night as far as "Beach Grove" and encamped. Stacked our arms and had just rested a few minutes when a courier came dashing up at a furious rate informing us that the Yankees were advancing by way of Hoover's Gap and that they had already engaged one regiment of our brigade who were sent out as skirmishers. The 302 Tennessee.

So we immediately set out for the scene of action. Again expecting to have a fight. We marched as far as Beach Grove and were there halted. We remained there about an hour without any Yankees making their appearance and then marched back. I think we have some cavalry spread along the front who every time they see a single Yankee come past, haste and report that the enemy are advancing in force and that is the way we are so often deceived.

General Breckinridge and all of his Division except our brigade are gone some where. I don't know certainly but I suppose they are gone to Mississippi. It is reported that the Yankees have twelve times assaulted Vicksburg and have been repulsed each time with heavy slaughter. I also learned that the Yankees have for three days been bombarding Cumberland Gap and I hope this attempt at this place will likewise prove a failure.

There is a good General in command in East Tennessee now General Simeon B. Buckner. I had as soon risk him as any in my knowledge, for he is every inch a hero and a skilled military man. It is expected that the Hon. C.L. Vallandingham from Ohio has been exiled from home sent through our lines and is now at Shelbyville, Tenn.

You can see from my letter that we are having a rather hard time of it after those scouting parties of Yankees and any day may have a considerable fight with them. So far the enemy around Murfreesboro have been quiet and don't seem inclined to make a general advance. Our brigade is now composed of six Regiments the following: the 18th Tennessee, 20th Tennessee, 26th Tennessee, 32nd Tennessee, 45th Tennessee and Newman's Batallion, he is also from Tennessee. I have no more news, as ever

Your brother,
H. Paine

- - - - - - - - - - - - -

LETTER NO. 13
HANIBAL PAINE TO MARY L. PAINE

Tullahoma, Tenn, June 28th 1863

Dear Sister

On my return from Knoxville to Wartrace, I found a letter from you awaiting my perusal, to which I shall attempt to give a responce this evening as you no doubt feel anxious to hear how things are going here. While we were gone to East Tenn the Yankees attacked Bates Brigade at Hoovers Gap and succeded in driving them away. They also attacked Genl Liddell at Liberty Gap and took the place.

Our Regt arrived at Wartrace day before yesterday evening. When we got there on the train our waggons were passing through town on the retreat. We halted them and immediately put our plunder off of the train into the waggons. Our Regt was immediately detained for provost guard duty in town. So I selected an encampment close by and we drew some rations and went to cooking.

Next morning by daylight everything was on the retreat and as I am now acting as quartermaster of course I had to accompany our train. We were very much bothered to get off with our waggons there were so many on the road in the way. But after a while we got started and got along very well until in the afternoon when the Yankees were about to cut us off and we had quite a time of it whipping up to get out of their reach. But we made good our escape and arrived at Tullahoma about two hours by sun.

That same evening their advance came within a mile of Tullahoma and formed in line of battle, but afterwards retired without any fight. All of our available force at that time present was thrown in line of battle and prepared to give them a warm reception. I am informed that Genl Bragg rode round Flat Rains where our Regt was posted, smiling and told them if they could only hold the place until night that we were safe, for by that time that his army would be here. I suppose he alluded to all those who have been at Shelbyville and other places and I think his words true for troops have been coming in every since and the whole army is falling back and concentrating at this point.

We are expecting a battle here any day, which will certainly not be long delayed if the Yankees continue to advance. They are said to be strongly reinforced and so far have come right ahead. But as our troops were falling back so far they have not offfered much resistance. I think it is Genl Braggs intention to make a stand here and if they come on we will soon have a desperate battle. I have heard no news from the front today. I am so busy I have scarcely time to write, so I must close.

As ever your Brother,
H. Paine

Near Chattanooga, July 7th/63

Dear Sister

As I failed to mail my letter after I had written it, I will write some more and send it still. Capt Howell arrived in Tullahoma the day before the evacuation of the place and immediately upon his arrival I quit the quartermaster business and joined my company for active duty in field. Consequently I have been with them through all the trials of retreat. We are encamped now six miles below Chatta on the N and C Railroad, but I don't think that we will remain here long. When I get settled I will write to you more fully, and if I can I will try and visit you some-time soon. Nothing more but remain

As ever your Brother
H. Paine

- - - - - - - - - - - - -

LETTER NO. 14
F. J. PAINE TO MARY L. PAINE
WASHINGTON, TENNESSEE VIA ATHENS

Sweetwater, Tenn, July 10th/63

My Dear Sister

I drop you a line this morning to let you know I arrived at this place in due time, and found the command still here, and hear no talk of them moving soon. I have no definite or reliable news from any point, we hear various rumors from different points but I do not know that any of them are considered reliable, except that Bragg has fallen back to the river. That I suppose is so.

We also have a report that Vicksburg has been evacuated, also that Pemberton and Johnson made an attack on Grant and routed his entire force, and that we are still in possession of Vicksburg. But the reports seem to be so contradictory that there is no telling any thing about certainly. But we will certainly hear in a day or two. I have been fearful for some time that they would finally suceed in taking Vicksburg, but I hope it may not be so.

We also have a report that seems to be generally believed that Wheeler and Forrest got in the rear of Rosencrans and made a dash into Murfreesboro, capturing and destroying two trains of cars, a large amount of commissary stores, and it is said they burnt a train of waggons numbering 700. If that is true it will cut off the supplies of the enemy and they will not be prepared for an advance for some time yet. It is also reported here and thought to be reliable that Genl Lee has captured Forty thousand of the enemy in Pennsylvania and that they are now on their way to Richmond. That if true is a good draw he has made upon them.

I have not heard from Hab since I came up. There has been a good many soldiers going up on the road but I have not learned whose command they belong to. I think Brown Brigade will be up if they have not come yet. I suppose Buckners force is all coming up into this department. I have not been able to learn anything about what the next move will be, but think things will develop themselves in a few days so I can form some idea of what the next move will be. I will write to you again in a day or two.

I have tried to buy some sugar to send home, but the Gov price now has gone up to one dollar per pound and I thought it better to do without than to give that price. There is soda here. I will send 2 pounds by some-one passing in a day or two. Write to me as soon as you get this direct to Sweet Water.

As ever your Brother,
F. J. Paine

- - - - - - - - - - - - -

LETTER NO. 15
HANIBAL PAINE TO MISS MARY L. PAINE WASHINGTON, TENNESSEE VIA ATHENS

Tyner's Station,
Aug 5th 1863

Dear Sister

I have concluded to drop you a line today in order that it may reach you by Fridays mail, knowing although I have nothing of interest to write, that the simple fact of knowing that I am still blessed with the enjoyment of good health will be of some satisfaction to you.

I find it rather hard living in camp after faring so well at home. We only draw bacon now two days out of every seven and five days of mean beef. The ration of bacon is one third of a pound to the man a day. The ration of beef one pound to the man a day. We draw two days of flour out of seven and five of corn meal. The ration of flour per day is one pound to a man. The ration of meal one and a fourth pound per day to the man, so the consequence is that we are about two days out of every seven without any meat, and merely have to live on corn bread.

So far we have always been able to get plenty of bread, but I call that rather hard living. It has never been so hard until since we left Middle Tennessee. I am going to try to send home to get something to eat if I can get any body off after it. I have sent up a detail for Lieut Knight a day or two since but am afraid it will come back disappointed. If he gets off I want to trouble you for a little of that old bacon, how much have you on hand that you can spare? And I will send for a good many other things, but I will not tell you what I want until I see whether he gets off or not. If he comes I will send a letter by him and let you know what I want.

I have no news to write concerning the Army. I have heard it said that our sappers and miners are pros-pecting a road out across the mountains in the direction of Sparta, but I don't know that there is any truth in the report, for it is merely a camp rumor. If true, it would seem that we were going to move in that direction after a while.

Tomorrow is the day of the Election. So it is close at hand. But I have not yet made up my mind who I shall vote for. I hear no news from Rosencrans. The cavalry I suppose which crossed the river have moved across the mountain in the direction of Sparta.

Give my respects to all. I hope our home may never be polluted by the presence of the invader, and may you all still be blest with peace and plenty.

Your Brother,
H. Paine

- - - - - - - - - - - - -

LETTER NO. 16
F. J. PAINE TO MARY L. PAINE

Link Creek, Tenn,
Aug 19th 1863

My Dear Sister

I am again seated to write you a short letter, merely that you may hear from me. For I know it is a source of pleasure at home to hear from me at any time. I neglected writing longer the last time than I intended, but I had so much to do I kept putting it off. I will try and do better in future.

We are still within three miles of Ebinazer. We only moved the camp three miles in order to get nearer forage, and to get rid of the flies which annoy the horses greatly when we remain long at any one place. Forage is getting very scarce here, we are now feeding some new corn, it is too green but we cannot get hay here and have to feed it in place of hay or oats. We are still getting some old corn which is much better than if we had to feed green corn altogether.

G.W. Calahan has the appointment of Chaplain now in our command and is taking a good deal of interest in it. He has a revival now going on. Has had a few pro-fessions, and quite a number at the anxious seat, amongst others Clay Darwin, Sam Sandersdale, Jus Whaley and several others of the same company. And they all seem to be very much affected and I think they are really in earnest. I have been busy generally and have not attended the meetings yet.

I have been staying very close in camp and trying to attend to my business since I came from home. Col Rucker and Neal have both been unwell since I returned and I have been in command of the legion part of the time which requires more attention than only one Battalion.

I have no news more than you have seen in the papers. There seems to be very little news published now from any quarter. I think Forrest is preparing for a move in some direction but I do not know when. I think likely it will [be] into Middle Tennessee.

I suppose Capt Darwin got home the day after I left on a seven days furlough and he has not returned yet. I hear that he is sick. If he gets sick every time he goes home I think he had better stay in camp.

I road out into the country a few miles this evening which is the first time I have been out of camp since I returned from home. I was hunting something to eat and succeeded in buying a nice ham and got a mess of watermelons. They have some as fine round here as I ever saw any where, though they sell very high.

I hope you are all getting along well at home and satisfied with doing the best you can. And if I could always know that this was the case I could be much better contented than I am, for at times when I think of it, I feel that I ought to be there. But on the other hand, when I take a different view of the condition of affairs I am obliged to admit that your condition is by far better than thousands, who but a short time ago worked much higher in the good of this world and I sincerely hope that you may all continue to even do as well as you have thus far.

I have recd no letter from home since I was there but am looking for one in a day or two as I wrote to Ann some days ago. I am still enjoying good health, and am always ready for my rations when I can get them, though amongst the officers they have been pretty short recently, as the commissary has no bacon and I will not buy beef for poor beef I never did like, but since roastinears have come in and apples ripened so they will do to fry I have been doing better.

There is an order issued from headquarters for the impressment of horses and mules and if an agent comes round there, call upon him for his authority and if he has it, and wants sorrell or the mule or both of them, tell them that they both belong to me and that I left them there to be worked. That I would have sold both but you could not get along there and carry on the farm without them and that you have no one there to get any more if they are taken, and if they still say they must have them ask five hundred dollars each for them and don't agree to take any less. And if they take them off, take what money they offer you, but don't agree to take it in full unless they give five hundred and take the name of the man in comd, and whose command he belongs to and write me all about it. They may not come there but they will be likely to if they go to that county.

Tell Ann she must pay the girls a visit for me occasionally during my absence, and keep me posted if any one is likely to take advantage of my absence and get in ahead of me. I hear of them marrying now and then through the country and some of my special friends there might do the same, and me not be apprized of it if some one doesn't look after my interests. I have no idea when I will get off home again, as it is uncertain where we may be ordered to at any time. If we remain in this vicinity I will come down to the association if I can get off.

If Ann will learn of some of her brethern when it is to be and write to me, I think I can fix up an excuse to get off about that time if we are anywhere in this vicinity. Write to me as soon as you get this and let me hear what is going on in Rhea. I have not heard ftrom Hab since I was at home. I will write to him in a day or two. I suppose they are still at Tyners Station. Give my love to all and know me as ever

Your Brother,
F. J. Paine

- - - - - - - - - - - - -

LETTER NO. 17
HANIBAL PAINE TO MISS MARY L. PAINE AT HOME, RHEA COUNTY, TENNESSEE POLITNESS LIEUT KNIGHT

Tyner's Station, Aug 13th/63

Dear Sister

I will send you a note by Lieut Knight, tho I have nothing to write. I have written to Jane and told her what I want you to send me. I send a box of pen points by Lieut Knight. I guess they are scarce in your country and will prove acceptable. There is near two hundred of them, and I send them for the use of you all. They cost ten dollars, but are cheap at that in comparison to what they retail at here. They sell here at twenty-five cents apiece. Sent to Augusta for these. If you will take care of these, you will have plenty to do the whole family for some time.

Your Brother,
H. Paine

= = = = = = = = = = = = =

NOTE: There are no letters from Hanibal or Flavius in 1864, but in 1865, Hanibal was again a prisoner of war. There is no indication of where or when he was captured or how long he was held a prisoner. One letter to his sister, Mary, has survived.

= = = = = = = = = = = = =

LETTER NO. 18
HANIBAL PAINE TO MISS M. L. PAINE CHATTANOOGA, TENNESSEE

Fort Delaware, Del. May 21st 1865

P.M. at Chattanooga will please forward immediately to Washington, Rhea County, Tennessee and much oblige.

My Dear Sister

Your kind communication was recd yesterday and its contents duly noted. The money you enclosed came safe to hand. Ann's and Jennie's letters have not yet been recd. I guess they will come in a day or two. I was gratified to hear from you all again and to learn that you were all well and prospering. You say Jennie and Ann each sent me ten (10) dollars. I would like to have thirty (30) more. You have acted prudently in not risking more than ten dollars in one letter. Send the rest in three different envelopes. If you cannot mail it in ten or twelve days at most from the date of this letter don't send it. If sent later I may leave from here and not get it.

If you are curious to know where I am going I will tell you I expect to come home. What do the people think is going to become of the prisoners? Are they expecting them to come home? Tell Buck I expect to be with him in the course of another month. I hope Jo is at home on this.

I suppose every one is taking the Oath where you live. It is a thing they will have to do when so requested, or they will be debarred from all the privaleges of loyal citizens and treated as alien enemies. What has become of the Negroes? I suppose you are aware of the fact that the are as free now as the whites. Do the people realize the fact that the Confederacy has "played out"?

I have been fortunate to receive some clothing from a lady friend in New York, not all I need but I can purchase what I can make out with with the money you send me cheaper than for you to send me clothes. You failed to tell me where to direct my letter, so be more thoughtful next time.

Your Brother, H. Paine

Address: Lieut H. Paine
26th Tenn Regt Infantry
Prisoner of War
Fort Delaware, Del. No. 29

RODDY REMINISCENCES

The following reminiscences were written by Wright Smith Roddy and his wife, Mattie Kimbrough Roddy, after they moved to Texas. Both sketches are among the files of the Rhea County Historical and Genealogical Society. There was also a letter describing Wright's activities, a copy of which was sent to Seth Tallent by Lloyd W. Roddy of Richland, Washington (a grandson of Wright and Mattie). Information from the letter has been added into the sketch.

WRIGHT SMITH RODDY

I was born in Rhea Co., East Tennessee, Jan. 17th 1845. My first school was at Macedonia Church. Then to several small schools untill I was about 11 years old. Then I was sent to Mars Hill Academy. Went there 2 years & I was sent to Sewee Academy in Meigs Co. about two years. Then went to Commercial school at Rhea Springs and then I stayed in my fathers store untill I went in the Army.

Joined Capt. Caywoods Com. B, 43rd Tenn. Vol. Nov. or December 1861. Col. J.W. Gillespie was Colonel. We served in East Tenn. that winter.

We served at Chattanooga when the Yankees tried to capture the place but failed. That was the first time I was under fire. We served under Gen. Marshall in S.W. Va., then we were ordered to Ky. & served General Bragg at Frankfort, Ky. We then fell back through Cumberland Gap to East Tenn. Took up Winter quarters at Kingston, stayed there about 3 weeks. Ordered then to Vicksburg, Miss. Served under Gen. Pemberton. We fought & defended the town untill we was forced to surrender 4 July to Gen. Grant. The loss was very heavy on both sides. The Army was paroled. Went back(?) --?-- untill ex-changed.

We were out again in a few weeks & met at Loudon, E. Tenn., served under Longstreet at Knoxville. We were mustered at Rogerville, E. Tenn. Served under Longstreet untill sent to Stanton, Virginia to reinforce Gen. Jones when the Yankees were pushing fast.

We met the enemy at New Hope Church & were badly defeated & lost one fourth of our men. Gen. Jones was killed. We fell back to Linchburg & were reinforced by Gen. Early. Drove the Enemy back to West Virginia mountains. Gen. Early then made a forced march down the Valy & Cross the Potomack river, Maryland & captured a Cart(?) stock & Rail trains stocked with clothing & Army suplies & returned back to Virginia.

We servd that summer & fall & never lost fight untill the fishing Creek fight & there nearly lost all. We was then ordered back to East Tennessee. Served that winter under Gen. Vaughn. Had a horse shot from under me at Morristown & was carried out by a Ky man named Campbell. We was badly defeated lost 1/3 our men. We attact the Yankees 2 weeks later at night & completely routed him. Captured 4000 prisoners, 400 wagons, all his guns.

Served untill General Lee surrendered. We were ordered to report to Gen. Johnson in North Carolina after the surrender. We was finally Payroled at Kingston, Ga. I had 2 horses shot from under me, one at White Fort, Va. & the other at Morristown, E. Tenn. I never was wounded.

I think I was in 150 engagements (small and large) in all. We left Kingston, Ga. for home about 150 miles & didnt have a Cent of money but the people were glad to help us along. Got home & found all well, all the fences burned up (& stock gone) but Mother managed to keep plenty to Eat & Wear. We got home in May 1865. I spent 3½ years in Army. Wasn't home any time during the War.

I then went to repairing fences & fixing up the place untill 1870. I came to Texas to look around, stayed that summer & returned to Tennessee, was married to Mattie Kimbrough June 1871. We then went to farming on Tenn. River. Lived there 2 years. Moved to Texas 1875. Been living here ever since.

(P.S.) After we came home my Father & myself were arrested & taken to Knoxville & tried for High Treason against the U.S. States & were equited. It cost us One Hundred Each, that Ended the Rumble(?)

MATTIE KIMBROUGH RODDY

I was born March 13, 1852, in Roane Co., East Tennessee, at the foot of Cumberland Mountain. Bellville was the name of our home and post office. I was the youngest of eleven children. My father was a farmer and a slave holder.

My earliest recollections are of this country life, so peaceful, so quiet, and yet so alive with industry, bustle and abundance. Almost every thing for home consumption was produced on the farm. Cotton, flax and wool enough to clothe the negroes. Cattle, hogs, sheep and poultry as well as fruit and vegetables filled the larder. Shoes were made from the beef hides and candles from the tallow. Coal oil was not known then.

On my fathers estate which extended for miles into the mountains were vast coal veins. Some of these he had opperating, having the coal dug and shipped down Tennessee river to Chattanooga. He also had in opperation a forge run by water by which he had iron made. He had his blacksmith shop. Amongst his negroes was a blacksmith, a shoe maker, a boss, and a fiddler.

The blacksmith did the work for the plantation, from the shoeing of a horse to the making of plows and waggons. The good old boss kept the younger ones straight and exercised his authority generally, and the fiddler officiated at all the merry making of both white and black, the corn huskings, and dances of which they were so fond.

The most pleasant relations existed between us. Their tasks were light, they were furnished comfortable homes, good food and clothing and were well taken care of when sich. In return they were faithful and true.

In this picture of memory "our old black mammie" was one of the figures. She shared with my mother the care I needed as a little child. Helped her to soothe our aches and pains and together we read her bibles and spelled out the long hard words. If I am so fortunate as to go to that better world, I expect to meet her there.

When I was a very small child, my father sent me with my older brother to a country school. When I was about nine years old I was sent to Knoxville, Tenn. to a very fine female academy. I was a little child to be sent from home, and I had many a heart ache, and was often home sick for the good old home down by the mountain, but the benefits I received from this school was life lasting. My teachers were most excellent.

About this time the war cry sounded. No one but those of us who lived in the south can tell how well we loved it. It seemed to defend their homes and rights was the only thing for an honorable southern man to do. And so they fought and bled and died.

Four of my brothers served in the southern army. Two were killed, and two came back to our desolated home. Came back to a broken hearted mother. My father had died in 1862. Their armies had foraged our country and confiscated all of our produce. We were without money, food and our clothes almost. Our fields had been ---?--- out to grow up in briers and sprouts and our negroes must needs leave us to obtain food which the governor furnished them.

Two of my brothers made a crop with two young oxen, the only thing we had left. They made an abundant crop and we began to live in peace, and the greatest thing was peace.

Then came the reconstruction days. Southern men were disfranchised. Carpet baggers came down on us and insults and tyranny were heaped upon our heads. But noble blood will tell. Our people have arrisen, they have forgotten and forgiven, and are loyal to our flag.

During the last two years of the war I was out of school most of the time. After the surrender I attended a private school in north Georgia for two years under my old teacher Mrs. Richardson and two exceptionally fine young ladies. After this I went to Martha Washington College in Abingdon, Virginia. One of the finest schools at that time in the south. This is a Methodist College, the school of the Holston Conference.

One year after returning from Martha Washington I was married at the age of 19 at the old home . . . After this we moved to Texas where we have lived a quiet life rearing seven children, who have grown to be fine men and women, a blessing and comfort to our old ages. Now we are only waiting till shadows are a little longer grown.

STEWART LETTERS

The following seven letters were included in the large collection of Lillard Papers housed at the Tennessee State Archives in Nashville. The two families became related when Texanna Lillard married William Stewart in 1861.

William (1828 - 1905) was the son of John and Lettie (Tillery) Stewart. There is no evidence that William served in the army during the war, but he was a member of the Meigs County Home Guard.

William's twin brother, Richard Stewart (1828 - 1892), was a member of Company I, (Vaughn's) 3rd Tennessee Regiment, as was brother, Martin V. (Van), who died on 26 August 1861.

Another brother, Matthew Buchanan Stewart (1834 - 1904), was a member of the same company, but later went with Sandusky's Company. A fourth brother, Levi Francis (1836 - 1881), belonged to Capt Boggess' Company.

LETTER NO. 1
TEXAS STEWART TO BROTHER
[NEWTON J. LILLARD]

June28th1861

Dear brothers

I will write you a few lines on Dicks letter and next week I will write again. Lee has been standing around me all this morning asking me to write to his Pa and Uncle Nute for him, says he wants you to kill all the mean abolition and hurry and come back home for he wants to see you bad. He talks a great deal about the war.

Crawford compay of Rhea starts Thursday they have quite a full compay I suppose several spok going over from Meigs. I hope you are all getting along as well as could be expected. brother Nute a certain young lady was here not long since Said certainly she would correspond with you if you wished it she kissed your type several times, put it in her pocket said she must take it home with her but you know I could not give it up no no. she is well posted can talk politics right ahead. Tom More and Sallie Wassun was married this week I suppose Dick will tell you about the Tom(?) Peak and Miss Hattie case.

Sister Jennie started to N.C. last Saturday Jessee Martin went with her to Knoxville, John went with her from there. her Ma is very low they do not think she will live long. Uncle Rogers started after Lizzie last Sabath week have not heard from him since he started he is going to stop and see his children he said.

Tell Mr. Boggess and Frazier to write to us we would be glad to get a letter from them any time. They are all as well as usal at Papas I believe Papa is very weak but still is going about Mary went home Monday Ell and Jennie went with her I am looking for Ell back today, mabe you sweetheart will come with her. The girls are making a small flag to take to Washington Thursday about as large as the one they presented to your company. I hope you will excuse this bad writing as it is in haste, so farewell for this time May the Lord bless you and protect you and may you get back safe, please write often. Lee says for his pa to be sure and write him a letter says he would keep it as long as he lives.

Your affectionate Sister
Texas Stewart

- - - - - - - - - - - - -

LETTER NO. 2
TEXAS STEWART TO SISTER
[JENNIE LILLARD ?]

Decatur Tenn
August 8th 1861

My dear sister

You no doubt think a little hard of me, not receiving no letter from me, I wrote about two weeks ago thought Mr Stewart had takened it to the office but he forgot it and I found it here on the table under some books. I will try and see that this one gets to the office. I was truly glad indeed to receive a letter from you, when Father came home he brought one from you one from Dick & one from Vern they were at Fairfax C.H. now they said evy thing quiet there then, but they did not know what moment they would be called on. there was not one of brother Nutes company killed or wounded. I could not feel thankful and humble enough my dear sister although I know they are our enemys and there is not anything you could name if they thought it would be a disadvantage to the south but what they would do, but still I have a feeling for them, for I know from all accounts there was a many an inocent man fell among the Northern troops. It was so hard to think they could not trust them to bury their dead. Beoureguard gave them the previlige the third time instead burying their dead they went to throwing up breastworks and entrenchments. the Southern troops buried a great many of them.

Mr Frazier said he was out on the battle field Wensday after the battle at Manassas, he said such a scene he never witnessed. I know it must have been an awful sight. Mr Boggess said he divided water with the wounded as long as he had a drop said he could not refuse them they beged so pitiful, he said he saw a great many lying there and not a wound about them, they was so exhausted and fatigued said several of their prisoners said they would rather be prisoners of the southerners than to fight for the northern tyrants. I see in the paper where three thousand of their three months soldiers have gone home, they say Pattersons or the most of them, their time is about out he is trying very hard to get to enlist again but they will not. some of the officers have been trying to compell their forces to remain. I do not think surely they expect to be successful for it seems like evy thing is against them. They say Geo H. Briges has gone I think it doubtful whether he ever reaches Washington City or not. some say James Gettys has started with his family we have not learned what rout Geo took but they say his family started by private conveyance, they took Nelson prisoner in the western part of Va, they say he gave his son that belongs to the Confederate army some money. I suppose some soldiers took Dr Euvrett out to hang him last week but some beg so hard for him they did not.

Papa received a letter from brother John first of this week. I have not been out there do not know what he wrote we did hear they were going to Knoxville to organize this week I have not heard of their going yet. I wrote him a long letter first of last week, he says they dont get news there very often, he was very anxious to heare all about the fights.

William Godsey started last Saturday for Nutes company. Van Stewart went with Mr Frazier and a Mr Melton. He said in his letter he was very well pleased, but said such a sight he never wanted to see again, he was out on part of the battle ground he and Mr Frazier did not get untill after the battle was over. Nutes company I suppose was in the hottest of the fight, they got there at 10 O clock in the morning and left the battle ground at 7 in the evening, some of the boys writing back said Nute went at it just like he did evry thing else, cool and calm.

Mrs Mary Thomas died this week was buried Wensday she was a daughter of Mr Neils she left an infant two weeks old it made me so sorry for the little thing it is such a pert child (a boy). I suppose you have herd Mrs Ernn McCorkle has a girl about three weeks old, I would like to see Ernn smiling.

Cousin Crate Buckner or Mr Buckner calls his baby Beaureguard (a girl), I have wrote to Tish and have received no answer yet, I hope you will let us hear from you often give my love to all the family and connections how I would like to see them all, tell your Pa he must come to Meigs, Papa would like to see him so much please write often your loving Sister

T. Lillard Stewart

Mr Stewart has just come in send much love to you, said as you was in bed that morning he left Papas he would shake your hand the more when he saw you how I wish I could see Tommy and you Kiss him for us and he must kiss you. You must not let him forget his aunt Tex.

- - - - - - - - - - - - -

LETTER NO. 3
T. L. STEWART TO BROTHER
[NEWTON J. LILLARD]

Decatur Tennessee
Nov 7th 1861

My dear brother

As the boys are going to start saturday, I thought I would commence tonight & perhaps I would get a long letter by that time, although there is not any thing of interest occurs very often Sure so we get out of something to write, I have wrote to you and Dick in the last two weeks some four or five letters.

Hugh Blevins arrived home last night he seems to be very weak. I saw him this evening Miss Almira Lillard presented a flag to Capt McKenzies company. We had a short speech from General Lane one from Cross and a very short one from Capt Hodge. David Blevins received the flag. He and James have had the Measels they are looking rather pale. There was quite a crowd in attendance today. Mr S Boggess and lady was down, I suppose the company at Tenmile was to be mustered into service today; I have not learned their officers yet.

Tomorrow the Society packs a box for your company. Cross addvised us to divide and send part to Kentucky, it is said the Texas Rangers came there destitute of winter clothing. I for one am perfectly willing to do so if your company do not need them, and again McKenzies Company are not all clothed, but any thing your company needs we are willing to try to get it to you. We have not received any letter from brother William yet. I do not know why it is he surely has wrote ere this.

We did not get our letters finished last night. Mr Stewart left soon this morning will not be back untill Saboth. I was at town this evening we had a great time packing up I think there was seven boxes in all and a great many things left out to send to Ky, there is a man from there now came after clothes for Crawfords company particularly he says he will take anything we want to send. Ten & Joanna are staying with me tonight, Pomp & Allison Lillard so we have quite a good crowd. I picked out this morning one bushell of the largest sweet potatoes to send but they said this evening there was no room for them I wish I could had sent them I know you and Dick would have been well pleased, perhaps we will have a chance to send them.

There has been a great revival going on up at Sewee Academy this week several professions, Mrs Luke Peak, finnie(?) & Lottie Peak, Parlie Moore one of Tom Stoeding girls, and one of the Lathams I did not learn which, Tex Boggess, I have not learned any others yet several of them are to be babtized tomorrow your good friend Sue Davis is going to the anxious seat regular they say she seems deeply convicted. I am truly glad to hear of a revival at Sewee, May the Lord still continue to bless them.

Jo & Ten say they would write some but have never wrote to a young gentleman and they would not know how to commence. told me to say something nice for them. I would like to see you and all the boys, but will try to contend myself the best I can. May the God of Battle bless you and your company, write often, we rite evry week and sometimes oftener.

Your loving sister
T. L. Stewart

LETTER NO. 4
WM STEWART TO RICHARD STEWART

Decatur Tenn
Nov 19, 1861

Mr Richard Stewart

Dear Brother I Reced yours of the 5th which give me much Satisfaction to hear from you & that you was well. it allways does me good to hear from you and the Boys, we have had very exciting times here for several days the Union men collected at Clifts for what purpose I donot know. Meigs McMinn & Rhea all collected together and Sent to Knoxville after troops. Several companys came down, Some Alabama Troops. the Linconites left quick for the Mountains & their homes, there are several companys of cavalry over there yet taking Some prisoners and Shooting Some down on the Mountains. The report is that they are collecting in the first district they have takeing their arms from them, it made them very mad they Say they will have Revenge if they have to burn every house in Meigs. I think they will cool down when they are turned out a --?-- Clift has gone over the mountain with about three hundred men they are on pursuit of him I hope they will catch him and hang him to a tree.

James Gates passed by my house last Saturday went down the lane and Saw Mcphersons Company coming with a flag with no stripes he turned back and Said he had forgoten part of his business in town. he goes on to town and took the other Road out through Nopone he must be guilty or he would have not run when he Saw the flag. he said he had been to Chattanooga. I think he had been to Clifts.

Rube McKenzie met a man in the Road this evning and took him Prisoner. he is from McMinn County lives in the Buttram Settlement. Rube was right he said he was his Prisoner he took him on his own responsibility. I think they taking Several in Meigs. I understand old Gates Bob & Jim was all taken up.

I will write to you again when I hear the facts. I have been out asking hands to Shuck corn to day. I dont think I will get much help without the women turns out. Cassy says she will help Shuck corn. I am only about half done gathering corn, ten acres of wheat to Sow yet Orleam(?) Wheat. We have had Some fair weather for work for two weeks back. Kate & Lize Says they have not Received that letter from you yet.

We are all well Father Mother and famely are all well. Mathy grows very fast. I havent heard from Buckanan for Some time. we was looking for him in Tenn this fall. I think that he is afraid to start to Move for fear he will be taken up on the Road. Hugh Blevins is improving Some Since he got home. Hugh commanded Doct Hodges Company in Rhea. he done very well. it has been reported that Vaughns Regment was coming to Ky. I recon Davis will not let you off Write often. I must close I want to go and help Frances Shuck corn to day. give love to all Your Brother William Stewart

Dick I will try and write you a long letter in a few days, you will ecuse me this time. I wrote to you last of last week this is only Tuesday write often cant you come to the shucking tomorrow

Texas

LETTER NO. 5
M. B. STEWART TO RICHARD STEWART

Decatur Tenn
November 21st 1861

Richard Stewart

Dear Brother We received a letter from you today dated the 13th and we was glad to here from you and here that you were still improving we are all in Tolerable halth at this time Mother has a very bad caugh

There is a great deal of excitement here at this time the Union men is geting verry badly scird they have been treat them very rough since they burt the Bridges they are disarming them all and taking a great many of them Prisoners and Kiling some of them I have taken two trips but got no fight I went down on the river to Jeff Mathes but found nobody there I then went to rhea to Cross road it was reported that they was fathering up there at Sale Creek camp ground but they left the night belore I got there I thought I thought when I got there we was a going to have a fight the pickets come in this as I got there and reported that there was a thousand Linkinites there and they had fired on our pickets and kiled one and wounded one you ought to have herd them holering and purrading their companies but when we got there it was a Alabama ridgement come up on the boat and got off at the mouth of Sale Creek and fired at our pickets they shot one of them through the foot so I will close noing that you will here all about it before this comes to hand give my best respects to all

Your affectionate Brother
M. B. Stewart

Nov 24th 1861

Dick I rote this letter on last thursday expected to Start it on Fryday but did not get it off I thought I would rite you a few more lines to night I have nothing new to rite to night they are still takin up the union men and takin their arms. Gov Harris has caled out thirty thousand of the malitia in west and middle Tenn says he would call them out in east Tenn but he dont think it necessary to call an unwiling People he sais we must give up our guns or he will make us go and take them they had done takin mine before his proclimation Mother sais she cant give up hern yet She may have it to do they take them to Nashville or Knoxville and have them valued I dont care whether I get anything for mine or not I have no gun now I wish you would make Cross buy you a good Pistol for that one he lost and send it to me I dont want you to buy it if he wont buy it let it go but I would like to have it

Father sais tell you he haes a big corn. Shooking on yesterday and got done he has been pulling corn and throwing out corn at the shuckung till it so Sweled his hand up a little Mother sais if you kneed any more socks to let her no in time I received your letter of the 16th instant and was glad to here from you

Dick you Spoke of coming home a bout Christmas we would be glad to see you if you dont come home I think I will come out a bout the middle of next month if there will be any chance to get to Van. rite to me whether the Yankees is there or not give my respects to all tell Steve howdy and tell him that I sean her to day she purty as ever So no more at present only remain

Your affectionate Brother
M. B. Stewart

- - - - - - - - - - - - -

LETTER NO. 6
JOHN STEWART TO RICHARD STEWART

Decatur Tenn
Nov 28, 1861

Richard Stewart

Dear Son I now seat myself to drop you a few lines to let you no that we are all well but your Mother She has had a very bad cold but is geting better I have nothing new to rite at present you rote to me to no if I hired Samps to Cross I did not hire him to any body I sent him to wait on you I suppose John Boggs sais that he whiped him once I didnt send him there for any body to whip but you I want you to make him do any thing you want him to do it is all a mistake about 17 hundred union men in hamelton Buck was there and he sais from the best information that he could get there was a bout 3 hundred but they scatered when they herd the southern men was coming on them they have caught a good many of them McKinsey Company is still over their they wont say that they have kiled any of them but say that some of [them] is laying stinking(?) in the mountains they have taken old Truhett Prisoner there a good many of them volinteerd in Hodge company I think they will haft to watch them verry close they leave the warehouse next Saturday at 12 oclock I dont think you need be uneasy about any fight here for I dont think ther will be any if we fight any now we will have to fight with sticks and rocks they taken all our arms both union and Southern men now Samps has been sending money home to his wife I want you to take his money and Buy him close if he has any to send home send it to me and I will take care of it till he comes home I dont want you to Buy his close out of your mony a tall he certainly can keep him self in close.

I received your kind letter of the 21st to Day and was glad to here from you and here that you was well I hope this may find you still injoying the same Mother sais if you need any thing to not fail to let her no it for you can have any thing you want Mathew sais you wanted to no how his Pig was doing he sais he dont no for he has never got it yet

Your affectionate Father
John Stewart

Dick I thought I would rite you few lines in answer to the few lines I got from you Day I have rote you all the news for Father only they have got one of the men that Burnt the Bridge at Calhoun I started you letter on monday I rote in it for you to make Cross Buy me a Pistol for that one he lost Dick want it and a good one to make him pay $25.00 and I will pay the Balance send it to me the first chance they have took my gun away from me I dont want you to buy it out of your money if he dont see cause to pay you for it let him rip rore

Dick rite often for you dont [know] how glad that we are to here from you So I will close give my best respects to all

Your affectionate Brother
M. B. Stewart

Father and Mother sais if you get sick to come home not to go to the hospital to come home and Bring Samps along to wait on you if you want to

- - - - - - - - - - - - -

LETTER NO. 7
WM STEWART TO RICHARD STEWART

Decatur Tenn
December 1st 1861

Mr Richard Stewart

Dear Brother I thought I would write you a few lines this morning to let you know that we are all well. I Hope that when this comes to hand it will find you in good health. I Sean a letter from you to Father I was very glad to hear that you was well but Sorry to know that you had to leave Centerville and go to Some other point. it Seems like when you get fixed up a little you have to move We are listening to hear of a Battle at Manassas every day, I hope if you have a Battle you will all go through Safe and have the privellige of Returning home and See your Friends,

Doct A.W. Hodge left for Knoxville yesterday he had about Sixty Men. he had a very good looking Com of men George Hail has gone in his Com. if George has good luck he will get off at last.

the excitement is calming down Some they have taken a good many prisoners to Knoxville & Nashville Court commences at Knoxville to morrow I am in hopes that the leaders will be hung. Clift has made his escape So far they have three of Old Lige Cates Boys prisoners Old Truitt & Several others down that way I dont believe that the union Men will do much damage in East Tenn towards fighting all the damage they will do will be by Burning Bridges & Houses. Some of them came up and Joined Hodges Company the Speaker Andy Goforth came up & Joined and is gone to Knoxville four prisoners from the Cross Roads Joined Hodge Com Twenty five Joined at Chattanooga as they went to Nashville I think there will be a Battle at Bowling Green or Collumbus Ky before long the Gens their Say they are Ready for any force they may Bring against them. the union men on the Mountain when our Boys would come up with them they would through down their guns and Run for life, that the way they fight.

I am getting along farming very slow at this time I will get done Sowing in Three days if the weather is good. I will have fifty acres of wheat Sowed Lewis Benton works very well Jones has not worked any for Some time nor will not work any next week. I will be late gethering Our corn. I will weigh our Hogs out next week or week after next I sold at 9 & go op. Pork is worth 10¢ at this time, wheat $1.25 Corn 50¢ delivered on the River.

I went down to town this morning and there was Sam Cox he got in last night Sam dont look well he has a bad Collor I was glad to See him he Said you was all well. he says he is comeing up to See us and then I will get him to tell me Some big tales. Sam says you could get to come home when you get Sick if you would. You know how we would be glad to see you do what you think is rite.

Father & Mother are both well and all the rest Dick & Pete are well Mathy Said you had wrote to him to know how large his pig was. the Shoats nearly all Died I told him he would have to wait till the old Sow had Pigs and then I would let him have one I wrote last thusday week to you I learn you have not Received it yet. Give my best Respects to all the Boys Wm Stewart

- - - - - - - - - - - - -

TAYLOR, CROSS, AND BLEVINS LETTERS

The following series of 81 letters was the property of Sarah Blevins Jones (1911 - 1994) of Decatur, Meigs County. The three families were connected by marriage and the letters are more meaningful when combined. A few letters and articles from ***The Athens Post*** have also been added. There are also several letters from the Lillard's included here.

Peach Taylor (10 September 1801 - 10 August 1886) and his wife, Mary Blevins (10 June 1807 - 13 July 1887), had three sons who served the Confederacy: Benjamin Franklin, John Blevins, and James Osborne. Their daughter, Mary, was married to Isaac Grundy Cross, son of Zachariah and Sarah (Hicks) Cross, on 24 November 1853. Isaac's brother, Absalom Looney Cross, is mentioned in several of the letters, but there are no letters from him. There are also several letters to and from Amanda Taylor, youngest daughter of Peach and Mary.

When the Home Guard was appointed by the Meigs County Court on 3 June 1861, Peach Taylor was one of the 30 members from Civil District 4. He was 60 years old at the time. Two of Peach's brothers-in-law, William S. Russell and William W. Lillard, were appointed to the Home Guard from Civil District 3.

Benjamin Franklin Taylor (7 May 1837 - 2 April 1862) enlisted on 3 May 1861 in Lillard's 3rd Tennessee Mounted Infantry. He was killed on 2 April 1862 by bushwhackers in Brimstone Valley, Scott County, Tennessee. Benjamin was a school teacher prior to the war.

John Blevins Taylor (18 October 1834 - 12 June 1902) was married to Ann Cross (1 June 1826 - 19 March 1915), sister of Isaac and Absalom, on 25 February 1858. His brother, James Osborne Taylor (28 June 1842 - 6 December 1895), was not married until after the war (1870 to Julia Amanda Findley). John and James enlisted on 19 July 1862 in McKenzie's 5th Tennessee Cavalry.

Artamisa Cross, sister of Ann, Isaac, and Absalom, was married to William S. Arrants in 1844 (see Letter No. 25). None of their sons were old enough to serve during the war.

Isaac G. Cross (born 12 September 1828), a Captain in Newton J. Lillard's Company, was killed in battle at Tazewell on 6 August 1862. His obituary appears after Letter No. 72.

The Blevins family included the brothers and sisters of Mary (Blevins) Taylor, who were all children of David and Sarah (Torbett) Blevins.

James Blevins (1802-1849) married Ruth Rockhold (1808-1891) and had the following children: Beersheba S., Alfred C, David M., William F., Hugh T., and Sarah A. Blevins.

Beersheba Stewart Blevins (1828-1903) married William Locke McKinley, son of John and Susanna (Locke) McKinley, on 1 April 1860 [see Letter No. 14]. William (1824 - 1897) served as County Court Clerk during the war. He was a lawyer and, after moving to Arkansas about 1870, became a Judge.

Dr. Alfred Carter (A.C.) Blevins (1831-1905) married Virginia Catherine Chattin on 10 May 1871. He studied medicine under Dr. John M. Lillard and Dr. John Hoyal before attending the Medical University of Nashville. On 4 July 1861, Alfred enlisted as first lieutenant of Company E (Crawford's), 26th Tennessee Infantry Regiment. After 12 months, he was made assistant surgeon of the 43rd Tennessee Regiment (Dr. James W. Gillespie, Colonel). About a year later, he was made Chief Surgeon of the 3rd Tennessee Regiment and served in that capacity until the close of the war.

David Massengale Blevins (1833-1911) enlisted in Compny I, 3rd Tennessee Infantry, in 1861. He took part in first Manassas and was captured at Vicksburg. He afterwards reenlisted and served until the end of the war. In 1880, David married Fannie D. Hoyle.

William F. Blevins (1835-1925) married Mary E. Russell (1842-1910), daughter of William S. and Susan (Blevins) Russell, on 11 May 1871. In July 1862, William joined W.W. Lillard's Company, 5th Tennessee Cavalry. He took part in the battles of Perryville (Kentucky), Chickamauga Creek, and the Georgia Campaign from Dalton to Atlanta, and was Second Lieutenant of his company. He returned home in the spring of 1865 after an absence of almost three years. During the 1870's, William served as Clerk and Master of the Meigs County Chancery Court, but moved to Darwin Station [Evensville] in Rhea County in 1883 [see Letters No. 3 and 37].

Hugh Torbett Blevins (1838-after 1911) was in the mercantile business with his brother, William, after the war. Hugh married Sarah McCorkle (1841-1891), daughter of Joseph and Elizabeth McCorkle, on 19 August 1868. Several of the letters to Benjamin F. Taylor [Nos. 15,23,38,43,53,65] were written by Sarah.

One letter [No. 55] from Hugh T. mentions the death of "Cousin Kit Blevins." James Kit Carson Blevins (1839/40-1861) was the son of Phillip M. and Harriet (Blakely) Blevins. He served as 2nd Corporal in Capt. N.J. Lillard's Company. Kit's brother, Argile Hardin Blevins (1842/44-1912), was a member of Capt. G.W. McKenzie's Company.

Sarah A. Blevins (1840-1927), daughter of James and Ruth, married Linneus Locke (1820-1891) on 3 September 1862 [see Letters No. 24 and 36].

Susan Blevins (1809-1887), sister of Mary (Blevins) Taylor, married William S. Russell (1804-1866) on 15 March 1828. He was the son of John and Sarah Rosanna (Sprowell) Russell. Severl of the children of William and Sarah are mentioned in the letters: John Thomas (1829-1882, married Tennessee McCorkle, sister of Sarah), Felix Grundy (1832-1899), Thomas J. (1837/38- ?), Mary E., and David A. or H. (1831- ? Texas)

Sarah R. (Sprowell) Russell, mentioned above, married second John Leuty. Their son, Thomas, married

Ester P. Eaves, and they were the parents of a frequent letter-writer, Kate Leuty [Mary Catherine Leuty, 1842-1865]. In one letter, Kate refers to her uncle, William S. Russell. On 27 April 1864, Kate married Matthew B. Stewart (1837-1904), son of John and Lettie (Tillery) Stewart. Matthew's two brothers, Richard (1828-1892) and Martin VanBuren (1840-1861) were mentioned in Letter No. 20.

Lucretia Blevins (1816-1869), another sister of Mary, married first Henson W. Thomas on 2 January 1834. Henson died after the birth of two children, Hugh T. and Sarah Thomas, and on 22 October 1845, Lucretia married William W. Lillard (1818-1881), son of John and Elizabeth (Taylor) Lillard. Elizabeth was the sister of Peach Taylor (children of Robert and Catherine Sevier Taylor).

Several letters were written by two daughters of William and Lucretia: Elmira (1841- ?) and Amanda C. (1843-1921). Elmira married W.A. Smith in 1867 and moved to California in 1873. Amanda, a school teacher, married Bartholomew K. Blevins, son of John W. and Elizabeth (Guinn) Blevins. The other two letter-writers, Crate Lillard and Texas (Lillard) Stewart, were sisters of Newton Jasper Lillard.

D.C. [David Crockett] Blevins (1839/40- ?), son of John Wilson and Elizabeth (Guinn) Blevins, served as 2nd Lieutenant in Capt. G.W. McKenzie's Company. He married Sousan O. Davis on 4 September 1867 in Meigs County.

Several letters were written by L.R. [Lysurgus R.] Blevins (1842-1863), son of Thomas Vance and Elvina (Gourley) Blevins. He served as 4th Corporal in Capt. N.J. Lillard's Company and was in the seige of Vicksburg. L.R. was killed at Marion, Virginia, on 6 December 1863. His brother, Jehu P. Blevins (1840-1917), was a member of the same company, and brother John "Johnny" Wilson Blevins (1845/46-1930) was with Capt. W.W. Lillard's Company. Another brother, Thomas Vance (1849-1899), married Amanda T. Taylor, daughter of Peach and Mary, on 4 December 1870.

LETTER NO. 1
BENJAMIN F. TAYLOR TO PARENTS

Knoxville, May 8th 1861

Dear parents:

With the greatest of pleasure I this evening avail my self of the opportunity of droping you a few lines to inform you how we are all getting along; we are all well and doing well, all in good spirits and plenty to eat, we had somewhat a disagreeable time during the wet spell. I do not know for certain when we will leave this place, we will organize the redgement tomorrow evening and perhaps leave next morning for Linchburg, Virginia, that is the move we are making today.

I G Cross arrived today with 18 more soldiers for our company and I never heared such a shout in my life as was sent up for him, troops are coming in every day the whole encampment is a live with men.

We came very near havin a sevier battle in Knoxville yesterday evening some of the redgement was in town and a gang of black republicans tried to impose upon them. I call them by that name because they deserve it. I could not if I was to try command language to express my contempt for such men as they are. 2 men were killed by the soldiers no man was hurt on our side, after those 2 men were killed they came running to camp after us to go and whip them out, we ran into the edge of town and formed ourselves in battle array to attact the citty, while we were preparin for the attact hundreds of the citizens came running to us and promised to surrender any man we wished for if we would not attact the town on this promices we returned to camp but verry much excited for sometime.

I have received 3 boquets since we left Athens one from a young lady in Louden and 2 from young ladies in Knoxville, our company has received the greatest name of any one that has passed up the road, they say we are the finest looking men they ever seen and their acts proove that they believe what they say, our company was invited to march into Knoxville last Saturday morning, we were received with great applause, several speeches were delivered and responded to by Mr. Frazier.

Their are thousands of troops passing up the road ever day, 15 hundred passed up from Mississippi on one train to day. Their has been 25 or 30 thousand passed up the road to Virginia in the last 3 or 4 days. I will have to close for the present, give my best love to Mary and Children, John Ann and children and all inquiring friends, it is not necessary to write to me until I write again. Your affetionate son B F Taylor

- - - - - - - - - - - - -

LETTER NO. 2
BENJAMIN F. TAYLOR TO PARENTS

Knoxville, May 12th 1861

Dear parents

It is with much pleasure that I this evening avail myself of the opportunity of dropping you a few lines to inform you how we are all getting along, we are all in fine health, I have not seen an hours sickness since I left Meigs County except a little cold and I am about well of it to day.

We will leave this place in the morning at 10 O clock for Linchburg, Virginia, their was a company of volunteers from Sullivan County came to camp thursday evening, several of the connections were in the company, one of the Massengills boys and D M Blevins, H T Blevins and E L Hodge started to Sullivan this Morning and are going to write us at Union Depot to morrow morning and join the redgement again.

We had a fine sermon to day as ever I heared, delivered by the Rev James Adkins and concluded by Rev Rodgers chaplin in Mexico. Frazier preaches this evening he is appointed chaplin of the redgement. Atkins and Rodgers brought out some nice pocket testaments and presented to us this morning, they were sent to us by the ladies of Knoxville. I had a verry fine one presented to me and I intend to keep it as long as I live and try to read it as often as possible, their are a great manny verry wicked men in the redgement but I hope that I will be able to shun their company.

Our company is the most sivil company in the redgement and has received far the best name in every respect. It it had not been for our company the others would not have received as good treatment as what they have by the citizens in Knoxville and in the surrounding country. I have seen young Muncy in Knoxville every day, he is a strait out cecessionist and Southern rights man.

W F Blevins note to me about some ink that I have in my trunk, I wrote to him to go and get it, if he should not receive the letter you can tell him to go and get it when ever he wants it. I have written several letters back to Meigs and toled them not to write to me until they heared from me again tell all that wish to write to me to write to Linchburg Virginia and I will receive their letters there. if their are any letters comes to Decatur for me brake them open and if their is any thing in them of any interest mail them to me if the Clevelin Banner is still comming to me you can take it out and use it for what ever you wish.

I do not know of any thing more at present to write to you as their has been letters sent back every day stating what was going on. I want you to write to me without fail and write soon as I will be glad to hear how you are all getting along, direct your letters to linchburg Virginia Colonel Vaughns redgement and 3rd lieutenant in Captain Lillards company, you had better get Mr McCorkle to back your letters give my best love to Mary and children John Ann and chil and to every boddy

your affectionate son

B F Taylor

- - - - - - - - - - - - - -

LETTER NO. 3
W. F. BLEVINS TO B. F. TAYLOR

Mr B.F. Taylor

I want your writing fluid as I am about out of ink, and I will pay you what it cost you, write to me and let me know whether or not I can get it if so I will go & get it, tell the boys we are all well, you must write when you will leave Knoxville, I am very lonsom hear, I had much rather be with you, though I am not with you in person, I am in feeling, I can say that you all have the best wishes of all that I heard speak about you, the Meigs Company has the prais in all quarters of the globe tell the Boys all to write to me, yours forever and a day longer

W F Blevins

- - - - - - - - - - - - -

LETTER NO. 4
CRATE LILLARD TO BENJAMIN F. TAYLOR

Meadow Spring,
May 17, 1861

Highly esteemed friend:

When I returned home from Washington I found your very interesting letter in waiting for me. I am truly glad that you are so pleasantly situated and keep so cheerful, but I think the remembrance of such a just cause you are engaged in, will enable you to endure that which the camp life deprives you of the comforts & luxuries of life. You are engaged in a noble and just cause for the peace and happiness of the home fireside, and for the rights and liberties of our own beloved and "Sunny South," for this many thankful hearts will bless you.

Our flag has a brave barer, one we are all willing to entrust in his keeping, for in doing so we feel confident that he will defend it with his life, and truly such is our opinion of all the company. We can readly and willingly entrust a banner to the keeping of such an intrepid band as the Decatur Guard.

I am not at all surprised at the company being cheered and applauded by the ladies and gentlemen, for I think they would be very dull of the appreciation of the noble & brave spirits, not to have recognized such intrepidity in the volunteers of Meigs, who could refrain from exclaiming Meigs now and forever, when they behold the Decatur Guards. Yes we are confident that we shall receive that banner again laden with honors and victory, reapedly the boys of Meigs God bless and defend them. Me thinks I hear each one of the company say never shall the polluted hands of an Abolitionist touch this sacred banner made such, by the tears of mothers sisters and friends as they presented and entrusted it in our keeping, in doing this act their prayers and entreatus ascended to the throne of Him who is the dispenser of justice, that the labors of the volunteers of Meigs may be crowned with greate success, gain victory and peace, finally restore them to their homes made lonely and desolate on account of their absence.

You cannot imagine how lonely and deserted Old Decatur looks. I almost dread to go there. I miss the volunteers so much. Oh it would be such a happy time if we could have the pleasur of seeing them, but we would not call them back from duty and their noble undertakings, with many wishes for yours and all the companys success.

I remain as ever, your true friend Crate Lillard

P.S. enclosed find a composition I suppose it is the one you wanted, I am ashamed to send it, but trusting in your kindness you will excuse its defects. Liny Hodge sends her love. Give mine to ----- ----- [no name]

Your Schoolmate C.L.

- - - - - - - - - - - - -

LETTER NO. 5
AMANDA LILLARD TO B. F. TAYLOR

Decatur, May 19th 1861

Dear Cousin.

With the greatest pleasure, I this Sabbath day for the first time in life take my pen in hand to answer your welcomed letter. I received your letter on the 1st, which I read with great pleasure. Was glad to here that you was well and well satisfied. I am well, at this time, and all the connections as far as known with exception of Ruth Blevins Jun, She has bin very bad, but is thought to be on the mend.

I am at Decatur this morning enjoying my self the best I can and you no thats not very well. You ought to be here on Som high hill to see the girls they has got on their old Split bonnets puled down over their face looking like they have just atended the burial of their last Sweetheart, every girl looks like a stewed witch (as I expect you knew that before you left).

It is raining at this time very heard and I cannot express my feelings just thinking about the poor solgers being out in such hard rain. But I hope that you are in some house out of the rain.

I have read about one 12 of letters since I came to Decatur all of the girls that had got letters from the boys got together and read each other letters and cryed talked over the many happy hours we had spent to geather. I have went to the door several times since I came to town expecting to see som one of my friends, But when I look out I view Seats vacond. But I hope you will com back to ocupy them before long. I received a letter from L h Cox, stating that you would be gon one year, thats a long time.

It appears like I cannot hear the rite of living in such a desolate and miserable place. If I should call it that. Frank I was glad to hear of the young ladies presenting you with such nice flowers But I knew that the Decatur boys would attract the attention of any young lady that the Sun ever shown on.

I have spent a few hours with your old sweetheart since you left Decatur, in all her chat and conversation, you was the object of her heart when I see you I will tell you her main Doubt let it suffice you when I tell you that I caught a beau last Sabbath. I tell you he is a pretty Shearp looking youth himself. He had on his Socks this time I guess. And a striped vest. He is talking of going to Knoxville to see all of the boys before they leave for linchburg. If he comes take him on to linchburg and make him fit for my fireside. Indeed he is a nice young man, But his beauty and conversation did not nor cannot make me forget my Spense that went off in Capt. Lillards gallant little band. I want you to speak [to] him for me you know who he is and therefore I shall not put down his name. Tell O, Tell him bless his heart.

Willy is lying here on the floor wanting to go to see his Sweetheart but it will not quit raining he says to tell you he is not dead yet. I called on Miss O Hodge this morning had a good deal of fun. She talked a good deal about you told me that she thanked you for the present you gave her. I must quit writing for this time. Tell T J and John Russell if they stick to their word that I will get a letter from them before long.

Give my love to N J Lillard and all the rest of the connections. Tell N J Lillard that Miss M.D. Blevins sends her love to him and also to E.L. Hodge, Layafette Mc. . . Tell all the boys howdy for me. Tell George Atchley that Bird P . . . Beat the drum for the home guard yesterday. He looked as brave as a Sheep and as Modest as a Soap troft. Tell Frank Lillard that Lizzie Blevins is still in the land of the living but looks bad. I expect it is on the account of his absence.

Frank Tell Newt to tell J A Love to tell Dick Stewart to tell John Russell to tell Hugh Blevins to tell T J Russell to tell Frank Lillard to tell Lafayette Mc . . . to tell Jesse Gwin to tell W A Smith to tell David B . . . Frank Mc . . . and Edward Hodges to play that good National Air called Yankeedoodle and leave the Doodle part out and think of me. Give my love to B Frazier also Stephen Baldwin And except a portion your self Write Soon and tell all the boys to write.

Your affectionate Cousin
Amanda Lillard

- - - - - - - - - - - - -

LETTER NO. 6
AMANDA TAYLOR TO B. F. TAYLOR

Decatur, May 22nd 1861

Dear brother.

I avail my self of the opportunity of droping you a few lines to inform you that we are all well and hoping when you receive theas few lines that they may find you ingoying the same good blessings. I have nothing of importants to write to you. We reseived your letter last thursday which give us grait pleather to hear from you and to hear that you all wr in good spirits. Elmira Lillards School begins hear next monday and I easpect to go to her. I want you to write to me while there. Isaac Cross is coming home or not if he is I should like to know it as quick as posabel. Mr Colvel is going to start a monday with his company and A.C. Blevins is a going to start in 8 or 10 days mosly belongs to his company and he say he is agoing Oald --?-- was wipt last monday in Washington they give him 39 lashes and cut the blood ever lick Mother says that she wants you to remember your creator and try to shun all weaked company. John and family are all well except Frank he hapened with a little accident he dropt a rock on his toe and mashed nearley off. Mary and the children air all well. I must bring my letter to a close I want you to write to me as soon as you get this letter we all send our love to you give my love to all my frinds Your loving sister

Amanda Taylor

- - - - - - - - - - - - -

LETTER NO. 7
N.J. LILLARD TO B.F. TAYLOR

Camp Cummings, May 31st 1861

Lieut. B.F. Taylor

Sir your on order to return to Camp Cummings on Sunday Next. Bring with you all the boys who are on furlough as we have orders to March to Linchburg Va at any hour. ---?--- I send you this order by Private J.T. Russell if the boys do not come willing, you must bring them by any means, do not fail to use your utmost indeavors to come up to time, be prompt in Complyance with this order. Respectfully Yours, N.J. Lillard, Capt.

Jacob Nance	John Taylor
James Parks	B.F. Lillard, Sergt.
J. H. Guinn, Corp.	H.T.V. Blevins, Sergt.
W.A. Smith	

There may be others if so bring them

- - - - - - - - - - - - -

LETTER NO. 8
B. F. TAYLOR TO PARENTS

Lynchburg, Va, June 11th 1861

Loving parents:

In great haste I this morning drop you a few lines as we are going to start from this place in a few hours for harpers ferry which is about 200 hundred miles from this place. We received orders yesterday to march as soon as we could get conveyance as our service would be needed very bad in 1 or 2 days.

I can say that I am glad to know that we are going where we can fight side by side with our brother Tennesseans and Kentuckeyans, Volunteers that never failed to gain bright victories upon every battle field where they were present. And Tennessee and Kentucky has volunteers on the field to day that can and will win victories that will give her honor in days to come. The boys appear more willing to start into battle than ever I seen youngsters to go to a party, they have no fears whatever.

And you need have no fears at home for we can whip them though they be 3 to our 1, every battle that has taken place they have had 3 or 4 to our 1 and the South has killed 5 or 6 to the North's 1; thats so, then why should we fear when we have all proof that the God of battles is on our side and will protect us.

There was a company came into camps from Kentucky last evening, they will go on with us to Harpers ferry, the place where all the Volunteers from Kentucky and Tennessee have gon for rendevouse.

I cannot write more at present, the boys are in tolerable health nothing rong but bad colds, I have sufered verry much with cold but am geting better. Tell Mary that Isaac has got well again he is appointed Adjutant of the redgement & Be Frazier chaplen, that shoes who has the best company.

If you write to me direct your letter to Harpers Ferry 1st E Tenn redgement in care of Capt Lillard, then I will have no trouble in getting it at all.

I remain as ever your affectionate son

B.F. Taylor

- - - - - - - - - - - - -

LETTER NO. 9
PEACH TAYLOR TO
B.F. TAYLOR AND ISAAC CROSS

At Home, June 16th 1861

Dear and affectionate Sons

I take this oppertunity to Inform You that we are all well at this time hoping when these lines reaches you to find you both well. I recd your letter on Yesterday which Gave me Greate Satisfaction to hear that you was all well I have Nothing of importance to write at this time.

Our Election is Over, Meigs County Voted Seperation & Representation 483. No Separation 253 Votes. the 4th District Voted Separation 128, and 3 against, 3 District 47 No Separation 68 for Separation, it is all rite the State has Gave Out from 60 to 70 thousand Supposed from the Best Calculations I do not know the Majority that the Union has Carried East Tenn by from 10 to 12 thousand I Suppose but dont know, it not worth My while to write about the Election You will Get the News before this letter reaches You.

Isaac Cross property Sold Pacing Mare Brought \$115, Sn--?-- & Colt \$140, 1 Waggon \$40.20, Gun \$18.20, the other not Sold. Uncle Billy and ant Susy is at my house to day the first time that Your Uncl has been from home Since You left Decatur. Mary and Children and William Arrants and wife is also here.

W W Lillard is preching in Buit(?) to day I am at home with a verry Sore leg So bad that Cant do any thing the rest all Gone to preeching the Connections is all well and people Generally.

I want you and Frank to take Good Care of Yourselves and Keep out of all Sorts of desapation. it will do My heart Good to here that the boys in Capt Lillards Company Sustains the Character that they have Established in Knoxville or at Camp Cummings. I want you & Frank to be Prudent and Conduct your Selves well and not Only You but the Balance of the boys in Capt Lillards Company and may the God of Battles Guard Guide and protect all of you is the Sincere prayer of Your affectionate Father.

Our harvest is on hand at this time, Your wheat Cut and we are in the Midst of Harvest and hands is Very Scears and hard to Get. Wheat is Verry fine the Best Crop Since that Good Crop Year, Our Crops looks fine all kinds of crops. Your Mother and Aunt Susan Sends their love you & Frank John & H--?-- and not only to you, But all the boys --?-- at Present but remains
Your affectionate Father Untill death Peach Taylor

- - - - - - - - - - - - -

LETTER NO. 10
WM S. AND SUSAN (BLEVINS) RUSSELL TO JOHN AND TOM RUSSELL

At P Taylors, June 16th 1861

Dear Sons

I take this oppertunity to inform you that we are well at this time and we hope when these lines Comes to hand to find you and Thos well we recd a letter from Thos last week which gave us much pleasure to here that you and Tom was well the Connections is all well.

I think it unnecessary to Say any thing about the Election because you will Get the News before this letter reaches you. I do not know what the result of the Election will Bring about in East Tenn, I am fearful it will bring more troubles I can not say what the result will be.

A. [Absalom Looney] Cross joined Capt Ragsdale Company of Cavellry from Chattanooga and is gone to Knoxville he started Yesterday Morning. Capt Boggas left for Knoxville thursday the 13th Inst with his Company if their is a few More Companies leaves Meigs their will [be] none left. Give our Compliments to all the boys.

If I Could leave I would be with you as soon as I could travel to your Camp. I want to be with you take Good Care of Yourselves, this is the first time I have been from home Since You left Decatur With Your Company. I have been employing my time in the field I am up with My work but I dont know how long I will be in this Condition, 3 Cheers Tenn 3 for Jeff Davis and 3 for the Southern Army. Good by

Wm S & Susan Russell

To John & Tom Russell
Capt N J Lillards Comp, 1st Regt, E Tenn Volunteers

- - - - - - - - - - - - -

LETTER NO. 11
AMANDA C. LILLARD TO B.F. TAYLOR

June 28, 1861

Dear Cousin

It is with a troubled and bothered mind I write. Why do you not answer my letter. Is it from the fact that you have never received my letter or did not it interest you enough to respond to its unworthy demands. The last letter you wrote me while at Knoxville. I didnt receive for two weeks after it was wrote. I sent to the PO every mail day with the expectation of getting a letter from my Cus. I so much admire untill my patients become worn out thought you never was going to write me again. But when I com to find out you had don wrote and Willie had taken it out of the PO and had forgotten to send it to me. So soon as I received your letter I answered it directed it to Lynchburg, do not know whether it ever reached you or not.

We are all well this morning and all the connections well as common. I received a note from Brillis yesterday evening Stating that you had a battle at New Creek which I was truly glad to hear that you came out conqueror in that battle and I do hope it will be so in ever one you have. Sorrow to here that one of our dearest little boys got wounded. I suppose it did not hurt him very bad or at least I hope it did not.

I stated in the above that we was all well which is not that away for my part. I have been Sick two weeks but is up and a bout at this time my face has faded considerable in the past two weeks.

Frank I saw a grate many of our girls down at Goodfield several from Decatur. I do not believe your sweetheart was on hand. June bugs are very scarce in these parts. The young Lady that was speeking about you and taking on goes by the name of Kate Leuty. I am looking for Dear Lizzie King home any day must I kiss her for you Seven times when she coms. I will be so glad to see her. Tell Edward Hodg I am waiting patiently for a lock of Lincoln hair which he promised to send me.

Excuse bad writing for I am in a hurry. I would like to write more. Tell my sweetheart that I am having a good and better But not the best time he ever heard of. My love to all, Your Cousin as ever and for ever.

Amanda C Lillard

Write Soon. Pinch Dave and Hugh for me

- - - - - - - - - - - - -

LETTER NO. 12
B.F. TAYLOR TO PARENTS

Camp Johnson Near Winchester
July 8th 1861

Loving parents:

Again I have the exquisite pleasure of droping you a few lines. We have just returned to camp from a small place called Buckles town where we were drawn up in the line of battle for 90 hours near 4 days. We started there on Tuesday evening reached the place Wednesday and returned last evening which was Sunday, it is 16 miles from this place. Our cause for going I suppose you have already learned, as some of the boys that were not able to go wrote back to Meigs concerning our trip.

On Tuesday the Federal troops attacked a place called Martinsburg 22 miles from this place, our force at that place was 2 thousand the federal force 15 thousand as I heared, in the fight 15 Southern troops were killed and 140 or 150 of the Northern troops and 41 taken prisoner, we taken 5 or 6 every day that we were gon making in all 82, among this number old John Brown's brother who was hung at Harpers Ferry, he is a doctor in the army.

We have three prisoners throwing up a brest-work near Winchester where we expect to have a fight in a few days. The ground that we are making our brest-work on is where George Washington fought one of his battles in the Revolutionary War, we are also camped on a farm owned by him in early life and use water out of his spring.

I did not give our reason for returning without a battle, when we were in 6 miles of Martinsburg we learned that the enemy were advancing on us we stoped and made prapations(?) to receive them they did not come but sent us word the next evening to leave or he would murder us. He said he would give us 10 hours to leave that place, Tennesseans 20 days to go home and Va troops 10, we disobeyed him verry much as we stayed near 4 days instead of 10 hours waiting for him to drive us off which we did not think he would do but the driving would have been reversed.

When our general which is Johnson found that Paterson which is the general of the forse at Martinsburg would not attact us he sent Paterson word to let the women and children out of town and we would make the attact the reply of the cowardly vilion was he would not let them out but intended placing them in front of the battle if we made the attact when their force was increased to 25 or 30 thousand and ours but 15 thousand that shows their pluck, we then fell back to Winchester trying to draw them after us but fear we will not be successful, our boys were verry mad because they could not get a fight out of them.

The Virginians swar that we have a regement of the bravest men they ever seen from any State, they give us the front when ever their is any fighting to do as they know we will not flinch.

I do not suppose it necessary to say any thing about the death of J A Love and P W Renyen as you will know all about it before this comes to hand. Their death is much lamented in the company as you may know but the best of friends has to be given up sometimes. The rest of the sick boys are on the mend all will get well soon I think. I am in as good health as ever I was, the boys say I am the healthiest looking one in the company. Isaac and all the connections are well.

Mother Capt Lillard sends his best respects to you says to tell you he would like to be there and eat a good dinner that you would get such as honey butter good cornbread and biscuit. I will have to close for the present so as to get this letter off to day. Give my love to John Ann and Children Mary and family and to all the connections.

Write to me soon and tell John to write, when I write home is as much to one as an other as you are all there together, direct your letters Winchester Va and they will be forwarded if we are gon as all the movements we make are known. I remain as ever, Your loving Son

B. F. Taylor

Mr. W.F. Blevins

I direct this to you that you may send it home immediately and to read if you wish comply with this request and you will oblige a good friend, give my love to your Mother and family. Your Cousin

B. F. Taylor

\- - - - - - - - - - - - -

LETTER NO. 13
AMANDA LILLARD TO B. F. TAYLOR

Coldwater, July 18th 1861

Dear and generous Cousin

It is with grateful pleasure that I resume my pen to respond to your dear and welcom Letter. Yours of 8th came to hand a few hours ago which I hasten to answer in my rough but best manner I can at present. I was glad to learn that you were in good health. Also glad to hear that those of the boys that is and has been Sick are on the mend hoping when this coms to hand it may find all well and doing as well as can be expected of Soldiers in Camp.

Your letter found us all in tolerable good health and all the connection So far as I know with the exception of Aunt Ann Blevins. I have not herd from her Since Monday, she has been bad and very bad. We have had Som Sickness in the past month in Meigs and up till now. It is thought by the Doctor that Mr William Eaves two children will die. With these exceptions all are well as common.

I was over at Decatur last Saturday and Sunday went over to See Mr Frazier and to be at the baptist Meeting. I did not get to See Mr Frazier which I am very sorrow he and wife was gon over the river.

I had a fine time at the Meeting considering every thing. Did not catch any beaus but that did not trouble me any as there was none I cared for. Bro John Waller an Sons were on hand. You should have Laughfed yourself good had you a been there and heard them sing bass to the top of their voices.

On Saturday they had Georg Marlory again for Drinking whiskey. At first he denied drinking any at Last proof was So clear that he acknowledged it all got up and told the brethren that he drank whiskey on such a day and he would drink it as long as he lived. he is still in the church.

I saw your Sweetheart Miss KL and read hear letter which you wrote her. You cannot imajin how she was taking on over its golden pages. I think she red it no less than five times while I stade with her.

Frank Lizzie has not com home yet or had not last Sabbath. When she coms I will kiss her as you requested (Instead of 7 times I am going to kiss her 14 times, which will be 7 times for you and 7 for me, what do you think of that).

Cousin the long ballad which you sent me I have read often it is so Stamped on my mind I think I will get up in the morning Singing one particular verse and especially the last line, Which is this, And we got their baggage and their cannon Singing Root She or doe. I laugfed my self good when I read it as I had never Saw it before. I thank you thrice for sending it. I thank you not only for the amusing ballad but thank you for such long letters. O, do write them often as nothing does me so much good as long letters from my dear Cousins and friends.

I reckin it is usless to Say any thing in reference to Mr Loves death as you know I esteemed him highly as a Gentleman and Schoolmate. I hope Heaven is his home. I suppose his Sister and Mrs Parks is taking it extreemly hard.

Cousin I must close for this time, as I feel confident I am not interesting you for I hear nothing thats good. I do want to see you all so bad what would I give if you were at home. I fear 1861 will be a year Long to [be] remembered. Give my Love two all the connections Say howday to Dave Hugh Tom and John Russell, Pinch Jimmy Blevins for me. Remember me to my Sweetheart, Excuse bad writing as I write in a hurry. Write when ever you have the chance, Long letters. Your Cousin and friend, True one at that. Amanda Lillard
Be a good boy keep death before you.

- - - - - - - - - - - - -

LETTER NO. 14
B. F. TAYLOR TO ----- McKINLEY

Fairfax Courthouse, Va.
July 30th 1861

Friend McKinley

I take this opportunity to send you a Ullogy of General Beauregard and General Johnston to us for our galantry at Manassas on the battle field. I think it is a splendid peace and think it will interest you with others of our friends. Perhaps you may receive a copy of this from someone else if so return this over to father.

There is not anything new or interesting in camp at this time. I learned today that old Abe had asked from Jeff Davis an armistice of 60 days, Jeff said he would give him the 60 days if he would ensure peace at that time and if not he would give him but 10. I will close for the present hoping to have something of more interest next time. Give my respects to your wife and other friends and except a good portion yourself. As ever your friend,

B. F. Taylor

Mack I would be glad to hear from you soon. Write immeditely, write to Manasses, we have to send there after our mail every day. Ben

[NOTE: The above letter probably was written to William Locke McKinley]

Head Quarters Army of the Potomac
Manassas, July 25th 1861

Soldiers of the Confederate States:

One week ago a Countless host of men organized into an army with all the appointments which modern art and practical Skill could divise invaded the soils of Virginia. Their people Sounded their approach with triumphant displays of anticipated victory. Their Generals came in almost royal State, their Ministers, Senators, and women came to witness the immolation of this Army and the Subjugation of our people, and to celebrate these with wild revelry.

It is with the profoundest emotions of gratitude to an overruling God, whose hand is manifest in protecting our homes and our liberties that we your Generals Commanding, are enabled in the name of our whole Country to thank you for that patriotic Courage that heroic gallantry that devoted daring exhibited by you in the actions of the 18th and 21st July by which the hosts of the enemy were Scattered and a Signal and glorious victory achieved.

The two affairs of the 18th and 21st were but the sustained and continued efforts of your patriotism against the Constantly recurring Columns of an enemy fully treble your numbers, and this effort was crowned on the evening of the 21st with a victory so complete that the invaders were driven disgracefully from the field, and made to fly in disorderly rout back to their entrenchments, a distance of over thirty Miles. They left upon the field nearly every piece of their Artellery, a large portion of their arms, Equipments, baggage, Stores &c, &c, and almost every one of their wounded and dead, amounting together with the prisoners to many thousands, and thus the Northern Hosts were driven by you from Virginia.

Soldiers! We Congratulate you on an event which ensures the liberty of Country. We congratulate every man of you whose glorious privalige even it was to participate in this triumphant of Courage and Truth to fight in the battle of Manassas. You have created an epoch in the history of liberty; and unborn Nations will rise up and call you "blessed." Continue this noble devotion looking always to the protection of a just God; and before time grows much older we will be hailed as the Deliverers of a Nation of Ten Million of people.

Comrads. Our brothers who have fallen have earned undying renown on Earth! and their blood shed in our holy cause is a precious and acceptable sacrifice to the Father of Truth and Right. Their graves are beside the Tomb of Washington, their Spirits have joined him in eternal Communion. We will hold the Soil in which the dust of Washington is Mingled with the dust of our brothers. We drop one tear on their laurels and move forward to avenge them.

Soldiers. We Congratulate you on a glorious triumphant and complete Victory. We thank you for doing your whole duty in the Service of our Country.

Signed Joseph E. Johnston
G. F. Beauregard

LETTER NO. 15
SARAH McCORKLE TO B.F. TAYLOR

Decatur, Augt 2d 1861

Kind Friend

Yours of the 12th inst was received some time since and as I now have an opportunity of sending you a few lines by Mr Godsey I have seated myself to write you. I would have written sooner but heard communications had stoped and supposed it was unnecessary to write.

We are all well at present, hope you enjoy the same blessing. We received intelligence of the great and glorious victory won at Manassas on the 21st. I was truly thankful that our side won the victory but at the same time grieved the loss of so many precious lives were taken. I can deeply sympathise with the bereaved ones whose hearts were made sad by the works of that day. I hope it will be the last battle that will have to be fought. I think it is enough to discourage the North so much that they will give up. I have nothing to write more at present. My love to all & a portion to yourself.

Your friend, Sarah Mc

Ten sends her love to all, says she loves them all & hopes they will all soon return home crowned with honor to enjoy once more the quite of home & dear friends.

Sarah [McCorkle]

Tell Brothers we did not know in time, we could send them any letters we had not time to write after we learned Mr Godsey was going. We will write as soon as we know where to direct our letters.

- - - - - - - - - - - - -

LETTER NO. 16
D.C. BLEVINS TO B.F. TAYLOR

Decatur, August 3rd 1861

Mr. B.F. Taylor, Dear Cousin

After So long a time I take the pleasure of acknowledging the receipt of your wellcome letter of 16th inst. I was verry glad to hear from you that you was well and had been well all the time Since you have been in Camp.

I hope you will excuse me for not writing sooner. the reason I didn't write Sooner was that I heard you was in a battle, and I was wating to hear the result. I wated patietally though the folks was all excited verry mutch. I told them to be patient and not be uneasy for the victory was ours and thank Heven when the nuse Com you had won the victory and none of you was hurt. There was a Jeneral rejoising in town and in fact every where when the nuse Came.

I expect you have hard time in Camp. But go --?-- I am Surtin you will be victorious on evry field and if you never fite another battle your victory at Manassas will make a brite place in the worlds history.

I havent any thing verry interesting with regard to our E Tenn brotherin. They are Still presisting in their unprincipled and phanatical Courses perpatrating deeds that would make even a devil Blush, they waylayed and murdered our Col the other day in the naberhood of Jamestown. So John Lillard writes, they allso threw logs and Chunks across the rail road the other Knight for the purpose of throwing the Cars off the tract loded with Volinteers we Cant find out who it was, if we do they will fair but midling.

The Alection Came off last thursday, havent heard how it went. I think Harris is alected Sertin. Welker is a luase, So far and we will get Southeran members to the legislature from this Senitorial and --?-- district. I have heard from Rhea Meigs McMinn and Munroe have all gon for the South. Meigs and Rhea run about three hundred majority each, Munroe 500 majority for the South Bradley union fall off of 300.

The hancuff Party is geting weaker in this Country. I think a few men fights in Virginia in favor of the South and we give them a little Slashing here at home and they will be all rite.

Give all the boys my regards. I would like to be with you and would have been with you had I not promised to wind up Sam and Nutes business.

Write me whether or not they will take in more volunteers after McElrath gets in with his recruits.

I will write you again. You must excuse this bad riten letter the people are mustering around here so, blowing the fife and coming out and So I cant rite. With my best wishes, I remain your friend and Cousin

D. C. Blevins

- - - - - - - - - - - - -

LETTER NO. 17
PEACH TAYLOR TO
I.G. CROSS AND B.F. TAYLOR

At home August Sunday 4th 1861

Affectionate Sons

With the greatest of pleasure I this Eaving Rite you a few lines to let you know that we have not forgotten you yeat, Nor Will till death. We are all well at this time, thanks be to God for his goodness & merces hoping these few lines may find you both Injoying good health and the balance of the Boys.

On last Tuesday I went to Town & got your letter and one from franklin that you Rote since the battle at Manasses, Which gave us greate Satisfaction and pleasure to here from you & here you was both enjoying good health. We was glad to here of the grate Victory one by the South, thare is More Rejoicing Over your grate Victory in that Batel than any One thing I have Ever herd in all of my life by all the true Sotherners people bouth Women & men thare prars are continuley assendand to the God of Battell to protect you and present you all till you Whupe the last Yankee Out & Mack them glad to Acknolledge the Southern Confedrecy independanc and give us our Just Rites. I want you to be good Boys and ask the God Heaven to be With you and preserve you all.

Mary and all the Children is well. John & Ann & Children is well. The health of this Cuntrey is generley good. Wash Godsey left Your house last Tuesday Very Mad he told his Father that She Said a hirlen was no better than a Negro, Which she denies and Said she never Misstreated him nor give him a angrey Word. One of Will Arances Boys was helping him Work at the time and you can lern the truth When you git back, his Crop is very indiferent it has bin a very wet season & hard to tend Weat land the Weat land Drounded out Several times and then Continued Weat untill two lait to maik Corn this is the 11th Augst all Still well. I Advised Mary not to leave hir Old house and try and git one of William Arants Boys to live with hir, I think he has promised hir one a while When he gits Well he has bin a little Sick but I lern is giting better. Your Aunt Ann B. Blevins Deceast this life the 28th July With the flux, was Sick Some 10 or 12 days.

Mr Vinson has got a Scool her and if Will would let one of his boys come and Stay with hir & gow to Scool this will be the best thing She can do. You nead not have any uneasness on that Subject as long as I live I will see She is takin good care of.

William A. Godsey started to Join your Company in Virginia on 2th of this instance. I Expect from What he said to me he will tell a very favorble tale on Washes Side, Moses Blevins left me the 7 June he joined Crawfords Company Some time before he left and tride to put Every --?-- in Wash he Could and he dun but little good the balance of the time and was at the point of quitting long before he did you will see how things has bin worked when you git back. Mr. Godsey and me Seteld the day before he started and gave me an Order on you for $19 Dollars fifty cts your property you wanted Sold at cost was all sold but one Waggin. A.L. Cross Sold the pason mare at privit Sale to Elzey Buttrum at $114 Dollars the black mare & Colt I got at $140 Dollars, John W. Smith got one Waggin $50.20 cts, the other Waggin was Run(?) to fortey Some Od Dollars and I did not let it sell. I have it in a good Shead at Binions in Decature.

Doctor Hogg Bout the Godsey gun $18.20, I have all the nots for the property that was Sold On nine Months time. You give me Some Recepts and papers before you left, Mary gave me Some Nots I have put them all away thare has not bin any money Collected that was oweing you yeat. I saw Mr Cealow(?) about the Wasson Debt and he told me it was --?--.

Colonel Cox Voted the Union ticket I am told Dead Out. The Union men is verry plenty here yeat and a grate taulk of ther Revolten but I think they had better lay still if they knew Which Side of there bred has the Butter On they are Refusen to give up the post Offis whare ever they hold them. Thare is three Company gone on to Kingsten to take posession of that Offes, I must conclude my letter, give my love and Respects to Captain Lillard and all his oficers and men in said Company, Your Respectful Father untill Death

Peach Taylor

- - - - - - - - - - - - -

LETTER NO. 18
KATE LEUTY TO B.F. TAYLOR

Decatur, August 22nd 1861

Respected friend.

Your very interesting and truly welcom letter at hand I this dreary evening resome my Seat to answer it although I have nothing to write that will interest you. It has been raining every day this week so I have been staying at home ever since Monday stayed at Mr. Lillards Sunday night Liz, Emma, Crate Lissa Sallie Mc and myself composed the crowd. We had a very interesting time. I have not saw the girls since Lizzie is at Washington, went over last Tuesday and Lissa and Emma are at your fathers went home with Amanda will come back Saturday.

Lizzie and me have been having some good fun since she came home, well you ought to have saw us last Sunday week, we had a gallant going to Church. (I did not say coming back) he went one direction, we went another, I did not think he would have treated us so badly.

I have moved my writing into another room, I was sitting in the far room got scared ran out at the front door came very near falling down over the rocks. I heard someone at the back door spoke several times to them, did not receive any answers thought it time to be leaving. I did not know but it was one of the Lincolnites for it is so dark I cannot see out doors, they are mean enough to travel at any time, night suits them better than daylight. There are some of as trifling ones in this county as can be found anywhere.

Aunt Susan Russell give Jacob Zeiglor fits the other day. She said what she pleased to him, he denied several things he has been guilty of, Uncle Billy set and listened at her but did not say anything.

Col McKinly is drinking, he run a union man out of town today in the hardest run, he treated him right I think for they ought not be allowed to associate with respectible people. I have no feeling for no such if he had been the right kind of man I would hated to heard of him being treated so. I think some of them will cool off after they hear Davis' proclamation if dont they had better or they will get cooled.

Cousin Mary Russell is teaching at the school house below Uncles. You kneed not be surprised if you hear of her being Mrs some body before long. Mr D was there last Sunday stayed until Monday. Mr James Martin from Texas is still here. I think he is trying to get to call you cousin from the moves he has been making.

I forgot to tell about Rev Housten Cate preaching for us at the baptist church. his wife seemed to be very much embarassed, did not raise her head. I had like to have fallen in love with a captain of a cavalary company who stayed all night here, he was a very well looking man and an old bachelor.

Recon I had better stop writing tonight as the colock has struck eleven for I know I have not interested you at all. May heavens richest blessing crown you with the best of consequence is the wish of your friend

Kate Leuty

Excuse the badly composed and blotted letter.

- - - - - - - - - - - - -

LETTER NO. 19
KATE LEUTY TO B.F. TAYLOR

Friday morning 23rd [August 1861]

This morning finds me in good health after getting such a scare last night.

Well Frank I do wish you could see Abel dress up in his cloth and chum(?) hat, how he can smile at the girls no use in talking, goes to church regular. I dont know which can smile the most him or Mr J. Davis, they are both flying around trying to get the girls to pay attention to them.

We have a very nice young gentleman with us, Mr. Tom Binyon (or little Tomy we call him), he is very kind to the girls the envelope I enclose this letter in he made gave to me, there is none in town.

Mr. Mayfield was over last week, called on Tenn said he was coming back next week to court would bring some good secessionest with him to protect the young ladies of Decatur as there would be so many union men here. I wouldn't be surprised if he would not like to be the protecter of one himself.

What has become of Mr. Allen. I have not heard anything from him since the pigeons flew, has he got over his mad fitt? I have not received that letter from Mr. Guthman yet. Give my respects to all my friends. I will stop Such nonsense. Your friend Kate

Please hand the enclosed to whom directed.

- - - - - - - - - - - - -

LETTER NO. 20
M.B. STEWART TO B.F. TAYLOR

Decatur, August 23rd 1861

Esteemed friend

I this evning avail myself of the opportunity of droping you a few lines to let you no that I am well, hoping these few lines may find you and all the rest of the Boys well. I have nothing of interest to rite at present, except that we have the best corn crop that we have had since my first recolection. I think we have plenty of corn to do us two or three years. I dont think you need to be uneasy about any thing to eat in the bread line but the Hogs is dying up mity fast here but we have more Jeff Davis corn and wheat than you ever saw.

Our union men has bin cuting up big for a while, but I recon they are knocking under faster than any set men you ever seen. there was a great stire a mong them a week or two ago, they gathered up on last Sunday was a week ago at Kingston and it was thought they were agoing to attact our Boys at Jim Town.

Monday morning James Weallen came down on the hunt of men and arms to go to their assistance. I went to town and we met at the court house to see whether we would go or not finely we concluded that it would be best for us to stay untill the union men started from below because they had bin meeting and driling nearly every day for the last week and we thought that they would come up the valley but it turned out to be a fiz(?)

They were aming to go to Kentucky and did go a heap of them. I would be glad if they were all gone for I do think they are the lowest down set of men I ever saw. I think Kentucky and old Jeffs proclemation will set them all right. Frank you ought to see them coming over since old Jeff issued his proclemation, I Say hurah for old Jeff. I think by the time that his forty days is out the union men will be like the mans flee when you go to put your finger on them they wont be there.

I am told that the Governor of Ky is going to call out his State Troops to make our union men leave there what went over there to get help to whip us. I am glad that if there is any whiping done they will haft to take it themselves. I am told that they are Starving over there and they are coming back some of them barefooted. I think when they get back they will behave themselves. I wont undertake to tell you all of their movements.

Frank you ought to be here to see some of them, they are the worst set of looking men you ever saw, you could tell them as far as you could see them and some of them you could allmost smell them. Frank Francis has the finest Boy you ever saw. He calls him Jeff, tell B.F. Lillard if he dont quit writing back here to my sweet heart I will come out there and give him the worst whiping he ever had.

Molley Rose(?) said to tell D.M. Blevins howdy for her. Frank I was glad to here of the victory you won at Manassas. I like to have been there and seen the Yankeys running. I had the pleasure of seeing one pair of the hand cuffs that they had to put on you Boys, but I am glad they didn't get them on you and I hope by the help of God they never will. it allmost made the hair stand on my head to look at them.

I must close for it is geting dark, tel Dick and Van howdy for me, tell Dick I received two letters from him yesterday and he told me to rite to him whether I was coming or not. tell him that I have not concluded for certain whether I will come or not, tell him I will write to him by mondays mail whether I will come or not. I would be glad to see you all and I think it is likely I will come, give my best respects to all and be sure to except a good portion your self. I remain as ever, your true friend M. B. Stewart

To B.F. Taylor. be sure and write immediately and tell all to rite for I am allways anxious to here from any of you.

- - - - - - - - - - - - -

LETTER NO. 21
B.F. TAYLOR TO PEACH TAYLOR

Fairfax Station,
Aug 26th 1861

Dear father:

This evening I have the pleasure of acknowledging the reception of your very kind and interesting letter which came to hand Wednesday evening last, and which was read over time and again and its contents carefully noted in my memory. It gratified me very much to hear that you were all alive and doing well, and do hope the same good blessings will continually be bestowed upon you all, what better could I wish for?

I have come to the conclusion that it is useless for us to write anything only conserning the health of the company as the newse we have these times are of but little or no interest whatever from the fact that it is like an old worn out song before our letters comes to hand.

In reference to our company they are as a general thing in verry good health, but with deep sorrow and regret I have to record the death of our brother Soldier M V Stewart who died this morning at half past 11 o Clock. He was complaining some 8 or 10 days but never taken down until 2 or 3 days ago and could help himself up in the bed until a few hours before he died, his death has throwen a damper over the entire compny. We intend trying to send him home but fear we will not be successful, we will know by morning. I cannot refrain sheading tears of simpathy for his aged parents brothers sisters and other relations, but all this availeth nothing in reference to restoring him to life and health again.

I will say nothing more about his death at present. Their has been some excitement in camp for the last 3 or 4 days but all from false allarms I learn. From the movements that are going on at this time I think there is a likelyhood of us being quartered at or near this point if the Yankeys do not make an attact on us which I do not think they will do, but if they should we will rout them again and quarter our selves in Washington City.

I believe I have nothing more of interest to write at this time. Tell Amanda that I received her letter the same day that I received yours and will answer it in due time, also one of my good old friend McKinley which I will answer in a few days. The reason I did not answer your letter immediately was because I had just wrote you one or 2 days before I received your letter and did not deem it necessary to write again so soon without I had something of more interest than I do have.

I feel to thank you for the good advise you gave me in reference to living right so that I might be prepared to die right, but I assure you father, it is a hard place to live as we should, their are so many things to lead us a stray. I will close for the night and write more in the morning as I was up all night last night with Van and am geting very sleepy.

P S: Tuesday morning Aug 27th 1861

All quiet in camp this morning, and the health of the company verry good. I am in as good health as I could wish for. I weigh 171 lbs and am stronger than I ever was in Tennessee. Isaac is healthier than you ever seen him and looks better. I do not think we will be successful in geting Van off home. I am going to set the boys diging his grave in a few moments in the Church yard where George Washington atended public worship in his time. The materiel that it is built of was imported from Urope by Lord Fairfax. I enclose a piece of the Pulpit to you.

I will now have to close as it is mail time. Give my love to Mother and all the family with Mary and children, John Ann and Children and execpt a good portion yourself. Write soon and write often. I remain as ever, your affectionate son

B. F. Taylor

P S: You can read this to Mr Stewarts family if you wish and have an opportunity.

- - - - - - - - - - - - -

LETTER NO. 22
D.C. BLEVINS TO B.F. TAYLOR

Decatur, Augst 27th 1861

Dear Cousin

Received your kind and interesting letter of the 16th inst this morning, was glad to hear from you, that you are well, and also of the improved condition of the Company. I hope you will remain So till your time is out. I now you have had a hard time Since you have been in Va. I wanted to Shier your toils with you and would have fain done so had I been able.

I have nothing interesting more than your folks and all the Connection are well. I handed over your enclosed letter to your father a few minuts ago.

The hand Cuff party in E Tenn are caming down some since they have met with their defeat in geting their arms throu Ky. They Stole off in little Squads across the mountain to orgenise, they say, and McGoffin is going to drive them back again by the hole sale. We are picking a few of them up and making them prisoners of them as they come back. So they are badley sceered and most of them are Submiting. I think it is on account of feer though.

Bridges and Nelson are both pretending to be Southeran Since they have been turned luse, and so is Broslin(?) since they Stoped his paper. I dont have any

Confidence in them at all, if they had a chance they would do more than they have ever done. I dont think we will have them to fight if McGoffin mentain his neutrality and let the Lincolnights come thru. I dont think they will fight by them selves.

Our Arrmey has gained a grate victory in Va, it seams as you say providence is on our side and we will be victorious on evry field, they had a battle nere Springfield. We give them a good whiping. Lyan was killed early in the day, our loss was from 200 to 300 killed and from 400 to 500 wounded. The loss of the enamy from 2300 to 3000. Our forces persued them and has Chaiced Zeigler and his forces clear out of the Country.

I am going to the war myself. Wm Lillard, G.W. McKenzie, Owen Martin and me are making up a Cavelry Company. Will orgenise next Monday and start shortley if we will be receivd, they are geting Crowded at Knoxville, teen thousand troops their.

If I get among them E T I will make them stand round sisten(?). I will rite you again if we get off Shortley. As I have nothing else interesting and Buck Stewart is going to leave for fairfax and I want to send my letter by him I will close. I wish you all good luck till you come home. I remain your true friend and School mate.

D.C. Blevins

P.S. tell J.K.D. Blevins I will write to him shortly. You must excuse this bad letter. I am in a hurry.

D.C. Blevins

- - - - - - - - - - - - -

LETTER NO. 23
SARAH McCORKLE TO B.F. TAYLOR

Decatur, Augt 28th 1861

Friend Frank.

Your of 15th was received yesterday. I was glad to hear from you & my friends generly in camp, as you may very well know nothing gives me as much pleasure, these dull times as a word or letter from my absent friends. Such I hope you all are, such I believe you to be, may it ever be my happy lot to retain such friendship as are possessed by the members of that noble company. I do not wish to flatter you or any of your fellow soldiers, I write from the impulse of my feelings. We are, all the citizens of Decatur, in as good health as usual.

I rejoice to hear of another glorious victory achieved by the chivalrous sons of the South. Thanks to the Supreme Ruler! that is another proof of His appobation of Southern Cause. The God of battle has been with our friends in the first & second conflict & should you be called soon again to another engagement may he be with you, watch over, and protect you from the enemies darts, with everyone that has so promptly volunteered his service to his country's cause.

I am pleased with the arrangements made by the company with regard to the band of music, think it will meet approbation of the people generly, they being so fond of music. I have not learned Dixie yet, I have not the words, & am not sure thay have the correct tune here.

Nothing would give me greater pleasure than to spend an evening with all you boys in camp, to hear you sing & talk with you all about every thing that has transpired in the last six months, but this cannot be, it will do to write about but may not be realized now, though I hope the time is not far in the future when that desire may be gratified. The girls are in right good spirits at present, I believe they have all determined to spend their time as pleasantly & also as useful as possible, they perform their routine of duties cheerfully, no doubt looking forward to a time when their absent friends will return to them, when their happiness will be as near perfect as mortals are allowed to enjoy.

Sallie, Kate, Lissa & Jane Smith passed the window just now going out to Mr Lillards to see Vern who arrived there yesterday.

I was at Mr Russells last week, they were all well. Mary is teaching school at Martins Schoolhouse. Ten & Vina went to Coz Bill Lillards yesterday. I sent your letter to the girls to read. Frank are you boys as generous in that particular as we girls? We allow each other to read our letters, that is, most of them.

Mr Russell received a letter from Dave last week, he writes Mr Rice's family is sick, Miss Taylor is very much dissatisfied, says she does not want to live there, die there, nor be buried there.

[NOTE: This is Mary Taylor, sister of Peach Taylor, who had moved to Texas with her sister and brother-in-law, Alexander and Lucinda (Taylor) Rice. B.J.B.]

Mr Abe Denton was in town last Thursday, going on home from Chattanooga, he says the Union feeling in Hamilton is growing beautifuly less. What is Frank Lillard doing these times. I never hear anything about him these days. Do you drill every day? How do you spend Sundays? Has Mr Frazier ever preached for you since the battle.

Have you heard about Hues Cates effort at preaching. Last meeting he & Mr Sandusky explained to the church that they had been called to preach, the church agreed to permit them to try their gifts at an exhortation. Huse arose on Sabbath selected his text and then proceeded but did not say much. Mr S did not try his hand that meeting. I guess he will be prepared by the time their Sacramental meeting comes in which will be in October. You will not be here to gallant Miss Read this time what do you suppose she will do.

This is court week but there will not be any court, the judge has written he will not be in attendance. Guess what I'm going to employ myself at this week. Well I bet you cant guess, I going to weave carpet, what do you think of that Old Abe! Tell Mr Cox the big Injun was in Decatur the other day looks larger than he did when he was here before. I've got my striped quilt finished aint you glad.

Hola has been visiting at Athens three or four weeks, Crate also has been there & at Cleveland. Lizzie

King returned home– "I'll write to Liz shore"! Now we will see whether you put that threat in execution, if it was made in sleep, Frank, you ought not to talk so loud in your sleep, some one might chance to hear you some time. I know you are wearied now reading my nonsense, you must not be mad with me for writing it. I have no one to talk to & I am compelled to kill time in some manner. That doubled & twisted Love was received with pleasure. Give my doubled & twisted & then doubled again love in return. Give my kindest regards to all the boys accept the best wishes of your unflinchingly

Sarah McCorkle

You must not think strange of my enclosing two letters in one envelope; these hard times I wish to be as economical as possible.

- - - - - - - - - - - - -

LETTER NO. 24
SARAH A. BLEVINS TO B.F. TAYLOR

Decatur, Sept 1st 1861

Cousin Frank

Hiley esteemed friend, I this beautiful Sabath morning resume my pen to write you; in answer to your kind letter reseaved several days or week you might say: (Oh! Frank for give me)

I am proud to say this Sabaths morn finds us all well as far as I know. I hope it may find you with the rest of my friends in good health. I have no news to write you that would interest you at present. There is not much sparking going on now nor will not be untill the Decatur Gard gets back, for the girls all say they will never Marry a man that will not fight for his country and southern rites, and thats so sartan.

Frank, on the 28th of last month there was great excitement in and around Decatur in consequence of apart of Capt Gass of Rhea and Capt Snow of Hamilton Co caverley companeys pasing thrugh here, I know not there business, but it is suposed that they are just skouting about to see and learn all they can consurning the union party, and to take the post office key from all the Linkhonnrites this is Just supposition.

I have read of the battle in Mo, and in Va and its where and find the the defeat of the enemy on all occasions; and it all sumed up it shoes like the God of battle is on your side and as long as he is your general you will conquer yes, conquer! he has said in his holy word; put your trust in me and I will repay thee, Concolen thought to think the great God and Angles are extending the arm of protection over and around you all; may he continue his blessing is the wishes of your umble Servent; with the rest of our friends in Decatur and vicinity, I know they all wish you all the good luck that hearts can wish for. I can go to church and hear the petition assending the hill of zion in behalf of the volunteers who have left their weeping mother brother and sister and friends to assist in defending their homes and fiersides.

May the God of peace be with you & all the rest of my kindred and friends & protect you during your stay there, & when you have served your time bring you to your home with peace pearched upon your victorous banner and frames of lorals with you is the prars of she who is trying to communicate her thoughts to one that my cousins I esteem greatly. I will bring my scribling to an quit -?-iss as I have to write to my sweet heart this evening; write soon and I will answer instanter. Yours affectinately

Sarah A. Blevins

N.B. give my love to those who may inquire after me if any such may be and especley to Mr M V St and your captain and 1st lieutenant. May plesent dreams accompany your slumber (My love to my dear brother).

Yours unflinchingly S A Blevins

- - - - - - - - - - - - -

LETTER NO. 25
ISAAC G. CROSS TO WILLIAM S. ARRANTS

Fairfax Station, Va.
Sept 4th 1861

Wm S Arrants Esqr

Dear Brother

I received yours of last month Yesterday and was glad to hear that you was well again and that my family are well, the first thing I look for when I get a letter is to see that my little fellows are all well. The health of the Company is much better than it has been for some time past.

We have just returned from scout of eight days, we have bearded the Lyon in his den, went in sight of Washington City, Alex[andria] and Arlington heights and fought their pickets for 8 days, we lost one man killed out of our regt from Capt Dill's Company. There is a continual fire going on between the Pickets day and night. Our line of pickets extended a long way up and down the Potomack. Takes about 2000 men on Picket at one time, our boys have more chracter for Dare Devilism than any troops in the Army.

You wold have laughfed to have seen them Down there on Picket cralling up through the weeds and along the fences like they wer creeping on a duck shoot and fall down and load again. They will not stand the flash of a Musket, I mean the Yankees. We are going down there again in few days, We have had some fine fun down there the citizens wer all union men and had run off and confiscated their rosten Ears Potatoes and Chickens and some times a fat Pig.

We will have some more fighting here before long and I think if we can give them another good troten we will have some chance for peace. Wise has give them fits in Western Va. Frank Martin says that as he came up yesterday he saw a whole company from the Captain down going to Richmond.

I want you to fix that matter if you can with Jerry without paying the money till I come home if you cannot tell Mary to give you $50.00 and pay it that much.

As Buck Stuart will be able to give you all the news and it is getting too dark to write, I will conclude. Send this to Mary so she can see that I am well. I dont suppose I will be at home till we are discharged, give my best respect to all and take to yourself the best wishes of a friend. I. G. Cross

- - - - - - - - - - - - -

LETTER NO. 26
B.F. TAYLOR TO PEACH TAYLOR

Fairfax Station, Va., Sept 5th 1861

Dear father:

This morning I have the opportunity of responding to the demands of your verry kind and highly apreciated letter which came to hand on the eavening of the 31st, but owing to Suraunding circumstances could not be answered sooner. Your letter found me at a place called Munson's Hill about 12 or 13 miles in the direction of Alexander and Washington City.

On Wednesday morning the 28th of Aug at daylit we were ordered into line to march to that point to whip the Yankeys off and take possession of the hill, it was taken without the loss of a single man, 2 or 3 slightly wounded. We are fortifying this hill and 2 others on each side of the one above mentioned. These hills command a view of Washington and a part of Alexander. It is about 7 miles to Washington and 5½ to Alexander.

We remained at that place 7 days and returned to our camp at the Station. Our picket guards were Stationed in 440 yards of the Northern picket with but a little field between. We Shot at each other day and night during the time we stayed. I had the pleasure of shooting at them several times myself but do not know whether I hit or not, we killed 8 or 10 among us so they say and but one on our side, he belonged to Capt Dills company, he was shot through the head.

We learned this morning that those who came and relieved us taken an other hill yesterday between Orlington hights and Alexander cuting off all communication between the 2 points, our loss was about 20 their loss 2 or 3 hundred. I fear the report is not true but they say it is reliable hop to God it is.

I cannot write more conserning the war at present. Mr Frazier and Buck Stewart can give the news better than we can write it. The money mentioned in your letter was not sent from the fact that the person we intended sending it by failed to get off and I requested Capt Lillard to send home after a note he had a gainst me and I would pay it off, in a few days they had another opportunity to send and the Capt failed to mark my money out. I was sorrow to hear of the mistake, hope this will be satisfactory.

I am going to send by Mr Buck Stewart $100.00 which I want you to use if you kneed it for anything or in any way, if you do not wish to use it in any way take the amount out that you let me have when I started and when I come home from Knoxville and lay the rest out in the way that you think will best promote my interest. I feel under ten thousand obligations for that noble pair of boots you sent in such favor will not be forgoten soon. They would have cost me 9 or 10 dollars here.

If you have an opportunity I want you to send me some bed clothing such as have the greatest warmth, say one blanket and one comfort is all the bed clothing I want, clothing for my self 2 pr socks, 1 pair slips and one or 2 pair of paints the most servisable and comfortable that I have at home. The reason I make this request is because I see in the papers that there is a man to be appointed in each county to bring such things to the Volunteers of each county. Pay yourself out of my money for the boots and other things you may send to me.

If you wish to send any of my letters to Texas send the one I wrote Brother John concerning the battle of Manases, perhaps it will be of more interest to them as they have not a full report of the battle.

You wished to know who was flag barer. It is caried by a Sargent and guard of corporals, no one appointed. I sent a --?-- cap by Virn Lillard that I captured off a retreating Yankey at Manases on the 21 July. If he has not sent it to you yet I want you to go and get it, It will be warm to ware this winter and very nice.

I will now have to close. I am a shamed of this badly writen and composed letter and hope you will look over it as I had to write in great hast. Give my love to Mother and all the family with all my connection and friends. I close hoping to hear from you soon.

Your affectionate son
B.F. Taylor

P.S. Tell Osburn & Amanda I will answer their letters in a few days. I am 8 or 10 letters behind with my friends and others, but will answer them all as soon as I can. I am in good health as I wish for, the health of the company is generally good Ben F

- - - - - - - - - - - - -

LETTER NO. 27
AMANDA LILLARD TO B.F. TAYLOR

Near Decatur, Sept 5th 1861

My Dear Cousin

Though a long period has elapsed since I last wrote you It was not because I'd forgotten you far from that but partly through neglect, And knowing you would get many letters giving a statement of all that takes place in Meigs, and surrounding Co, so excuse me for not writing sooner.

I am at a loss what to write you that would be interesting or new. First, the people of Meigs are well as common some sickness here and there occasionally; not very dangerous but Margaret Blevins, she has the fever bad and very bad at that. I don't think she will ever get well, though she may. Your folks or a part of them has had the chills, though I understand they are much better.

Frank, the excitement in Meigs was very grate last week from the fact that the Soldiers was passing every day going through to Rhea Co. The opinion of some was that the born Secessionists and black hearted union men would have a battle at X roads on yesterday. Do not know how it turned out, but I have not heard from there today. If they do fight, I hope the Secession flag will continue to float over her gallant boys, and that they may crush and crumble those that supports the banners of the old Stars and Stripes.

You ought to be here and see how the unions men look. I don't believe one union man in Meigs could look a Seceisionist in the face two seconds to save his own life; they look like they want to hurt(?) --?-- da--?-- in which to conseel themselves for one year.

The young ladies of Meigs are going to pay the Soldiers in Rhea a visit this week, probably next Saturday and I hope I will make one of the number. O, I do wish you and the other boys I mean our Decatur boys was hear to go with us, how much pleasenter the time would pass off. But we have got a little use to going a bout with out the company of gentlemen.

I guess against you com back we will not know any thing about entertaining young gentlemen. We have had preeching in town yesterday and today. Mr. Husted Cates delivered one of his best sermons; also Granvill Sandusky. They did very well you know.

I wish you could have been on hand (you had better think Castes preached from his text). Rev Roy preeched a very good sermon this morning, he prayed the best prayer I ever heard for the protection of Soldiers.

I have been at Uncle James Lillard's ever since yesterday morning enjoying myself finly. Saw more frins since Ive been here than all put together that I have saw in 5 months. This morning Sunday as it was Lizzie, Crate and myself had a candy pulling before meeting time and I laugh till I couldnt laugh any longer. Lizzie is saving you some candy untill you come home. Miss --?-- was out at your house last monday also Emma K that looks brotherly; Miss Kate L was at meeting today --?-- catch any beau, we heardly ever get any only those on the Ribbon --?--.

So you not think that it is hard times Crate did this line, I hooked one the other day and I wanted to choak him with a Pap-?-. I will as to close soon a -?-ohn had com after us I didn't expect to go home this evening. Give my love to all the boys, write soon a long letter and I will do better the next time. Be a good boy dear. From your Cousin Amanda Lillard

My best respects, your true friend, Crate

- - - - - - - - - - - - -

LETTER NO. 28
I.G. CROSS TO *THE ATHENS POST*
(published 4 October 1861)

Camp Blair, Va. Sept 21st 1861

Dear Post:

Two months ago today was fought the memorable battle of Manassas. Not having an opportunity to visit the place since that time till today, by permission of Col. Vaughn I set out early in the morning, accompanied by Dr. E.D. Gilbert, by the way of Centerville, to take a view of the battle ground. But on our arrival at the place, there was no comparison between the two days, except the beautiful sun that shone most brilliantly and warm. Instead of the loud hoarse sound of the cannon, the shrilling whistle of the missles of death, the dark clouds of dust and smoke, the stern, firm, deep tones of the commanders of brigades and regiments, and the crashing sound of cavalry, nothing but the songs of the little birds and the occasional voices of parties strolling over the wasted field in search of the spot where some loved one had fallen. Instead of a hostile enemy, maneuvering back and forward, nothing marked the place but the little mounds that covered the fallen soldier.

It is not altogether pleasing to the reflecting mind to visit the sanguinary field. For amid victory, there is a disposition in the feeling heart to say, would to God the blow could have been averted. The place around where Sherman's Battery was taken sends up a tremendous stench yet, owing to the number of horses killed there and the shallow depth the slain were buried. A most notable fact the citizens told me, there had not been a vulture on or about the ground since the battle, which is proved by the decayed carcasses of the horses.

On a travel over the field, it seems the line is a semicircle from where Sherman's Battery was taken, around in the direction of the Blue Ridge. You can trace the line to where the 8th Georgia Regiment fought so bravely by the timber that is scarred, and the occasional post that has been erected to mark the spot where this or that officer fell. Among other marks, in a large pine thicket where almost every saplin had been struck, and some four or five times, we found a beautiful marble slab erected to the memory of Capt. (blank) of the 8th Georgia Regiment.

On our search, we came round to the line where our Brigade had fought, and where I learnt for the first time the spot on which the Federal Col. Cameron fell. It was some satisfaction to know that he had fallen, probably by the hands of the people upon whose homes and brethren he was helping to fix the shackles of military despotism. I mean Maryland, as the 1st Maryland line belongs to our brigade; and a noble band they are. Here we poured the ganling fire into the enemy's rear as they retreated through the field now marked by many graves, which show that our boys took good aim.

THE TURN OF THE TIDE—FIRST MANASSAS, JULY 21, 1861.

After following the line round to the place where Capt. Morelock was wounded and obtaining some momentoes, we returned to our starting point and visited the place at which Col. Bartow fell, which is marked by a beautiful marble post, with the inscription, "They have killed me, Boys, but never give up the fight." It will be remembered that he fell just as his noble hand was about to capture the celebrated Sherman Battery, as I was in forty or fifty yards of it.

After calling on an old darky friend hard by and getting some cool water and a splendid dinner, we wended our way to camp, much pleased with our visit.

I.G. Cross

- - - - - - - - - - - - -

LETTER NO. 29
PEACH TAYLOR TO B.F. TAYLOR AND I.G. CROSS

Meigs County, September 22nd 1861

Dear Sons

I am again permitted through the kind providence of God to Answer your kind and affectinate letter Dated the 15 and 16th Instance which gives us grate Satisfaction to learn that you & Isaac was bouth in the land of the living Injoying the Comforts and blessing of this life and in good health With all our relations and friends in Captain Lillard Company for we claim them all as our friends and Neighbors hoping when these lines comes to hand they may find you all Well and doing well in the Service of our beloved South and may the God of heaven continuly bless you with health and strength and preserve your lives to git home to the Imbraces of your friends and Relations at home again.

Your letter I am answering came to hand yesterday, I allso received your letter you sent by Mr Sturt and one from Isaac with one hundred Dollars Each of you sent. This letter I want to be of Equeall use to you both. I Received the Cap you Sent by Vern Lillard. We are all in as good health as could be expected, Onley Osburn & Amanda they have had the Chills for the last two Weaks of and on, Osbourn is going a bout and has not had any chill for the last 10 or 12 Days. Amanday has had them Stop twist but Every few Days they come back. She has had a Chill to Day.

We have had the Wettest Summer and fall So far I Ever have Seen in my life, the Wet Weather Branches is Still Running flush. the health of the Countrey is generally good. Onely chills or Ague(?) John and Ann & children is all well.

Osburn Wrote you a letter last Monday before I got our last letter and stated Something about sending you some Close & Bed Close in a few Days. Your Mother and Mary is making you & Isaac a Suit of muset(?) Jeans as you requested in your letter. We will have it maid and attended to as you Directed Soon, With all the bead close & Waring Close you & Isaac Sent for. M T Vincen is making Isaac Boots he sais they Will be Worth Six Dollars.

I here of a grate many a going to send things to there friends thare best Object to sending for 8 or 10 Days untill you are settled as we are Expecten you to have another hard battell. We are allways glad to here from you but more so when we here of a battell on Tusday & Saturday the Post office is allways croyded to hiere from you and it dont matter hos writs we are glad to hear from you or any of you.

I have not seen Mr Frazier since he come back he has bin on the --?-- Ever since he came back this is Tusday the 24th I comenced Writing on Sunday Evingin but Oing to the health of Mary Cross & children I did not finish till to Day.

September the 24 1861

Mr I.G. Cross. Dear Son

After my best Respects to you and to Company I Wish to inform you of the health of your family. On this day was a weake John & Sary both had a chill. Mary got Sum midisin and gave them and yesterday they both mist thear chill and is better. Mary has bin here Ever Since they have bin Sick.

On Saturday She thout She had a lite chil was not very well I thaut is best not to finish my letter till I knew how things wor abut to work With hir an yesterday Mary Child a gain this is nothing Elce but every other day Ageue. She will stay here on till they all git better and maby till you git back if you ever live to see that Day.

I want you bouth & all of you to act prudently and put your trust in the God of battle who is the best of all friend who can be presant to Administer to your Wants When your earthly friends Can not.

A.L. Cross was here last Sunday was a weake his Company was stationed at Post Oak Spring, but would leave in a few days he staid only two days he is well.

We have had as continual Confusion with the Union men in the lore end of this county & the lore end of Rhea & Hambelton County. Ever Since the State went Out of the Union thare has bin four companeys stationed at the Cross Roads in Rhea Ct for three weeks past 2 hors Companeys and 2 foot Companeys. I was Down in Camp yesterday they have taking a grate many of the Union men and leaders of the party and maid them take the Oath. What they Did not take prisoner they came in gave up, I think they had better flee to the Sitey of Refuges for We are after them Strait Out.

I will give you the names of there Companey. J. Crawford maid up of Meigs & Rhea Counteys boys mostley Rhea. E. Bougus of Meigs County boys these two part Companeys left yesterday for Fourt Trusdail by the way of Nashville the 2 hos Companey are Still thare a wating Orders they have 25 or 30 Dozen with the Measels Mostley in Captain Gasses Company Maid up of Brday & Meigs Countey boys 8 of this Company is from the Decature Destrict.

I think if a few more leave we will not be able to gether our Big Crop of Corn in the Cuntery. Captain Snow of Hambleton is the other Company. I lerned yesterday that some one has taken old Dugan as a prisoner on Saturday to Knoxville, I allso learn theare has been a Battell by our forces and the Union men at Barbers Ville in the eadge of Kentuckey, Our men gained the Victrey With Out Much lost Killing and taking prisners Severl hundred they takin one man Went Over from Kingston by the name of Bard. Mr Speare of ---?---
--ey and Dr Truiet are bout over in Kentuckey heading a Company. Spears has bin sendin letter to his Sun and his Sun distribting to the Union men. They have taken him. I must close for the present, but Remains your affectionate till Deth

Peach Taylor

- - - - - - - - - - - -

LETTER NO. 30
I.G. CROSS TO JAKE TAYLOR

Camp Blair, Va.,
September 27th 1861

Dear Sir

I received yours of the 18th inst, and was glad to hear that you was all well. This leaves me in tolerable health, I have been a little unwell for a day or two but am getting better, nothing more than cold I suppose. We got in from Maysons hill last night nothing very strange occured while we wer there, had no fighting to do. Maysons hill is about two miles from Munsons from whare I wrote you before. The Yankees came out the other day above Falls Church but on the approach of our troops they ran into their holes. We would go over occasionally while up there and get the latest northern papers from thar Pickets. One gave Hugh Blevins went over and one gave him 25 cts and he gave him a plug of tobacco. There is no shooting between the Pickets at Mayson Hill.

Tell Mary to see Jack Davis and get him to cut the Coat. I want a Military Coat. The pants tell her she knows how to make them. Tell her to get Blue silk velvit about one inch and a half or inch and quarter wide for the stripe up the leg. Tell her That Dr Gilbert will attend to the bringing them up. I fear if they are started without someone with them I will never get them. Tell her if their is no other chance to send them as first Directed. Tell her that she need not send me a blanket. I have three. As I had a letter written for Mary when I received yours and give pretty much all the news and as you will get them at the same time I will not write much more.

I would like to be at home a while and see you all. Tell your Mother to have that Supper ready I will be there in six or seven months. I want you all to keep writing more and longer. Tell John I want him to take those steers & pay Hunter for them or sell them and pay for them. Yours very respectfull

I. G. Cross

- - - - - - - - - - - -

LETTER NO. 31
B.F. TAYLOR TO AMANDA TAYLOR

Camp Blair, Va., Sept 28th 1861

Loving Sister:

This beautiful Saturday eavening I have the pleasure of drafting you a few lines in answer to your kind and highly interesting little letter which came to hand some days or weeks ago. I hope you will pardon me for not writing sooner from the fact that I have wrote to others in the family and what I write to one I write to you all because you are all near and dear to me by the ties of nature, and though we are at this time separated by many long miles some high mountains and deep rivers yet we are nearer than ever before in feeling.

I have but little to write this evening that will be of any interest to you as I wrote yesterday eavening to Osburn giving all the news that would be of any interest. I stated in my letter to Osburn that we had orders to cook 5 days provisions and be ready to march at a moments warning. We have not started yet but are still under the same orders, it may be that we will not go atall, that I cannot tell.

Osburn stated in his letter to Isaac that Mother and Mary wished to know how we wanted our coats cut. We want them cut frock coats and cut uniforme stile, Mr Frazier will see to that. J A Davis has our measures like he cut our coats before we left he will do the cuting. I want my coat cut larger than the one he cut before we left for Knoxville, larger in every respect and longer in the tail and sleavs. I will write to him or Frazier about that.

I do not think I will nead the pants Mother speaks of making and nead not make them without she wants to as the other 2 pr she speaks of sending I think will do me until we return though they will be warmer than what I have. I will now close as I wish to write 2 or 3 other letters and perhaps one to my sweet heart or june bug as we some times call them.

I want you to write to me immediately after reception, commence your letters as you see my letter is commenced. I mean in reference to the caption and begin all proper names with a capitol letter such as the name of individuals particular states rivers mountains and the like, when you do not know how to spell a word go to the dictionary or grammer in the back of the spelling book. Mandy do not think from this that I thought your letter unworthy of notice, far from this I assure you. Your letter was well writen and composed for your practice and chance, far beyond my expectation I assure you. I did not think you would be able to write half such a letter as you did. Being so well pleased with your letter I am willing to give you all the instruction I can.

I want you to write often & improve all you can, study your books all you can such as the spelling book and english grammer. I want you to make a good schollar of your self. I will do all I can for you when I return. Take pains with your writing. I will now close hoping to hear from you immediately. My love to you all. Your loving brother

B. F. Taylor

- - - - - - - - - - - - -

LETTER NO. 32
KATE LEUTY TO B.F. TAYLOR

Decatur, Sept 29th 1861

Esteemed Friend.

I have once more had the pleasure of reading another kind and interesting letter. You cannot imagine how much pleasure it is to read a letter from those who have left their homes and gone to fight for our liberties suffering the hardships of Camp life for surely you all must have more hard service to perform than any other regiment in the Southern army. We never hear from you but what you either have just returned from or are preparing to go out on picket duty. But with all this you have been very fortunate so far and I sincerely hope may continue to escape all the Yankey bullets that are constantly Whizzing around your head.

Since I last wrote you another one of our school mates (Meg Blevins) has died. On the 22nd at 11 oclock after suffering 7 weeks death relieved her of the sorrows of life, we hope transplanted her to a clime where troubles will come no more and where all sorrows are healed.

I should have liked very much to heard you rather seen you shoot that one as you say you think it is the one that shoot Mr. Baldwin. I hope it was the same one. I wish you could all be here at the meeting which is next week so you could help Wallen(?) sing pretty little angel and hear Houston Cate preach another sermon on the blockade. I know it would amuse you to see him in the pulpit.

Frank you do not know how much you are all missed here when we go to church there are so many vacant seats it looks very strange not only at church but every where else the corners all look so lonesome where you used to all seem to enjoy your selves so often those familiar voices are hushed for awhile, but hope it wont be long till you will all return here to mingle again with your kind friends an relatives who would appreciate your society so much, for myself I can say the happiest hours of my life have been spent with you all who are now off protecting our homes and firesides.

Rachel Howell said give you her best wishes says you are one of her favorites among the young gentlemen of Meigs, says she hopes your life will ever be as brilliant and bright as the stars that shine in heaven at night.

I will not write any more to night as Tenn McCorkle has called over to stay all night and wishes to write some on the next page. I remain as ever your true friend. Kate Leuty

Lissa said to tell you could beat any body singing and playing Dixie and the Southern wagon wants you to take good care of Ed and when you return home she will sing and play for you.

- - - - - - - - - - - - -

LETTER NO. 33
TENNESSEE McCORKLE TO B.F. TAYLOR

Decatur, Sept 29th [1861]

Dear Friend Frank

You will no doubt be somewhat surprised at seeing a strang hand writing in Kates letter. I have called over to stay all night with her and she was writing and asked me to write some to you. I did not know whether it would be very acceptable to you or not but being as well aware of your generousity and leniency I make an effort to write a few lines.

There is nothing of interest going on here at present, the people are in very good health at present about here. I have been gone on a visit up in Monroe County, was gone nearly three weeks, did not enjoy myself as well as I have done frequently during visits that I have taken previous to this from the fact I could not hear from you all soo oft as when at home and that is the greatest pleasure I have thes days hearing from my absent friends at least I am egotistical enough to flatter myself that I have friends among you, yes I believe I have friends there that have been my friends even from infancy up some that I have associated with from my earliest recollection and there are also friendships of a more recent date that I prize very highly and wish to retain so long as I am permited to live.

I hope you may all be spared to return home again to mingle with kind friends and relatives that would appreciate your society very much and also to renew your associations with the girls if you feel inclined so to do if not as it was formerly in what ever way you would enjoy yourselves most. The girls about here all seem somewhat like old women, they are a good deal more serious than they were previous to your departure, I think they will liven up when you all return.

I must tell you what a joke I have on Kate. I was over here this evening before supper and she had on her dirty dress and when I came back after supper she had changed dresses neat and clean colar her silk apron, had her hair combed very nicely and had come round in the room next to Miss Pass with a light pretending that she intended to write some and all the while she was just looking for Tommy. I did not mean to tell but it sliped. Suspecioning her to be expecting him I steped up rather heavily knocked on the door with a stick I had in my hand. She came and opened the door and was blushing tremendously.

He has been calling I understand very regularly and for all I know this may have been the eavening set apart for her to give the answer it looks that way from the blushes you just ought to seen how flumexed(?) the gal looked when she saw it was just me. He is a nice boy I have been loving him a little myself but think from appearances my cake(?) is dough(?)

Frank, I hope you will excuse my presumption in writing to you without your requesting me to do so, if you consider this writing of a few words in responce I would be happy to hear from you and if not you can treat it with silent contempt. I could write you more foolery if time and space would permit, but I fear I have already sorely taxed your patience with my scrawl. I remain as ever your affectionate Friend

Tenn McCorkle

- - - - - - - - - - - - -

[Stationary used for Letter No. 34 is reproduced on top of following page]

LETTER NO. 34
B.F. TAYLOR TO PEACH TAYLOR

Camp Blair,
Sept 30th 1861

Dear father:

At this late hour of the night I have the pleasure of droping you a few lines in answer to your kind and affectionate letter which came to hand by to days mail. It found me with the entire company in good health. I will say with the exception of 2 or 3 who are a little puny. I was truly sorrow to hear of the bad health of the family, I mean Osburn and Amanda with Mary and her family, but I do hope that their health will be better soon if not at the present time. This is all I can do is to wish for better things. I am glad she is at your house and think it would be best for her to stay with you especially while they are sick so that you can see that they have all the necessary attention paid to them.

Father I have but little to write to you that will be of much interest as every thing is lying so low at this time but from what can be seen and heard I think those who live to tell the story will have plenty to write about in a few days. Jeff Davis arrived at this place on this evenings train and went out to Fairfax to night which is about 3 miles from our camp.

And other evidences we have of something going to be done soon is that our generals have been holding private consultations every day and almost every hour for 4 or 5 days past. General Beauregard was heard to say the other day that their would be a move made in less than 6 days that would astonish the entire world. This is hearsay I cannot vouch for its truth, I mean what Beauregard said.

Our force is withdrawn from those hills where we have been picketing for the last 5 or 6 weeks. The Yankeys now have posession of them and out as far as Falls Church. I think the object in withdrawing them was to get the Northern force scatered as much as pos-

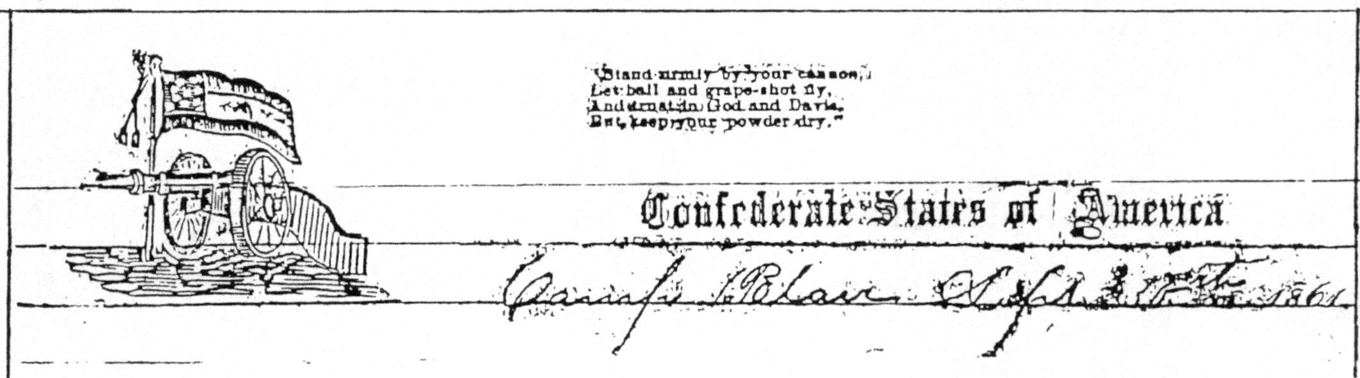

possible so that we would have a better chance at Washington City and Orlington hights.

It is now growing late I will close for to night and write more in the morning before mail. Good night to you all.

Tuesday Morning October 1st 1861

This morning finds us in good health and all quiett in camp. I have nothing new to write this morning and will close in a few minutes. As to the coat triming you can get all that is necessary in Decatur or Washington with the exceptions of the buttons Stars and shoulder stripe. I can get them here and get Mat Benson to put them on when the coat comes. Tell Jack Davis to go to any of the stores and get such trimings as he neads for the coat, to work the button holes and I will get Benson to set the buttons on when it comes. I already have the shoulder straps. I will now close, hoping to hear from you soon. I will write soon again if I have the time, as often as twice each week to some of you. My best love to you all, Your loving son

Lieut B.F. Taylor
Co I, 3rd Regt Tennessee Vol

- - - - - - - - - - - - -

LETTER NO. 35
JOHN B. TAYLOR TO I.G. CROSS AND B.F. TAYLOR

Meigs County, October the 2, 1861

Mr. Isaac G. Cross.
Dear brother

This eavening seat my self to try to write you a few lines to let you know that I had not forgotten you and to let you know how we are all doing at present. I as to my part is well Ann and the children is well. Mary H. Cross has been chilling some few times but has got it stoped on her Sary and John has been chilling a few times and is litely chilling ocasionly yet. Doctor hodg [Hodge] was at my house yesterday and gave them some quinine and I think that it will all be over in a few days. Emily and James Grundy is well and just as mischievous as any other two. James O. Taylor and Manda is chilling ocasionly yet when ever they take an over gorge of vietles. Father and Mother is well with the exception of their growling Mood.

We had the pleasure of a visit paid by Mr A.L. Cross on yesterday, he came steping in for breckfast yesterday morning he remained with us until after dinner he then said he would gow down to Russells and stay all night and then next morning would Start back to camp at postoak Springs where he would get with his and the other company and then these two companys would start to Cumberland gap, and from thence to Kentuckey he allowed. Absalom looks as well as you ever saw him and appears to be well pleased with his trip he has the same office that he had when he went to Mexico. Corporal you know.

So no mor upon that subject you wrote about your oxens and hogs we sold the oxens to Solomon Henry for the same you gave for them on a credit bearing interest from date and William Henry Security to it your hogs I am fatning my self one half for the other I have thirteen of them. I will make them so fat that there will not be an eye at either ends of them.

When your corn is fit to gather I intend to gather it if you desire it and will get some hands and crib it rite up. I will throw it in my crib and yours with the Shuck on and will build cribs at the lower end of the bottoms for my self. I will now write a few lines to B.F. Taylor and wish when you read this that you will hand it to him.

Lieutenant B.F. Taylor Esq

Dear brother. I again after so long a time since I last wrote you I drop you a few lines to let you know that I have not forgotten you. I am well at present and hope when these few lines comes to hand that you may be found enjoying good health and doing well. I have thought time and again that I would write but there was always something turned up to hinder.

I will just say to you that Ann has maid a bed comfort to send to you and since she finished it Mother has been pursuading us not to send it for she intended to send the one she has any how hers is lined with a blanket and hours with domestick but is a good heavy comfort and I want to send it to you if you kneed it. I intend to send you a pair or two of socks if you kneed such as a flannel shirt. I will get it and send it to you, your suit of jeans you sent for will bee prepaired as soon as posible it is going up with a kind of vien your Bead Cloathing and other things you sent for will be on the first chance or pasing.

I will tell you how the Cecession brethern served our old brother dugin at the close of his prayer at Cedar Springs, they arrested him and made him walk to Athens and from there to Knoxville to try him for the deeds done in the body. I want you and Isaac G Cross to write to me Soon and I will try to do better next time.

Yours respectfully

John B. Taylor

- - - - - - - - - - - - -

LETTER NO. 36
SARAH A. BLEVINS TO B.F. TAYLOR

Decatur, Oct 10th A.D. 1861

Cousin Frank

I am afforded this glorious privlidge of acknowling the resept of your very kind and much aprectiated letter which was read time and again, its contents carfreley noted to my memory. Happy to know that I am still remembered by my intimate friends and acquantances; and more over those that have gon in defence of there southern independence.

It is hard to part with those dear friends that in days past and for ever gon that fild the friendlay family sircle and made time so swiftley glide away. Oh! that times war now as they once were, but alas; that time is gone never more to return. The love ones has bid farewell to friends and home and taking up the line of march to the tented field on the battle plains to blockade the northern invader that was once our friends but know our foes from invading the sunie South a thing that never shall be accomplished by the rebles as long as Jacksons blood is permitted to flow thru the vaines of southern sons, and if prayors and tears will help the cause on I know we will be aded by the great god the ruler and protecter of all good; for it looks as if he has been with us in the gaining of the grate and glorious victorious in the Mo battles; and the great victory on the Manassas plain and every where elce that the southern troops has been attacked; (the hand of ombipance can accomplish more in one hour) than old Abe Lincoln and his cabnet and minion of forces can accomplish in a sentry of years. And if the great --?-- is for us who can be against us.

There banner has bin made to train in the dust before our faces; they had to surender to that, and their two hundred and fifty thousand dollar in specie to be unberied that they had stolen from the southern bank.

As I before said their banner has bin maid to trail in the dust, and ours has not, it has always been able to hold her head above the breeze and will continue to do so as long as the brave sons of Tennessee and her sister states can list the name of a Washington or a Jackson, or even the word secession and our southern rites.

I glory in our brave confederate states they are out numbered by the fedrel and their population are three to one and perhaps more for ought I know, that maks no differance you have whiped them time and again and caused them to run and leave their dead and dying their wounded, their provisions their bagged and nearley there all, this has been dun by eaven on the soil of Mo, Ky, and Va the stat of our forfathers fought the strugle of our one independence, and this once glorious union to save.

This epistol leaves me and --?-- friend well with the exception of your sister Amanda & Mary Cross two youngest children, they are chilling every day and Amanda every other day. So no more at present but remain as ever your affectionate Cousin

Sarah A. Blevins

Tell all the boys houdy for me and D M B & H B in particular.

- - - - - - - - - - - - -

LETTER NO. 37
W.F. BLEVINS TO D.M. & H.T. BLEVINS

Decatur, Oct 11th 1861

Dear Brothers

I am blessed with the oportunity of droping you a few lines to inform you that we are well and entertain the hope that this may find you in good health, this leaves us all the conection well as far as I know. I have nothing that would be of much intrest to you at present, more than there is considerable excitement in this section about the war this 30,000 call has excited this country very much there is being mad in this county two Company one cavalry and one infantry, the cavalry has been organized and will leave in three days or two weeks the officers of which are as follows: G W McKenzie Capt, W O Martin 1st Lieut, W W Lillard 2nd, D C Blevins 3rd, they havent elected ther non comissioned officers, they will get a full company, (the other) the infantry is headed by A W Hodge, R W Lillard, I R Binyan & others, it will be some time before they will get off but I think will finally get a good company.

I havent heard from Alfred since he left home, but there has been some letters received from Ky, stating that they were all in good health & also stating that they were fortifying a place called Bowling Green, the place wher they are now stationed as to myself they have been after me to volunteer & go with them. I have as yet refused & think I will continue so untill I hear from you and see whether or not I can get in to business where you are, my health is not first rate since the cold & rain that came affect my Rhumatism.

W.F. Blevins

Cou Frank: I want you to see to having that sore foot well attended to and I will be under lasting oblegation to you. Sallie

- - - - - - - - - - - - -

LETTER NO. 38
SARAH McCORKLE TO B.F. TAYLOR

Decatur, Oct 25, 1861

Friend Frank

This gloomy looking morning finds me seated to answer, in my weak manner, your kind note which was received yesterday. If I do not make my scroll interesting contribute it not to want of inclination, but want of matter for I believe though it were gotten up in an imperfect manner, nattural to me it would be interesting to you merely because it was from your native county & neighborhood.

I do not know of much sickness in the country except measels & hooping cough. Jenniny is just recovering from a spell of measels & her sister Sarah, I understand is taking them. No other case in town that I am aware of.

Messrs Perry & Runyon reached home last Sabbath they informed us of your return to near Manassas, we did not think for a moment that it was cowardice that prompted that move, for we all know you are as brave men as ever trod the soil of Virginia.

On yesterday about three O'clock Adjutant Cross & Sgt Gwinn rolled into our village, you can probably imagine what running there was among us to meet them, it makes our very souls glad to see our friends from camp comming & especially members of the Decatur Guards. God bless them, there are some of the cleverest, kindest, & biggest souled boys in that Company. I believe, in fact, I know it, that ever went into a tented field to fight for their Countrys Freedom, their own Independence their homes & friends. You may think I am endeavoring to flatter you boys but if I designed doing such a thing I am aware it would be a vain effort, but, "From the abundence of the heart, the pen writeth."

We still have very gloomy weather, we had a pretty heavy frost on the morning of the 24, it realy begins to look like Winter, the leaves are turning brown & falling to the ground, then will come our loneliest time, while it was warm & dry we could kill time by outdoor amusements, but in the dark, & dreary days of Stern winter we can only gather around the fireside & dream over past happy hours or build air castles, which will be as frail as the web which the spider forms to imprison the unconcious insect as it passes on its innocent errand; & which I have no idea will ever be realized.

While we are thus passing the time I would just turn my mind for a short space of time & think, what will you boys be passing your time, at times probably shivering with cold around your camp fires while the winds whistles his mournful tune around from the North where all worst enemys dwell, & again you may be traversing the surrounding country through snow, ice and rain, in pursuit of those detestable Yankees who have been the cause of all these troubles which have set the whole country in such confusion & uproad. But those vile hearted Leaders will some day, & it may be erelong, reap an abundant reward for all their crimes. They will surely be "weighed in the scales, and found wanting" when the time arrives for meeting out justice to all.

I was not very greately surprised at learning you were ignorant of my meening in referance to writing to that young lady as the threat was made during sleep. It was while you were at Knoxville one night when you had an unusually uncomfortable pallet. You no doubt wonder where I received my information; well I heard it from some one who came home while you were incamped at that place.

I am indeed happy to hear of Cinnings good success in Virginia hope his fondest anticipations may be realized, with satisfaction to all parties concerned. So Miss Kate need not expect to get any more cinnimy. I suppose Capt. McKinzies Comp met here Thursday last to receive their banner, but for some cause which I have not yet been able to ascertain the thing did not take place. The Capt received a letter from Gen Gillespie today which stated that he would muster them into service next Friday.

It is thought I.R. Binyon & Dr Hodges Comp will also be mustered in in that time. After these two Comps leave the men will be like angels visits in Meigs, dont you think? My impression Meigs will have done her part admirably, if Bradly would turn out as many she would show a much more praisworthy spirit than the way she is doing.

The men of Cleveland have been travelling round through this county purchasing all the homemade Janes, & heavey goods of other kinds suitable for men clothing, to carry away & speculate on among the soldiers; this shows a fine spirit does it not? They did not get anything here from anyone only Abel; he sold them his Janes.

Tenn requests me to write for her– she has received your letter was much pleased to hear from you & will answer in about a week when she gets up some news.

Give my best wishes to all and except the Friendship of Yours

Sarah McCorkle

Please say to Mr Cox I will write him as soon as I get something of interest & give him my compliments until I have something more important to present.

- - - - - - - - - - - - -

LETTER NO. 39
N.J. LILLARD TO ISAAC G. CROSS

Centerville, Va., Oct 26th 1861

Dear Adjt

Yours 23rd Inst, recd this evening glad to hear from you & the Boys. Sorry however to here of Simon Misfortune hope nothing Serious. We have herd the news of the Leesburg fight; we whiped them badly. Gen Evan fought them with four Regiments, they had 12; he taken Six pr Cannon, prisoners near 800, killed wounded & drowned a great many, the news this morning is that the Federals have Crossed at Leesburg again with a force of Fifty thousand & that ours was fighting them yesterday, there has been none of our troops down from this point except one or two Regiment we supposed they were gone on Pickett duty.

Dick is better, Massingale is not so well as when you left, think they both will be up in a few days. the fight upon the Potomac is Confirmed --?-- which you have in abundance. We have no positive Marching orders, But have been ordered to send off all Extra Baggus & be ready to move in 30 Minutes, What direction We know not.

Gen Elsey has been very sick and not much better now. I held on Yesterday an election in Co R. Acre was Elected 1st Lut, Miller 2nd Sr & Bullock 2nd Jr All Satisfied believe, Andeson & Smith Run against Bulloch beat them 10 Votes, they tied at 23 each, Everett & Shemoy(?) have both Resigned. Well what do you think Leut Acre Bro was amongst the Leesburg Prisnors he Seems much affected about it.

You must write me often while in Tenn. We want to here from you every Mail. The prospect for a fight is Some better than when you Left, When it will occur It is not known that Yankie is no further than Falls Church in any force. Your friend Respectively

N.J. Lillard

- - - - - - - - - - - - -

LETTER NO. 40
D.C. BLEVINS TO B.F. TAYLOR

Decatur, Novr 8th 1861

Dear Cousin

I have wated some time for an answer to my last letter but nothing came to hand. I hope you havent forsaken me. I think I now the hard ships of Camp life and the bad chance you have to write. So you are execsible(?). I would like to hear from you once more before I leave for Ky. I havent any nuse at all more that Liet Cross can tell you when he returns soon.

We expect to have pretty warm times in Ky and probably pretty hard, but we intend to meet it Squair up like Solgiers and never flinch. We cant bair the idea of Ten being invaded and let back upon us those E Ten tories that have run off from their own State and homes to take Shelter under Lincolns new(?) folleing(?) Banner no never.

Our Companey was mustered into Service on the lst Inst. We will go to Ky before long as Soon as we get drilled. When you hear from the McKinly Rangers you will hear of us doing Something. I wish you grate Success, hop you will get home Safe.

Give all the boys my best respect and except a good portion to your Self. Write to me as soon as this comes to hand, fair well. Your true friend and Cousin.

D. C. Blevins

- - - - - - - - - - - - -

LETTER NO. 41
ELMIRA LILLARD TO B.F. TAYLOR

Mr B.F. Taylor
3rd Tenn Reg Volunteers
Commanded by J C Vaughn, Fair Fax C H, Va

Friday night, Nov the 8th 1861

Ever remembered Cousin.

I know We ought to be thankful that We are spared even to Write to each other, But I cherish the hope that the day is not far distant When We can lay aside the pen and speak face to face. Frank you musnd think hard of me for not Writing sooner, because We have been so busy and another thing I had nothing that would interest you.

I have been waiting for Captain McKenzies Company to start and it is not gone yet; but think they will get off in a few days. They will probably go to Charleston to guard the Bridge. Captain McKenzie has got a good Company. O. Martin 1st Lieutenant, Pappa 2nd, Cousin D.C. Blevins 3rd, noncommissioned not elected yet.

We had quite a fine time in Decatur yesterday. The Company met for the purpose of receiving their Flag, and to start to Loudun. When the Mail came and brought them the news that tents could not be had for them yet a While, but was ordered to receive their Flag and be in rediness.

I had the honor of presenting it to them. Cousin Mary A. Blevins by my side supporting the Banner prepared. Cousin D.C. Blevins, in behalf of Captain McKenzie, made the reply in his peculiar pleasing manner, After which, We had a speech, or Speeches from General Lane, Doctor Hodge, and I.G. Cross. Amanda and I stayed all night at Aunt Ruths. We had quite a mery time, and would have been moreso had Cousin Hugh been able to have participated. I.G. got in a good way laughing and playing with the Girls as if he was a bout eighteen. When I left town this eve, he was packing up those boxes of clothing and contributions.

[NOTE: the speeches given by Elmira and David will be found in PART I in an article dated 15 November 1861. B.J.B.]

I expect to have to go to pulling corn in the morning. the Lord only knows how we will get along this winter without Pappa or John either. But I know you will help us hoe the corn next Summer when you all get home.

We got a letter from brother Hugh dated October the 12th, he was then at fort Smith, Arkansas, with the Texas Cavalry. Says he is well prepaired for the trip has plenty of good cloths and the best horse in the company. his address is H.T. Thomas, Capt Dyes Co., Fort Smith, Texas Rangers, Commanded by McCullock.

Well Sit I went to dry my writing and burnt my Letter, and Spoilt its disfigur. I am getting sertes kinder Sleepy as I did not sleep much last night, and expect you are wearied anyhow, So I will quit by giving you every appureance of my love and rememberance of my Cousin Ben. Good night

Elmira Lillard

I hope it will not be long until I hear from you again. E.L.

LETTER NO. 42
KATE LEUTY TO B.F. TAYLOR

Decatur, November 9th 1861

Dear friend Frank

This dark and gloomy morning I am afforded the pleasure of responding to your more than welcome letter of Oct 30th which came to hand a day or two ago giving the gratifying inteligence you was enjoying good health.

This evening Willie, Mr N J Lillard and Adjt Cross will leave up again for Va. I am always glad to see any of you come home but it seems like you get to stay so short a time with us we hate so bad to part now as at first.

We were all very much surprised to see Hugh Blevins step in at the door last Wednesday night. The girls were all at aunt Ruths at quilting, Sallie B. Tenn McCorkle and me had come down stairs were sitting around the fire talking very busy when we heard a tap at the door but did not pay much attention only said come in. The door opened and as a matter of course all eyes were looking to see who would enter but none recognizing him except me when he spoke I knew his voice. I could of heard aunt Ruth and Sallie hollowing a half a mile when they found it was him in a few minutes the house was crowded to see what was the matter.

We had a very interesting time here last Thursday. Capt McKenzies Company met for the purpose of leaving this place for Loudon were disappointed about getting camp equipage did not go. The flag was presented by Miss A Lillard. She made a nice speech. Lieut Dave Blevins replied after which there were speeches delivered by Gen Lane, Adgt Cross and Dr Hodges, every thing passed off as it always does here in Meigs.

Well I have no news of interest to write more than you will hear from those who are going. Amanda Lillard says you can inform her gissard(?) tinger(?) up there he need not suffer any fears about her and Mr Martin for he is going off in a few days.

Cousins Millie and Sallie Russell are here came last Thursday Mr. Martin also as he is generally on hand when they are had his horse ordered when he found they were going to stay sent it back and is here yet, think he is trying to spark Mary.

This is the time of the meeting I wrote you about that Parson Cates wife was to be baptised. She will have a soft time it has been raining all day and has the appearance of continueing. Amanda says she will do all she can if she is here to prevent them from kissing(?).

You say if your letters are too long and wearisom for me to inform you long letters are the kind I love to receive. I have never received one too long yet if they were six times as long I would not then get wearied.

Our new Circuit rider preached for us last Sabbath evening. I like him very well --?-- the acquaintance I have come(?) here in Friday and stayed untill Monday, he has only been married two months his wife is with him, she has the appeaeance of being a fine little woman. His name is Moore. Give my love to all and accept the best wishes of your true friend

Kate Leuty

LETTER NO. 43
SALLIE [McCORKLE?] TO B.F. TAYLOR

Decatur, Nov 21st 1861

Friend Frank

Your kind letter has been to hand a few days & tonight affords me the first opportunity of acknowledging the reception of the same. It found me & the people generly in the enjoyment of good health.

I have been expecting by every mail since I read your letter to hear of you leaving that point but am glad I can say that I have not yet heard it unless it was to come back to Tenn, which I presume is a vain hope.

We have been having some fun in our neighhood with the Lincolnites the men have been riding hither & yonder for about two weeks almost continueally after our enemies in this & Rhea. It was thought about the middle of last week that there would be war sure enough.

The northern force, but they happened to be farthest south this time, was collected at Sail Creek Campground ready & waiting to do battle on a grand sale, I suppose; but when the Southern men got sufficiuent force together to meet them they had mysteriously disapeared, run of course, as you know they always do. They scattered themselves about promisciously through the mountains, but our folks have succeeded in taking several of them prisoners. Eight passed through here this morning going to Knoxville, plodding along through the mud with chains on like as many cattel. Don't you suppose they felt greatly humiliated!

They left for Knoxville last Monday with 30 or 40 prisoners. Some of them have given up their arms, others who did not hand theirs over were compelled to do so. Some men had one gun & two revolvers, they had them concealed in straw & leaves in the woods; no two pieces were found in one place. This was in the 1st district of this county. Capt McKenzies Comp is in Rhea yet scouting through the mountains after the rascals.

The great desire seems to be to find Clift who is supposed to be sneaking about in the mountain gorges. They have orders from head quarters to take him dead or alive, if alive I suppose he will not see the sun rise many more times. Mr Pleas Miller below here lay out four days & then came out & told them he could not live that way & wished the Union was in some very warm place.

I imagine Genl Scott will enjoy private life exceeding well after being instrumental in the performance of so much good during this campaign, but hope his prayer will not be answered to the utmost extent, Dont you?

The girls are intent making themselves new cotting [cotton] dresses to wear this winter. You can hear spinning wheels & looms in almost any direction you will turn these days. It reminds me very much of the Revolutionary War, that was in my young days when I spun & wove all my frocks, & had two threads of turkey red in that one I wore to church.

You need not think I mean to make sport of the industry I see around me. I approve of it. I am of the impression a note from you would be very acceptable to the young lady in question though I have never heard her say so in plain words. She sayed when I told her what you wrote, that she thought you might as well write to her as Kate or me, & you know the old adage says "Actions speak louder than words." Nothing more of interest. Excuse this short letter.

Your true friend
Sallie

- - - - - - - - - - - - -

LETTER NO. 44
D.C. BLEVINS TO B.F. TAYLOR

Decatur, Novr 23rd 1861

Dear Cousin

Yours of the 17th Inst at hand. I am verry glad to hear from you, of your good health, and allso of the Company. May God bless you with the Same till your Safe return home. I expect I was labering under a mistake a bout the time I wrote you. I did write Some of the Boys, that I didn't now whether I would get their letters or not if they write me from the fact we had marching orders, and I didn't now when we was going. Then I hope you will excuse me for grumbling a little, and write me as often as you can, and I think probably I will get the letters. Tell all the boys to write to me and I will have them forwarded.

I havent much nuse, we have whiped out the union men generally, taking a hundred prisoners. Our Company has Captured 4 horses; Lut(?) Lillard got Cliffs horse. The Governur has ordered out the militia in Middle and West Tenn. I think he will order them out in E Ten in a few days. I think he ordered out the middle and West Tenn to have them in redaniss. So if the E T refused he can make them go, we will have warm times but we intend to envade through the best we can. Let things come as they may. We intend to keep the invaders off our Soil, they have Sent those prisoners to Nashville. Cant see what will become of them. One thing I no they cant take the oath any more.

I except your proposition, it would be a pleasure to me to receive letter from you while I am in Camp. So write to me and when ere I am I will give you my PO, and we will Corespond during the War, for I expect to remain a Volunteer if I have my health till the War is ended, except my best wishes, give my respects to all the boys, tell Sam Cox to write to me. Respectfully

D. C. Blevins

- - - - - - - - - - - - -

LETTER NO. 45
B.F. TAYLOR TO PEACH TAYLOR

Near Centerville, Va.
Nov 25th 1861

Kind and loving Father

To night I have the opportunity of droping you a few lines as it was your request that I write at least once a week. I have no war newse to write you that will be of any interest. All is verry quiet in camp at this place. The entire force was taken out to day at this place the line of battle formed, and each brigade and regt asigned their place to fight should an attack be made at this point. The sight was verry beautiful indeed to see almost the entire force of such a large army drawn up in line at one time.

We had orders at this time to be ready to go on picket in the morning at 8 o'clock and will not write any more for the present as I have a bad chance to write and am writing on my knee. The company is generally in good health. Isaac and myself are in good health. I will write again as soon as I return from picket which will be in 4 days. Give love and best wishes to all, your son

B.F. Taylor

- - - - - - - - - - - - -

LETTER NO. 46
TENNESSEE McCORKLE TO B.F. TAYLOR

Decatur, Nov 25th [1861]

Dear Friend Frank

I received your very kind and more than welcome letter in due time. Not withstanding I have been some what slow about answering it. I do not want you to think I thought it unworthy corespondence from me. I have no news that will interest you but will give you the best I have. We are all in good health at present, the health of the people in the country is very good.

Today was the circuit Preachers time to preach here it was his second time. I think he is a very good Preacher and hope he will be liked more by the people here than Swisher was.

We had a call meeting at the Baptish Church last Sunday. Rose said Philip and the Eunich was Baptised. I thought it was Hustons wife and Amanda Elder. You know that is a quotation that Rose always comes over when he goes to Baptize any one. The most amusing part was that Houstons wife came very near falling down before she got out of the water.

Well Frank while I write the cold winds of November is whistling around it makes me feel very sad to think how many of my fellow beings are exposed and will perhaps have to be out on duty many sick and perhaps more boisterous and hard weather than it is now. When I reflect on the cause and those who have been instrumental in bringing on this shameful state of affairs, I am wicked enough to wish them dead.

Our last week papers seem to be more in hopes that peace will be made in a short time than they have been for sometime past. I wonder that it might be so. The long cold winter evenings are now here and it is a gloomy prospect for some of us to look at but our lonlyness will be nothing to compare with the privations and suffering you all who have been so patriotic will have to undergo.

Enough on that subject. I did not want you to think I was -------?------- [line not legible] I was not aware until yesterday that things had progressed so far that you had ordered(?) Pap--?- hand(?) your(?) paper to Miss Lizzie. It seems that it is the case for he handed it to her yesterday.

I wish you could be here tomorrow evening. We are goimg to have a quilting to make a comfort for the Soldiers, Say(?) to Mr J T Russell for me that I am under lasting obligation to him for writing me so often and that I will answer them Christmas eavening --?--. Give my Best to Dave and Mr Baldwin and accept the love of a good friend.

Tenn

- - - - - - - - - - - - -

LETTER NO. 47
KATE LEUTY TO B.F. TAYLOR

Decatur, Dec 10th 1861

Dear friend

This evening after taking a pleasant moonlight stroll this lovely moonshine night I seat myself to answer yours which came to hand several days ago. The weather has been very pleasant here for several days. I never remember of seeing as warm and dry weather this time of the year before. It makes one feel like spring was here. The birds are singing their sweet songs, but I fear this pleasant weather will not continue long.

On last night I was to a quilting at Mr Wesley Lillards helping to quilt a comfort for him to take to camp. We had four young gentlemen with us more than has been at any of our quiltings this fall. There was a soldier left here ---?--- ---?--- he expected fight in Rhea County such ---?--- to an Alabama regiment yesterday one of his company came after him they were both at the quilting and Tom Cox and Tomy Binyon, these four composed the crowed of gentlemen.

All of the young men except two have volunteered and gone from here. Last week the mail boy Volunteered at Athens went off and left no one to bring over the mail so we did not get any news until they sent after the mail Sunday evening.

Since I commenced writing Hugh Blevins has arrived from Bowling Green there is a great deal of sickness there they brought several home last week dead among them was Mr. John McClanahan. a few days before Jim Gipson was brought dead. It is said the average forty dying a week.

Dr Hodges company is at Knoxville. I received a letter from brother Bill to day he is very well pleased with camp life he wrote they would go into Gen Gillespies reg which will be organized tomorrow, the Dr has a nice company, they are all civel except two or three. I think he will make a good Captain. Dr. Gilbert belongs to the Co, he is trying for the place of assistant Surgeon.

Christmas will soon be here but how dull it will be. We have been thinking some of you would come home to spend a few days but since there has been some letters received yesterday we have almost give out looking for any of you.

I will close my uninteresting letter for I know I have failed to interest you. Accept the Kindest wishes of your unchanging friend.

Kate Leuty

- - - - - - - - - - - - -

LETTER NO. 48
KATE LEUTY TO J.P. BLEVINS
AT CENTERVILLE, VA.

Decatur, Dec 11th 1861

Dear friend

Your kind and interesting letter has been received and read with interest. I now seat my self to answer although I have nothing to write that will be likely to interest you. You know Decatur always has been a dull place about news but is much worse now since there is so few of us left.

A few weeks ago it look like we would have a battle or two to write about but I believe they have give out fighting this time. Capt McKenzies company is still at the X Roads I do not know how long it will remain there did hear yesterday they had orders to go to Knoxville but it is so hard to hear the truth now a days. I do not put much confidence in anything I hear untill I know it is so. An other company has left our midst and are now at Knoxville (Capt Hodges). They have been gone nearly two weeks they will go into Gen Gillespies regiment it is to be organized to day.

We have had very pleasant weather for several days but this morning the appearance of snow and is much colder than usual for a few days it has looked spring. I hope the weather has been pleasant in Va.

I noticed a letter in the Banner from Col Vaughn stating his reg was still doing picket duty. I know it is hard on you when you have to be in snow and cold mud. I think the way he wrote he has a hope of coming to Tenn to take up winter quarters.

The health of the Country is very good. No more at present. As ever your friend

Kate Leuty

- - - - - - - - - - - - -

LETTER NO. 49
ISAAC G. CROSS TO PEACH TAYLOR

Centerville, Va.,
Dec the 14th 1861

Dear Parent.

I write you in great haste this morning as the Capt is going to start I and Frank both in good health– no news hear of interest– every thing quiet on this line we will probably make arrangement for winter quarters next week, I have not heard directly from home since I left, I have writen several letters but received no answer, I was sorry to hear of you loosing your mare. Tell Mary I would love to hear from her and the children.

W F Blevins spoke to me almost what they owed you. You will please settle what they owe you as I am owing them for the fruit I bought from them and you can have a credit for what you owe me. Tell Ap if he goes to Chat I want him to look into my fruit Acct tell him I think he ought to write to me, write to me soon.

I am Sir very respectfully your obedient son

I. G. Cross

- - - - - - - - - - - - -

LETTER NO. 50
AMANDA C. LILLARD TO B.F. TAYLOR

Coldwater, December 14th 1861

Dearest Cousin Ben

Your dear letter enclosed with Capt Lillard was received this evening; also yours of 10th November was received no longer than last Sabbath, a long time on the roads. I had com to the conclusion that Miss Kate had stolen all your attention, but I shal not grumble at you any more, but know my letters are on the road some where.

You supprised me in your letter when you said you thought I did not deem your letter worthy of an answer. Now dont write that any more or I shall flog you when you return.

In yours of 10th from the way you writen I infer that you doubt my friendship or(?) neather(?) hold out that idea, consider me your best friend in Meigs & when you return home I will tell you all about it.

Well Cousin as to news. I havent any in store worth your attention. I was over at Decatur to day. Saw all of your sweethearts, Kate is as pretty as ever, the next time I see Lizzie K [King], I will comply with your request in the best manor I can.

Your sis Amanda was at Town to day she said they was all well & of coars doing well. The confusion among the Ladies of De I shal not attempt to discribe.

Christmas is fast approaching & what kind of a time we will have I cannot tell, but imagine it will be a dry one unless som of you boys return, if so you will be received with Shouts & Clapping of hands by all.

Frank, Cattie Locke is going to get maried in a few days to Dr somebody [Dr. Marion C. Clark] I have forgotten his name. I think she might awaited untill this war is over, what do you think a bout it. I anticipate several weddings at the close of this campeign. I must close. Tell Van C. his family are all well. Give love to all & receive the kindest regards & love from your friend & Cousin

Amanda C. Lillard

P.S. How does my spark get along, does he make a good soldier, Yes I know he does. Yours Truly A.C.L.

- - - - - - - - - - - - -

LETTER NO. 51
D.C. BLEVINS TO LIEUT. B. F. TAYLOR

Smiths X Roads,
Dec 17th 1861

Dear Cousin

Yours of the 6th Inst at hand. I was glad to hear from you of your good health and that you are geting along fine generally. I havent much nuse. The connection are all well as far as I know.

We are geting along verry well in Camp. Still arresting tories. I have been on the Scout for Six days with a Squad of men, traveled over Waldens ridge and Cumberland mountains, arrested twenty odd men and pressed these malingers into Service, So we have Some boys to wate on us.

I returned to Camp yesterday, have been buisey to day taking depositions. Lut Lillard will Start to Knoxville with Some of the prisoners to morrow and Some has volunteered. We have to Send the proof up with them. So it keeps us buisey all the time Scouting hunting up witnesses or taking depositions.

I havent much nuse from Ky, they are expecting a fight at Bolling Green. Zollicoffer had a fight with the Yankes and tories the other day killed 14 or 15 of them and they run as usual, no loss on our side.

I learn by dispatch that Charleston SC was half burnt by the enemy, a few days ago, forget the date, Some Ses it Caught by axident or Some trator Set it on fire, and our forces being ingaged with the enemy, Couldnt put it out till it done grate damage.

I am Sorry but it Cant be helped, if they will Come out on the land we will Show them where they Stand, God grant that we had an navie Strong enough to Sink the last Yankey vessel to the bottom of the Ocian, then they might bost of their power in the ocine in Stid of their power on the hi Seas, but my wishes are that we may yet be as we are on the land, their Superiors on the water.

I must close, our School Guirls with whom we have Sported(?) away So many happy hours are all doing fine, times are not now as they ust to be I use to have my fun with my School mates at old Decatur Academy, but now I have fun with my fellow Soldiers around the Camp fire or while traveling over the mountains in persute of tories, but I hope we will all live to See peace restored to the Country and enjoy life as we use to enjoy it in a land of Liberty. give my respects to all the Company and except my best regards your self.

Your Cousin and true friend
D.C. Blevins

- - - - - - - - - - - - -

LETTER NO. 52
J.P. BLEVINS TO L.R. BLEVINS

Richmond, Va., Thursday night
Dec 19th 1861

Dear Brother

It is made my unpleasing duty to inform you of the death of Cousin Kit [Blevins]. He died at ½ past 12 O'Clock to day of Typhoid fever. You wrote me he had gone off to the hospital but did not know where he was. I tried to find out whether he was in Richmond or not but cold find nor hear anything of him until this morning when to my great astonishment W.A. Buckner came in to my room hunting for me.

I went immediately to see him. When I entered his room Buckner asked him if he knew me, when he told him in a very low whisper my name; though, one could Scarcely understand any thing he said from the fact that he had been past Speaking above his breath for two or three days. I stayed by his bedside until about half past 12 O'Clock, when he died. Bill & Buckner said they had done all they could for him but all they could do would not save him. W.A. Buckner went to try to get to take him home, but could not get off. I got all his things, his Shawl, Blanket, Knap sack, clothes &c except what we used to put him away. I am writing home to Uncle Phillip about him, which of course will be sorrowful news to him.

I will go up and see him again in the morning before he is buried. The boys says they have all that dies in that hospital very decently buried.

Thursday evening Dec 20th

W.A. Buckner & myself tried again this morning to try to get to take Kit home but there was no chance. He was buried to day at 12 O'Clock in Oak Wood Grave Yard. We had him put away as well as we could. He was buried very decently. I went out with them to the grave yard about 1½ miles from where I am staing. I feel as well as usual to day but I dont think I am stout enough to go into camp yet for a few days. As I have to write a letter to Uncle Phillip yet this evening I will close. Write Soon and give me the news if you have any. Write whether there is any prospect for a fight Shortly. After my best respects to you and all I remain your Brother

J.P. Blevins

Lysurgus if there comes a letter to camp before I get there from Uncle Phillip you must send it to me immediately.

J.P.B.

- - - - - - - - - - - - -

LETTER NO. 53
SALLIE McCORKLE TO B.F. TAYLOR

Decatur, Dec 22nd 1861

Mr Taylor

I received your welcom note dated 8th & now will endeavor to answer it. It found me with all my friends so far as I am able to learn in the enjoyment of very good health. The people generly in virrily are enjoying good health. This I suppose is a great blessing for physicians are scarce now a number of them having gone into the service. I was sorry to learn you was suffering so much with headaches, which I know gives the victim great pain, allthough I never had an attack myself in my life.

We have had three weeks or more of as pleasant weather as we could desire. But this morning is disagreeable, it is raining slowly looks like we were going to have a protracted spell of weather. Well it is the time now for rain & mud, tomorrow is circuit court here & Christmas comes Wednesday they tell me. I am not anticipating any fun myself, though I hope it may be a merry Christmas to all who are in the spirit to enjoy it. I wish you to write me how you boys spent that day. Quite different I am sure it will be from the last one.

What a change twelve months has brought about! One year ago we were all together enjoying each others society, little thinking that the next aniversary of that noted period would find our friends associates & relatives scatered, as it were, to the four winds. But look forward to a brighter day. God in His kind Providence has seen fit to preserve the lives of nearly all of our associates, for which we should be thrice thankful, seeing as we have so many [who] have fallen victim either to the sword or disease. Let us then look to the brightest side of the picture, always endeavor to be cheerful ourselves and render those arround us happy. I will drop this subject.

There have been more nice young gents in town the last week than I have seen in a coons age. Capt Lillard arrived Friday evening. He is looking nice I assure you as well as all the others that have been & are now at home from that company. The Capt looks like he has grown taller since he left home, if all you boys have improved as much during your absence as those we have seen, we girls we [will] be perfectly crazy when you all return. You all, or several, of you wrote in the summer about being so much sun burnt we would scarcely recognize you. I cannot believe(?) it. I am of the opinion that you only write that to find what effect it would have on us girls.

Willie B reached home yesterday he tarried awhile at Union. Miss Minerva Frazier is in our village has come I suppose to hunt Christmas.

Bettie Buckner was over last Sabbath, she has grown some since she attended school here. There is a protracted meeting in hands at Sewee Academy at present; they have a disagreable time though I hope they may experience a warm meeting. No one is in attendance from our burg. Misses Mahala & Clara E Cates went up yesterday. Your Mother was in town yesterday.

I would be exceedingly glad to hear of peace being made but would be sorry if it should be at the cost of so many presious lives as we know would be sacrificed should a general engagement take place between the contending armies.

Six more prisoners were taken on to Knoxville from Rhea last week, dont think E Tenn will be cleared of Lincoln followers before long. We hear now & then of more bridge burners being hanged. Give my best wishes to all who will accept & receive for yourself a good share from your true friend

Sallie McCorkle

- - - - - - - - - - - - -

LETTER NO. 54
B.F. TAYLOR TO AMANDA T. TAYLOR

Camp Walker near Manassas
Thursday Night Dec 26th 1861

Affectionate Sis:

After a delay of several days I have the privelege of droping you a few lines in answer to your verry kind letter. Your letter was verry interesting to me from the fact that I find in your last letter that you are making great improvement. I do not want you to say you are a shamed to write to me, for you know their is no information but what I would give you in reference to writing or anything else when ever it is in my power and would take a great pleasure in so doing.

I was truly proud of your expression that you would do the best you could, that done me more good than the finest written letter that ever was wrote could have done. It is the kind of a motto I like, and it will make a lady of you some day if you will always keep it in view and work up to it. I want you to write to me at least once a week whether I have time to write to you that often or not, but I will promise to answer immediately ever letter you write me as we will not have but little more service to do this winter and will have nothing to do but write to any one that will write to me. So please to write at least once a week to me. It will be practice to you.

I believe I have no late war newse to write you that will be of any interest. I suppose you have learned ere this time of our new encampment. We are 1½ miles from Manassas Junction on the railroad, or about 2 hundred yds from the road. We have our winter quarters pretty well finished, will finish them this week, if no bad luck more than I know of at this time. I have a verry good and comfortable house nearly done to night will finish it this week.

Cos Hugh T Blevins came to camp last Monday. We were all verry glad to see him return to camp. Well I will close as I have nothing more worth writing and will write soon again. Give my love and best wishes to all the family. Tell them to write to me soon or I will come to the conclusion that they have forgotten me entirelly. Write soon your self, Write without fail.

In conclusion please accept the best wishes of your good friend and brother. The health of the company is verry good, also my health and Isaacs are verry good.

B.F. Taylor

- - - - - - - - - - - - -

LETTER NO. 55
HUGH T. BLEVINS TO AMANDA TAYLOR

Camp Walker, December 26th 1861

Manday, Dear Cousin

For the first time in life I attempt to drop you a few lines, though having nothing of much interest to write I will contract my letter. I arrived in camp last monday, was eight days on my rout, layed over at Knoxville Union & Lynchburg. I enjoyed my trip vissaly(?) & am now in good health. The company is in tolerable health.

Sorrowfully I have to relate the death of Cousin Kit Blevins who died on the 29th instant, he was properly cared for as I learn. His absence from us by death has thrown a gloom across our vision, but he has only paid the debt we all owe. I was much greaved on account of his being away from his parents & friends, but one thought that gives me consolation is that hes [he has] died in the service of our country, defending our rights.

We are gowing into winter quarters, are Busily building our little huts, have labored very hard to day & am somewhat tired. B.F.T., David & myself are puting us up a fine house about twelve feet square & will lay the flore with dirt, we intend to live at home & board at the same house. We would like very much to have the Ladies of Meigs visit us this winter at least against Valentines day when we could have fine time dancing on our earthen flower.

The boys say that yesterday was Christmas. I recon it was but I worked all day hard. Great is the contrast between the consumption of yesterday & any other Christmas that I ever before witnessed the day passed quiet unknowtised. I hope this is not the case with you all who it has been my hapy lot to pass so many pleasant hours during past Christmases. I hope the time is not far distant when we will be purmited to mingle together at our homes in purfect peace.

I must close for the present. I hope you will not be offended at receiving these few lines by way of B.F. letter excuse me this time & I will try to do better the next. Give my love to the family to John & family, Mary Cross, allso to the girls every where & particularly my wife. You must write & I will answer promptly. As ever your Cousin

H.T. Blevins

P.S. You will excuse my bad writing as my hands are very sore & swelled on account of hard labor building our houses.

- - - - - - - - - - - - -

LETTER NO. 56
PEACH TAYLOR TO B.F. TAYLOR

Meigs County, December the 29th 1861

Deare Sun

I am again permitted through the kind hand of God of Droping you a few lines in Answer to your kind letters I have Received since I last writen to you. I Received them about 8 Days ago and have failed to answer them till the present owing to the pussh of my bussiness. We ware alle glad to heare from you and more so to learn of your good health, Which is the greatest Blessings can be bestoed on any being in this life and more So While you are enjoying a Camp life and Distance from home and heare friends hoping and trusting in God that you may still be preserd and injoy good health and git Safe home to the Imbraces of your friend at home.

We are all enjoying Good health and has bin for some time the health of this Countrey at present is very good. I have none newes of interest to write you, the Union Men of Tennessee is all Mached(?) up, Captain McKinzays Company is stille at the Crosse Roads they have not got Ol Cliff as yeat.

Captain McClinden(?) sent after Colonel Cox & Dentons and at the nest of the Union Men in that -?-ate and maid them go to Clevlin and take the Oath the Colonel objected to the trip at first but finley got Ready and Obaid the call Very Much Against his Will as they war Ordining men came after him.

I Received the few lines you Sent by Captain Lillard and $140.00 Dollars Which you wanted me to keep till further orders unless me or John or some of the family Wanted to use it. Your Mother has lifted Ten Dollars of your money to pay for things she has bout and sent you. I have paid John Ten Dollars the other day which he said you Owed him on the Dearmon Debt. I paid Jack Davis Ten Dollars & twentey five cents he Said you Owed him and tock his Receipt. I lifted a note H.T.V. Blevins held on you for fifteen Dollars. I allso paid a tax against you for 80 cts, the balance of your Money I have still got and will keep Safe till you Direct me Other Ways. I under stud by A. Denton you owed him sum and I tole him I would pay him but has not seen him Since he did not tell you anything about the Debt till I asked him.

You wanted me to look round and see whare I could git you a nowber(?) one young horse these is as Scarse all most as hens teeth and varyes from one hundred & eighty five to two hundred Dollars. Your Uncle W.S. Russell has a good horse he Bout some 2 mones agoy a Yellow Clabanck, I do not nowe at what price. I will look Round for this kind of Stock till I heare from you again and then Write more about them and the prices.

I am Dun Soeing Wheate and getherin Corn but has not my Rent Husked Out in the bottom. I Maid a good Crop for the healp I made 55 loads with side bords, tell Isaac that Mary and all the Children is well and has bin for some time tell him she is purty ashey(?) on hering of his making up another Company tell him I have gethered his Crop all but the new ground he maid 15 loads of my Waggon.

A L Cross is Walkin about and mending. Corn is Worth 60 cts Pork 10 cts gross. I have Writen Mr Rice several letters and have had no Answer from them since Polley Taylor Writen. Captain Lillard & S Cox well Start back to Mary(?) Weak.

Your Mother is going to send the froot [fruit] and Butter you sent for. I must conclude my letter. Give my best love and Respects to all the Boys, Your Father Till Death

Peach Taylor

- - - - - - - - - - - - -

LETTER NO. 57
KATE LEUTY TO B.F. TAYLOR

Decatur, Jan 1st 1862

My dear friend.

This new years morning I am afforded the pleasure of spending a few minutes in reply to your very interesting letter which came to hand a few days ago. I have put off writing thinking I would have something new to write about that would interest you but have not everything is as dull here as usual. We have not had any Christmas. There is not but fear in town to day the young gentlemen have gone to Smiths X roads. Capt McKenzies Co leaves there tomorrow for Knoxville.

Last Saturday evening myself and several of the girls went up on Sewee to meeting they have had a fine meeting held 10 days there were nine conversions, Six of them were baptized Sunday morning.

Yesterday Minerva Frazier, Crate Lillard, myself and Jim Blevins, Sam Cox and another young gentleman went down to Dentons Store and Mr Coxs. It was a pleasant day. I enjoyed the visit fine. Minerva has been over nearly two weeks & will not go home for some time yet. We would be glad if it was so you could be here to spend a few days with us if it was so all of you could come home what a fine time we would have going to parties.

Well what has become of young lawyer what carries the documents in his pocket wonder if he has any more suits on hand which he intends to have decided at the April term.

How did you enjoy yourself while on picket did you get to see that girl? I told the Capt what you said to tell about the Lady. I hope you have had a plesant Christmas. I will close as I know I have failed to interest from the fact there is nothing going on here to interest any one. Accept the best wishes of your unchanging friend.

Kate Leuty

P.S. New years gift. Kate

- - - - - - - - - - - - -

LETTER NO. 58
N.J. LILLARD TO B.F. TAYLOR

Decatur, Jany 3rd 1862

Dear Adjt Dr P & Leut Taylor

I write you a few lines this Morning but guess I will be with you before it reaches you. I have nothing to write more than Christmas pass off with out much smoke. Capt McKenzie Co will be here to night enroute for Knoxville to organize their Bat. Floyd Brigade has gone to Bowling Green, Bro Bill is here from there says they will have a fight pretty soon he thinks.

Bradley County will have some 7 or 8 Co in the field pretty soon. I will start home next tuesday. Hope you will have quarters done ere I reach there. All is well. Yours Respectfully

N.J. Lillard

- - - - - - - - - - - - -

LETTER NO. 59
ISAAC G. CROSS TO PEACH TAYLOR

Camp Walker, Va.,
Sunday, January 5th 1862

Dear Parent

It is with no small degree of pleasure that I write to inform you that I am in fine health. I was weighed this morning and am heavier than ever before in my life, weighing 162½ and still a fattening. I will soon be as fat as Butram.

I have just read a letter you wrote to Frank and was very well pleased to heare that my folks as well as yours had all got well. Also to hear that our corn crops had turned out so well. Tell Mary not to fret two much about me making up another Company for I will be at home in due time. I have about 50 in my Company and will get it up beyond a doubt but I am going to come home before reentering the service. I dont think that I could remain at home satisfied while the war is going on when I see as good a chance to reenter the service as honorable as I can at the present.

As for news I have but little that would interest you. There has been some talk of an advance but I put but little confidence in any thing I her till I know it to be so. I see in the papers that McClelland is quite low with Typhoid fever and more talk of his being superseeded that dont look much like an advance does it.

I am taking the daily Richmond Dispatch which I am going to send to you and with it I will inclose a few lines which will give all the news you can pay the postage and get the dailey news both from here Richmond and the North. You can hand them over to Ap John & the Neighbors So you can all get the news. If you will call upon McKinley you can get one I sent him giving the Correspondence between Lone(?) Lyon and Seward in reference to the Masson and Slidell Case. Hoping to hear from you soon, I remain as ever yours

I.G. Cross

- - - - - - - - - - - - -

LETTER NO. 60
B.F. TAYLOR TO PEACH TAYLOR

Camp Walker near Manassas, Va
Sabbath Night, Jan 5th 1862

Affectionate father:

With my usual degree of pleasure I am again seated for the purpose of drafting you a few lines in answer to your kind letter which came to hand a few hours ago. I was truly glad to hear of you all being in good health and getting along so well. This is always the most important newse to me that I can receive.

As to war newse that will be of any interest to you I have none. It is true there is some little excitement in camp to night. On Thursday night the Yankey drove our pickets in at post (No 6) where our Regt always do their picketing. This eavening the newse came that they were advancing on us how true it is I cannot tell, thoug I do not believe the report. But on the other hand we have some good reasons to vouch for its correctness.

As to newse from Ky you perhapse have later than we have here. Our last report stated that the forces at Bowling Green were advancing. In fact the entire force in Ky were making an advance movement. We have gone into winter quarters within 1½ or 2 miles of the Junction. We have a verry nice situation for our quarters.

We are quartered on the railroad leading from Manassas to Alexander. We have our quarters finished and have moved into them, they are verry comfortable I assure you. Cozs D.M. Blevins and Hugh T. Blevins with myself have us a nice little cabbin finished off with good beds in it. We live as comfortable as rats, or in other words we live at home and board at the same house.

Well, I will drop this subject as it is not of much interest. Those debts you spoke of paying for me were all correct and just, as to the Jack Davis debt I owed him some but did not know how much it was. You spoke of an account that D. Denton held against me, I do not know precisely what it is but it is between 10 and 15 dollars about 12 I think. I want you to pay it off or any other small account you can find against me. Any debt amounting to 25 or more dollars I will settle when I return.

I owe Uncle William Russell for 2 Months board for which I have never Settled with him, and I must acknowledge that I am a shamed of it. It was through negligence of me that I did not settle with him before I left. I want you to go and pay it out of the money you have there of mine and make some appologes for me.

Tell Mother I was glad to hear that she had used my money to pay for things she bought and sent to me instead of working and scratching around to pay for them which I was fearful she would do. I want her to use it to pay for any thing she sends to me or an thing she needs for her own use. She is entirely welcome to it or any of you that wish to use it.

As to buying a horse for me. You can look around and see what you can do go and look at Uncle W S Russells horse see what he is worth and what you can get him for, money down, also give me a description of the horse and his age, and I will write you what to do as I will be better settled by that time what I intend to do. It may be that I will come home a few days in the corse of 2 or 3 weeks from now if there is no prospect of a fight at this point, though it is verry uncertain I assure you.

Well as it is getting verry late and I have nothing more to write I will close. The health of the company is only tolerable good. D M Blevins has been very sick for 3 or 4 days but is some better tonight. The Doctor thinks it is the fever thing. I hope he is mistaken and that he will be well soon. My health is verry good, Isaac is also in good health. Give my love and best wishes to all and accept to thy self a good portion of the same. Your affectionate Son

B.F. Taylor

Write immediately after reception of this.

- - - - - - - - - - - - -

LETTER NO. 61
AMANDA TAYLOR TO B.F. TAYLOR

Meigs County, January 5th 1862

Dear Brother

This Rainy Sabath morning after meditating upon the hard ships you doubtless ar under going to day in order to gain our liberty the libertys of our sweet suny south and to assist in driving back those that wold invade our onst happy homes and firesides, I to day take grate pleasure in droping you a few lines to inform you that we ar all well hoping this may find you all enjoying the same blessing.

You wanted to know what was the mater with us all that we did not write to you on my own part I can say it is just be cause I have neglected my duty for neglegence is my onley plea for Frank I know it is not for want of esteem for as a brother I esteem you hyley and wold ask you to forgive the past and in the future I will try to do better.

I will have to excuse the matter for John as he has had a very sore thimb but it is about well now. We hav had a very pleasant winter so far thar has bin very little rain comparing to that which is common in this Country thar has been no snow werth naming but to day has some appearance of it it appears like providence has smiled up on the people here that has had thar Corn to gather and take care of fore it has bin a one Horse business nearly all the time as thare is no hands to be hired people are nerley dun gathering now.

John has 4 or 5 load in the field yet he has raised a fine crop he thinks he raised between one thousan and 12 hundred bushel of corn and the finest seete [sweet] potatoes just get away we picked out some of the largest and best of them to send to you when Isaac was her but he cold not take them all so John bought a half bushel of chesnuts for you if thare is any chance of geting them to town to morrow you Shad hav them yet.

The shirts that John Spoke of sending to you he tryed to get flanel but cold not get a yard that is none to be had ether for grone folks nor babes poor little things. I dont no what will become of em with out the sheep gives a heap of wool next year.

Well I recon that it as much of that as you will care a bout and it is geting late and i hav to write a letter for Mary. Ap is here with us yet but says he intend to go back to camp when Capt McKenzie Company goes to Kentuckey, tho he is not well anuff to do servis but thinks best to go as the hav not herd from home since he left I expect he will be discharg tho he dos not like the idea of it.

I will close for the presant hoping to hear from you soon. So no more but remains your friend and Sister until death.

A Taylor

- - - - - - - - - - - - -

LETTER NO. 62

Hd Qrs 4th Brigade,
Jan 6. 1862

Orders

The E Tenn Vols will furnish a Lieut two non com officers & 30 men provided with one days rations ten spades & tweny axes to report to Capt Tremaux 8th Regt at 9 O'Clock to morrow morning at the R.R. Crossing near Camp Walker. By order of Col Hill

To Chestney
aaase

- - - - - - - - - - - - -

LETTER NO. 63
D.C. BLEVINS TO LIEUT. B.F. TAYLOR

Knoxville, Tenn
Jan 13th 1862

Dear Cousin

I drop you a few lines this morning in answer to your letter I received a few days ago, nothing new, we came to Knoxville las Wednesday Organised Our Regt same day. John Rogers was Elected Col, White of Chattanooga Lut Col and Mr Maclin of Washington Co Mager, the health of our Company is good and allso the health of the Regt. Ours is the only Regt Cavalry organised in E Tenn.

They are all fine men and if they will arm us write we will do the government some good. I saw Thomas Russell & D.M. Blevins as they passed down on the train on their way home. I must come to a close we have marching orders cant tell where we are going out after the tories I guess. Except my best regards

D.C. Blevins

- - - - - - - - - - - - -

LETTER NO. 64
PEACH TAYLOR TO
I.G. CROSS AND B.F. TAYLOR

Meigs County,
January the 18 1862

Deare Suns

With pleasure I am again Seated for the purpose of droping you a few lines in answer to your kind letters which came to hand this Day Dated 5th of January Which gave us grate satisfaction to here that you and Franklin were in good health and I hope all the balance of the Connection and friends injoying the Same blessings.

I wold suppose you injoy good health from what you say you weigh 162½ lbs and still fatting and would seen be as fat as Butram. I shall be Sory to heare when you git so fat that you cant cross your legs like Butram, this is the secont letter I have Received from you since you left home last.

Your first letter stated that you wanted me to settell the amount of the note I held on Blevins boys in a Debt you owed them I have seen W. Blevins onct or twist since and he hase never said an thing a bout the mater as yet to me

David Blevins & Thomas Russell got home this Eaving a week ago. I have not seen either of them Since they got home I under stand David is not entirley well yet. Captain N.J. Lillard has come back from Knoxville Sick and is not yet well as I under Stand. I have not seen him since he came back home.

You must Excuse me for not writing you sooner. I have had more to doe than I could attend two. We finished huskin the last of the Rent Corn yesterday, the Crib is plum full Corn is Worth 60 cts and still advancing, pork 12 cts– meat. I have nothin more of Intrist to Wright you Onely We are all Well and the health of the Countray good.

Mary & the Children is in good health and has bin for sum time. John Taylor & famuley is all well but little Susen has bin a litell unwell for some time. The Connection & friends is all well so fare as I have any Knolledg. A.L. Cross has got so he can gowe about with out his Crushes he started to Chattanooga this Morning he will see Mr Powel for you this time and write you from there he said.

tell Franklin I Received his letter the same time I Received yours and Will Answer it in a short time, When I can have more time and see Russell an the boys that has come home [from] camps, if Franklin starts home Wright me a few days before hand.

I want you bouth and all of you to take good Care of your selves, We have nothing to fear while you are blest with good health which a lone Comes from the hand of God, for which you Should be very Thankful and I trust Will. I must conclude my letter but Remains your Father and friend till Death

Peach Taylor

- - - - - - - - - - - - -

LETTER NO. 65
SARAH McCORKLE TO B.F. TAYLOR

Decatur, Jan 18th 1861 [1862]

Mr. Taylor, Your Honor.

Precisely two weeks from the time your letter was written it was received & the contents examined with greate satisfaction as such a feeling attends the perusal of all letters received from my friends. If you should be considering me negligent about responding should this reach its destination the above explanation will I hope appease your wrath should any be aroused.

I think I can & do duly appreciate my part of the praise in your kindness you have seen fit to bestow upon the ladies of the good Old Meigs. I concur with you in your opinion of the patriotism which they possess, I believe there is a good share of that honorable feeling in our native county & I am proud that such is the case; & in the mean time many of them are not wanting in that other tract which you ascribe to them if I do say so myself. Though of that portion of the subjects wish to be excused.

Christmas past without much ado among us about Decatur, we had one party in our village which was about all that transpired of any interest. A great contrast was perceptable between this & last Christmas Holy days, however it is useless to dwell upon this melancholy subject.

I look forward to a time in the future, which I hope is not far distant when we will all be happy to compensate of all the troubles we have been made to experience. Sometimes I see such flattering news in the papers of the speedy termination of the existing contest, that I am buoyed up with hope & at other times it is to the reverse.

However I suppose it is a chastisement to the people for their wickedness, as you know in ancient times they were frequently punished for their wickidness & I dare say we are not more righteous at the present day. While our dark hearted enemies in the North are the principle leading cause of all this present trouble I doubt not that there are some little errors committed in the South.

Mr Cor(?) Denton has the Measels. Willie Leuty came home last Monday with the same disease, neither dangerous I suppose. Mr N.J. Lillard has had a tolerably serious time with his throat though he was improving at last accounts. D.M. & T.P. arrived last Sabbath. D.M. is able to walk about, & he rode out [to] Mr W.W. Lillards last week.

I was greatly surprised when I learned Thomas was coming home, he was the last one I thought would come before his time was out. We girls would be most happy to accept your invitation to visit you young gents in your newly erected houses. Nothing would give me greater pleasure than to see your arrangements in cooking, & washing the dishes & I know I should be amased to see you making up your beds, & verious other things that you have never been accustomed to doing. But it is useless for me to think of such a thing.

Inasmuch as I have written you all the news I have on hands I will desist for the present. Give my compliments to your mess & to all others who will accept & tell them all to not forget their friend Sallie away down South in Dixie. Your true Friend

Sarah McCorkle

P.S. Sallie Blevins requests me to say to you next time she writes to you & that other fellow whats got a white head you will answer her. Sallie

- - - - - - - - - - - - -

LETTER NO. 66
N.J. LILLARD TO B.F. TAYLOR

Decatur, Janry 20, 1861 [1862]

Dear Ben

I write you a few lines this morning, all is well around Decatur. Nothing of Interst. I think I will go out to Town this evening and mail this Letter. I have had pretty hard Brash, think I will start home in about a week If I keep on mending. Len Guinn arrived here on yesterday looking rather thin think he will recruit very fast.

Col Lillard has Just arrived Looking fine. Say the boys are all in pretty good health. Sam & Jim Lamar are with you in this, there is Some eatibles in those Boxes for Mess Nor(?) look out for them. the girls are all very Saucy Indeed, I think If I stay here Many More days I will Marry Some of them if they dont Mind. All Joins in Sending Love to you and say three months is not a long time to wait as 12. I would be glad to be with you but prudeance a Vise we(?) not(?) to be to hasty in returning home.

Decatur is a very Lonesome place Indeed. You would become disgusted with it directly. I have not been there for 15 days and have no desire to go down. The weather is very warm indeed. I sweat all the time night & day, have had no snow yet. Give love to all the boys. Yours as ever

N.J. Lillard

- - - - - - - - - - - - -

LETTER NO. 67
W.O. MEW(?), SURGEON,
TO
CAPTAIN [I. G. CROSS] OF COMPANY I,
3rd REGIMENT TENNESSEE VOLUNTEERS,
C. S. A.

= = = = = = = = = = = = =

[Envelope and contents of above reproduced on following pages]

= = = = = = = = = = = = =

Gen'l Hospital, C. S. A.,

Lynchburg, Va., Jany 21, 1862

Captain:

The following named Soldiers have, this day been discharged from the Hospital, and ordered to report to you immediately for duty. The Quartermaster has furnished transportation.

Francis J. A. Pearce, W. D. Martin, Jas. R. Parks

Co "I" 3rd Reg. Tenn. Vols

Very Respectfully, Y'r ob't Serv't

[illegible]

Surgeon in Charge.

Captain of Co "I"

3rd Reg. Tenn. Vols

GENERAL HOSPITAL

RICHMOND, Jan 2[illegible] 1862

SIR, Priv M. V. Copeland 3rd Tenn Reg [illegible]

is this day discharged from the General Hospital to return to duty.

[illegible]

IN CHARGE OF GENERAL HOSPITAL

LETTER NO. 68
B.F. TAYLOR TO I.G. CROSS IN DECATUR, TENN.

Clinton, Tenn, Tuesday evening
March 18th 1862

Mr I G Cross

Sir in haste I drop you a few lines to let you know our where abouts. We are now encamped in sight of Clinton have the nicest encampment we have ever had since we have been in the Service, Wood water and every thing else is so convenient. We left Knoxville Sabbath morning and reached this place last eavening about 2 hours by sun, how long we will remain here I cannot tell, perhaps some time. We are taking up some prisoners occasionaly. We had out a Scouting party to day and taken 3 or 4. I will have to close it is so dark I cannot see how to write. We have learned nothing yet from Capt McKenzies Company. You had better come to this place first if you do not hear of us any more. I will write soon, give my best wishes to all. Yours with due respect

B F Taylor

- - - - - - - - - - - - -

LETTER NO. 69
B.F. TAYLOR TO PEACH TAYLOR

Clinton, Tenn March 20th 1862

Dear father

In haste I to night drop you a few lines to let you know what we are doing. We are still encamped in sight of a town called Clinton in Anderson County on Clinch river. We will take up the line of march in the morning at 8 Oclock for Jacksborough 20 miles from this place, and perhapse cross the mountain into Ky. From best infor-mation it is the intention of our comanders to cut off a small force of about 3 or 4 thousand Yankeys that have crossed the mountain and are trying to get in behind our force at Cumberland Gap.

We are certain to get into a frolic in a few days, and I am of the opinion that you will not hear of the 3rd Tenn geting scared to death before we are hurt as has been the case with some of the soldiers out in that neck of the woods, and if they whip us they will have to do some right hard fiting first. Our force at this point is 16 or 17 hundred infantry and 4 or 5 hundred Cavalry making in all about 2 thousand. Our Regt is the front of the Brigade.

The scatering Southern men in this section of country are flocking to our standard and going with us to morrow to help fight and pilot us through the mountain.

We are not going to take any tents or extry bagage of any kind. They are Stored up in Clinton and will be a guard left with them. I am going to leave orders with the guard from our Co to ship my trunk to Locks ware house if the boat comes to Clinton any more. You can enquire there for it and see if it comes, we have taken one trunk between us that held all the clothes we will want until our time is out. I believe I have wrote all the newse that is necessary for the present.

The health of the company is verry good. Tell Isaac if he has not gone to come to Clinton as he can learn of us at that place. Our Commussary will be there for the present. Give my best wishes to all and excuse bad writing, we have no ink with us. I will write again the first opportunity.

Yours affectionately
B F Taylor

- - - - - - - - - - - - -

LETTER NO. 70
ISAAC G. CROSS TO PEACH TAYLOR

Loudon, Tenn, March the 25th 1862

Dear Sir

On my arrival here this evening I learned that the Regt was again ordered to Kingston. We will get there tomorrow evening. I will go down in the Morning. Floida Cavalry was turned back from here to day about 200 --?-- crossed the River when the order met them to Return to Chattanooga to await further orders.

No Yankees on this side of the mountain the fight at the Gap turns out to be a very little thing. Report say that they undertook to get artillery up the side of the Mountain to shell our fortification but a few shots from our batteries run them back. We had one man killed and two wounded, their loss was from 25 to 50. Some of our boys passed down on the train and report all the boys doing well.

I swaped my stud off this Morning and I think I made splendid swap. I got a Roan Horse about 15 hands high 9 years old one eyed and works fine and travels pretty well. I would not have Road that horse an other day, for him. I could not pass any one on the Road with a horse. If Jesse Martin had not been with me I never would have got him along at all he made one lounge with me broke the girth and we all came in a pile. I gave 30 dollars to boot and was glad to get the chance. The horse I think would suit you fine on the farm he is heavy and very gentle in fine order. I will write in a few days from Kingston. Yours truly

I G Cross

- - - - - - - - - - - - -

LETTER NO. 71
KATE LEUTY TO B.F. TAYLOR

Decatur, March 28th 1862

Dear Friend Frank

I once more have the pleasure this beautiful spring morning of spending a few moments in reply to your very interesting letter of the 23rd.

I have no news to write that would be likely to interest you. Mr. Baldwin is very sick sent for Dr Hoyle, he came over this morning. I have not heard today how he is whether any better or worse. Cousin Tom is getting well but Gundy(?) has been sick.

The militia met again last Monday and drew. Willie Blevins, Calvin Genno and Grundy Russell drew to go. Every body got drunk (with a few exceptions) had two or three fights. They cut up worse than when you was here. I think it would suit A Vincent better to go back to the Co and fight Yankees instead of stay here drinking whisky and fighting. Him and Mr. Cooly fought he hurt Mr Colley very bad, both were drunk.

Capt Sanduckys Company met on that day and elected their commissioned officers. Mr. William Moore beat Mr. Frazier for first Lieut. Mr. Fike and Houston Cates tied for Second and D Grigsby was elected third. Mr Moore carried the whiskey around generaly that was the cause of Mr Frazier getting beat.

The next morning the ladies gathered themselves together, marched up to the Grocery opened the door and rolled the barrel of Whiskey out in the street, and poured it out. Wrote an advertisement and put on the door that if he bought any more then they intended to treat it the same way.

Bettie Buckner has been over staying nearly a week since you left. She is just as same as ever. Liz myself and her spent some pleasant hours together think I will go over and spend a few days with her before long.

If you remember I promised you a mess of beans last Spring before you left here but failed to fulfill my promis so when you return home I will give them [to] you. I have been making garden for a few days past think will raise that many beans if no more.

I will close knowing I have already wearied your patience. I subscribe myself as ever Your true friend

Kate Leuty

= = = = = = = = = = = = =

In the above letter, Kate mentions the problems with whiskey. Several articles in ***The Athens Post*** also described the situation (see also an article dated 2 May 1862 in Part I of this book):

DECATUR
[28 March 1862]

A friend writing from Decatur, Meigs County, on the 26th says: The vending of "ball-face" in our little town having become such an intolerable nuisance to all civil people, the ladies of the Town assembled yesterday, in broad daylight, and poured all the liquor out of the barrels, bottles, &c., of the Grocery, and put up a notice that any more brought here will meet with the same fate.

We hereby approve the spirited act of our fair friends at Decatur, and trust their examples will be followed by the ladies of other towns and villages. Tippling houses are not only nuisances to a community, but smell rankly to heaven. We like an occasional glass of good liquor, and, perhaps, sometimes take more than the apostle recommends for the stomach's sake and our other infirmities; but we never entered one of those places yet, where women's tears and orphans' wails are manufactured by wholesale, that we did not imagine we could see in the background the flaming portals of hell and hear the howlings of the Apocralyptic Beast with Seven heads and ten horns.

- - - - - - - - - - - - -

A short item in the ***Athens Post*** of 2 May 1862 stated that "Since the establishment of the whiskey blockade, the price for milch cows has advanced 50 per cent."

NOTE: The above letter from Kate Leuty was the last correspondence to or from Benjamin Franklin Taylor. The following article appeared in ***The Athens Post*** on 11 April 1862 and notes his death.

A FIGHT IN SCOTT COUNTY

"We learn through a letter received in this city yesterday, that a detachment of Gen. Longstreet's forces, consisting of part of Col. Vaughn's regiment, part of the 2nd Alabama regiment and a body of cavalry, all under the command of Col. Vaughn, encountered a body of jayhawkers near Huntsville, in Scott County, on Tuesday last, who scattered, took to the woods and commenced "buskwhacking." Lieut. Taylor, of Capt. Lillard's Company was killed, and three others of Colonel Vaughns force. . . ."

There is a headstone for Benjamin in the Taylor Cemetery in Meigs County, but an obituary has not been found. A letter written by John T. Russell, verifies that his body was returned from Scott County for burial [letter was included with B.F. Taylor's official records].

State of Tennessee) I, John T. Russell, Clerk of the
County of Meigs) County Court, within and for the County and State aforesaid do hereby Certify that Peach Taylor is the legally appointed Represetative or Administrator of B.F. Taylor deceased that said Deceased was third or Second Lieutenant of Company I, Commanded by Capt. N.J. Lillard in the third Regiment Tennessee Volunteers Commanded by Col. J.C. Vaughn in the Army of the Confederate States of America and that I was a member of the same Company and Regiment and know the above statements relative to the position and service of the said B.F. Taylor to be true; but was Discharged prior to the Death of the said Deceased and Cannot Certify as to that further --?-- that I was present at the interment of him the said Deceased . . . the 2nd day of September 1862

[signed] John T. Russell

==============

LETTER NO. 72
I. G. CROSS TO *THE ATHENS POST*
(published 4 July 1862)

HEADQUARTERS, 3rd Tennessee Volunteers,
Camp Taylor, June 27, 1862

Sir: Having learned that some of the parents and friends of some of the members of my Company are accusing me with acting in bad faith to them, at the expiration of our twelve months, and was instrumental in retaining them in the service. Whoever has made such representations were wholly ignorant of the facts, or they are guilty of a gross falsehood, which will appear from the following communication. – and as I have always entertained the best of feelings for the members of the Company, and for those of their friends and relatives at home, I wish it published for their own satisfaction as well as a vindication of my course.

CAMP VAN DORN, June 19, 1862

Major H.L. Clay, A.A. Gen.–

Dear Sir: I beg leave to communicate to you without passing it through intermediate commanders, for there has been two communications addressed to you in relation to my Company, and sent up, and there has been no answer received. I will here state that they demanded a discharge at the expiration of their twelve months and refused to do duty, but agreed to do duty until they could get an answer to the communication addressed to you on the 6th instant, inquiring whether they were held under the Conscript Act, they having learned that it was suspended. Since that time a great many of them have left and gone to their homes. They are anxious to go into the cavalry service, and if I could have permission to mount then there will be no difficulty in getting them to return to the Company. If I can not get permission to take my Company into the cavalry service, I want to know what course I shall pursue with those who are absent. Hoping to get some infor-mation soon, I remain, sir, your ob't serv't.

I. G. Cross, Capt.
Company I, 3rd Reg't Tennessee Volunteers

Which was returned with the following indorsement:
Capt I.G. Cross, commanding Company I,
3rd Reg't Tenn Vols.

The Conscript Act has not been suspended, and your men will continue in the performance of their duties. Those men who are absent without leave will be reported and published as deserters. You will inform them that they must return immediately to duty.

Thomas H. Taylor, Col.
Commanding Brigade

Now, in view of all that I have done, I think it unkind in any one to create an impression that I have done any thing that was subversive of the rights of many.

I remain, sir, very respectfully. Your ob't servant, I. G. Cross

----

NOTE: This is the last communication from Isaac G. Cross. The following obituary was published in ***The Athens Post*** on 8 August 1862 [he was buried in Lower Goodfield Cemetery and his grave is marked with a stone]:

ISAAC G. CROSS

The body of Capt. I.G. Cross, who was killed in the fight at Tazewell on the 6th, reached this place [Athens] on Saturday and was taken to his home in Meigs County for interment. When the war commenced, Capt. Cross was among the first to volunteer, and was elected First Lieutenant of the first company raised in Meigs County– commanded by Capt. Newt. Lillard– He was in the battle of Manassas, and in all the engagements and skirmishes in which the 3rd Tennessee Reg't has participated. When the regiment was re-organized, he was elected Captain of the Company in which he had served for twelve months as Lieutenant, Captain Lillard being elected to the office of Lieut.-Colonel.

He was shot through the head in the early part of the fight on the 6th, while cheering his comrads to the struggle. He was a good man– true in the field, and true in all the relations of life. The country has lost tens of thousands in this bloody struggle, but, humble and unpretending though he was, no better and braver soldier has fallen than Captain Cross. Let us cherish his memory, and not forget his bereaved widow and orphaned children.

- - - - - - - - - - - - -

THE FIGHT AT TAZEWELL
***The Athens Post*, 8 August 1862**

The fight on the 6th, at Jones' Spring, near Tazewell, was not so large an affair as at first reported, though the fighting was severe while it lasted. It seems that the most of it on our side was done by Vaughn's foot cavalry, the bloody 3d Tennessee. We copy from the Knoxville paper of the 10th:

We learned that the enemy numbering seven regiments, and being parts of three brigades, were posted in two strong positions, a little distance apart, on Walden's Ridge. Our infantry, approaching the enemy by a flank movement on the extremely rugged crest of the Ridge, for a considerable distance, on a very hot day, were much exhausted, but attacked both positions with great energy. After an artillery duel for two or three hours, our brave troops charged in two bodies, on the enemy, Barton's brigade and two regiments of Taylor's charging one position and Rains brigade charging the other, right in the face of the enemy and greatly exposed.

But our troops did not get more than 200 yards, when the enemy fled precipitately, in disorganized parties to Cumberland Gap.

Our troops, overcome by excessive heat, were too much exhausted to pursue them beyond the town of Tazewell, and the greater part of the enemy escaped. Parts of two regiments, however, were cut off, and one officer and fifty men were captured by us; the rear scattered through the woods, and, being fresher, escaped.

Our loss was Lieut. Col. Gordon, commanding 11th Tennessee Regiment, captured, eight or ten men killed, and 20 or 30 wounded. We understand that Col. Gordon had passed over from the spur his regiment occupied to another occupied by the 42d Georgia Regiment, to confer with Col. Henderson, of the latter, on the plan of attack, and, in returning, he was captured, having probably taken a wrong trail, which led him within the enemy's line.

The following is the list of casualties, as published in the Register of a subsequent date:

Company A, commanded by Lieut. Jno D. Milligan:
  Killed– Private J.P. Colyer
  Wounded– Corporal Jas Donohoe
  Slightly Wounded– Private J.M. Horner, J.G. Watkins, shoe shot off
Company B, commanded by Lieut. O. S. Morgan:
  Killed– Wm Smith
  Wounded Slightly– Corporal L. Millens
  Stuned Slightly– T.C. Harlow
Company C, commanded by Captain J.N. Fender:
  Killed– None
  Wounded Slightly– G.W. Smith, L.H. Parker
Company D, commanded by Captain D.F. Gaddis:
  Killed– Private A.A. Gollahair
  Arm Shot Off– Thomas Dunn
  Wounded Severely– M.W. Collens
  Wounded Slightly– L. Mowry, J. Rymen, J. York, and H.H. Runions
Company E, commanded by Lieut. Wilkerson:
  Killed– None
  Mortally Wounded– Private James Favis
  Severely Wounded– Sergeant S. Elliott
  Wounded in the Thigh– Sargt. Maj. J.M. Singleton
Company F, commanded by Lieut. James Giddeons:
  Killed– None
  Slightly Wounded in the Hand– Lieut. Giddeons
  Wounded Slightly– Private J. Cook
Company G, commanded by Lieut. James Giddeons:
  Killed– None
  Wounded Severely– Private Wm McMinn and Vandra Mostiler
  Wounded Slightly– P.C. Towey
Company H, commanded by Captain Marr:
  Killed– None
  Slightly Wounded in Finger– Private Luke Landers
Company I, commanded by Captain Isaac G. Cross:
  Killed Early in the Fight– Capt. Cross
  Wounded Mortally, will die– Private Wm Correll
  Severely Wounded– S. Price
  Slightly Wounded– Wm Meeton
  Very Slightly Wounded– Wm Smith
Company K, commanded by Lieut. Wm Lee:
  Killed– J. L. Monjoy, Musician
  Severely Wounded– Anderson Morgan, Dennis Love

- - - - - - - - - - - - -

LETTER NO. 73
JAMES O. TAYLOR TO PEACH TAYLOR

Knoxville, Jan. 6th 1863

Dear father.

I embrace the present oportunity to drop you a few lines by which you may learn that I am well and hope this little note may find you injoying a similar blessing. I have nothing to write of interest to write you. I have taken a considerable trip in the counties of Scott & Caswell which wereed me to Some extent. I am tolerable well pleased with servis, though its very hard, but hope to survive the story & when the Cloud of fanaticism blows away that we will have a peace more glorious than has ever been before.

I send Mandy & Mary a pare of Hoes by George R Ladd which was captured in Scott Co. I will clos for the present hoping to hear from you soon. I am your obedient son

J O Taylor

\- - - - - - - - - - - - -

LETTER NO. 74
JAMES O. TAYLOR TO AMANDA T. TAYLOR

Union Co. Tenn, Jan 23rd 1863

Dear Sister

I have a few spare moments in which to drop you a few lines, by which you may learn that I am in only moderate health at present have been sick for a few days but am geting better am now able for duty, was taken with cold chills with an akeing in my limbs & vomiting occasionaly, it resulted in a light tuch of the Jaundice, but have no uneasiness about me now for I will do well. I would liked to have been at home while sick but was impossible at that time we were in the Mountains when I was at my worst.

I will come home the first opertunity but cant tell when for all furlows are revoked at present, we have marching orders to Move at 8 oclock the time is now up, I must close for the present hoping to hear from you soon but I ask an intrest in the prairs of the good men and women of Meigs to protect and guide me through the present dificulty & hope there prairs will be answered in behalf of the South that we may have a speedy Peace it is said that the prairs of the ritious availeth much I believe had it not been for the prairs of the good people that our Cause would have gone by the bord(?) but hope for better times that we may return home & enjoy ourselves under our Vine and fig tree. I am your affectionate brother

J O Taylor

\- - - - - - - - - - - - -

LETTER NO. 75
L. R. BLEVINS TO AMANDA TAYLOR

Camp Near Vicksburg, Miss
Jan the 13th 1863

Miss Amanda Taylor

Mutch Esteemed Cousin I drop you a line to knight As I hav a chance of sending it by Capt Allen To let you know that I am well and hoping this may reach & find you well I havent anything mutch interest to rite you cas I rote you a few days ago and rote Most all the important News. I rote to you from Jackson I wer in hope that we would get to stay their a while but we onley got to stay three days and then we came to this place and a place it is. It is a place that I dont like in the least we hav to use Branch Watter and it moody the most of the time and the Country is very broken and sandy and the wether is too warm to soot me for Winters. But still I will have to put up with whatever comes as long as I stay in the servise.

Well Mandy, When you see my spark kiss her for me and tell her to ceap cool. Well I must close as it is getting late you will pleas excuse this short and impurfect letter rite when an opportunity serves you. Give my best love to all and receive the best to your self from your Cousin in haste

L.R. Blevins

\- - - - - - - - - - - - -

LETTER NO. 76
L. R. BLEVINS TO AMANDA T. TAYLOR

Vicksburg, Miss, Jan the 25th 1863

Miss A.T. Taylor

Mutch Esteemed Cousin I am blest to day with an opportunity of trying to Answer yours of the 17th Inst which found me well and getting a long as well as could be expected under the sircumstances. I am very mutch obliged to you for the Suspenders that you sent me as they are very scarce.

Well Amanda, perhaps you would like to know how I like this portion of Dixie land, well I dont think that I can boast of my --?-- for being at this place it is a very inconvenient place the Country is some what broken and the water is very bad. We have to use branch watter and it mudy the most of the time and it rains too mutch to soot me. So no more on that subject but now for the war.

The Yankees are tollerable plenty hear and we may hav them to fight before long, they are landing troops on the opposit side of the River from Town and It is Supposed they will try to cross the river at some point below so as to attact below and abov at the same time but they will hav some trouble as they will hav to cross under the fier of our artellery so no more on that subject.

The General is all rite, all though I havent saw him since I received your letter. I hav Nothing more to rite you at present worth your attention. You will pleas escuse this short and imperfect letter as it is the first time during life I have attempted to try to rite.

This leaves me and pat well rite when an opportunity servs you giv my best lov to all and pleas receiv the same to your self, So After my best wishes to you I remain your Cousin in hart

L.R. Blevins

P.S. Give my best Respects to your Father and Mother and also to Mary Cross and Ann Taylor.

- - - - - - - - - - - - -

LETTER NO. 77
L.R. BLEVINS TO AMANDA TAYLOR

Camp Near Vicksburg, Mississippi
February the 26th 1863

Dearest Amanda

Your very kind note of the 13th Inst came to hand to day and was red with mutch pleasure and I now am permitted to try to answer the same and I regret very mutch that I havent something that would interest the same. I havent mutch war news more than our men captured one of the Yankees Gunboats knight before last a few miles below this place. It wer an iron clad. Our boats bursted it up so it wer sunking befour the Yanks would surrender it.

Our boats wer three in number that wer engaged in the fight they faught a bout twenty seven minutes. Our men taken one hundred and twenty prisners that wer on the boat. I hav heard of onley two men being kilest in the engagement and one or two being wounded. They belonged to the thirty first Tennessee Regiment. Their being too or three companys of that Regt sent down the River on a boat some time since to warn our transports that wer down below that the Yankes had Run the blockade with one of their boats and they wer returning on one of our boats when they got in the fight did I say when they got in the fight yes but not so they wer onley on the boat as sharp shooters and I dont know as they did very mutch of the fighting as small arms could do but little with a Gun Boat, so thats all.

I think by the time we get to or thre of the yanks boats they will not be so cean to runn the blockade with them as the one mentioned in the above is second won that we hav taken. I hav no more war news worth relating at present I believe.

It is with regret that I shal inform you that their has bin a great deal of dissatisfaction in our Regiment for the last few days on account of the Rations that we hav bin drawing for the last few days the ---cat(?) that we hav bin getting is beaf of a very infer article their fore i think they hav a rite to complain but I think it will all come rite in a short time.

Well Amanda you wanted to know whether I had pict me out any one of them Demapolis Girl for me wife or not. now let me say one word rite their and that is when the Demopolis Girls are pestern your mind so just think of Little Billey of Alabama and perhaps your trobled mind will all come rite a gain.

I also find in yours of the same date that Miss Sallie Neal wer all rite on the last time that you saw her I wer glad to hear of hur being all rite but I am thinking she has gon by the with me as she has laid claim on Pat and if that be so I shal forfeit my claims at once. So thats all on that subject.

I have nothing more to rite at present only it has bin Raining all day as hard as an --?-- So I will cloas giv my best wishes and love to all the family also to all that will receiv it and retain a good portion to your self. So I will close hoping to hear from you soon I remain your cousin in hart

L. R. Blevins

P.S. W.A. Smith sends his compliments to you and Parents and says he hopes you with other Girls of Meigs will not think the Girls of Demopolis Ala has won off the attachments of Co I (or Boys) from you all, time will prove all things. The Major wants to know whether he won that dollar or not if he did he says you can send it to him in case of wind it will be very comfortable his respects to all. he says you will understand what dollar it is he won or lost. he wants to know whether you done what you promised to do for him or not.

- - - - - - - - - - - - -

LETTER NO. 78
L. R. BLEVINS TO AMANDA T. TAYLOR

Vicksburg, Miss. Apr the 3rd 1863

Dearest Cousin.

I have the pleasure of addressing you this evening. Your very interesting letter of the 22nd of the last Inst came to hand yesterday. It found me in a feble stat of helth and I am yet unwell but I feel mutch better to day. I think that I will be all rite again in a day or too. I have no news worth your attention to rite you at this time all seems to be quiet at this place. It is Rumored in camp that we will leav hear in a short time. I now not where too but some think we will come back to North Alabama or to Tenn but I place but little relianc on the rumors but hope it may be true as summer is close at hand.

Well Cous I found in the contents of your letter that it wer reported their that our Regt war all under Guard for not doing duty well that is all falce I know I will admit that their was one Company of our Regt Under guard a few days for refusing to do duty but they have bin relieved and Our Regt are in better helth and finer spirit than they hav bin in some time. We are getting tollerable plenty to eat at present e nough as I think to ceap us from suffering.

Well Cous I Ast Capt Allen the question you rot for me to ask him he denies the charge and says their is not a word of truth in it. And requested me to hav it soped at where it is. It rather --?-- the Boy.

You wanted to know what Congress wer doing well they havent bin doing very mutch latly, but standing Guard and going on picket. I handed Pat the letter to read for himself what you wanted me to tell him. Also W.C. Smith you wanted me to give your lov to your sweet Hart but I could not do that not knowing who he he well I must close for this time you woll pleas excuse this short and ill composed letter.

I heard to day that D.M. Cox wer ded but I cannot believe the report from the fact that Mr W L Grigsby got a letter from John Stewart the 27 or 8 which said nothing about it. Give my love to all that will except of it & retain a good portion to your self. I remain your Cousin in hart

L. R. Blevins

A.C. Blevins sends his love and best wishes to you and Father and Mother. They Boys are jenerly Well.
P.S. You will pleas let me know in your next who Mary and Henry Clay is and Kisain and all a bout them if you pleas. Rite soon.

Apr the 4th 1863

I am most well this morning. Nothing strang(?) on hand Capt Allen talks of comming to Tenn in a Short time if he can get off.

L. R. Blevins

- - - - - - - - - - - - -

LETTER NO. 79
JAMES O. TAYLOR TO PEACH TAYLOR

Camp Near Williamsburg, Whitly Co.
Kentucky Apr 20th 1863

Dear Father and Family.

I this Eavning have the opportunity of dropping yo a few lines to inform yo that I am well and have bin so ever since I come from home the Company is all in good health. We had a very bad acssident in Grahams Company to day when one of his men was setting Righting to his father and had just sind his name to hit when another of his men was setting greesing and rubbing hus gun and let it go off and shot the man right through the hart and he never spoak.

I roat a letter home this morning was a week ago and I haddent started my letter but a few Minets when a Dispatch came in from the pickets that the Yankeys was advancing upon us we was ordered in line until the enemy came in three quarters of a mild of us and then we fell back to Tinenot the Yankeys have fell back to Loudon about twenty nine miles from this place I under stand that there is a force their of about three thousand we were on a scout yesterday and were in twenty two miles of them I dont know where we will go from this place I think that we will cross the river to night and go up that direction I have nothing more of intrest to right at preasent.

I want yo to send me forty dollars by John when he comes up so I must close give my love to Mary and children, Ann and children and to all that will except of it.

J.O. Taylor

- - - - - - - - - - - - -

LETTER NO. 80
L. R. BLEVINS TO AMANDA TAYLOR

Antioc Church, 10 miles S.E.
Vxburg, Miss, May 11th 1863

Kind Cousin

After my compliments I procede to write you a few lines in answer to your kind letter of the 21st which was recd a few days Since and its contents duly noted. This note will leave me together with all Co "I" in tolerable good health and I hope it will find you all the same.

I have but little of interest to write at present except some little excitement which has preveiled through out our army during the last ten days. About the first of this month the Feds crossed a pretty large force across the River below Grand about 45 miles below Vxburg and on the 2nd they attacted our forces (which was small) at that place and oweing to the smallness of our armey thare and reinforcement so fare away our small but brave band and after 10 or 12 hours hard fighting was forced to abandon their position with a pretty heavy loss in killed wounded & missing.

One Brigade Genl (Tracy) was killed besides many other brave Officers and men. Our brigade was Ordered to their assistance but notwithstanding we marched day and night hard we did not get there in time to save our army there from a retreat. We arrived on the line late in the evening and about 10 oclock at night the entire army was Ordered to retreat in the direction of Vicksburg.

Accordingly before 12 the retreat was in full progress (So says the boys I was not able to be with them) and was continued all night and next day which brought us across Big Black (a River some 20 miles below Vicksburg) and which was the third night, and as we had some natural advantages we was permited to stop and sleep and take some refreshments. We fell back some 10 miles during the next two days which brought us where we now are.

Our forces are distributed at diffrent places and on a line from Warenton 10 miles below Vicksburg on the Miss R to Bovina 15 miles from Vicksburg on the R Road leading to Jackson at the latter place the Federals were expected to attempt to cut us off, but as yet they not made any peticular demonstrations in that direction, Nor is the whereabouts of the main Badg of their army known to me.

We (the 3rd) have been on picket at Hamond Ferry for the last five days untill today, we returned to camp this morning. A Yankey came down to the River (Big Black) to get some water and some of our boys were hid in the bushes, Saw him and made him get on a log and come across the River to them, he said the Feds started this morning to Jackson but I place but little confidence in what he says but should it be true they will have a warm time of it. We have a pretty good force in that direction.

On the night of the 2nd the yanks attempted to land some Rations in flat boats towed by a tug boat past our Bateries but before they had passed half our gun boats loading and all was in flames and the crew beging for assistance which was sent as soon as the fireing from our guns could be stoped. 22 of the crew was taken 2 or 3 drowned.

The boats were carying two hundred thousand Rations for men and horses all burned, but I must close Soon I would like to be at home where I could se Kisam and all the other folks and Galls the Boys too. Remember me kindly to your Pa Ma and all the family together with all Connection and friends, then hoping to hear from you soon I close by Subscribing Myself Yours truley

L. R. Blevins

P.S. W.A. Smith says he thanks you for the Complimentary remarks on the Beauty &c of his spark if she be such but says he knew very well that that was the case before you told him so. he prizes your Judgement Receive his Kindest regards and extend the same to your Pa & Ma.

- - - - - - - - - - - - -

LETTER NO. 81
J.O. TAYLOR TO PEACH & MARY TAYLOR

Camp Near Bigcreek,
Whettley Co, Tenn
May 30th 1863

Dear Father and Mother

I this Morning have the opportunity of dropping you a few lines to let yo know how we are all getting along the Company is in Moderate health. I have nothing of intrest to right to yo as we have no chance of gitting any reliable News in camp. We are hear pastering hour horses and send two Companies out tow the top of Pine Mountain on Picket and they stay three days distence about 18 Miles from this place.

I suppose we are put in Scots Brigade and will be releaved in a few days and report at lenours the colonel got a dispatch that he would be releaved by this eavning at the furthest.

We have had a little rain for the last day or two for the first time in about three weeks, it had got very dusty until it raind the Wheat crop looks fine in this country. I think there will be a great deal of Wheat raised. I want yo to Manage so as to git me a pair of boots maid a gainst the last of August if yo posable can git the leather and git them maid I think my boots will Probaly do me untill that time

I want yo to right to me how yo are getting along farming and how your croops look, tell John Blevins he must excuse me for not righting to him as I cannot get any postage stamps right soon give my best respects to all that will except of it.

J. O. Taylor

- - - - - - - - - - - - -

LETTER NO. 82
JOHN B. TAYLOR TO PEACH TAYLOR

Anderson County,
August the 5th 1863

Dear Father

I this Morning drop you a few lines to let you know how we are getting along, my health is very Bad altho I am going about. I have Been taken some medisin and think I will get Better in a day or two. James O. Taylor is still on the --?-- Mend and is mending verry fast he has got So he can walk about over the house and has a fine stomache to eat but is verry cautious about Eating too Much. I think we will be able to move from this place By the first of the weak, we will gow to the Convalescence Camp over about Concord on the Railroad and then I think we will get to come home in a few days to recruit our selves and horses.

My horse taken the lung feaver about two weeks ago and has very near gave up the Spirit, he may get well but he wont be able to travel very soon. Father I would say to you if you have any Spare Horse Save him for me and I will pay you as much as any one else. I learned you had Bought you a fine horse and I thought perhaps Old Jim had got well again and you could spair the one you Bought.

Father I have no news of Interest to wright to you. Our Brigade hasent made it pay very well this time they have been pasing hear two or three days a perfect Sceddlle(?) I think they Say they done fine until they got to Richmond they had captured a good many prisoners and severald hundred Mules and horses, Burned a great deal of Comissary Stores and many things belonging to the government, but they ventured too far and the Federals got after them so tight they had too skedadle leaving all their captured Stock and a good many of our men taken prisoners.

Some of them Says that Colonel Mackenzies Regiment Was all Captured they was cut off at Winchester and hasent been heard of Since others say that McKenzie is coming out less injured than any other Regiment in the Brigade. I cannot tell how it is yet But I am afraid they are Captured, we will hear all about it in a few days and I will write again.

I will close for the present do not Bee uneasy about us for if Either of us gets worse I will Seend you word so no more at present. Hoping this may find you all Enjoying good health.

Affectionately Yours & Wright as soon as you get this.

John B. Taylor

- - - - - - - - - - - - -

LETTER NO. 83
JOHNEY BLEVINS TO AMANDA TAYLOR

At home Sept 2nd 1863

Cousin Amanda

I write you a line this eavening in hast, and would like to write agreadal [a great deal] but have not time, when I left home this morning I expected to see you again before I left but it was all a mistake, though I hope I will some time.

I will leave in the morning for Charleston, we expect to meet Col McKenzies Regment there and then we dont know where we will go to, I will close as I have but a few more hours to spend in old Meigs. Tell her some good word for me and how well I love her, be careful Manda and dont let the Yanks get you.

Your friend & cousin
Johney Blevins Good By

- - - - - - - - - - - - -

LETTER NO. 84
JOHNEY BLEVINS TO AMANDA TAYLOR

April 20th 1864

Cousin Amanda

You will on this lonesom morning premit me to drop you a line, I will not attempt to give you any thing like a regular letter as Osborn has wrote to you. He will write you a few lines to let you know that I have not forgot those of my friends that is far from me this morning, And that I am well and enjoying myself as well as could be expected under present circumstances, hoping this may find you enjoying a like blessing. Well Manda you can but imagine how I would like to be in Old Meigs today, I think I could enjoy myself far more better than I have in days that is past and gone. I hope the time is not far distant when we shal drive the invading foe from off our soil, though the cloud appears dark at this time. You may all look for me when you se me coming. I expect to fight our enemy until the last song is sung, hoping to hear from you soon, I will close.

Johney Blevins

- - - - - - - - - - - - -

LETTER NO. 85
HUGH T. THOMAS TO AMANDA TAYLOR

The poem below was included in a letter written on 17 February 1869 from Wartrace, Tennessee, where Hugh was living at the time. He was the son of Henson and Lucretia (Blevins) Thomas. It was evident that he was still bitter about the war (author unknown):

THE GOOD OLD REBEL

I am a good Old rebel
Now thats just what I am
For this fair land of freedom
I doo not care a damn
I am glad I fit against it
I only wish weed won
And I dont want no pardon
For any thing I've done.

I hate the Constitution
This great republic too
I hate the freedmans buro
In uniform of blue
I hate the nasty eagle
With all his brass and fuss
The lying thieving Yankies
I hate um wuss and wuss

I hate the Yankee nation
And ever thing they do
I hate the declaration
of Independence too
I hate this glorious union
Tis driping with our blood
I hate the Striped banner
I fit it all I could

I followed old Masa Robert
for four years near about
Got wounded in three places
And starved at point lookout
I caught the Rheumatism
camping in the Snow
But I cild a chance O Yankey
And would like to cill Some more

Three hundred thousand Yankeys
are now in Southern dust
Wee got three hundred thousand
Before they could get us
They died of Southern fever
Of Southern Shell and Shot
I wish it was three million
In Sted of what wee got

I cant take up my musket
And fite them any more
But I aint a going to love them
Now thats a Sartin Shore
And I dont want no pardon
For what I was and am
I wont be recon Structed
I doo not care a dam

INDEX

- C -

- D -

- E -

- F -

- G -

- H -

- Mc -

- M -

- N -

- O -

- P -

- Q -

- R -

- S -

- T -

- V -

- W -

www.ingramcontent.com/pod-product-compliance
Lightning Source LLC
Chambersburg PA
CBHW080238270326
41926CB00020B/4295

* 9 7 8 0 7 8 8 4 8 7 1 5 6 *